"The Catholic Commentary on Sacred Scripture is a landmark achievement in theological interpretation of Scripture in and for the Church. Highly recommended for all!"

—**Michael J. Gorman**, St. Mary's Seminary and University, Baltimore

"I welcome with great joy the launch of this collection of commentaries on the Bible because the project corresponds perfectly to a pressing need in the Church. I am speaking about exegetical studies that are well grounded from a scholarly point of view but not overburdened with technical details, and at the same time related to the riches of ancient interpretation, nourishing for spiritual life, and useful for catechesis, preaching, evangelization, and other forms of pastoral ministry."

—**Albert Cardinal Vanhoye, SJ**, Pontifical Biblical Institute, former secretary of the Pontifical Biblical Commission

"By bringing together historical background, exegetical interpretation, Church tradition, theological reflection, and pastoral application, this series promises to enkindle thoughtful discussion about the implications of the New Testament for lived Christian faith in the Church today. Its accessible format and multi-angled approach offer a model for teaching and ministry."

—**Katherine Hayes**, Seminary of the Immaculate Conception

"This series promises to be spiritually and doctrinally informative, based on careful, solid biblical exegesis. The method and content of this work will be helpful to teachers of the faith at different levels and will provide a reliable guide to people seeking to deepen their knowledge and thereby nourish their faith. I strongly recommend the Catholic Commentary on Sacred Scripture."

—**Cormac Cardinal Murphy-O'Connor**, Archbishop of Westminster

"The Catholic Commentary on Sacred Scripture is clearly written, sticks to the facts, treats the Bible as true history, and does not get lost in idle speculation and guesswork about the sources of the Gospels and the other books. Homilists will find here the pearl of great price and the treasure hidden in a field. Laypersons who are looking for a truly Catholic interpretation of the Bible will find it here. Those who want to know more about God's holy word in the Bible will want to purchase the whole set."

—**Kenneth Baker, SJ**, editor, *Homiletics and Pastoral Review*

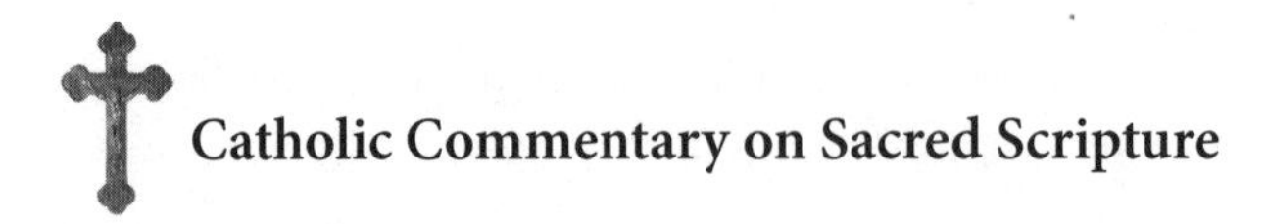

Catholic Commentary on Sacred Scripture

The Gospel of John

Francis Martin and
William M. Wright IV

BakerAcademic
a division of Baker Publishing Group
Grand Rapids, Michigan

Published by Baker Academic
a division of Baker Publishing Group
P.O. Box 6287, Grand Rapids, MI 49516-6287
www.bakeracademic.com

Printed in the United States of America

Library of Congress Cataloging-in-Publication Data

Martin, Francis, 1930–
The Gospel of John / Francis Martin and William M. Wright IV.
pages cm. — (Catholic commentary on sacred scripture)
Includes bibliographical references and index.
ISBN 978-0-8010-3647-7 (pbk.)
1. Bible. John—Commentaries. 2. Catholic Church—Doctrines. I. Title.
BS2615.53.M37 2015
226.5′077—dc23 2014044232

Imprimatur:
Most Reverend David Allen Zubik, DD
Bishop of Pittsburgh
August 25, 2014

The *Nihil obstat* and the *imprimatur* are declarations that a work is considered to be free from doctrinal or moral error. It is not implied that those who have granted the same agree with the contents, opinions, or statements expressed.

18 19 20 21 22 23 24 10 9 8 7 6 5 4

Contents

Illustrations

Editors' Preface

> The Church has always venerated the divine Scriptures just as she venerates the body of the Lord. . . . All the preaching of the Church should be nourished and governed by Sacred Scripture. For in the sacred books, the Father who is in heaven meets His children with great love and speaks with them; and the power and goodness in the word of God is so great that it stands as the support and energy of the Church, the strength of faith for her sons and daughters, the food of the soul, a pure and perennial fountain of spiritual life.
>
> Second Vatican Council, *Dei Verbum* 21

> Were not our hearts burning [within us] while he spoke to us on the way and opened the scriptures to us?
>
> Luke 24:32

The Catholic Commentary on Sacred Scripture aims to serve the ministry of the Word of God in the life and mission of the Church. Since Vatican Council II, there has been an increasing hunger among Catholics to study Scripture in depth and in a way that reveals its relationship to liturgy, evangelization, catechesis, theology, and personal and communal life. This series responds to that desire by providing accessible yet substantive commentary on each book of the New Testament, drawn from the best of contemporary biblical scholarship as well as the rich treasury of the Church's tradition. These volumes seek to offer scholarship illumined by faith, in the conviction that the ultimate aim of biblical interpretation is to discover what God has revealed and is still speaking through the sacred text. Central to our approach are the principles taught by Vatican II: first, the use of historical and literary methods to discern what the biblical authors intended to express; second, prayerful theological reflection to understand the sacred text "in accord with the same Spirit by whom it was written"—that is, in light of the content and unity of the whole Scripture, the living tradition of the Church, and the analogy of faith (*Dei Verbum* 12).

The Catholic Commentary on Sacred Scripture is written for those engaged in or training for pastoral ministry and others interested in studying Scripture to understand their faith more deeply, to nourish their spiritual life, or to share the good news with others. With this in mind, the authors focus on the meaning of the text for faith and life rather than on the technical questions that occupy scholars, and they explain the Bible in ordinary language that does not require translation for preaching and catechesis. Although this series is written from the perspective of Catholic faith, its authors draw on the interpretation of Protestant and Orthodox scholars and hope these volumes will serve Christians of other traditions as well.

A variety of features are designed to make the commentary as useful as possible. Each volume includes the biblical text of the New American Bible, Revised Edition (NABRE), the translation approved for liturgical use in the United States. In order to serve readers who use other translations, the most important differences between the NABRE and other widely used translations (RSV, NRSV, JB, NJB, and NIV) are noted and explained. Each unit of the biblical text is followed by a list of references to relevant Scripture passages, Catechism sections, and uses in the Roman Lectionary. The exegesis that follows aims to explain in a clear and engaging way the meaning of the text in its original historical context as well as its perennial meaning for Christians. Reflection and Application sections help readers apply Scripture to Christian life today by responding to questions that the text raises, offering spiritual interpretations drawn from Christian tradition or providing suggestions for the use of the biblical text in catechesis, preaching, or other forms of pastoral ministry.

Interspersed throughout the commentary are Biblical Background sidebars that present historical, literary, or theological information and Living Tradition sidebars that offer pertinent material from the postbiblical Christian tradition, including quotations from Church documents and from the writings of saints and Church Fathers. The Biblical Background sidebars are indicated by a photo of urns that were excavated in Jerusalem, signifying the importance of historical study in understanding the sacred text. The Living Tradition sidebars are indicated by an image of Eadwine, a twelfth-century monk and scribe, signifying the growth in the Church's understanding that comes by the grace of the Holy Spirit as believers study and ponder the word of God in their hearts (see *Dei Verbum* 8).

Maps and a glossary are located in the back of each volume for easy reference. The glossary explains key terms from the biblical text as well as theological or exegetical terms, which are marked in the commentary with a cross (†). A list of suggested resources, an index of pastoral topics, and an index of sidebars are included to enhance the usefulness of these volumes. Further resources, including questions for reflection or discussion, can be found at the series website, www.CatholicScriptureCommentary.com.

It is our desire and prayer that these volumes be of service so that more and more "the word of the Lord may speed forward and be glorified" (2 Thess 3:1) in the Church and throughout the world.

Peter S. Williamson
Mary Healy
Kevin Perrotta

Note to Readers

The New American Bible, Revised Edition differs slightly from most English translations in its verse numbering of the Psalms and certain other parts of the Old Testament. For instance, Ps 51:4 in the NABRE is Ps 51:2 in other translations; Mal 3:19 in the NABRE is Mal 4:1 in other translations. Readers who use different translations are advised to keep this in mind when looking up Old Testament cross-references given in the commentary.

Abbreviations

†	indicates that the definition of a term appears in the glossary
AB	Anchor Bible
ABD	*Anchor Bible Dictionary*. 6 vols. Edited by David Noel Freedman. New York and New Haven: Doubleday and Yale University Press, 1992
ABRL	Anchor Bible Reference Library
ACCS	Elowsky, Joel C., ed. *John*. Ancient Christian Commentary on Scripture: New Testament 4a–b. Downers Grove, IL: InterVarsity, 2006–7
b.	Babylonian Talmud
BDAG	Bauer, W., F. W. Danker, W. F. Arndt, and F. W. Gingrich. *A Greek-English Lexicon of the New Testament and Other Early Christian Literature*. 3rd ed. Chicago: University of Chicago Press, 2000
Catechism	*Catechism of the Catholic Church* (2nd ed.)
Denzinger	Denzinger, Heinrich. *Compendium of Creeds, Definitions, and Declarations on Matters of Faith and Morals*. 43rd ed. Edited by Peter Hünermann. Latin-English. San Francisco: Ignatius Press, 2012
DS	Denzinger, Heinrich. *Enchiridion symbolorum, definitionum et declarationum de rebus fidei et morum*. Edited by Adolf Schönmetzer. 1965
FC	Fathers of the Church
LCL	Loeb Classical Library
Lectionary	*The Lectionary for Mass* (1998/2002 USA ed.)
LXX	†Septuagint
NABRE	New American Bible, Revised Edition
NIV	New International Version
NJB	New Jerusalem Bible
NRSV	New Revised Standard Version
NT	New Testament
OT	Old Testament
PG	Patrologia Graeca. Edited by J. P. Migne. 162 Vols. Paris, 1857–86
PL	Patrologia Latina. Edited by J. P. Migne. 217 Vols. Paris, 1844–64
1QS	*Rule of the Community* (of the †Dead Sea Scrolls)
11Q19	*Temple Scroll* (of the Dead Sea Scrolls)
RSV	Revised Standard Version
SBLSymS	Society of Biblical Literature: Symposium Series

Books of the Old Testament

Gen	Genesis
Exod	Exodus
Lev	Leviticus
Num	Numbers
Deut	Deuteronomy
Josh	Joshua
Judg	Judges
Ruth	Ruth
1 Sam	1 Samuel
2 Sam	2 Samuel
1 Kings	1 Kings
2 Kings	2 Kings
1 Chron	1 Chronicles
2 Chron	2 Chronicles
Ezra	Ezra
Neh	Nehemiah
Tob	Tobit
Jdt	Judith
Esther	Esther
1 Macc	1 Maccabees
2 Macc	2 Maccabees
Job	Job
Ps	Psalm/Psalms
Prov	Proverbs
Eccles	Ecclesiastes
Song	Song of Songs
Wis	Wisdom
Sir	Sirach
Isa	Isaiah
Jer	Jeremiah
Lam	Lamentations
Bar	Baruch
Ezek	Ezekiel
Dan	Daniel
Hosea	Hosea
Joel	Joel
Amos	Amos
Obad	Obadiah
Jon	Jonah
Mic	Micah
Nah	Nahum
Hab	Habakkuk
Zeph	Zephaniah
Hag	Haggai
Zech	Zechariah
Mal	Malachi

Books of the New Testament

Matt	Matthew
Mark	Mark
Luke	Luke
John	John
Acts	Acts
Rom	Romans
1 Cor	1 Corinthians
2 Cor	2 Corinthians
Gal	Galatians
Eph	Ephesians
Phil	Philippians
Col	Colossians
1 Thess	1 Thessalonians
2 Thess	2 Thessalonians
1 Tim	1 Timothy
2 Tim	2 Timothy
Titus	Titus
Philem	Philemon
Heb	Hebrews
James	James
1 Pet	1 Peter
2 Pet	2 Peter
1 John	1 John
2 John	2 John
3 John	3 John
Jude	Jude
Rev	Revelation

Introduction

Pope St. Gregory the Great compared Scripture to a "smooth, deep river in which a lamb may walk and an elephant may swim."[1] These words certainly apply to the Gospel of John. Within its pages are found divine teachings articulated with simple images such as water and light, memorable stories composed with literary and dramatic skill, and glimpses into the very mystery of God, proceeding from the most profound mystical illumination. Like the loaves and fishes multiplied by Jesus, the Gospel of John provides a superabundance of spiritual teaching, edification, and challenges to all its readers, whether beginners or experienced.

Before embarking on this study of John, it will be helpful to consider some introductory matters. We will, therefore, examine the Gospel's authorship, historical context, and literary genre. We will then discuss the Gospel's literary structure and characteristics, its relationship with other biblical writings, and its major theological teachings. We will conclude with some remarks about reading John's Gospel today.

Authorship

The Gospel does not explicitly name its author, and so it is necessary to engage in guesswork based upon evidence from the Gospel itself and from early Christian tradition.

All discussions of this Gospel's authorship involve the anonymous figure called "the disciple whom Jesus loved" (21:7), usually referred to as the Beloved Disciple. The Gospel says that he was an eyewitness to Jesus' life (19:26, 35),

1. Gregory the Great, *Moralia* 1.4 (PL 75:515).

and his testimony has been preserved in the Gospel (21:24–25) by himself or a secretary. He first appears at the Last Supper, as the one reclining next to Jesus (13:23), and is then depicted in three other scenes: with Jesus' mother at the foot of the cross (19:25–27), with Peter at the empty tomb (20:2–10), and at Jesus' resurrection appearance in Galilee (21:1–23). He could be "the other disciple" with Peter at Annas's house after Jesus' arrest (18:15–16; if so, he has ties to the Jerusalem priesthood). Some have argued that he is the unnamed disciple who first comes to Jesus with Andrew after having followed John the Baptist (1:35, 40). The Gospel contains evidence that its author knew the geography of the Holy Land, especially Jerusalem, before the Roman destruction of Jerusalem in AD 70 (4:3–6; 5:2; 8:20; 9:7; 10:23) and was very familiar with Jewish religious practices, liturgies, and traditions of biblical interpretation (2:6; 7:37–39; 8:12).

There are two major theories about this disciple's identity.[2] The major opinion from Christian antiquity until the nineteenth century was that the Beloved Disciple was John the Apostle, son of Zebedee.[3] This well-known member of the Twelve is named in the †Synoptics (e.g., Mark 1:19–20; 3:16–17; 9:2), Acts (3–4), and Paul (Gal 2:9), but he is never mentioned explicitly in the Fourth Gospel, although there is a mention of "Zebedee's sons" in 21:2. Strong evidence for identifying the Beloved Disciple with John the Apostle is the agreement on this point among second-century Christians. For instance, St. Irenaeus, who wrote in the 180s, stated that John, "the Lord's disciple who had also *rested on* [Jesus'] *breast*, issued the Gospel while living at Ephesus of Asia."[4] Irenaeus learned about John from St. Polycarp, a bishop who knew and was taught by John the Apostle.[5] Recent scholarship has located the attribution of the Fourth Gospel with John the Apostle in the "traditions of the presbyters," or elders, which date to the late first or early second century.[6]

Many scholars today are not inclined to assign much historical weight to second-century traditions about Gospel authorship. The major scholarly opinion today is that the Beloved Disciple was not a member of the Twelve Apostles. In this view, the author was another disciple of Jesus during his ministry, likely a

2. See R. Alan Culpepper, *John, the Son of Zebedee: The Life of a Legend* (Minneapolis: Fortress, 2000 [1994]).

3. For argumentation, see Craig S. Keener, *The Gospel of John: A Commentary* (Peabody, MA: Hendrickson, 2003), 1:82–115.

4. Irenaeus, *Against the Heresies* 3.1.1, in *St. Irenaeus of Lyons: Against the Heresies*, trans. Dominic J. Unger, OFMCap, Ancient Christian Writers 64 (New York: Paulist Press, 2012), 30.

5. Irenaeus, *Against the Heresies* 3.3.4.

6. See Charles E. Hill, *The Johannine Corpus in the Early Church* (Oxford: Oxford University Press, 2004). Hill's fresh reconsideration of the second-century evidence renews the identification of the Beloved Disciple as John the Apostle as a very intriguing possibility.

former follower of John the Baptist (the anonymous disciple in 1:35, 40), and who may also be John the Elder, the author of 2–3 John (on the relation of the Gospel to the Letters of John, see below).[7] Those who take this position point out that the Gospel does not record any of the Synoptic stories that feature John the Apostle, such as the transfiguration. The Gospel also sets the Beloved Disciple alongside Peter in order to showcase his special status: only the Beloved Disciple knows the identity of Jesus' betrayer (13:24–26); he is present at the cross whereas Peter denied Jesus (18:17, 25–27; 19:25–27); he outruns Peter to the empty tomb and first arrives at some degree of Easter faith (20:2–8); he first recognizes the risen Jesus speaking to the disciples from the seashore (21:7). If he is the other disciple in 18:15–16, he obtains access to the high priest's house and then has Peter admitted. This highlighting of the Beloved Disciple's role leads some scholars to infer that he was an outsider to the Twelve.[8] This theory, however, requires an explanation as to why this Gospel would have been wrongly associated with John the Apostle at such an early date and by people who claim to have known him personally (e.g., Polycarp). Whoever the Beloved Disciple was, he may not have been the only person involved in the composition of this Gospel. Internal tensions in the text suggest that the Gospel may have been composed over time, with multiple hands involved in the process. John 3:22 says that Jesus and his disciples were involved in baptizing, but 4:2 says that Jesus himself was not doing the baptizing. In John 16:5, Jesus says, "Not one of you asks me, 'Where are you going?'" Yet Peter asked this very question in 13:36. Moreover, John 21:22–23 refutes a mistaken belief, circulating among some Christians, that the Beloved Disciple would survive to see the †Parousia, and the need to refute such a belief may have been occasioned by the fact that the Beloved Disciple had died by the time of the Gospel's final editing. Like other ancient writers, New Testament authors sometimes employed secretaries who did the actual writing of a composition (see Rom 16:22; 1 Pet 5:12). It is possible that the Beloved Disciple was the authoritative teacher, whose testimony has been recorded in the Gospel by one or more of his disciples.

The ancient evidence is complex and ambiguous, and it prevents us from arriving at definitive conclusions about the Beloved Disciple's identity or the Gospel's authorship. An intriguing possibility, proposed by C. K. Barrett and

7. See Oscar Cullman, *The Johannine Circle*, trans. John Bowman (Philadelphia: Westminster, 1976). On the association of this disciple with John the Elder (or Presbyter), see Martin Hengel, *The Johannine Question*, trans. John Bowden (Philadelphia: Trinity Press International, 1989); Richard Bauckham, *Jesus and the Eyewitnesses: The Gospels as Eyewitness Testimony* (Grand Rapids: Eerdmans, 2006).

8. One could also derive the very opposite conclusion from the same evidence: his prominence and constant association with Peter suggests that the Beloved Disciple is to be counted among the Twelve (Acts 3:3; Gal 2:9).

developed by John Painter, is that the Beloved Disciple is John the Apostle, the son of Zebedee, whose traditions and work were shaped into the Fourth Gospel by one of his disciples.[9] This hypothesis accounts for the ancient traditions about authorship while also accounting for the evidence that the Gospel underwent some editing in its composition history. For the Gospel's author, "John," what is ultimately important is not his own personality but the risen Lord to whom he bears witness through his Gospel, and "his testimony is true" (21:24).

Historical Context

Various indications in the Gospel suggest that it was written for Christians in a Greco-Roman setting, perhaps in Ephesus, where Irenaeus and others say that John resided.[10] Early Christian tradition identifies John as the last of the four Gospels written, and scholars usually date it to the 90s AD.

The Gospel of John is steeped in the Jewish world of the first century. The author was almost certainly a Jew from the Holy Land, for, as mentioned above, he knows its geography, including details about places before their destruction in AD 70, as well as many Jewish liturgical and biblical traditions. Some aspects of its theological style, such as symbolism of light and dark, resemble the Jewish theological thinking found in the †Dead Sea Scrolls. But the Gospel also implies that its intended readers were Gentiles or at least Jews not from the Holy Land. John often provides the translation of Semitic terms (e.g., Rabbi, 1:38; †Messiah, 1:41; Cephas, 1:42) and the meaning of cultural details (4:9), which Jews who lived in the Holy Land would have known but Gentiles and perhaps Jews outside the land would not. Moreover, the Gospel often categorizes participants in the account as "the Jews," which, as Richard Bauckham has noted, is a label by which †Jews were spoken about to Gentiles.[11] If we draw on the letters of John, 3 John gives evidence that some members of the Johannine churches were converts from Gentile paganism, for the names mentioned in 3 John—Gaius (1), Diotrephes (9), and Demetrius (12)—are Greco-Roman, not Jewish.

Much discussion of the Gospel's historical setting involves speculation about the history of the Johannine community, that is, the church or network of churches in which the Beloved Disciple was the authoritative teacher and in which the

9. C. K. Barrett, *The Gospel according to St. John*, 2nd ed. (Philadelphia: Westminster, 1978), 133–34; John Painter, *The Quest for the Messiah: The History, Literature and Theology of the Johannine Community* (Edinburgh: T&T Clark, 1991), 72–73.

10. Irenaeus, *Against the Heresies* 3.1.1.

11. Richard Bauckham, *Testimony of the Beloved Disciple: Narrative, History, and Theology in the Gospel of John* (Grand Rapids: Baker Academic, 2007), 230n96.

Gospel was composed. The starting point for much of this speculation is the odd Greek word *aposynagōgos* (literally, "one out of the †synagogue"), a term that in all early Christian literature appears only in John (9:22; 12:42; 16:2). In the account of the man born blind, John says, "The Jews had already agreed that if anyone acknowledged [Jesus] as the Messiah, he would be expelled from the synagogue [*aposynagōgos*]" (9:22), and during the Farewell Discourse, Jesus predicts that this will happen to his disciples (16:2). It is difficult to determine what historical realities *aposynagōgos* might reflect. In the view of many scholars, the term reflects the situation of some Jewish followers of Jesus in relation to their local synagogue, not in the time of Jesus but later in the first century. If so, the appearance of the term only in this Gospel may suggest that some among John's readers had had a tumultuous separation from their local †synagogue as a result of their confession of Jesus' messiahship. Such a separation would help explain the negative nuance of the term "the †Jews" in some passages in the Gospel, for these experiences in the later first-century would have shaped the Gospel's account of the animosity between Jesus and some of his fellow Jews in the time of his public ministry. On the issues related to John's way of speaking of "the Jews," see the sidebar on p. 101.

Genre

Like the other Gospels, John is best categorized within the genre of Greco-Roman biography or "Life" (*bios*).[12] The first-century Greek author Plutarch wrote many such biographies, and in his *Life of Alexander the Great* he explains some features of this genre:

> I do not tell of all the famous actions of these men, nor even speak exhaustively at all in each particular case, but in epitome. . . . For it is not Histories that I am writing, but Lives; and in the most illustrious deeds there is not always a manifestation of virtue or vice, nay, a slight thing like a phrase or a jest often makes a greater revelation of character. . . . I must be permitted to devote myself rather to the signs of the soul in men, and by means of these to portray the life of each.[13]

Several things in Plutarch's description of a "Life" resemble features of John's Gospel. First, a "Life" is *selective* in what it narrates about a person. It is not intended to give a comprehensive account of a person's words and deeds. John

12. See Richard A. Burridge, *What Are the Gospels? A Comparison with Greco-Roman Biography* (Cambridge: Cambridge University Press, 1992).

13. Plutarch, *Alexander* 1, in *Lives*, vol. 7, trans. Bernadotte Perrin, LCL 99 (Cambridge, MA: Harvard University Press, 1919); see Paul J. Achtemeier, Joel B. Green, and Marianne Meye Thompson, *Introducing the New Testament: Its Literature and Theology* (Grand Rapids: Eerdmans, 2001), 65.

likewise affirms that Jesus did much more than what the Gospel reports: "There are also many other things that Jesus did, but if these were to be described individually, I do not think the whole world would contain the books that would be written" (21:25). Second, Plutarch talks about how he, as an author, *shapes the material*. He writes "in epitome," or summary, and aims "to portray the life" of his subject. Similarly, John, like the other Gospels, has a deliberate literary arrangement. The rationale for this arrangement is theological rather than merely chronological. Thus, for theological purposes, John deliberately locates Jesus' clearing of the merchants from the temple as the first event of his public ministry, an event that likely occurred near the end of his public ministry, where the †Synoptics place it. Third, a "Life" is written for the *formation of its audience*. By reading the account of the subject's words and deeds, a reader should learn moral lessons about virtues to be imitated and vices to be avoided. Similarly, John says that his purpose in recounting the actions of the risen Jesus is for his audience's faith and spiritual formation: "These are written that you may [come to] believe that Jesus is the Messiah, the Son of God, and that through this belief you may have life in his name" (20:31).

Yet this purpose of drawing the reader to faith in Jesus highlights a major difference between the Gospels and Greco-Roman "Lives." The subjects of Plutarch's Lives are dead figures from the past. For John and the other New Testament writers, Jesus is not a dead figure from the past. On the contrary, Jesus has been resurrected to glorified life. He is the living and eternal Son of God, who is present spiritually to his Church and active in his disciples' lives. The Gospel does not simply recount the words and deeds of a historical figure but is also the means of a genuine encounter with this risen Lord, whose words and deeds are "living and effective" (Heb 4:12) in the present.

When we read John, we should be mindful that we are reading a theological interpretation of Jesus' life. The Gospel itself indicates that it views the life of Jesus in retrospect, with the illumination provided by the Holy Spirit after Jesus' resurrection (2:22; 12:16). For John, history and theology are deeply entwined, and people can understand the meaning of Jesus only through the interior action of the Holy Spirit (16:13). John has composed his account of Jesus' life so that its spiritual significance can be handed on to his audience.

Structure and Literary Features

The Gospel begins with a Prologue (1:1–18), which is possibly an early Christian hymn or homily. The Prologue provides the key for understanding the entire

Gospel by framing it in terms of the eternal relationship between the Father and the Son and in terms of the Son's mission of salvation.

The body of the Gospel can be divided into two major sections.[14] John 1:19–12:50 comprises what is often called the Book of Signs. These chapters narrate a three-year ministry of Jesus, which centers on his public revelation of the Father and himself as the Son. John's account of Jesus' ministry features lengthy discourses, miraculous †signs, and controversies. These chapters are called the Book of *Signs* because of their emphasis on revelation. John calls Jesus' miracles "signs" because they point to and reveal spiritual realities and truths about Jesus. To see the signs properly is to be led to the reality of Jesus that they reveal. The second major section, often termed the Book of Glory (13:1–21:25), narrates, among other events, the Last Supper, in which Jesus delivers his farewell address to his disciples, and then his death and resurrection. These chapters are called the Book of *Glory* because they center on the events of Jesus' passion, death, and resurrection, through which he supremely reveals the glory of God: the infinite exchange of love between the Father and the Son.

The Gospel's theological content is closely related to its literary form. As Gail O'Day writes, "In order to understand *what* John says about Jesus and God, then, one must attend carefully to *how* he tells his story."[15] These are some of the Gospel's more prominent literary features through which the Evangelist articulates his theology:

- Pairs of opposites: John often uses pairs of opposites that have theological meaning, such as light and dark, faith and unbelief, life and death.
- Special vocabulary: John sometimes invests seemingly ordinary words with deep theological meaning, such as "remain," "the world," "receive."
- †Irony: this is a literary device in which one thing seems to be the case, but another thing, often its exact opposite, is actually the case. A great example is John's presentation of the cross. On the surface, Jesus' death on the cross seems to be his ultimate defeat and humiliation. But in fact, the cross is God's victory, in which Jesus accomplishes the Father's saving work.
- Misunderstanding: throughout the Gospel, people fail to understand Jesus, and this prompts him to elaborate on his teaching, as in his dialogue with Nicodemus (3:1–15).

14. See Raymond E. Brown, SS, *The Gospel according to John*, AB 29 (New York: Doubleday, 1966), 1:cxxxviii–cxliv.

15. Gail R. O'Day, "The Word Become Flesh: Story and Theology in the Gospel of John," in *What Is John?*, vol. 2, *Literary and Social Readings of the Fourth Gospel*, ed. Fernando F. Segovia, SBLSymS 7 (Atlanta: Scholars, 1998), 69.

- Words with double meanings: John sometimes uses Greek words that have multiple meanings, with more than one meaning in mind. For example, the Greek adverb *anōthen* (3:3) can mean both "from above" and "again." Jesus' pronouncement that one must be born *anōthen* plays on both meanings: one must be born *again* (a second birth) in a manner that is of heavenly, not earthly, origin (*from above*).
- Symbolic characterization: John leaves some individuals unnamed to invest them with a theological or symbolic meaning (e.g., Jesus' mother, the Beloved Disciple).

Relationship to Other Biblical Writings

The Gospel of John is closest in theology and literary style to the three Letters of John. Like the Gospel, 1 John does not name its author, but 2 and 3 John claim to be written by "the Presbyter," or Elder. The Gospel and Letters of John are stylistically similar in their special theological vocabulary and pairs of opposites. The Letters were likely written after the Gospel, and they elaborate on topics found in the Gospel (e.g., the love command in 1 John 5:1–5).

Also included among John's writings is the Book of Revelation, whose visionary is named "John" (Rev 1:9). Revelation's theology, literary style, and genre are significantly different from the Gospel and Letters of John. Revelation is an †apocalypse, a literary genre centered on the revelation of heavenly mysteries, which are expressed in vivid symbolism, set against the Roman persecution of Christians in the late first century, and this persecution does not appear as a concern in the Gospel or Letters. Yet there are some curious similarities between the Gospel and Revelation. For instance, these are the only two New Testament writings to call Jesus "the Lamb" (John 1:29; Rev 5:6) and "the Word of God" (John 1:1; Rev 19:13). These are also the only two New Testament writings to cite clearly the oracle in Zech 12:10: "They will look upon him whom they have pierced" (John 19:37; Rev 1:7).

Also significant is the relationship between John and the †Synoptic Gospels: Matthew, Mark, and Luke. On the one hand, John and the Synoptics have much in common. They give the same basic account of Jesus' life: a public ministry of itinerant teaching in Galilee and Judea, miracles, and controversies, ending in his crucifixion and resurrection. All four Gospels feature many of the same individuals: Jesus' mother, John the Baptist, Peter, the Twelve, Mary Magdalene, Caiaphas, Pilate. In addition to the passion and resurrection narratives, John and the Synoptics have some stories in common (e.g., the multiplication of the loaves followed by Jesus' walking on water in Mark 6:34–52; John 6:1–21).

On the other hand, there are also some noticeable differences between John and the Synoptics. In the Synoptics, Jesus often teaches in parables and short pithy sayings. But in John, Jesus teaches in long enigmatic discourses and does not tell any Synoptic-like parables. The Synoptics imply that Jesus' ministry lasted one year, but John's mention of three Passovers suggests a ministry of three years. In the Synoptics, most of Jesus' ministry takes place in Galilee, whereas John narrates much of Jesus' ministry in Judea.

The critical question is how to explain these similarities and the differences. Does John know and use the Synoptic Gospels in his writing? At the minimum, John knows many of the same traditions about Jesus that are found in the Synoptics. For instance, John does not narrate the call of the twelve apostles (e.g., Luke 6:12–16), but he first mentions the Twelve rather abruptly with the expectation that the Gospel's audience already knows who they are (6:67, 70–71). If John knows any of the Synoptic Gospels, he does not use them in the same way that Matthew and Luke use Mark. Of the three Synoptics, Luke is the most likely candidate that John might have known (or perhaps Luke knew a version of John), for there are some points of contact unique to John and Luke: an individual named Lazarus (Luke 16:19–31; John 11:1–44), the family of Martha and Mary (Luke 10:38–42; John 11:1–44), the possession of Judas by Satan (Luke 22:3; John 13:27), Pilate's threefold acquittal of Jesus (Luke 23:4, 14, 22; John 18:38; 19:4, 6), Peter's visit to the empty tomb (Luke 24:12; John 20:2–10), and the risen Jesus' appearance to the disciples on Easter Sunday night in Jerusalem (Luke 24:36–43; John 20:19–25).

As for theology, we could say with Luke Timothy Johnson, "What is left implicit in the synoptic Gospels is made explicit in [John]."[16] In the Synoptics, Jesus often calls God "my Father" (Matt 7:21; 10:32–33; 20:23), but only occasionally does he call himself "Son" (Matt 11:27; 24:36; see also 21:37). In John, however, Jesus often refers to himself as "the Son." John presents Jesus as using the title "Son" with greater frequency in order to set forth more directly and dramatically the mystery of his relationship with God, whom he called "Abba, Father" (Mark 14:36).

Major Theological Teachings

John's Gospel is centered on God. From the very first verse, we are given a glimpse of the inner life of God as an eternal communion of life and love between God the Father and his Son, who is also his Word (1:1). The world, which God

16. Luke Timothy Johnson, *Writings of the New Testament*, 3rd ed. (Minneapolis: Fortress, 2010), 471.

created through his Word, has become a place of spiritual darkness and sin, enslaved by Satan, who is called "the ruler of this world" (12:31). Out of love for sinful humanity and his desire to save them from sin and reconcile them to himself, God, through his Word, forms Israel as his special people and teaches them about himself and his will (1:9–11; 12:41). The divine Word's work in the world takes on a previously unimaginable form when he becomes †incarnate, united to a human nature, in Jesus of Nazareth.

Jesus' whole life and mission is grounded in his relationship with the Father. Jesus is the Son, the one sent by the Father, to reveal him and accomplish his saving work. All that Jesus says, he has heard from the Father (8:38, 40; 18:37), and he does only that which the Father has given him to do (5:19; 10:37–38; 14:11). Jesus' whole life—his person, words, and deeds—is a revelation of the Father, of himself as the Son, and of the infinite love between them.

Jesus' mission to reveal the Father and accomplish his saving work culminates in his perfect gift of self on the cross. For John, the cross of Jesus reveals that "God is love" (1 John 4:8). The Father gives his all, his Son, out of love for the world and for its salvation (3:16–17). The Son, incarnate in Jesus, in turn gives his all back to the Father. He is perfectly obedient to the Father, seeking to do only his will (4:34), and in a supreme act of love and obedience, he lays down his life on the cross for the world's salvation (10:17–18; 14:31). In Jesus' cross, the eyes of faith are able to see the glory of God: the Father gives his all in the Son, and the Son gives his all in return to the Father. In this eternal exchange of perfect and total self-sacrificial giving, we catch a glimpse that "God is love."

As the Word made flesh, Jesus offers to draw human beings to share in this eternal exchange of life and love, the divine communion. People either accept or reject this offer of salvation and eternal life through their acceptance or rejection of Jesus. The incarnation is thus an occasion of judgment (3:19–21; 9:39). Those who reject Jesus also refuse his offer of salvation and eternal life with the Father. This is a choice to remain in sin, leading to future condemnation (8:24; 12:47–48). However, to those who receive the divine Word in faith and discipleship, Jesus gives the "power to become children of God" (1:12). He enables his disciples to become the Father's children by giving them a share in his own life and relationship with the Father as the Son.

This participation of Jesus' disciples in the divine communion is fully realized only in eternity, but it is genuinely, though imperfectly, enjoyed by the disciples in the present. By drawing his disciples into communion with himself and the Father, Jesus also draws them into communion with each other. In this way, the divine communion becomes the spiritual foundation of the Church. What binds the disciples to Jesus and to the Father and to each other is the Holy Spirit, whom the risen Jesus sends to dwell within his disciples (14:16–17; 20:22). As God dwelling in Jesus' disciples, the Holy Spirit impresses the reality of the risen Jesus onto their hearts and empowers them to be witnesses of his love. The disciples are to love and obey Jesus as he loves and obeys the Father (15:10). As the Father sent Jesus into the world, so Jesus sends his disciples into the world (15:26–27; 17:18, 21, 23). Through their love, faithful obedience, and unity, Jesus' disciples bear witness to an unbelieving world about the Father's love, revealed in the death and resurrection of his Son and made present and transformative by his Holy Spirit.

Reading the Gospel of John Today

At the end of the Gospel, the risen Jesus appears to the doubting Thomas, who demanded tangible proof of his resurrection. The scene concludes with the risen Jesus declaring, "Blessed are those who have not seen and have believed" (20:29). Like every generation of Christian believers after the first one, we are included in Jesus' beatitude: we have not seen the risen Jesus as Thomas did, and yet we believe.

The evangelist goes on to say about his accounts of the resurrection appearances: "These are written that you may [come to] believe that Jesus is the Messiah, the Son of God, and that through this belief you may have life in his name" (20:31). For John, only a personal encounter with the risen Jesus brings about faith in him as the risen Lord. Since 20:31 states that the Gospel has been written to cultivate such faith in its readers, it implies that readers can truly encounter the risen Jesus by reading the Gospel in faith. The Gospel is a way that later generations of Christians, who have not seen Jesus physically, can nevertheless truly encounter him and so believe in him.

As we approach the Gospel with an eye to encountering the risen Lord through it, we do well to imitate those habits that the Gospel teaches are appropriate to receiving the Lord. Like the disciples in the narrative, the Gospel invites its readers to approach its content with faith and humble receptivity to the Word (1:12; 8:31–32). Just as the disciples, who did not truly understand Jesus without the Holy Spirit (12:16; 16:12–15), we too are we invited to open ourselves to the Spirit's action within us. Let us, therefore, approach the Gospel with faith, receptivity, and docility before the "Spirit of Truth," who, as Jesus promised, "will guide you to all truth" (16:13).

This commentary follows the interpretive approach prescribed by the Second Vatican Council in its Dogmatic Constitution on Divine Revelation (*Dei Verbum*) and reiterated by Pope Benedict XVI in *Verbum Domini*. Our goal is a theological interpretation of John's Gospel that integrates its historical and literary dimensions as well as its reception and interpretation in the Church's tradition and faith. We hope that this exposition of John's Gospel will help readers come to know and love the risen Lord more deeply and allow the Holy Spirit to impress his reality upon their hearts. While we write from the perspective of Catholic faith and for a general Catholic readership, we also know very well the treasure to be found in studying Scripture with and learning from our non-Catholic friends. We hope that all our non-Catholic readers might find in these pages much that is valuable and edifying.

Outline of the Gospel of John

I. The Prologue (1:1–18)
   A. The Eternity of God (1:1–2)
   B. The Word's Activity in Creating (1:3–5)
   C. The Word's Activity in the World and in Israel (1:6–13)
   D. The Incarnation of the Word (1:14–18)
II. Successive Days of Revelation (1:19–2:12)
   A. The First Day of Revelation: John the Baptist, the Lord's Witness (1:19–28)
   B. The Second Day of Revelation: The Baptist's Testimony to Jesus (1:29–34)
   C. The Third Day of Revelation: The First Disciples (1:35–42)
   D. The Fourth Day of Revelation: Disciples in Galilee (1:43–51)
   E. Glory Revealed on the "Third Day": The Wedding at Cana (2:1–12)
III. Jesus' First Trip to Jerusalem (2:13–3:36)
   A. The Temple, Old and New (2:13–25)
   B. Dialogue with a Scholar and John's Reflection (3:1–21)
   C. The Baptist's Final Testimony and John's Reflection (3:22–36)
IV. Encounters with Jesus in Samaria and Galilee (4:1–54)
   A. A Samaritan Woman's Faith Journey I: Gift of Living Water (4:1–15)
   B. A Samaritan Woman's Faith Journey II: Worship in Spirit and Truth (4:16–26)
   C. A Samaritan Woman's Faith Journey III: Reaping the Fruit of Evangelization (4:27–42)

- D. A Galilean Gentile's Faith Journey: Jesus Heals an Official's Son (4:43–54)

V. The Obedient Son, Lord of the Sabbath (5:1–47)
- A. Jesus Heals on the Sabbath (5:1–9)
- B. The Controversy Begins: Working on the Sabbath (5:10–18)
- C. The Work of the Father and the Son (5:19–30)
- D. Witnesses to Jesus (5:31–40)
- E. The Accusers Accused (5:41–47)

VI. Jesus and Passover: Food for Eternal Life (6:1–71)
- A. Jesus Provides Bread for a Multitude (6:1–15)
- B. Theophany upon the Sea (6:16–21)
- C. Setting Up the Discourse: Context, the Basic Principle, and God's Work (6:22–29)
- D. The Bread of Life I: God Is Giving the Bread of Life (6:30–34)
- E. The Bread of Life II: The Father's Gift (6:35–40)
- F. The Bread of Life III: Yielding to the Father (6:41–47)
- G. The Bread of Life IV: The Bread Is Jesus' Flesh (6:48–59)
- H. Rebellion among Jesus' Followers (6:60–71)

VII. Jesus at the Festival of Tabernacles I (7:1–52)
- A. Jesus Goes to the Festival on His Own Terms (7:1–13)
- B. Who Is Jesus That He Can Say and Do These Things? (7:14–30)
- C. Jesus Announces His Departure (7:31–36)
- D. Rivers of Living Water (7:37–39)
- E. Divisions in the Crowd and the Leadership (7:40–52)

VIII. Jesus at the Festival of Tabernacles II (7:53–8:59)
- A. Jesus and a Woman Caught in Adultery (7:53–8:11)
- B. The Light of the World (8:12–20)
- C. The Obedient Son Reveals the Father (8:21–30)
- D. The Jerusalem Debate I: Jesus Brings True Freedom from Sin (8:31–36)
- E. The Jerusalem Debate II: Affiliation and Action (8:37–47)
- F. The Jerusalem Debate III: Greater Than Abraham and the Prophets (8:48–59)

IX. The Light of the World: Illumination and Judgment (9:1–41)
- A. The Light Illumines One in Darkness (9:1–7)
- B. The Questioning Begins (9:8–12)
- C. The Pharisees Debate: Sin or Sign? (9:13–17)
- D. In the Dark (9:18–23)
- E. Sight and Blindness (9:24–34)

F. The Fullness of Sight (9:35–38)
G. The Verdict (9:39–41)

X. The Good Shepherd and the Festival of Dedication (10:1–42)
A. The Shepherd Discourse I: Introducing the Imagery (10:1–6)
B. The Shepherd Discourse II: Interpreting the Imagery (10:7–21)
C. At the Festival of Hanukkah (10:22–30)
D. Blasphemy? (10:31–42)

XI. The Resurrection and the Life (11:1–54)
A. The One You Love Is Ill (11:1–6)
B. Lazarus Has Died (11:7–16)
C. The Resurrection and the Life (11:17–27)
D. The Grief of the Son of God (11:28–37)
E. The Dead Hear the Voice of the Son of God (11:38–44)
F. Plans and Prophecies (11:45–54)

XII. Jesus Goes to Jerusalem for His Passover (11:55–12:50)
A. Setting the Stage for Jesus' Arrival (11:55–57)
B. Mary Anoints Jesus for Burial (12:1–11)
C. The King of Israel (12:12–19)
D. The Hour Has Come (12:20–26)
E. The Hour of God's Triumph and Glory (12:27–36)
F. Foretold in the Scriptures (12:37–43)
G. Summary of the Book of Signs (12:44–50)

XIII. On the Night before He Died (13:1–30)
A. The Footwashing (13:1–11)
B. An Example for the Disciples (13:12–20)
C. Judas's Betrayal (13:21–30)

XIV. Farewell Discourse I (13:31–14:31)
A. Glory Revealed in Love (13:31–38)
B. Going to the Father (14:1–7)
C. Seeing the Father (14:8–14)
D. God Will Dwell in the Disciples (14:15–24)
E. Knowing Jesus' Love for the Father (14:25–31)

XV. Farewell Discourse II (15:1–16:4a)
A. The Vine and the Branches (15:1–8)
B. Bearing Fruit through Divine Love (15:9–17)
C. Confrontation with the World (15:18–16:4a)

XVI. Farewell Discourse III (16:4b–33)
A. Conviction from the Spirit (16:4b–11)
B. The Spirit of the Living God (16:12–15)

- C. Sadness Will Give Way to Joy (16:16–24)
- D. Things to Come (16:25–33)

XVII. Jesus' Prayer of Communion (17:1–26)

- A. Jesus Prays for the Glorification of Father and Son (17:1–8)
- B. Jesus Prays for His Disciples in Their Mission to the World (17:9–19)
- C. Jesus Prays for the Unity of His Church (17:20–26)

XVIII. The Hour Begins (18:1–27)

- A. Jesus Goes to His Arrest (18:1–14)
- B. Jesus before Annas and Peter's Denials (18:15–27)

XIX. The Trial before Pilate (18:28–19:16a)

- A. Scene 1 [Outside]: What Charge Do You Bring? (18:28–32)
- B. Scene 2 [Inside]: Jesus' Kingship and Kingdom (18:33–38a)
- C. Scene 3 [Outside]: Barabbas or Jesus? (18:38b–40)
- D. Scene 4: The King Is Crowned (19:1–3)
- E. Scene 5 [Outside]: Pilate Presents the King (19:4–7)
- F. Scene 6 [Inside]: "No Power over Me" (19:8–12)
- G. Scene 7 [Outside]: The Verdict (19:13–16a)

XX. No Greater Love (19:16b–42)

- A. The Crucifixion (19:16b–22)
- B. Jesus' Garments (19:23–24)
- C. The Family of God (19:25–27)
- D. Loving to the End (19:28–30)
- E. Blood and Water (19:31–37)
- F. The King's Burial (19:38–42)

XXI. Encountering the Risen Lord (20:1–31)

- A. The Empty Tomb (20:1–10)
- B. Mary Magdalene's Movement to Easter Faith (20:11–18)
- C. The Disciples' Movement to Easter Faith (20:19–25)
- D. The Movement to Easter Faith of Thomas and Future Believers (20:26–31)

XXII. The Church's Witness to the Risen Lord (21:1–25)

- A. The Risen Lord and the Church's Mission (21:1–14)
- B. Peter's Witness to the Risen Lord (21:15–19)
- C. The Beloved Disciple's Witness to the Risen Lord (21:20–25)

The Prologue

John 1:1–18

There is a special power in the words with which John begins his Gospel. What makes this hymnlike Prologue to the Fourth Gospel so profound is John's vision of the Word of God, in relation to whom all creation and history exist and have meaning (see Col 1:15–17). The divine Word was with God the Father from all eternity, was at work in creation and in the history of Israel, and then became †incarnate in Jesus. The Prologue is thus a summary of God's dealings with the world before and in the incarnation of the Word, Jesus.

The Prologue begins with the eternity of God (1:1–2) and moves to the creation of the world (1:3–5). John then recounts the divine Word's activity in the world and particularly in the history of his people Israel (1:6–13). We are then given to contemplate the incarnation: the Word of God becomes a human being in Jesus without loss of his divinity. The incarnate Word completes the Father's plan of salvation when, through his cross and resurrection, he fully reveals the Father and opens the way for humanity to enter eternal life with God (1:14–18). The rest of the Gospel plays out these themes introduced in the Prologue.

The Eternity of God (1:1–2)

[1]In the beginning was the Word,
and the Word was with God,
and the Word was God.
[2]He was in the beginning with God.

OT: Gen 1:1–5; Wis 9:1–9; Isa 55:10–11

NT: 1 Cor 8:6; Col 1:15–20; Heb 1:1–4

Catechism: knowing God, 36–38; the Trinity, 252–56

Lectionary: Christmas during the Day; Second Sunday after Christmas; Christian Initiation apart from Easter Vigil

1:1–2 The opening lines of the Gospel present the ineffable mystery of God: **In the beginning was the Word**. Throughout the Old Testament, we find many passages about God's word. In the book of Isaiah, the Lord says,

> Just as from the heavens
> the rain and snow come down
> And do not return there
> till they have watered the earth, . . .
> So shall my word be
> that goes forth from my mouth;
> It shall not return to me empty,
> but shall do what pleases me,
> achieving the end for which I sent it. (Isa 55:10–11)

The prophet Jeremiah speaks of his call: "The word of the LORD came to me: / Before I formed you in the womb I knew you" (Jer 1:4–5). In Genesis, God creates the world by speaking (Gen 1:1–5), and other texts present God as creating through his word: "By the LORD's word the heavens were made; / by the breath of his mouth all their host" (Ps 33:6).

The Word also came to be identified with God's wisdom: "Lord of mercy, / you who have made all things by your word / And in your wisdom have established humankind" (Wis 9:1–2). Some biblical texts personify God's wisdom as a heavenly figure who was present when God created (Prov 8:27–31; Wis 9:4). John invites us to have creation in mind by beginning his Gospel with the same words that opened the creation account in Gen 1: "In the beginning."

Shortly before Jesus' birth, many Jewish holy people and mystics reflected on the Lord in light of his creating and governing the world, actions that can be regarded as "the footprints" God leaves in the world.[1] The Jews knew the Lord (†YHWH) as God, the creator and ruler of all, and they fiercely defended his uniqueness as the only one worthy of worship. Biblical texts cited above also display thinking about God's Word: the divine Word can instruct a prophet, be sent on a mission, or be involved in creation. And yet, God's Word is not a creature, like an angel or servant. In the Old Testament, the Word is greater than these, but not a separate deity. We could say that the word shares God's unique identity (who God is) in such a way that God's unity is not compromised.[2]

1. See Catechism 32, 36–38.

2. Richard Bauckham, *Jesus and the God of Israel: God Crucified and Other Studies on the New Testament's Christology of Divine Identity* (Grand Rapids: Eerdmans, 2008), 1–59. Throughout the commentary, we will at times employ this notion of "sharing God's identity" set forth by Bauckham.

When the full reality of Jesus' identity is revealed, first through his own claims and then definitively through his resurrection and outpouring of the Holy Spirit, all becomes clear. What was variously attributed to God's Word, wisdom, or †Torah (law) in the Old Testament and Jewish thought now comes to be seen as attributable to the divine Word, who is one with and yet also distinct from God the Father.

While John is certainly thinking of God's Word in the Jewish tradition, his Greek word for "Word," *logos*, had an established history in Greek philosophical thinking.[3] Plato and Aristotle used the term *logos* for thought and speech that was rational.[4] For the Stoics, *logos* was the part of the universe that made it reasonable and thus understandable by humans. Combining elements from Greek philosophy and Jewish religion, the Jewish theologian Philo of Alexandria, a contemporary of the New Testament authors, wrote of God's *Logos* as an intermediary between the material world and God, who is absolutely beyond the world.

Evoking creation in Gen 1, John tells us that the Word already **was**. In effect, John is saying, "No matter when the beginning of all creation was, at that point the Word already was. He is eternal like God. He existed before all created things."[5] John expresses the relationship between God and the Word as one of distinction and unity.[6] On the one hand, **the Word was with God**; literally, the Word was "toward God." In the beginning, there was this relationship, an unimaginable fire of love, between God and his Word: the Word was turned "toward" God's face, and this turning toward was reciprocated. So there are two. On the other hand, there is a unity: **the Word was God**. Everything that God is, the Word is: they are one—and yet they are two. Once again displaying the mystery of the divine communion, John concludes, the Word **was in the beginning with God**.

The Word's Activity in Creating (1:3–5)

[3]All things came to be through him,
and without him nothing came to be.
What came to be [4]through him was life,
and this life was the light of the human race;
[5]the light shines in the darkness,
and the darkness has not overcome it.

3. Thomas H. Tobin, "Logos," *ABD* 4:348–56.
4. Ibid., 348.
5. See 1 Cor 8:6; Col 1:15–20; Heb 1:1–4.
6. Catechism 252.

OT: Gen 1:26–31

NT: 1 Cor 8:6; Col 1:15–20; Heb 1:1–4

Catechism: creation as a work of the Trinity, 290–92; image of God, 362–68

Lectionary: Christmas during the Day; Second Sunday after Christmas; Christian Initiation apart from Easter Vigil

1:3 The divine Word is the agent by which God created everything: **All things came to be through him, and without him nothing came to be** (Wis 9:1; 1 Cor 8:6; Col 1:16; Heb 1:2). The expression "through him" suggests cooperation in the act of creation.[7] God the Father gazes on his Word, who is his perfect expression, "the image of the invisible God" (Col 1:15), "the refulgence of his glory, the very imprint of his being" (Heb 1:3). The Word perfectly reflects all that the Father is, expressing all that can ever be created. God the Father creates what he sees imaged in his Word, and thus nothing came to be without the Word.

1:3c–4 **What came to be through him was life.** There are different levels of life in the world: plants, animals, humans, and angels. While human life has some things in common with animals, we are created "in the image of God" (Gen 1:27). Human beings are animated by the light of the *Logos*, so that we have a soul with the capacity to be in relationship with God by knowing and loving him: **this life was the light of the human race.**[8] The imagery of light appears throughout Scripture to refer to God's radiant splendor (Exod 13:21; Ps 4:7; 36:10; Isa 60:19–20) and his instructions for living (Ps 119:105, 130). John's Gospel employs light symbolism to present Jesus as "the light of the world" (8:12; 9:5), who reveals the Father and his will and offers the gift of eternal life.

1:5 John continues, **The light shines in the darkness, and the darkness has not overcome it.** In the Fourth Gospel, darkness is a symbol for sin, understood broadly as the spiritual condition of alienation from God (see sidebar on p. 163). This darkness, or evil, is not an eternal force or "stuff" opposite God, as in the heresy called Manichaeism (see Catechism 285). Rather, we can think of evil as a corruption in something originally good or as the absence of some good that ought to be present.[9] Moreover, the verb translated "overcome" can also mean "comprehend." The spiritual darkness can neither overpower the light nor understand the light and its ways.[10]

7. Catechism 291–92.

8. Catechism 362–65, 367.

9. St. Augustine, *Confessions*, trans. Henry Chadwick (New York: Oxford University, 1998), 7.12.18. All citations of this work are taken from this translation.

10. Consider the inability of the fictional demon Screwtape ("Letter 19") to understand that love is God's genuine motive in his dealings with humanity; C. S. Lewis, *The Screwtape Letters* (1942, repr., New York: HarperCollins, 2001), 99–103.

The Word's Activity in the World and in Israel (1:6–13)

[6]A man named John was sent from God. [7]He came for testimony, to testify to the light, so that all might believe through him. [8]He was not the light, but came to testify to the light. [9]The true light, which enlightens everyone, was coming into the world.

> **[10]He was in the world,**
> **and the world came to be through him,**
> **but the world did not know him.**
> **[11]He came to what was his own,**
> **but his own people did not accept him.**

[12]But to those who did accept him he gave power to become children of God, to those who believe in his name, [13]who were born not by natural generation nor by human choice nor by a man's decision but of God.

OT: Exod 19:3–8; Hosea 11:1–4; Isa 43:1–8
NT: Rom 1:18–32
Catechism: Old Covenant, 121; Word in Israel, 707–16; human reason and will, 1701–9
Lectionary: Christmas during the Day; 2nd Sunday after Christmas; Christian Initiation apart from Easter Vigil

1:6–8 The Evangelist introduces the last and greatest of the prophets: **John** the Baptist, who **was sent from God**. The Baptist's primary role in the Fourth Gospel is to be a witness to Jesus: the Baptist **was not the light, but came to testify to the light**. The purpose of his testimony **to the light** is **so that all might believe through him**. The Gospel later declares that Moses and the whole of Scripture bear witness to Jesus (1:45; 2:22; 5:39). The Baptist appears here as a representative of all who "testify to the light," meaning the whole prophetic tradition. Israel's prophets, to whom "the word of God came" (1 Chron 17:3), spoke his will and announced his coming. The Baptist completes this prophetic witness to the light: he came so that the light "might be made known to Israel" (1:31).

1:9–10 The Evangelist traces the active presence of the Light, or Word, in creation and especially in Israel. He first speaks of creation at large: **the true light, which enlightens everyone, was coming into the world**. All human beings are illumined by the divine Light in our capacity to reason, to know the truth.[11] As St. Thomas Aquinas teaches, "The light of natural reason itself is a participation of the divine light."[12] Our natural ability to know the truth "whereby we

11. Catechism 1701–9.

12. St. Thomas Aquinas, *Summa theologica* 1, q. 12, a. 11, reply obj. 3, trans. Fathers of the English Dominican Province (New York: Benziger Brothers, 1947–48). All quotations of his *Summa theologica* will be taken from this translation.

discern what is good and what is evil . . . is nothing else than an imprint on us of the divine light."[13] Human beings can know the truth and discern good from evil by our own natural abilities, which are themselves gifts from God. Wherever there is truth or goodness in the world, there is a trace of the divine Word. As St. Justin Martyr writes, "Everything that the [pagan] philosophers and legislators discovered and expressed well, they accomplished through their discovery and contemplation of some part of the Logos [i.e., God's Word]."[14] The Light, which **was in the world**, is the divine Word **through** whom the world was made.

However, the world preferred to ignore the Light: **the world did not know him**. As St. Paul writes in Rom 1:18, human beings, despite the witness to God in creation, "in their wickedness suppress the truth."[15] Although the Fourth Gospel does not have an explicit account of original sin, it affirms that the world, which God created good (see Gen 1:31), has fallen into sin, spiritual darkness, for refusing to acknowledge and receive the divine Light.

1:11–13 Among the nations of the world, God chose a special people as his own: the people Israel. God entered into a †covenant with them (Exod 19:3–8) that "has never been revoked" (Catechism 121), because "the gifts and the call of God are irrevocable" (Rom 11:29). The divine Word was close to them in a particular way, and many drew close to him.[16] But many of **his own people did not accept him**. The word "accept" means to receive in faith, to receive the Word into one's self and allow him to transform one's life. As evidenced in the Old Testament, many Israelites refused to hear the Word that was spoken through the prophets. They persisted in sinning and "forgot" the Lord (Hosea 2:15). As a consequence, the Lord meted out the covenantal punishment of exile and scattering (Deut 28:63–64), breaking up the people, the twelve tribes of Israel, and scattering them among the Gentile nations (2 Kings 17:6–7, 12, 23; 25:8–11). However, the ever-faithful Lord promised through the prophets that he would redeem his people from their sin and punishment in a great, future act of salvation—a new exodus (Isa 43:1–8; Jer 16:14–15).

While many did not accept the divine Word, some Israelites **did accept him**. John combines the faithful in Israel's past with those who accept the Word in his own day, the new Israel (John 1:47). He then specifies the gift that the Word gives to those who accept him: **he gave power to become children of God, to**

13. St. Thomas Aquinas, *Summa theologica* 1–2, q. 91, a. 2.

14. Justin Martyr, *Second Apology* 10, in *Writings of Saint Justin Martyr*, trans. Thomas B. Falls, FC 6 (New York: Christian Heritage, 1948), 129.

15. Our translation; compare NABRE, "suppress the truth by their wickedness."

16. Catechism 707–16.

"The World" and Dualism in John

BIBLICAL BACKGROUND

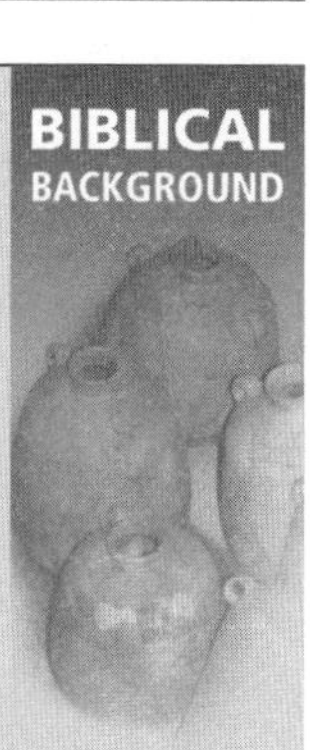

The Fourth Gospel uses the expression "the world" in a variety of senses. "The world" can mean creation. God created the world through his Word (1:3, 10), and in light of Gen 1, the world is essentially good. God's unimaginable love for the world is the reason he sent his Son into the world to save it (3:16–17). But the very fact that the world needs to be saved points to a deeper theological sense in which John uses the term "the world" to designate human beings and their world as they reject and rebel against God by sin. This second use of "the world" illustrates a stylistic feature of John's writings, known as dualism. Dualism is the way in which John often frames matters in pairs of opposites, such as light and darkness, life and death, truth and lies. John often uses the category "the world" in a dualistic way, contrasting it with the Father, Jesus, and his disciples. When "the world" is used in this dualist way, it is a fundamentally a spiritual category—that is, John is not primarily talking about creation as such. Donatien Mollat puts it this way:

> At the heart of this world [used in a negative sense], the author of the Gospel uncovers an irreducible core of resistance to God. He has the intuition of a formidable power of negation and refusal, which exceeds human limits and plunges its roots into a dark center of hatred and lies (8:44; 1 John 3:12). His gaze discovers a pit of "darkness" to which man is moving and in which he is plunged by his sin ([see] 13:30).
>
> The dualistic context is not for John a cosmic or metaphysical context. It is a spiritual structure which sets forth a reality of the moral order and which demonstrates at what depth salvation intervenes, what struggles it must face, what an abyss of pride and rebellion it must overcome. Johannine dualism is inscribed within a world of liberty and choice. The notion of "world" serves to unmask the demonic universe of refusal and rejection.[a]

a. Donatien Mollat, "Jean L'Évangéliste (Saint)," *Dictionnaire de Spiritualité*, vol. 8 (Paris: Beauchesne, 1974), 200; and *St. Jean: Maître Spirituel* (Paris: Beauchesne, 1976), 26, our translation.

those who believe in his name. The people of Israel were already considered God's children: "Thus says the Lord: Israel is my son, my firstborn" (Exod 4:22).[17] Their privileged identity as God's chosen people was bound up with physical generation, creating kinship, and with †Torah observance. But John speaks of a new kind of generation, a spiritual generation, which comes about through faith in the Word and by a unique, direct action of God himself. Such people are **born not by natural generation nor by human choice nor by a**

17. There are many texts in which Israel calls God our/your "father" (Deut 32:6; Isa 63:16; 64:7, etc.) and where the people of Israel are called God's children or "son" (Wis 2:13–18; 5:5; Hosea 11:1–4).

man's decision but of God. The reason for this new development appears in the next verse.

The Incarnation of the Word (1:14–18)

[14]And the Word became flesh
and made his dwelling among us,
and we saw his glory,
the glory as of the Father's only Son,
full of grace and truth.

[15]John testified to him and cried out, saying, "This was he of whom I said, 'The one who is coming after me ranks ahead of me because he existed before me.'" [16]From his fullness we have all received, grace in place of grace, [17]because while the law was given through Moses, grace and truth came through Jesus Christ. [18]No one has ever seen God. The only Son, God, who is at the Father's side, has revealed him.

OT: Exod 33:18–23; 40:34–38
NT: Phil 2:6–11; Heb 1:1–4
Catechism: incarnation, 456–63, 470
Lectionary: Christmas during the Day; Second Sunday after Christmas; Christian Initiation apart from Easter Vigil

1:14 John presents the heart of the Christian mystery and the cause of our becoming "children of God": **the Word became flesh.** It is the mystery of the †incarnation: the divine Word, who from all eternity is turned toward God and is himself God, has become completely human in Jesus.[18] God, the creator and ruler of all things, has now become part of creation. The divine Word, who was "in the form of God, . . . emptied himself, taking the form of a slave" (Phil 2:6–7).

In the incarnation, the divine Word **made his dwelling among us**. The phrase "made his dwelling" (Greek *skēnoō*) evokes the language used to designate God's "dwelling" among his people in the Old Testament (†LXX *skēnē*). God dwelt with his people in the wilderness tabernacle (Exod 25:8–9) and in the first Jerusalem temple, built by King Solomon (1 Kings 8:10–13). God's wisdom made a home in Israel (Sir 24:8), and Ezekiel spoke of a future temple to be established in connection with God's end-time, or †eschatological, act of salvation (Ezek 37:27–28; 48:10). Thus God dwelt among his people in earlier

18. Catechism 461–63.

The Glory of the Lord

BIBLICAL BACKGROUND

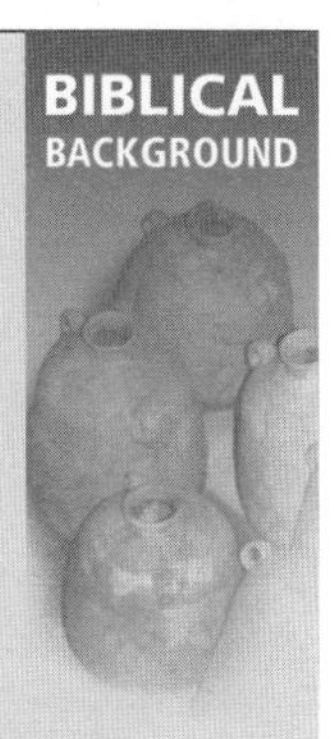

Scripture often speaks of "the glory of the LORD," a perceptible and utterly awesome manifestation of God. The glory is "God himself insofar as he is revealed in His majesty, His power, the glow of His holiness, the dynamism of His being."[a] The "glory" was an overpowering spectacle; the Hebrew word for "glory" (*kabod*) is related to the verb for heaping weight on something (*kabad*). The glory of the Lord often appeared in the form of fire and cloud at places of God's dwelling. The glory was manifested at Mount Sinai (Exod 24:17), and when the wilderness tabernacle was finished, "the glory of the LORD filled the tabernacle" (40:34). When King Solomon built the Jerusalem temple, "the glory of the LORD had filled" it (1 Kings 8:11). Ezekiel had a vision of the glory of the Lord leaving Solomon's temple before it was destroyed (Ezek 10:18–19; 11:22–23) and a vision of the Lord's glory returning to dwell in a new temple in the end times (Ezek 43:1–5).

a. Donatien Mollat, "Glory," in *Dictionary of Biblical Theology*, ed. Xavier Léon-Dufour, 2nd ed. (Gaithersburg, MD: Word Among Us; Boston: St. Paul's Books and Media, 1995), 202.

times, but now he does so in a previously unimaginable way: he dwells among us as a man, Jesus of Nazareth.

As the new, unparalleled place of God's dwelling, the incarnate Word is the fullness of God's revelation. John makes this claim with his statement, **We saw his glory**. The Scripture speaks of the Lord's "glory" as a perceptible manifestation of his awesome presence. By seeing **his glory**, John refers to a sensible revelation of God himself in Jesus, the incarnate Word.

What John previously articulated in terms of God and the Word, he now expresses more deeply in the intimate, family language of **Father** and **Son**. The Father's **only** Son is **full of grace and truth**, the Lord's "loving-kindness and faithfulness" for which he is praised throughout the Scripture (Ps 25:10, "mercy and truth"; 117:2, "mercy" and "faithfulness"). Recall that in 1:12 the divine Word enables those who receive him in faith "to become children of God." The family language of Father and Son sheds more light on this reality: Jesus is the Son, and to become a child of God means to share in Jesus' own divine life as the Son.

1:15 The Baptist, who was previously mentioned as the summit of prophetic witness (1:6–8), now gives explicit witness to the Son: **This was he of whom I said, "The one who is coming after me ranks ahead of me because he existed before me"** (see v. 30).

Saint Teresa of Avila on Devotion to Christ's Humanity

Saint Teresa recounts reading some books claiming that "corporeal images, even when referring to the humanity of Christ, are an obstacle or impediment to the most perfect contemplation." These books were arguing that real growth in the spiritual life can happen only when a person is totally separated from any kind of material image of God. However, Teresa came to learn that the humanity of Christ, expressed in images of him, is not an obstacle but a great help for growth in holiness:

> I thought the humanity was an impediment [to prayer]. . . . I had been so devoted all my life to Christ, . . . and thus I always returned to my custom of rejoicing in this Lord, especially when I received Communion. I wanted to keep ever before my eyes a painting or image of Him since I was unable to keep Him as engraved in my soul as I desired. Is it possible, my Lord, that it entered my mind even for an hour that You would be an impediment to my greater good? Where have all my blessings come from but from You? . . . [You sent someone to correct my thinking and You let] me see You so many times [in mystical visions] . . . so that I would understand more clearly how great the error is, and tell many persons what I just said, and put it in writing here.[a]

a. St. Teresa of Avila, *The Book of Her Life* 22.1–4, in *The Collected Works of St. Teresa of Avila*, trans. K. Kavanaugh, OCD, and O. Rodriguez, OCD (Washington, DC: ICS Publications, 1987), 1:191–93.

1:16–17 The Evangelist then begins his own witness to the incarnate Word as the fulfillment of God's saving plan. The **fullness** of the Son is his being everything the Father is ("the Word was God") except that he is distinct from the Father (he "was with God," 1:1). **From** this divine relationship **we have all received, grace in place of grace**. John sees salvation history as marked by two great gifts from God. The first is God's gift of the †Torah to Israel: **the law was given through Moses**. As the psalmist prays, "How I love your law, Lord! / I study it all day long" (Ps 119:97). The second and even greater gift is **grace and truth**, the fullness of divine revelation **through Jesus Christ** (Heb 1:1–2). The relationship between Torah and Jesus is not to be understood as bad followed by good, but as good followed by better. The "better" is a direct, living encounter with the Word incarnate through the Holy Spirit; the "good" was a real but partial encounter with the Word through the Torah—an anticipated participation.

1:18 **No one has ever seen God**, "who dwells in unapproachable light, and whom no human being has seen or can see" (1 Tim 6:16). Even Moses, after he prayed that he might be allowed to see God (Exod 33:18), was granted only a fleeting glimpse of his "back" (33:23), for God declared, "You cannot see my face, for no one can see me and live" (33:20). God is so awesome and magnificent that the direct sight of him would so overwhelm us that we would die. But now, **the only Son, God, who is at the Father's side, has revealed him**. The Son, who is God's Word and Wisdom, has become a human being in Jesus of Nazareth without any loss of his divinity. In Jesus, people can see, hear, and touch God himself directly. As Pope St. John Paul II taught, in Jesus we see "the human face of God."[19] By receiving his revelation, we can begin to know the truth of Jesus' words: "Whoever has seen me has seen the Father" (14:9).

Reflection and Application (1:1–18)

John's Prologue presents the mystery of the incarnation: God became human in Jesus. This mystery infinitely surpasses human comprehension. The history of Christianity offers many instances of intellectual and spiritual shipwrecks that occurred when the mystery was not respected. In the early Church, on the one hand, some were so taken with the divinity of the Word that they minimized or denied the genuineness of Jesus' humanity. These gnostics (who have modern New Age successors) attempted to spiritualize Jesus and make of him some sort of benign force in the universe, thus denying his real humanity. On the other hand, some have not accepted Jesus' divinity but considered him a good man, a great religious teacher among many others.

In order to hold on to both the divinity and the humanity of Jesus, we need to become better acquainted with his living reality as he is present in our everyday lives. We can strengthen our grasp of his incarnation and deepen the experiential dimension of our faith by taking a few simple steps. First, we can spend time in prayer every day and during that time read the Bible (praying John's Prologue is a great place to start). Second, we can guard our minds from the busyness and anxiety that distract us by making time for silence in our day. Reducing our consumption of mass media helps us to avoid the excess of information that only confuses the mind and paralyzes the will. Third, we can open ourselves up to the will of God, for as St. Paul declares, "This is the will of God, your holiness" (1 Thess 4:3). Fourth, we can live a life that takes the incarnation of our God seriously by attending Mass, frequenting the sacraments, and finding a way to care for the poor, for they are Christ among us in a special way: "Amen, I say to you, whatever you did for one of these least brothers of mine, you did for me" (Matt 25:40).

19. John Paul II, "Angelus: Feast of the Baptism of the Lord," January 11, 2004.

Successive Days of Revelation

John 1:19–2:12

The first major section of the Gospel, "The Book of †Signs" (John 1–12), narrates Jesus' public ministry. Within the Book of Signs, the first subsection (1:19–4:54) contains a series of incidents and dialogues that occur as Jesus travels back and forth between Judea and Galilee. Throughout this section, the invitation to faith in Jesus is offered to different people.

John 1:19–51 contains a sequence of four days of revelation in which different aspects of Jesus' identity are revealed. This sequence of days of revelation reaches its high point and completion at the wedding feast at Cana (2:1–12). In this sequence of days, John introduces us to Jesus, whose identity and role in the divine plan is given in a series of titles, such as the Lamb of God, †Messiah, Son of God, and †Son of Man.

The First Day of Revelation: John the Baptist, the Lord's Witness (1:19–28)

[19]And this is the testimony of John. When the Jews from Jerusalem sent priests and Levites [to him] to ask him, "Who are you?" [20]he admitted and did not deny it, but admitted, "I am not the Messiah." [21]So they asked him, "What are you then? Are you Elijah?" And he said, "I am not." "Are you the Prophet?" He answered, "No." [22]So they said to him, "Who are you, so we can give an answer to those who sent us? What do you have to say for yourself?" [23]He said:

"I am 'the voice of one crying out in the desert,
"Make straight the way of the Lord,"'

as Isaiah the prophet said." [24]Some Pharisees were also sent. [25]They asked him, "Why then do you baptize if you are not the Messiah or Elijah or the Prophet?" [26]John answered them, "I baptize with water; but there is one among you whom you do not recognize, [27]the one who is coming after me, whose sandal strap I am not worthy to untie." [28]This happened in Bethany across the Jordan, where John was baptizing.

OT: Deut 18:15–20; 2 Kings 1:3–8; Isa 40:1–5; Mal 3:23–24
NT: Matt 3:1–12; 17:10–13
Catechism: John the Baptist, 717–20
Lectionary: Third Sunday of Advent (Year B)

1:19–21

The Evangelist introduces us to the **testimony** or "witness" of John the Baptist. Testimony, or witness, is an important term in John's Gospel. Instead of using the term "evangelize," John speaks of "witnessing," which in a Christian context suggests not only personal, firsthand knowledge but also risking one's all.[1]

A delegation **from Jerusalem** arrives, **sent** to find out whether John is, or thinks he is, one of the end-time figures whom Jews were expecting. There was no uniform expectation for a messianic figure in Jewish antiquity, and the various titles in this section (†Messiah, Elijah, the Prophet) reflect the diversity of end-time expectations. The Baptist openly acknowledges, **I am not the Messiah**, God's promised deliverer.

The Jerusalem delegation then asks, **Are you Elijah?** Some biblical texts prophesied that Elijah the prophet would return before God's end-time action to save his people and punish the wicked. The prophet Malachi describes Elijah's role in the end times:

> Now I am sending to you
> Elijah the prophet,
> Before the day of the LORD comes . . . .
> He will turn the heart of fathers to their sons,
> and the heart of sons to their fathers. (Mal 3:23–24; see Sir 48:4, 10)

As described in Matthew and Mark, John the Baptist's manner of life and dress were patterned on that of Elijah (compare 2 Kings 1:8 and Matt 3:4). Here the Baptist denies that he is *literally* the prophet Elijah; yet in the †Synoptics,

1. The Greek term for "testimony" (*martyria*) underlies our English word "martyr."

Fig. 1. Jordan River

Jesus speaks of him as Elijah (Matt 17:11–13) in the sense of acting "in the spirit and power of Elijah" (Luke 1:17).[2]

The Baptist also denies that he is **the Prophet**. In Deut 18:15, Moses says, "A prophet like me will the LORD, your God, raise up for you from among your own kindred; that is the one to whom you shall listen." This text formed the basis for the expectation of a †Prophet-like-Moses, a messianic figure to come, and later in the Gospel, many people think of Jesus in this role (6:14–15; 7:40).

1:22–23 After the delegation asks the Baptist to identify himself, he responds in words that were then stirring many hearts in Israel: **I am "the voice of one crying out in the desert, 'Make straight the way of the Lord,'" as Isaiah the prophet said**. The Baptist is quoting the opening lines of Isa 40. This text is cited in the †Dead Sea Scrolls, where it expresses the desire for "the consolation of Israel" (Luke 2:25)—the hope that God would fulfill his promises to save his people from their †covenantal punishment and suffering.[3] By applying these words to himself, the Baptist awakens in many hearts the expectation that the promised time of salvation is close.

1:24–28 Not only are "priests and Levites" (1:19) in the Jerusalem delegation but also †**Pharisees**. Their question, **Why then do you baptize?**, searches for the basis of

2. Catechism 718.
3. In the Dead Sea Scrolls, see 1QS 8.12–14.

the Baptist's authority and the reason for his activity. The Baptist responds by pointing to the dignity of **the one who is coming** and the fact that he himself is beneath the status of this one's slave (**whose sandal strap I am not worthy to untie**). The first day closes with the specification of the geographical location of the Baptist's activity: **in Bethany across the Jordan.**

The Second Day of Revelation: The Baptist's Testimony to Jesus (1:29–34)

[29]The next day he saw Jesus coming toward him and said, "Behold, the Lamb of God, who takes away the sin of the world. [30]He is the one of whom I said, 'A man is coming after me who ranks ahead of me because he existed before me.' [31]I did not know him, but the reason why I came baptizing with water was that he might be made known to Israel." [32]John testified further, saying, "I saw the Spirit come down like a dove from the sky and remain upon him. [33]I did not know him, but the one who sent me to baptize with water told me, 'On whomever you see the Spirit come down and remain, he is the one who will baptize with the holy Spirit.' [34]Now I have seen and testified that he is the Son of God."

OT: Exod 12:1–13; Lev 1:10–13; Isa 11:1–9; 52:13–53:12

NT: Matt 3:13–17; 1 Pet 1:17–21; Rev 5:1–14

Catechism: Jesus, only Son of God, 441–45; Jesus' baptism, 535–37, 1223–25; Lamb of God, 608; Christ's death as the definitive sacrifice, 613–14

Lectionary: Second Sunday of Ordinary Time (Year A); Christian Initiation apart from Easter Vigil

1:29 The Prologue indicated that the Baptist's primary role is "to testify" or bear witness to Jesus (1:6–8, 15). On this second day, Jesus appears in the Gospel for the first time, and the Baptist gives his testimony about him.

The Evangelist begins with a turn of phrase that is a recurring pattern in the Gospel: someone *sees* another person and *says* something about him or her (1:29, 36, 47; 19:26–27).[4] This is a formula of revelation in which one person sees another and then reveals that person's role in God's plan. In this first instance, the Baptist **saw Jesus** and **said, "Behold, the Lamb of God, who takes away the sin of the world.** The title **Lamb of God** combines several biblical allusions.[5] First, the lamb is central in the Passover liturgy, which celebrates the exodus, God's mighty act to save the Israelites from slavery in Egypt (Exod 12:1–13).

4. Michel de Goedt, "Un schème de révélation dans le Quatrième Evangile," *New Testament Studies* 8 (1962): 142–50.

5. Catechism 608.

New Testament writers depict Jesus as the new Passover Lamb, whose sacrificial death brings about deliverance from sin and reconciliation with God (John 19:14, 36; 1 Cor 5:7; 1 Pet 1:19; Rev 5:9). Second, the title "Lamb" resonates with the temple's sacrificial system in which lambs, as well as other animals and items of value, were offered to God in worship as sacrifices. Thus "Lamb" alludes to the animal sacrifices by which the people's sins were ceremonially purged and reconciliation with God was attained (Lev 1:1–13). Jesus, however, is not just one more liturgical sacrifice: he is the Lamb, who definitively lifts off the whole mass of sin and evil that presses upon the whole human race, and he brings about complete reconciliation with God (see sidebar on p. 163).[6] Third, the book of Isaiah describes a Suffering Servant of the Lord, who goes to his death to obtain forgiveness for others' sins as "a lamb led to slaughter" (Isa 53:7). Since Jesus talks about his death with reference to the Suffering Servant (John 3:14–15; 8:28; 12:32; see Isa 52:13), we can see in the title "Lamb" an allusion to the Suffering Servant.

1:30 The Baptist next refers to Jesus' divine dignity: **A man is coming after me who ranks ahead of me because he existed before me.**[7] These words recall the Prologue. The divine Word existed eternally with God the Father from before creation (1:1). The preexistence of the Word is why the Baptist repeats his testimony from 1:15, "This was he of whom I said, 'The one who is coming after me ranks ahead of me because he existed before me.'"

1:31–34 The Baptist also acknowledges that he did not recognize Jesus, even though his vocation was to speak out so **that** the One to come **might be made known to Israel**. It was when he baptized Jesus that he saw the Spirit descend and rest upon Jesus and recalled God's words to him: **On whomever you see the Spirit come down and remain, he is the one**. The Holy Spirit's descent and remaining upon Jesus fulfilled God's promise in Isaiah 11:2 of an ideal future king: "The spirit of the LORD shall rest upon him." Through this promised king, "the earth shall be filled with knowledge of the LORD" (Isa 11:9). The One on whom God's Spirit rests will bring peace and fill people with the knowledge of the Lord because he **will baptize with the holy Spirit**. That is, Jesus will send God's Spirit to dwell in and purify his people—something God had promised to do in the end times (see sidebar on p. 47). Anointed with and possessing the Holy Spirit, Jesus is able to pour the same Holy Spirit out upon humanity.[8] After seeing the Spirit descend and remain upon Jesus, the Baptist testified to Jesus' true reality: **He is the Son of God.**[9]

6. The phrase "take away the sin" reflects the common biblical metaphor that likens sin to a burden or weight. See Gary A. Anderson, *Sin: A History* (New Haven: Yale University Press, 2009).

7. Compare Matt 3:14–15.

8. Catechism 536.

9. Catechism 444.

The Biblical Promise of the Holy Spirit

BIBLICAL BACKGROUND

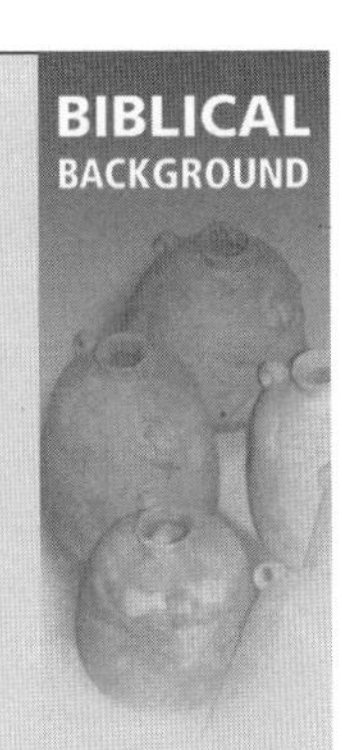

Many biblical prophets teach that when God works his definitive act of salvation at the end of time, he will pour out the Spirit (Isa 32:15; 44:3; Ezek 36:24–28; 39:29; Joel 3:1–2; Zech 12:10). Ezekiel says that God will put his own Spirit within his redeemed people when he makes a new †covenant with them: "I will put my spirit within you so that you walk in my statutes" (Ezek 36:27). Similarly, God says through the prophet Joel,

> I will pour out my spirit upon all flesh.
> Your sons and daughters will prophesy,
> your old men will dream dreams. . . .
> In those days, I will pour out my spirit. (Joel 3:1–2)

The expression "pour out the spirit" is a way of referring to a future manifold blessing. Among the blessings connected to the outpouring of the Spirit are the following: reconciliation with God (Isa 44:3–5; Ezek 39:29); purification from sins and re-creation by God (Ezek 36:25–27; 37:9–10, 14); creation of obedient hearts that are receptive and capable of love and petitionary prayer (Ezek 36:26–27; Zech 12:10); profound inner knowledge of God and his teaching (Jer 31:31–34; Ezek 36:24–28); and charismatic gifts, such as prophecy (Joel 3:1–2). When this promise was fulfilled at Jesus' death and resurrection, it was revealed to be the personal presence, within the faithful, of the Holy Spirit himself, who enlightens them, empowers them, and gives them joy.

The Third Day of Revelation: The First Disciples (1:35–42)

[35]The next day John was there again with two of his disciples, [36]and as he watched Jesus walk by, he said, "Behold, the Lamb of God." [37]The two disciples heard what he said and followed Jesus. [38]Jesus turned and saw them following him and said to them, "What are you looking for?" They said to him, "Rabbi" (which translated means Teacher), "where are you staying?" [39]He said to them, "Come, and you will see." So they went and saw where he was staying, and they stayed with him that day. It was about four in the afternoon. [40]Andrew, the brother of Simon Peter, was one of the two who heard John and followed Jesus. [41]He first found his own brother Simon and told him, "We have found the Messiah" (which is translated Anointed). [42]Then he brought him to Jesus. Jesus looked at him and said, "You are Simon the son of John; you will be called Cephas" (which is translated Peter).

Pope Benedict XVI on "Baptism in the Holy Spirit"

> The Holy Spirit consecrates the person and at the same time makes him or her a living member of the Mystical Body of Christ, sharing in the mission of witnessing to his love. And this takes place through the Sacraments of Christian initiation. . . . Today I would like to extend the invitation to all: let us rediscover, dear brothers and sisters, the beauty of being baptized in the Holy Spirit; let us recover awareness of our Baptism and our Confirmation, ever timely sources of grace.[a]

a. Pope Benedict XVI, "Homily at the Regina Caeli on the Solemnity of Pentecost," May 11, 2008. The expression "baptize in the Holy Spirit" refers to the grace of being interiorly aware of the action of the Holy Spirit. See Francis Martin, *Baptism in the Holy Spirit: A Scriptural Foundation* (Steubenville, OH: Franciscan University Press, 1986).

OT: Gen 17:3–8; 32:24–31
NT: Matt 16:13–20
Catechism: desire for God, 27–30; the title Christ, 436–39
Lectionary: Second Sunday of Ordinary Time (Year B); The Preparation and Baptism of Adults

1:35–36 The third day begins with the same "see and say" revelation formula that opened the previous day (1:29). With **two of his disciples** standing by, **John** sees **Jesus walk by** and again declares his role in the divine plan: **Behold, the Lamb of God**.

1:37–39 Then something new happens. Having **heard** the Baptist's testimony about Jesus, these two begin the journey of discipleship: they **followed Jesus**. Then **Jesus turned** and with his first words in the Gospel, asks them a question that confronts every person: **What are you looking for?** Responding to him, but thinking of Jesus more as a teacher than as Lord, they ask, **Rabbi [Teacher], where are you staying?** Jesus' response is both an invitation and a promise: **Come, and you will see**. The two disciples **stayed with** Jesus all **that day**, until **four in the afternoon**. The Greek verb translated as "stayed" (*menō*) is theologically significant in John. The same verb is translated elsewhere as "remain." Jesus uses this verb to denote his intimate relationship with the Father, the divine communion (14:10; 15:10), into which he calls his disciples (15:9). When the two disciples **saw where he was staying**, they not only learned where Jesus was lodging in an earthly sense, but they also began to discover his true, spiritual abode with the Father.

1:40–42 **Andrew** is one of these two disciples. Just as these two came to Jesus through the Baptist's testimony, we now see them bringing others to Jesus through their own testimony. Andrew **found his own brother Simon**. Andrew tells Simon that he and his companion **have found the Messiah.** While it is difficult for us to imagine the impact of this claim on a first-century Jew, its meaning is clear: God has come to honor his promises to Israel in this man.[10]

Andrew then **brought** Simon **to Jesus**, and we again find the "see and say" revelation formula in which one person sees another and then says what his or her role is in God's plan (1:29, 36). **Jesus looked at** Simon **and** declared, **You are Simon the son of John; you will be called Cephas.**[11] Jesus thus declares to Peter his role in God's plan: as Abram became Abraham (Gen 17:5) and Jacob became Israel (Gen 32:29), so now Simon becomes *Kēphas*, "the Rock," the foundation of the Church that Jesus will build (Matt 16:18). At the end of the Gospel, Jesus will entrust his sheep to Peter and give Peter a unique share in his role as the good shepherd (21:15–19).

Reflection and Application (1:35–42)

When Jesus first speaks in the Gospel, he asks the two disciples, "What are you looking for?" (1:38). This same question confronts everyone: What are we seeking in life? What will make us truly happy and fulfilled? An important element of the gospel is that only in God do human beings find their perfection and fulfillment (Catechism 27–30). God made us in such a way that only he, and no created things—although they are good too in their own way—can completely satisfy our deepest longing. As St. Augustine famously put it, "You stir man to take pleasure in praising you, because you have made us for yourself, and our heart is restless until it rests in you."[12] We are invited to identify ourselves with these two disciples in the Gospel and heed Jesus' invitation: "Come, and you will see" (1:39). For it is only in coming to Jesus, the Word made flesh, and abiding in him that we will find the fulfillment and happiness for which we were created.

The Fourth Day of Revelation: Disciples in Galilee (1:43–51)

[43]The next day he decided to go to Galilee, and he found Philip. And Jesus said to him, "Follow me." [44]Now Philip was from Bethsaida, the town

10. Catechism 436.

11. "Cephas" is from *Kēphas*, the Greek form of the Aramaic word *Kepha'*, which like the Greek word *petra* (leading to the name "Peter") means "rock." Paul refers to Simon Peter by this Aramaic name in 1 Cor 1:12; 15:5; Gal 2:9, 11.

12. St. Augustine, *Confessions* 1.1.1.

of Andrew and Peter. [45]Philip found Nathanael and told him, "We have found the one about whom Moses wrote in the law, and also the prophets, Jesus son of Joseph, from Nazareth." [46]But Nathanael said to him, "Can anything good come from Nazareth?" Philip said to him, "Come and see." [47]Jesus saw Nathanael coming toward him and said of him, "Here is a true Israelite. There is no duplicity in him." [48]Nathanael said to him, "How do you know me?" Jesus answered and said to him, "Before Philip called you, I saw you under the fig tree." [49]Nathanael answered him, "Rabbi, you are the Son of God; you are the King of Israel." [50]Jesus answered and said to him, "Do you believe because I told you that I saw you under the fig tree? You will see greater things than this." [51]And he said to him, "Amen, amen, I say to you, you will see the sky opened and the angels of God ascending and descending on the Son of Man."

OT: Gen 28:10–19; Ps 32:1–2; Dan 7:13–14
NT: Mark 1:16–20; Luke 6:12–16
Catechism: angels, 328–36
Lectionary: St. Bartholomew; Feast of the Archangels; For Vocations of Priests and Religious

1:43–44 After gathering these disciples, Jesus traveled north **to Galilee**. On the previous days (1:29, 35), the call of the disciples took place through the witness of another. The first two disciples went to Jesus after hearing the Baptist's testimony, and then Peter was brought to Jesus through Andrew. Now, in a pattern similar to the call stories in the †Synoptics (see Mark 1:16–20), Jesus himself calls **Philip**: **Follow me**. Philip's home was **Bethsaida**, a rather large town on the northeast tip of the Sea of Galilee and also the hometown of **Andrew and Peter**.

1:45 **Philip found Nathanael** there (Nathanael has been traditionally identified as St. Bartholomew, one of the Twelve Apostles; see Luke 6:14) and declared Jesus' messianic identity: **We have found the one about whom Moses wrote in the law, and also the prophets, Jesus, son of Joseph, from Nazareth**. After encountering Jesus, Philip sees in him the fulfillment of God's promises in Scripture to act on behalf of his people. Behind and above all the great figures in the history of God's people, there is a unifying reality, foreshadowed in the lives of the patriarchs and prophets, hinted at in Israel's "poor" ones who are especially faithful to and reliant upon the Lord (Ps 10:17; 14:6), and glimpsed in the righteous kings. He is the one to come, the object of mystical longing. He is the one described in prophecy, anticipated in prayer, and praised by sinners for his mercy. He is the one about whom Moses and the prophets wrote, and—Philip declares—we have found him! He is Jesus from Nazareth.

1:46 Nathanael, however, is somewhat let down, because he judges Jesus by his human origins: **Can anything good come from Nazareth?** This topic of Jesus' identity in terms of his origins appears frequently throughout the Gospel (7:27–28; 8:14; 9:29–30). Philip's response to Nathanael's condescending skepticism echoes that of Jesus to the first two disciples: **Come and see.**

1:47–50 The "see and say" revelation formula again appears (1:29, 36, 42): **Jesus** sees **Nathanael coming** and says **of him, "Here is a true Israelite. There is no duplicity in him."** Nathanael is a faithful son of Israel, one of whom the psalmist can say, "Blessed is the man to whom the LORD imputes no guilt, / in whose spirit is no deceit" (Ps 32:2). Nathanael asks how Jesus knows him, and Jesus gives evidence of knowing much more than he can guess: **Before Philip called you, I saw you under the fig tree.** Some biblical texts speak of being in the shade of a fig tree as a symbol of the peace of the messianic age (Mic 4:4; Zech 3:10).[13] Jesus' words strike Nathanael as a prophetic announcement that he will himself have a place in the messianic age, and Nathanael responds with an acclamation of Jesus as †Messiah: **Rabbi, you are the Son of God; you are the King of Israel.** Only when Jesus rises from the dead will the full content of these titles be manifest. Yet Nathanael has made a great stride toward understanding, and he is rewarded by a solemn promise from Jesus: **You will see greater things than this.**

1:51 Jesus says, **Amen, amen, I say to you, you will see the sky opened and the angels of God ascending and descending on the Son of Man.** These words, which are addressed to all disciples because the "you" is plural, are the last step in the successive revelation of Jesus in this chapter, and they open up into the rest of the Gospel. From the beginning of the narrative in 1:19, a series of titles has been given to Jesus by others: "Lamb of God" (1:29, 36), "Son of God" (1:34, 49), "Rabbi" (1:38), "Messiah" (1:41), "the one about whom Moses wrote" (1:45), "King of Israel" (1:49). The last title in the sequence, †Son of Man, is especially important, because it is the title by which Jesus refers to himself.

The mention of angels ascending and descending from heaven upon something alludes to the †theophany, or appearance of God, to Jacob at Bethel (Gen 28:10–19). God appeared to Jacob in a dream and extended to him the †covenantal promises made to Abraham and Isaac. When he awoke, Jacob said, "How awesome this place is! This is nothing else but the house of God, the gateway to heaven!" (Gen 28:17). Jacob anointed a stone there with oil and named the place "Bethel," which means "the house of God" (28:18–19).

Jesus combines two important themes from this Jacob story into his title "Son of Man." The first is revelation. At Bethel, the Lord revealed himself to Jacob in a dream; now he reveals himself directly and physically in Jesus. The

13. Craig Koester, "Messianic Exegesis and the Call of Nathanael (John 1.45–51)," *Journal for the Study of the New Testament* 39 (1990): 23–34.

The Son of Man

BIBLICAL BACKGROUND

In all the Gospels, Jesus often refers to himself as the Son of Man (in John, 3:13–14; 5:27; 6:27, 53, 62; 8:28; 9:35; 12:23, 34; 13:31). The phrase Son of Man (Hebrew: *ben 'adam*) is often a synonym for "human being" (Isa 56:2; Ezek 2:1). The more pertinent background to Jesus' use of this title is Dan 7:13–14. Daniel receives an †apocalyptic vision of God's final defeat of evil in which "One like a son of man" appears on the clouds and receives God's everlasting, universal kingship (Dan 7:13–14). In other Jewish apocalyptic writings, the Son of Man was regarded as a preexistent heavenly figure, who was God's end-time agent to defeat evil and execute divine judgment (e.g., *1 Enoch* 46:3–5; 62:5–16; *4 Ezra* 13:3–13, 25–26). Jesus' use of "Son of Man" in the Fourth Gospel draws on this background to present himself as the †incarnate revelation of God, who has come down from heaven and whose coming into the world effects judgment.[a]

a. See Francis J. Moloney, SDB, *The Johannine Son of Man* (Rome: Libreria Ateneo Salesiano, 1976).

second theme is God's dwelling place. Jacob referred to the site where the Lord appeared to him as Bethel, "the house of God." Now, "the Word became flesh / and made his dwelling among us" (1:14). Jesus is the direct, physical dwelling of God among human beings; because God has taken on human nature in Jesus, Jesus reveals God in a new, unsurpassable way. The incarnate Word is the new "house of God," where the glory of the Lord is present and sensible, and he is "the gateway to heaven" (Gen 28:17). The fulfillment of Jesus' promise—the revelation of God in Jesus who becomes humanity's gateway to heaven—will be the substance of the rest of the Gospel.

Reflection and Application (1:43–51)

The four days recounted in (1:19–51) contain an unfolding revelation of Jesus Christ. Intimately connected with this revelation of Jesus is the call to discipleship. At first, two men followed Jesus on the word of the Baptist. They met Jesus and stayed the whole day with him. One of them, Andrew, was then able to make an act of faith in Jesus and bring Peter to him. Jesus himself called Philip, and Philip called Nathanael. In all these stories, people acted on a deep, intuitive attraction to Jesus.

Jesus calls every one of us to intimacy with him. His call summons us to step out of our comfort zones and obey him. At first, the call may be simply

The Angels

LIVING TRADITION

When we recite the creed at every Sunday Mass, we profess God as the Creator of "all things visible and invisible." The "invisible" creation is the spiritual—that is, the nonmaterial—creation, composed of creatures that are pure spirit, known as angels.

"The existence of the spiritual, non-corporeal beings that Sacred Scripture usually calls 'angels' is a truth of faith" (Catechism 328). "With their whole beings the angels are *servants* and messengers of God. Because they 'always behold the face of my Father who is in heaven' (Matt 18:10), they are the 'mighty ones who do his word, hearkening to the voice of his word' (Ps 103:20)" (Catechism 329). "From its beginning until death, human life is surrounded by their watchful care and intercession (cf. Matt 18:10; Luke 16:22; Ps 34:7; 91:10–13; Job 33:23–24; Zech 1:12; Tob 12:12)" (Catechism 336).

to begin a prayer life, to break off a pattern of sin, or to be reconciled with someone. Since it is a divine call, it has a mysterious attraction and bears a promise, which at first may be only dimly heard. If we take a step in the direction of Jesus—if we begin to pray, start to act on something we know he wants—then we, like the first disciples, will come to know him better and to "remain" with him.

Glory Revealed on the "Third Day": The Wedding at Cana (2:1–12)

[1]On the third day there was a wedding in Cana in Galilee, and the mother of Jesus was there. [2]Jesus and his disciples were also invited to the wedding. [3]When the wine ran short, the mother of Jesus said to him, "They have no wine." [4][And] Jesus said to her, "Woman, how does your concern affect me? My hour has not yet come." [5]His mother said to the servers, "Do whatever he tells you." [6]Now there were six stone water jars there for Jewish ceremonial washings, each holding twenty to thirty gallons. [7]Jesus told them, "Fill the jars with water." So they filled them to the brim. [8]Then he told them, "Draw some out now and take it to the headwaiter." So they took it. [9]And when the headwaiter tasted the water that had become wine, without knowing where it came from (although the servers who had drawn the water knew), the headwaiter called the bridegroom [10]and

said to him, "Everyone serves good wine first, and then when people have drunk freely, an inferior one; but you have kept the good wine until now." [11]Jesus did this as the beginning of his signs in Cana in Galilee and so revealed his glory, and his disciples began to believe in him.

[12]After this, he and his mother, [his] brothers, and his disciples went down to Capernaum and stayed there only a few days.

OT: Exod 19; Deut 16:9–12; Isa 62:1–5; 66:7–13; Zeph 3:14–18; Amos 9:9–15

NT: Mark 3:31–35; Luke 1:26–38; Eph 5:29–32; Rev 21:1–10

Catechism: Mary as our Mother, 967–70; marriage, 1612–13; old law and new law, 1961–67; Mary's prayer, 2617–19

Lectionary: Second Sunday of Ordinary Time (Year C); Common of the Blessed Virgin; Marriage

It is striking that in this narrative about a wedding, we hear nothing of the bride, and the groom appears only briefly at the very end. This oddity suggests that John sees more in this event than is first visible. The wedding at Cana illustrates John's ability to retain the earthly dimension of an event while showing it to reveal a divine mystery. John thus displays the kind of theological vision that the theologian Henri de Lubac recognized in the spiritual interpretation of Scripture: "The spiritual meaning, then, is to be found on all sides, not only or especially in a book, but first and foremost *in reality itself*."[14] The divine mystery is present in and revealed through the concrete realities of salvation history. By the enlightenment of the Holy Spirit, John sees in the Cana miracle a beginning of God's revelation and salvation in Jesus. He carefully narrates this event to help us see that the interior dimension of Jesus' compassionate gesture for the banquet's host is really the initial unfolding of the final act in the Father's saving plan, a plan promised and made to Israel "in partial and various ways" (Heb 1:1) but now made known in his Son.

2:1 After four days enumerated in John 1, the Cana account begins, **On the third day**. The mention of the third day is open to several interpretations.[15] The interpretation we will develop here is that the third day alludes to the giving of the law on Mount Sinai in Exod 19 and its celebration in Jewish tradition.[16]

14. Henri de Lubac, *Catholicism: Christ and the Common Destiny of Man*, trans. Lancelot C. Sheppard and Sister Elizabeth Englund, OCD (San Francisco: Ignatius Press, 1988), 169.

15. If "the third day" is added to the four-day sequence in John 1, seven days are narrated in 1:19–2:11. This could be an allusion to the seven-day account of creation in Gen 1, which was already alluded to in John 1:1–18. The divine Word, through whom "all things came to be" (1:3), now enters the world, incarnate in Jesus, and begins the work of the new creation by gathering disciples to himself.

16. See Francis Martin, "Mary in Sacred Scripture: An Ecumenical Reflection," *The Thomist* 72 (2008): 525–69; Francis J. Moloney, *Belief in the Word: Reading John 1–4* (Minneapolis: Fortress, 1993), 53–57, 91–92.

Festival of Weeks, or Pentecost

BIBLICAL BACKGROUND

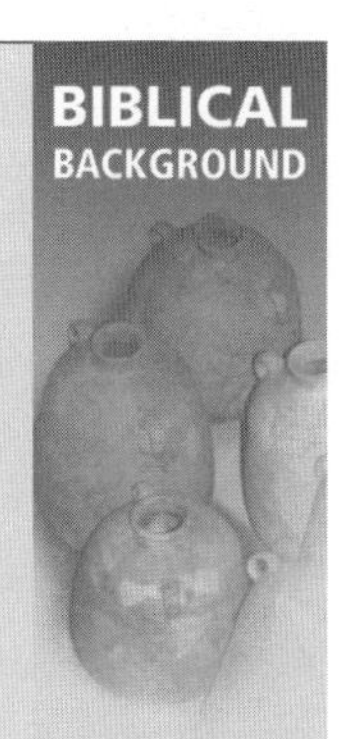

The Festival of Weeks (Hebrew: *Shavuot*), or Pentecost, was a Jewish liturgical festival that celebrated God's gift of the spring harvest. Seven weeks were counted from the sabbath after Passover, and on the fiftieth day ("Pentecost" comes from the Greek word for fifty) there would be a pilgrimage celebration in Jerusalem (Exod 34:22–23; Lev 23:11, 15–16; Deut 16:9–11). Pilgrims would offer to the Lord two loaves made from the flour of the newly harvested wheat, along with other sacrifices, to thank him for his providential care in giving them land and food (Lev 23:17–19). Just as other agricultural festivals came to commemorate events in salvation history, Pentecost came to be a celebration of the Sinai covenant and its renewal. While this connection of Pentecost and the Sinai covenant does not appear in the Old Testament, evidence for it is found in the book of *Jubilees* 5:10–6:31 (ca. 150 BC). Luke's account of the Holy Spirit's descent on Pentecost (Acts 2:1–4) has numerous allusions to the covenant making at Mount Sinai.[a]

a. See Roland de Vaux, OP, *Ancient Israel: Its Life and Institutions* (New York: McGraw Hill, 1965), 2:493–95; Luke Timothy Johnson, *Acts of the Apostles* (Collegeville, MN: Liturgical Press, 1992), 41–47; E. P. Sanders, *Judaism: Practice and Belief, 63 BCE–66 CE* (Philadelphia: Trinity Press International, 1992), 138–39.

After leading the Israelites out of slavery in Egypt, Moses brings them to Mount Sinai, where the Lord offers a †covenant relationship to Israel. The people Israel respond, "Everything the Lord has said, we will do" (Exod 19:8). The Lord then tells the Israelites that he will appear to them three days later, and he instructs them to prepare for his appearance on the third day: "Be ready for the third day; for on the third day the Lord will come down on Mount Sinai in the sight of all the people" (Exod 19:11; see 19:15). "On the morning of the third day" (19:16) the Lord appears on Mount Sinai in his awesome power and reveals his "glory" (Deut 5:24).

God's giving of the †Torah and the covenant at Mount Sinai came to be commemorated liturgically on the Jewish Feast of Pentecost (see sidebar above), and some elements of the Jewish interpretation of this event resonate with the Cana narrative. For instance, a second-century Jewish commentary on Exod 19, the *Mekilta* of Rabbi Ishmael, enumerates a series of days in preparation for God giving the Torah on "the third day," and this numbering is similar to John's listing a sequence of days (1:29, 35, 43) in preparation for "the third day" (2:1).[17]

17. *Mekilta Bahodesh* 3.1–3 on Exod 19:10–11 reads: "And the Lord Said unto Moses: 'Go unto the People, and Sanctify Them To-Day.' This was the fourth day of the week. And Tomorrow. This was the

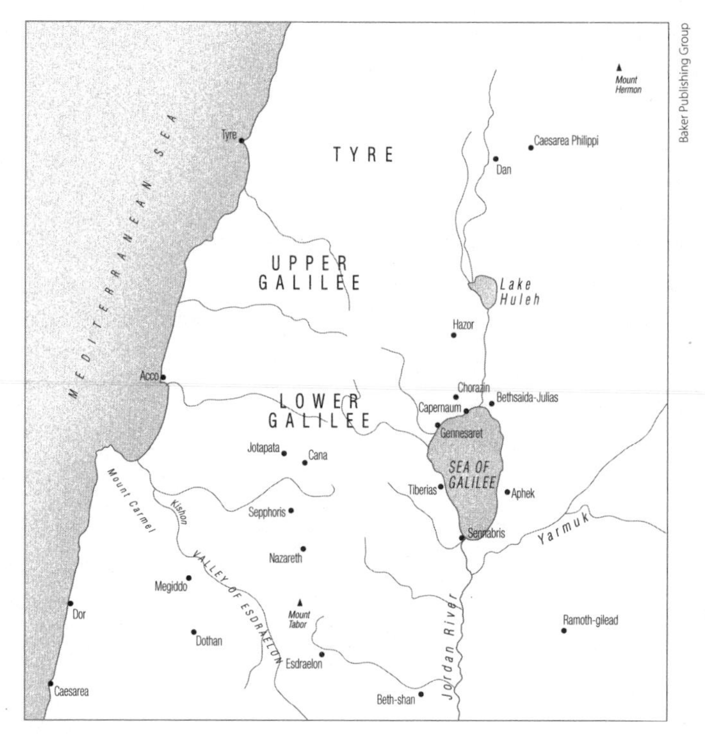

Fig. 2. Map of Galilee

There was a wedding on the third day **in Cana in Galilee**. This Cana is most likely Khirbet Cana, located about nine miles north of Nazareth. Beyond being the simple report of a wedding banquet, this notice recalls the biblical prophets' likening of the covenant relationship between God and Israel to a marriage (Hosea 2:16–25): God is the groom, and his people Israel are the bride.[18] Isaiah uses marriage imagery to talk about God's definitive, future act of salvation to redeem his people from sin and reconcile them to himself. God's saving action is grounded in his covenant faithfulness and love: "For your husband is your Maker; / the LORD of hosts is his name, / Your redeemer, the Holy One of Israel" (Isa 54:5). When God performs this saving action and renews the covenant, the resulting situation is likened to a wedding: "As a young man marries a virgin, / your Builder shall marry you" (Isa 62:5). The Sinai covenant, God's promise of

fifth day of the week. And Be Ready against the Third Day. This was the sixth day of the week on which day the Torah was given" (in Jacob Z. Lauterbach, ed., *Mekilta de-Rabbi Ishmael* [Philadelphia: Jewish Publication Society of America, 1933], 2:210).

18. *Mekilta Bahodesh* 3.118–19 characterizes the appearance of God at Mount Sinai on the third day and the †covenant that followed as a wedding.

a definitive act of salvation, and its marriage imagery come together here to form a rich context within which John invites us to contemplate the wedding of Cana.

2:2 The first person mentioned as attending this **wedding** is **the mother of Jesus**; **Jesus and his disciples** are mentioned after her. Several things about John's presentation of Jesus' mother are significant. First, she appears only twice in the Gospel: at Cana and at the foot of the cross (19:25–27). Her presence in these two episodes is not an accidental curiosity. The two incidents point to spiritual truths about the mother of Jesus that do not readily appear in a surface reading of the text. Moreover, John never refers to the Blessed Mother by her proper name, Mary, but only as **the mother of Jesus**. By leaving her unnamed, John allows her to have a larger symbolic role in the Gospel. Scripture often personifies the people of God as a feminine figure, such as the Lord's covenantal bride. In the Old Testament, Israel is personified as "daughter Zion" (Ps 9:15; Isa 62:11; Zeph 3:14) or as the children of Mother Zion (Isa 66:7–9; see also 60:1–7), and in the New Testament, the Church is personified as the bride of Christ (2 Cor 11:2; Eph 5:29–32; Rev 19:6–8; 21:2, 9). At Cana, the mother of Jesus appears as the embodiment, in a single person, of the faithful, obedient people of God. Just as the people Israel expressed perfect faithfulness to God at the covenantal wedding at Mount Sinai—"We will do everything that the Lord has told us" (Exod 24:3; see 19:8; 24:7)—so too the mother of Jesus instructs those present at the wedding to "Do whatever he tells you" (2:5; compare Luke 1:38). The mother of Jesus is the model of those obedient to God: she both displays and encourages perfect covenant faithfulness and love for God.

2:3 A problem arises at the wedding and needs resolution: the **wine** runs **short,** and **the mother of Jesus** brings this need to her Son. Running out of wine would be a cause of embarrassment for the host of the wedding banquet. Thus Mary's notice that **They have no wine** implies a request for Jesus to help their friends. But the biblical overtones of the story suggest that the **wine** has a spiritual meaning beyond simply being the drink required at the wedding (see comments on 2:9–10 below).

2:4 Jesus' twofold response to his mother has been much discussed. The first part, **Woman, how does your concern affect me?**, literally reads, "What to me and to you, woman?" "What is this to me and to you?" is a Semitic expression that creates a distance in interest or understanding between two parties. Here, in addition, it serves to place the relationship between the two parties on a new basis. While the title "woman" was a typical way of addressing women in antiquity,[19] it was not a form of address for one's own mother. In this first part

19. See John 4:21; 8:10; Matt 15:28.

of his response, Jesus in a certain sense distances himself from an exclusively mother-son relationship, as he is recorded to have done in the †Synoptics.[20] Yet through the culturally surprising address of his mother as "woman," Jesus also reestablishes the relationship between them on a different basis: discipleship and the accomplishment of God's saving work.

In the second part of his response, Jesus tells his mother, **My hour has not yet come**. This is the first time that Jesus speaks of his †hour, a frequently recurring topic in the Gospel. Jesus' hour is the time of his cross and resurrection, when he fully reveals the Father's love and accomplishes his saving work. It is also grammatically possible to read Jesus' words here as a question, "Has not my hour already come?"[21] Understood in this way, Jesus would be announcing that the hour to inaugurate his saving work is now, and its completion will be at the cross when Jesus again addresses his mother as "Woman."

2:5 Mary shows that she accepts her new relation to Jesus as his disciple who has a special role as a companion in his work. Recognizing this shift in their relationship is the key to understanding the full dimension of the narrative.[22] Jesus' **mother** tells **the servers, "Do whatever he tells you."** These words assign Mary a twofold role. First, she is the model disciple, subordinate to her Son. Her words echo Israel's response to God's offer of the covenant: "Everything the Lord has said, we will do" (Exod 19:8; see 24:3, 7). Mary instructs the servants to listen to her Son as the people Israel listened to the Lord at Sinai. Second, by first bringing the host's needs to Jesus and encouraging the servants to be docile and obedient to him, Mary is an intermediary between her Son and the members of the household. As St. Thomas Aquinas writes, Mary "assumed the role of a mediatrix [in two ways]. . . . First, she intercedes, with her Son. In the second place, she instructs the servants."[23] The mother of Jesus presents the needs of the people to Jesus, and she encourages the people in the ways of discipleship, instructing them to obey Jesus.

2:6 The mention of the **six stone water jars there for Jewish ceremonial washings** recalls the ordinances about ritual purity in the Torah. Ritual purity was a

20. In the Synoptics, Jesus corrects those who tell him that his relatives are present and wish to see him: "Whoever does the will of God is my brother and sister and mother" (Mark 3:35; see Matt 12:46–50; Luke 2:48–49; 8:19–21). Doing God's will is what Mary is invited to do in a superior way in the Cana wedding.

21. Albert Vanhoye, "Interrogation johannique et exègese de Cana (Jn 2:4)," *Biblica* 55 (1974): 157–67.

22. So too B. F. Westcott, *The Gospel according to St. John* (London: John Murray, 1902), 36.

23. St. Thomas Aquinas, *Commentary on the Gospel of John* 2.1, section 344, in *Commentary on the Gospel of John*, trans. Fabian Larcher, OP, and James A. Weisheipl, OP, introduction and notes by Daniel Keating and Matthew Levering (Washington, DC: Catholic University of America Press, 2010), 1:135.

condition that allowed a person to be near God's presence.[24] Moving into a state of ritual purity often involved washing oneself or various items with water. It is not clear what specific purification washings are meant here, but they nevertheless fit within the general allusions to the Sinai covenant in this story.

2:7–8 Jesus gives the servants two commands: **Fill the jars with water** and **Draw some out now and take it to the headwaiter.** In both cases, the servants heed the advice of Jesus' mother and do exactly as he says. The servants **filled** the water jars **to the brim**. Jesus will turn this huge amount of water—between 120 and 180 gallons—into wine! Such a large quantity, more than one could expect for a wedding banquet, subtly suggests a deeper meaning to these events beyond simply meeting the need for more wine. An abundant supply of wine appears in many biblical texts speaking about God's †eschatological act of salvation. When God brings about the definitive salvation of his people, there will be great celebration, with a superabundance of wine. Amos says, "The mountains shall drip with the juice of grapes, / and all the hills shall run with it" (9:13); later Joel declares, "On that day, / the mountains will drip new wine" (4:18).

2:9–10 Then **the headwaiter tasted the water that had become wine**, but he did not know **where it came from**. However, **the servers knew** that Jesus was the source. The headwaiter then **called the bridegroom**, and his words both conclude the narrative and proclaim its meaning.

According to ordinary human practice and expectation, **Everyone serves good wine first, and then when people have drunk freely, an inferior one**. But the Lord does not work according to human ways or expectations: "My thoughts are not your thoughts, / nor are your ways my ways" (Isa 55:8). The headwaiter concludes that something new and unexpected has happened: **but you have kept the good wine until now**.[25]

We can now draw together the different biblical allusions in this account and glimpse the spiritual meaning of this event. Through his prophets the Lord promised a definitive act of salvation by which he would redeem his people from sin and renew the covenant. This New Covenant was likened to a marriage between God and his redeemed people, and in this new, perfected state of affairs, God would meet and vastly exceed his people's needs, such that no one would want for anything. Hence the prophets described it as a time of great prosperity, including such things as an superabundance of good wine. In this seemingly

24. A helpful discussion of various purity laws in Jesus' day is in John P. Meier, *A Marginal Jew*, ABRL (New York: Doubleday; New Haven: Yale University, 2009), 4:342–52.

25. The mention of "good wine" may be another connection with the Feast of Pentecost. Among the †Dead Sea Scrolls, the *Temple Scroll* (11Q19 19.14) describes the celebration of Pentecost with an offering of "new wine." See Joseph A. Fitzmyer, SJ, *Acts of the Apostles*, AB 31 (New York, Doubleday, 1998), 235.

simple event at a wedding, John invites us to see a great mystery: God's great, end-time act of salvation to fulfill his promises and renew his covenant is being accomplished in his Son Jesus. God's covenant marriage with his people on the third day at Sinai is being renewed in the eschatological marriage of the †Messiah with his people, personified by his mother, on the third day at Cana. The water of the Sinai covenant is not being thrown out, but it is being transposed into the wine of the Gospel in the new context of the Word made flesh.

2:11–12 The miracle at **Cana** was **the beginning of** Jesus' **signs**. John refers to Jesus' miracles as **signs** because these mighty deeds of divine power reveal or point to spiritual truths about Jesus through sensible means. Jesus' †signs are an extension of his †incarnation.[26] Just as Jesus' humanity reveals his divinity, so also do his signs reveal **his glory**, his divinity. Jesus' transformation of water into wine discloses his fulfilling God's promises of salvation and covenantal renewal. Just as "the glory of the LORD" was revealed to Israel at Mount Sinai (Exod 24:16–17), so too at Cana is his glory revealed in this sign performed by the incarnate Word.

After witnessing this sign, Jesus' **disciples began to believe in him**. Faith in Jesus goes hand in hand with the proper apprehension of his signs as disclosing spiritual mysteries. Jesus' disciples already have some rudimentary faith, as evident in their discipleship and their various affirmations about Jesus in John 1. They are able to see the Cana miracle as a sign, and now, moving beyond a series of affirmations, they begin to believe **in** Jesus personally. Faith goes beyond assent to doctrinal claims, moving to a personal commitment of trust in God himself. As we shall see, the disciples' faith remains imperfect throughout the Gospel (see John 13–16). It reaches maturity only after Jesus' resurrection, with the assistance of the Holy Spirit.

John adds that Jesus, with **his mother, [his] brothers, and his disciples, went down to Capernaum and stayed there only a few days**. The order of those listed is significant, because it is the inverse of how the account started. The Cana narrative began with mother of Jesus named first (2:1), but now Jesus, her Son and Lord, appears in the leading role.

Reflection and Application (2:1–12)

The Mother of Jesus. At Cana, we see Mary as the model of the Church. Her words to the servants, "Do whatever he tells you" (2:5), express the same disposition that she voiced to the angel Gabriel at the Annunciation: "May it be done to me according to your word" (Luke 1:38). In both cases, Mary's words

26. Catechism 774.

Saint Augustine on the Water Turned into Wine

> There was prophecy in ancient times, . . . but that prophecy, when Christ was not understood in it, was water. For, in water, wine is somehow latent. . . . [The] lack of understanding is taken away when you have passed over to the Lord, and what was water becomes wine for you. . . . Understand Christ there [in the Old Testament], and what you are reading not only becomes savory, but it also intoxicates, shifting the mind away from the body, so that, forgetting things that are past, you stretch yourself forth to those things that are before you.[a]

a. St. Augustine, *Tractates on the Gospel according to John* 9.2. Unless otherwise noted, all citations of Augustine's *Tractates* will be taken from Augustine, *Tractates on the Gospel according to John*, trans. John W. Rettig, 5 vols., FC 78–79, 88, 90, 92 (Washington, DC: Catholic University of America Press, 1988–95).

recall those of Israel at Mount Sinai: "Everything the Lord has said, we will do" (Exod 19:8; see 24:3, 7). The mother of Jesus displays the disposition that all believers should have toward God: humility, receptive openness to God's will, and lively obedience. These are the basic attitudes of discipleship, and they are fundamental for growing in holiness. We also see Mary acting as an intercessor who mediates between Jesus and the members of the household. She presents the needs of others to her Son, and she instructs others to obey him. Mary has a unique role in salvation history because it is only through her that the divine Word became flesh so as to accomplish the work of salvation.

The Sacrament of Marriage. This Gospel is one of several readings offered for the sacrament of marriage. Commenting on the Cana miracle, the Catechism states that the Church "sees in it the confirmation of the goodness of marriage and the proclamation that thenceforth marriage will be an efficacious sign of Christ's presence" (1613). God instituted marriage as a visible sign of his permanent covenantal love for his people (Gen 2:23–24; Eph 5:29–33). Given our various imperfections and weaknesses, married life can be tough work. Marriage can be even tougher when it is lived out apart from God. The first lesson for married couples is to make sure that "Jesus [is] . . . invited to the wedding" (2:2). If we invite Jesus into our marriages and family life and ask him to enable us to live out our commitments in faithfulness and love, he will transform the water of ordinary married life into the wine of sanctification. God's grace will permeate the joys and difficulties of our marriages, and they will become the means by which spouses grow together in holiness, bearing fruit in our families.

Jesus' First Trip to Jerusalem

John 2:13–3:36

The Gospel records four visits of Jesus to Jerusalem for Jewish religious festivals (2:13; 5:1; 7:10; 12:12). During this first trip, Jesus starts his public ministry with a dramatic, prophetic action in the Jerusalem temple, the most important institution in the most important biblical city (2:13–25). A prominent Jewish leader named Nicodemus, who realizes that there is something extraordinary about Jesus, pays him a visit, and Jesus engages Nicodemus in a dialogue to lead him to a deeper faith (3:1–15). After a proclamation by the Evangelist about Jesus' role in salvation history (3:16–21), we are given John the Baptist's final testimony about Jesus (3:22–30) and another theological reflection from the Evangelist (3:31–36) that sums up themes in John 3.

The Temple, Old and New (2:13–25)

[13]Since the Passover of the Jews was near, Jesus went up to Jerusalem. [14]He found in the temple area those who sold oxen, sheep, and doves, as well as the money-changers seated there. [15]He made a whip out of cords and drove them all out of the temple area, with the sheep and oxen, and spilled the coins of the money-changers and overturned their tables, [16]and to those who sold doves he said, "Take these out of here, and stop making my Father's house a marketplace." [17]His disciples recalled the words of scripture, "Zeal for your house will consume me." [18]At this the Jews answered and said to him, "What sign can you show us for doing this?" [19]Jesus answered and said to them, "Destroy this temple and in three days

I will raise it up." [20]The Jews said, "This temple has been under construction for forty-six years, and you will raise it up in three days?" [21]But he was speaking about the temple of his body. [22]Therefore, when he was raised from the dead, his disciples remembered that he had said this, and they came to believe the scripture and the word Jesus had spoken.

[23]While he was in Jerusalem for the feast of Passover, many began to believe in his name when they saw the signs he was doing. [24]But Jesus would not trust himself to them because he knew them all, [25]and did not need anyone to testify about human nature. He himself understood it well.

OT: Exod 12:1–28; Ps 69; 84; Jer 7:1–15; Zech 14:16–21
NT: Matt 21:12–17; Mark 14:55–59; 15:29–30
Catechism: Jesus and the Temple, 583–86; Holy Spirit prepares for Christ, 1093–98
Lectionary: Third Sunday of Lent (Year C); Common of Dedication of a Church

2:13 After a short sojourn in Capernaum, **Jesus went up to Jerusalem**, and the text implies that the disciples accompanied him (2:12, 17, 22; 3:22).

For the first time in the Gospel, we meet with direct notice of a Jewish liturgical feast: the **Passover of the Jews** is **near**. As an observant Jew, Jesus makes a pilgrimage to Jerusalem and enters **the temple area**. The temple was the most important institution and building in Jewish life. It was the place where God dwelt among his people in a special manner, and thus it was a central factor and component in Jewish life. The temple was God's house, the place where he made himself known, instructed his people, and received their worship. As the psalmist sang, "How lovely your dwelling, / O LORD of hosts! / My soul yearns and pines / for the courts of the LORD" (Ps 84:2–3). The temple operated under the auspices of the high priest and the priestly aristocracy in Jerusalem.

2:14 Upon entering the temple precincts, Jesus saw **those who sold oxen, sheep, and doves, as well as the money-changers seated there**. Since Passover was a pilgrimage festival, it attracted an international crowd of pilgrims, which swelled the population of Jerusalem with hundreds of thousands of people.[1] The temple's Court of the Gentiles would have been inundated with pilgrims, who were given entrance to the temple precincts in successive waves. Since foreign coinage often carried the image of emperors or kings (Mark 12:15–17) and such images were considered a violation of the law (Exod 20:4), the pilgrims needed to exchange their currency to pay the temple tax and buy sacrificial animals in

1. See Joachim Jeremias, *Jerusalem in the Time of Jesus: An Investigation into Economic and Social Conditions during the New Testament Period*, trans. F. H. and C. H. Cave (Philadelphia: Fortress, 1969), 77–84; E. P. Sanders, *Judaism: Practice and Belief, 63 BCE–66 CE* (Philadelphia: Trinity Press International, 1992), 125–28.

Passover and Unleavened Bread

BIBLICAL BACKGROUND

Passover is the Jewish liturgical feast that commemorates the exodus, when God saved the Israelites from slavery in Egypt (Exod 12:1–28). There came to be attached to Passover a seven-day Festival of Unleavened Bread (Exod 12:18–20; Lev 23:4–14; Deut 16:1–8). Passover was one of three annual liturgical feasts that required Jewish men to make a pilgrimage to Jerusalem. Central to the Passover liturgy was the sacrificial slaughter of the Passover lamb (Exod 12:3–10). A Jewish pilgrim would present a lamb to the priests in the temple, who would slaughter it as a sacrifice (see commentary on 19:14a). The lamb would be returned to the pilgrim, who would eat it that night "with unleavened bread and bitter herbs" (Exod 12:8).[a]

a. See Sanders, *Judaism*, 132–38.

money acceptable in the temple (hence the money-changers). Pilgrims would have their Passover lambs ritually slaughtered and offered in sacrifice for the nation (hence the sheep and birds).

2:15 Jesus then **drove** out those who supplied pilgrims with the proper temple coinage and the animals for the Passover sacrifices. The †Synoptics locate the temple incident shortly before Jesus' passion, during the only visit of Jesus to Jerusalem during his public ministry mentioned in the Synoptics (Matt 21:12–17). But John, for theological reasons, places this event at the start of Jesus' public life.[2]

2:16 Several things in Jesus' command, **Take these out of here, and stop making my Father's house a marketplace**, provide insight into John's theological understanding of the temple incident. Of the four Gospel accounts of this incident, only John has Jesus calling the temple **my Father's house**. This unique phrase reveals that John understands Jesus' action here in terms of his relationship with the Father. Jesus is the Son of God, and his relationship with the Father legitimates his astonishing action, which disrupts the business related to sacrificial offerings (and implies a claim to have control over the temple). By disrupting

2. The placement of this event in the †Synoptics is more plausible from a historical point of view, since Jesus' public demonstration in the temple (Court of the Gentiles) at Passover time could not be ignored by the authorities and likely precipitated his arrest and execution. While such a divergence from the actual sequence of events may strike us as a serious defect in a narrative, the ancients' relation to time and space was very different from our own. See Eviatar Zerubavel, *Hidden Rhythms: Schedules and Calendars in Social Life* (Berkeley: University of California Press, 1985).

the sacrificial system, Jesus symbolically announces changes to come in the worship of God. Just as the water of Sinai was transformed into the wine of the gospel at Cana, so will the worship of God be transposed into the worship of the new †covenant, "worship in Spirit and truth" (4:24).

Only in John's account does Jesus speak of the commerce in the temple as turning it into a "marketplace." This could be a subtle allusion to the end-time vision in Zech 14. There the prophet envisions the day of the Lord, when he will come in power to rescue his people, defeat their enemies, and establish a perfect state of affairs in the world. God will so sanctify his people that they will have no need to purchase animals for sacrifices in the temple: "No longer will there be merchants in the house of the LORD of hosts on that day" (Zech 14:21). Jesus' command that the commerce in the temple must stop could be a prophetic indication that the Lord has now come with the salvation for his people that Zechariah foretold.

2:17 Jesus' **disciples recalled the words of scripture, "Zeal for your house will consume me."** The quotation is from Ps 69:10, but John has a subtle but very significant difference. In the ancient Greek version the text reads, "Zeal for your house consumed me" (Ps 68:10 †LXX), but in John the verb is in the future tense, "will consume me." Jesus' zeal for his Father is one of the principal reasons that he will be consumed on the cross.

By placing the temple incident at the start of Jesus' public ministry, John provides a lens for viewing the whole of Jesus' life and work. For the first time in the Gospel, Jesus speaks of his relationship with the Father. The Father is the source of Jesus' authority and his mission of salvation. His claims about his relationship with the Father and his actions that follow from it will be the cause of controversy between him and the Jerusalem religious authorities throughout his life and will lead to his death.

2:18–19 The temple authorities (**the** †**Jews**) then challenge Jesus: **What sign can you show us for doing this?**[3] They are looking for some †sign from God that would provide sanction for Jesus' provocative actions in the temple. Jesus gives them an answer: **Destroy this temple and in three days I will raise it up**. The Gospels report that Jesus connected his actions in the temple with a statement that prophesied the temple's destruction. His words and deeds in the temple recall the prophet Jeremiah, who threatened the destruction of the first Jerusalem temple if the people of Judah would not repent of their sins (Jer 7:1–15).[4]

3. On John's use of the term "the Jews," see the sidebar on p. 101.

4. The allusion to Jeremiah is clearer in the †Synoptics, where Jesus refers to the temple as "a den of thieves" (Matt 21:13; Mark 11:17; Luke 19:46) much as the Lord, speaking through Jeremiah, asked, "Has this house which bears my name become in your eyes a den of thieves?" (Jer 7:11).

These prophetic words of Jesus must have been quite memorable because they reappear, in a misunderstood (and twisted) form, in accounts of Jesus' trial and crucifixion in Matthew and Mark (see Mark 14:56–59; 15:29–30).

2:20 The temple authorities, however, do not understand, and they issue a further challenge: **This temple has been under construction for forty-six years, and you will raise it up in three days?** The construction work referred to is the renovation and expansion of the temple started by Herod the Great in 19 BC. In fact, the temple was still receiving its final touches in AD 70 when it was destroyed by the Romans.

2:21 The temple authorities think that Jesus is talking about destroying and rebuilding the actual temple building, but John provides us with the intended spiritual meaning of Jesus' words: **He was speaking about the temple of his body**. The Evangelist has taught that the †incarnate Word is the new dwelling of God in the world: the divine Word "made his dwelling among us" in Jesus (1:14). Similarly, when Jesus alludes to Jacob's dream at Bethel (which means "the house of God"; 1:51), he suggests that his disciples will see that the incarnate Word is the "house of God," the place of divine revelation. The bodily resurrection of Jesus—the raising up of the temple of his body after death—will be the sign that provides the Father's confirmation and sanctioning of all that Jesus said and did (see comments on 20:20).

2:22 Like the temple authorities, Jesus' disciples did not understand his words at the time. But **when he was raised from the dead, his disciples remembered that he had said this, and they came to believe the scripture and the word Jesus had spoken**. In 2:17 and 12:16, the disciples are said to remember. This activity goes far beyond simple recollection. At the Last Supper, Jesus tells the disciples that the Holy Spirit "will teach you everything and remind you of all that [I] told you" (14:26). The disciples' remembering will be guided by the Holy Spirit in them after Jesus' resurrection. The New Testament writings often speak of Jesus' resurrection as the key to fully understanding the Scriptures in their depths. In Luke 24 the risen Jesus, standing in the midst of his disciples, "opened their minds to understand the scriptures" (Luke 24:45; see 24:25–27). When John tells us here that the disciples came to believe the scripture, he probably refers to the whole Old Testament, which, when read in light of Jesus' resurrection, clearly speaks of the death and vindication of the †Messiah.

2:23–25 Jesus also performed some miraculous **signs**, and as a result, **many** festival pilgrims **began to believe in his name**. Jesus' miraculous signs are a way by which people come to believe in him, but these actions must also be seen in

Origen on the Mystery of the Temple and Christ's Body

LIVING TRADITION

Both, however, (I mean the temple and Jesus' body) according to one interpretation, appear to me to be a type of the Church, in that the Church, being called a "temple" [Eph 2:21], is built of living stones, becoming a spiritual house "for a holy priesthood" [1 Pet 2:5], built "upon the foundation of the apostles and prophets, Christ Jesus being the chief cornerstone" [Eph 2:20].

And through the saying, "Now you are the body of Christ and members in part" [1 Cor 12:27], (we know) that even if the harmony of the stones of the temple appear to be destroyed, [or,] as it is written in Psalm 21 [22:15], all the bones of Christ appear to be scattered in persecutions and afflictions by the plots of those who wage war against the unity of the temple, . . . the temple will be raised up and the body will arise on the third day after the day of evil [Eccles 7:15] which threatens it and the day of consummation which follows. For the third day will dawn in the new heaven and the new earth [Rev 21:1], when these bones, the whole house of Israel [Ezek 37:11], shall be raised up on the great day of the Lord, once death has been conquered [1 Cor 15:54]. Consequently, the resurrection of Christ too, which followed from his passion on the cross, contains the mystery of the resurrection of the whole body of Christ.[a]

a. Origen, *Commentary on the Gospel of John* 10.228–29, in *Commentary on the Gospel of John: Books 1–10*, trans. Ronald E. Heine, FC 80 (Washington, DC: Catholic University of America Press, 1999), 305–6.

the proper light. Sometimes in the Gospel, people are drawn to Jesus simply because they are bedazzled by his miracles. They see him as a wonder-worker and do not understand that the miracles are signs, revealing spiritual truths about him and his work. Jesus **would not trust himself to** such people, for he **knew** what lies within the **human** heart. He saw that their interest in him was shallow, a "house [built] on sand" (Matt 7:26).

Reflection and Application (2:13–25)

In this scene Jesus does some startling things. He symbolically takes control over the temple and announces changes to come in the worship of God. By speaking of his body as the temple, Jesus establishes himself as the center of divine worship. John links the disciples' grasp of what Jesus did and said to their post-resurrection interpretation of Scripture (2:17, 22). In both cases, Jesus comes to light as the center of both liturgy and Scripture. These same theological beliefs are expressed in the liturgy of the New Covenant. The heart of New Covenant worship is the Eucharist, the one sacrifice of Christ on the cross made present sacramentally. Likewise, the Scripture readings at Mass are arranged so that the worshiping community may see God's actions in salvation history in relation to Christ and experience their transforming power. There are readings from the Old Testament, the Psalms, and the New Testament; and we stand for the Gospel reading to show its central importance. The Church's worship of God centers on Jesus, who is the fulfillment of God's saving plan recounted in Scripture, whose sacrifice reconciles sinners to God and provides spiritual food for our souls.

Dialogue with a Scholar and John's Reflection (3:1–21)

[1]Now there was a Pharisee named Nicodemus, a ruler of the Jews. [2]He came to Jesus at night and said to him, "Rabbi, we know that you are a teacher who has come from God, for no one can do these signs that you are doing unless God is with him." [3]Jesus answered and said to him, "Amen, amen, I say to you, no one can see the kingdom of God without being born again from above." [4]Nicodemus said to him, "How can a person once grown old be born again? Surely he cannot reenter his mother's womb and be born again, can he?" [5]Jesus answered, "Amen, amen, I say to you, no one can enter the kingdom of God without being born of water and Spirit. [6]What is born of flesh is flesh and what is born of spirit is spirit. [7]Do not be amazed that I told you, 'You must be born from above.' [8]The wind blows where it wills, and you can hear the sound it makes, but you do not know where it comes from or where it goes; so it is with everyone who is born of the Spirit." [9]Nicodemus answered and said to him, "How can this happen?" [10]Jesus answered and said to him, "You are the teacher of Israel and you do not understand this? [11]Amen, amen, I say to you, we speak of what we know and we testify to what we have seen, but you people do not accept our testimony. [12]If I tell you about earthly things and you do not believe, how will you believe if I tell you about heavenly things? [13]No one has gone up to heaven except the one who has come down from heaven, the Son of Man. [14]And just as Moses lifted up the serpent in the desert, so must the Son of Man be lifted up, [15]so that everyone who believes in him may have eternal life."

[16]For God so loved the world that he gave his only Son, so that everyone who believes in him might not perish but might have eternal life. [17]For God did not send his Son into the world to condemn the world, but that the world might be saved through him. [18]Whoever believes in

him will not be condemned, but whoever does not believe has already been condemned, because he has not believed in the name of the only Son of God. [19]And this is the verdict, that the light came into the world, but people preferred darkness to light, because their works were evil. [20]For everyone who does wicked things hates the light and does not come toward the light, so that his works might not be exposed. [21]But whoever lives the truth comes to the light, so that his works may be clearly seen as done in God.

OT: Num 21:4–9; Isa 52:13–53:12; Ezek 36:24–28

NT: Rom 6:1–11; 8:14–17

Catechism: faith as a grace, 153; name of the Holy Spirit, 691; symbols of the Holy Spirit, 694; baptism, 1214–16; Baptism makes us a new creature, 1265–66

Lectionary: Fourth Sunday of Lent (Year B); Trinity Sunday (Year A); Triumph of the Cross; Christian Initiation apart from the Easter Vigil; Baptism of Children

3:1

While in the environs of Jerusalem, Jesus receives a respectful visit from a distinguished guest. We have not a confrontation but a dialogue between Jesus and **a ruler of the †Jews**. Nicodemus is a **Pharisee** belonging to a prominent wealthy family, several of whom were devout †Pharisees.[5] The dialogue contains a kind of symbolic language that resembles the Prologue (1:1–18) and is suitable for a learned audience. Another important feature of this dialogue, and indeed most of the dialogues in John, is misunderstanding. Nicodemus has difficulty grasping what Jesus teaches. Jesus speaks of spiritual, supernatural things, but Nicodemus tends to think in terms of earthly, natural things. Jesus seeks to lead Nicodemus into a deeper understanding, to raise his natural thinking to reckon with spiritual realities. In this way, Jesus wishes to communicate a vitally important lesson for all believers: the new, eternal life that he has come to bring is a pure gift from God that totally exceeds our natural abilities.

3:2

Nicodemus **came to Jesus at night**. Since **night** can be taken literally as meaning after sundown, this meeting is not necessarily a clandestine encounter but a respectful visit. Given John's use of light and dark symbolism, however, **night** can also symbolize Nicodemus's initial state of unbelief and misunderstanding. Later in the Gospel, John speaks of some Jewish authorities who believed in Jesus but did not acknowledge him "openly in order not to be expelled from the †synagogue" (12:42). Joseph of Arimathea seems to have been one such person (19:38), and Nicodemus may also be included in this group. Nicodemus appears twice more in John: in 7:50–52, where he defends Jesus somewhat before other

5. Richard Bauckham, *Testimony of the Beloved Disciple: Narrative, History, and Theology in the Gospel of John* (Grand Rapids: Baker Academic, 2007), 137–72.

Pharisees, and in 19:39, where he finally manifests his allegiance to Jesus by bringing a huge amount of precious spices to Jesus' burial.

In their first encounter, Nicodemus acknowledges to Jesus, **We know that you are a teacher who has come from God, for no one can do these signs that you are doing unless God is with him**. The "we" to whom Nicodemus refers may be a group of disciples who have accompanied him in his visit, for a "ruler" would hardly have come alone. In light of his being a "ruler" (3:1), Nicodemus's use of "we" could be an authoritative singular, expressing his authority in this group.[6] Nicodemus has made an honest conjecture about Jesus based on his †signs (2:23): Jesus is a teacher sent by God. Nicodemus may not grasp things fully, but he is moving in the right direction.

3:3 Jesus seems to acknowledge that Nicodemus has at least partially understood the significance of his signs. But in order to grasp the signs as a revelation of Jesus and his work, one needs to receive a new spiritual life. Jesus, therefore, raises the discussion to a higher level: **Amen, amen, I say to you, no one can see the kingdom of God without being born from above**. John's Gospel sometimes uses a word that has two rather different meanings in order to teach something related to each of those meanings. Here, the Greek word *anōthen* means both "from above" and "again." Accordingly, this birth of which Jesus speaks is both heavenly in origin ("from above") and a second birth ("again"). Jesus teaches that human beings need to receive a new, spiritual life from heaven. Not to receive this new life means failure to experience ("see") the kingdom, the reigning of God as king in Jesus.

Although the †Synoptics record Jesus' preaching of the kingdom of God as the core of his message, the phrase "kingdom of God" occurs only twice in John's Gospel, both times in this episode (3:3, 5). However, the theme of Jesus as king is prominent in John's passion narrative. The Evangelist, writing many years after Jesus' ministry, shows a deep spiritual understanding of the substance of Jesus' teaching about the kingdom. For John, the kingdom, or God's kingly rule in the world, is in Jesus himself. As Benedict XVI puts it, "The new proximity of the Kingdom of which Jesus speaks—the distinguishing feature of his message—is to be found in Jesus himself. . . . He himself is the treasure; communion with him is the pearl of great price."[7] In order to see God's kingly rule in Jesus, one must be born again, from above.

3:4 Nicodemus, however, does not understand. Jesus spoke in spiritual terms of a new heavenly birth, but Nicodemus is thinking in earthly terms of physical

6. So Richard Bauckham, *Jesus and the Eyewitnesses: The Gospels as Eyewitness Testimony* (Grand Rapids: Eerdmans, 2006), 377–78.

7. Joseph Ratzinger (Pope Benedict XVI), *Jesus of Nazareth: From the Baptism in the Jordan to the Transfiguration*, trans. Adrian J. Walker (New York: Doubleday, 2007), 60–61.

birth: **How can a person once grown old be born again? Surely he cannot reenter his mother's womb and be born again, can he?** The tone of his response is unclear. It may be a total lack of comprehension, even touched with sarcasm. Or it could also be a rabbinic mode of discourse, which draws an extreme conclusion from a speaker's statement in order to force the speaker to explain himself more fully. Obviously, a man cannot be born physically from his mother twice, and so Nicodemus invites Jesus to clarify his teaching.

3:5 **Jesus** develops his initial statement: **Amen, amen, I say to you, no one can enter the kingdom of God without being born of water and Spirit**. In 1:33, the Baptist had testified that the one coming after him "will baptize with the holy Spirit." With the solemn phrase "Amen, amen, I say to you," Jesus speaks of the fulfillment of the Baptist's witness. This second birth from heaven is baptism, which is an action of the Holy Spirit. Through the water rite, the believer is joined to Jesus' death and resurrection (Rom 6:4–5) and receives the indwelling Holy Spirit. If **the kingdom of God** is Jesus himself, then to **enter the kingdom** is to be given a share in Jesus' own divine life. By means of baptism, we are born into communion with Jesus and the Father through the Holy Spirit.

This birth of **water and Spirit** also alludes further back to God's promise through Ezekiel. The prophet taught that when God works his great act of salvation, he will cleanse his people with "clean water" and put his "spirit within" them (Ezek 36:25, 27). God will give his redeemed people a "new heart and . . . a new spirit" (36:26), hearts that are receptive and capable of love. God thus promises to form an obedient people by putting his Spirit within them. John develops this symbolic connection between water and the Holy Spirit throughout the Gospel (see 4:10, 13–14; 7:37–39).

3:6 Nicodemus had been thinking about natural birth, while Jesus has been talking about spiritual birth. The two are analogously related, but they are ultimately of distinct orders: **What is born of flesh is flesh and what is born of spirit is spirit**. This is the heart of Jesus' message to Nicodemus and to the world, and its basic principle was set forth in the Prologue: "But to those who did accept him he gave power to become children of God, to those who believe in his name, who were born not by natural generation nor by human choice nor by a man's decision but of God" (1:12–13). Through faith and baptism, believers are born into a spiritual life as children of God, sharing in Jesus' own life as the Son (compare Rom 8:14–17). This new heavenly life is a gift from God, not a matter of physical descent or human choosing.

3:7–8 Jesus uses a parable-like statement to illustrate the gracious, mysterious work of the Spirit in a person's being born from above. **The wind blows where it wills, and**

LIVING TRADITION

Saint Justin Martyr on Natural and Spiritual Birth

Justin Martyr (ca. 100–165) grew up in a pagan home and explored various philosophies before becoming a Christian. After becoming a Christian teacher and writing a number of works, including two defenses of the Christian faith addressed to Roman authorities, St. Justin was beheaded by Roman authorities.

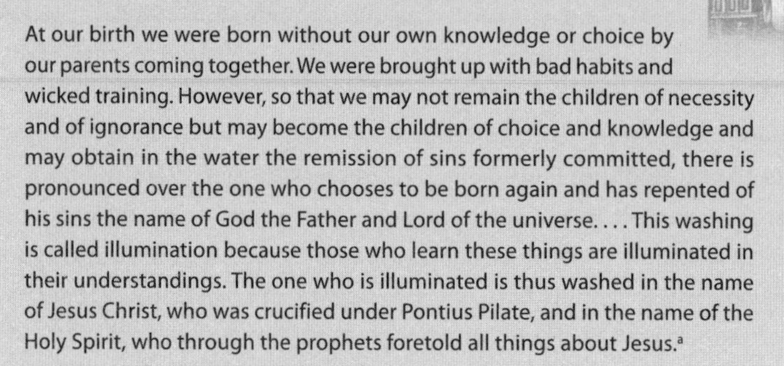

> At our birth we were born without our own knowledge or choice by our parents coming together. We were brought up with bad habits and wicked training. However, so that we may not remain the children of necessity and of ignorance but may become the children of choice and knowledge and may obtain in the water the remission of sins formerly committed, there is pronounced over the one who chooses to be born again and has repented of his sins the name of God the Father and Lord of the universe. . . . This washing is called illumination because those who learn these things are illuminated in their understandings. The one who is illuminated is thus washed in the name of Jesus Christ, who was crucified under Pontius Pilate, and in the name of the Holy Spirit, who through the prophets foretold all things about Jesus.[a]

a. Justin Martyr, *First Apology* 61 (in *Ante-Nicene Fathers*, 1:183), in ACCS 4a:109.

you can hear the sound it makes, but you do not know where it comes from or where it goes; so it is with everyone who is born of the Spirit. There is a play on words here as in 3:3, because the Greek word translated as "wind" (*pneuma*) also means "Spirit." Just as the wind eludes human mastery, so does the Holy Spirit. Everyone born from above grows in the new divine life to the degree that they experience and accept the free and gracious work of the Holy Spirit in their lives.

3:9–10 Now Nicodemus realizes that he is in the presence of someone who himself is "from above." More docile and intrigued than before, Nicodemus asks, **How can this happen?** Jesus' reply—**You are the teacher of Israel and you do not understand this?**—is not an insult but a challenge, inviting Nicodemus to open himself up to these realities that fulfill the biblical tradition. Nicodemus first addressed Jesus with an authoritative "we" (3:1–2). Now Jesus responds with his own authoritative "we": **We speak of what we know and we testify to what we have seen**; that is, Jesus speaks of what he received from the Father, **but you people do not accept our testimony**.[8]

8. So Bauckham, *Jesus and the Eyewitnesses*, 378–79. Other scholars see in the contrast between "we" and "you" a reflection of the conflict between John's community and his local synagogue over the person and status of Jesus. See "Historical Context" in the introduction to this volume.

3:11–13

There is much more for Nicodemus to learn: **If I tell you about earthly things and you do not believe, how will you believe if I tell you about heavenly things?** In a very important statement, Jesus points to the source of his authority and teaching: **No one has gone up to heaven except the one who has come down from heaven, the Son of Man.** Jesus first used the title †Son of Man when he promised believers that they would see him as the place where God dwells among humanity, reveals himself, and opens up heaven to them (1:51). Added here is the teaching that the Son of Man has come down from heaven. Only the Word made flesh can reveal the Father and speak of heavenly realities because only he has come down from heaven and will return there. Jesus has come to make known to us the heavenly realities of which earthly realities such as natural birth are models and figures. By doing the Father's saving work, Jesus will give us a share in what is heavenly.

3:14–15

Jesus employs a biblical figure to explain how he will reveal the Father and bring us eternal healing: **Just as Moses lifted up the serpent in the desert, so must the Son of Man be lifted up, so that everyone who believes in him may have eternal life.** This is the first of three occasions in the Gospel where Jesus refers to his death on the cross as being "lifted up" (also 8:28; 12:32).[9] The verb "lifted up" (*hypsoō*) has a twofold meaning. It can mean lift up in a literal sense, as in Jesus being physically lifted up from the ground on the cross. It can also mean lift up in the sense of exalt. Jesus uses the word in both senses. Jesus' being lifted up in ignominy from the ground while on the cross will also be the moment of his exaltation, when he preeminently reveals God's love. Like the title "Lamb of God" (1:29), the mention of "lift up" is an allusion to the Suffering Servant in Isa 53. In the †Septuagint text (†LXX) of Isa 52:13, the Lord says that his servant will be "lifted high"—using the same Greek verb—"and be exceedingly glorified." The same Servant, "like a lamb led to slaughter, . . . took away the sins of many" (Isa 53:7, 12 LXX).[10] The Son of Man, who will be lifted up, is also "the Lamb of God, who takes away the sin of the world" (John 1:29).

Jesus unfolds the mystery of his cross by referring to the bronze serpent raised up by Moses in the wilderness (Num 21:4–9). In that incident, the Lord afflicted the Israelites with fiery serpents as a punishment for their rebellious complaining, and the Israelites then appealed to Moses to intercede for them. God instructed Moses to make a bronze serpent and affix it to a pole. When an Israelite gazed at the symbolic portrayal of the effects of his sin, the bronze

9. These three "lifting up" statements are comparable to the three Passion Predictions in the †Synoptics (as in Mark 8:31; 9:30–31; 10:32–34).

10. Our translation of the LXX.

serpent, he was granted healing and life (21:9). Similarly, whoever gazes in faith at the ultimate effect of human sin, the crucifixion of the Son of God, is changed and given life eternal. This vision of faith looks through the †sign to the spiritual reality. Thus a living faith experience of heavenly realities becomes the means of entry into eternal, divine life. With this biblical example for Nicodemus, Jesus opens up the possibility of a spiritual understanding of his own tradition, inviting Nicodemus to genuine faith in him.

3:16–17 Having set forth Jesus' teaching about eternal life, which his cross makes available and into which believers are born by the Spirit's action, the Evangelist now penetrates to the heart of this Gospel's message: **For God so loved the world that he gave his only Son, so that everyone who believes in him might not perish but might have eternal life**. The Father's love for the world leads him to give his only Son, his all, for the world's salvation. The world is under condemnation and in spiritual darkness on account of sin, but the Father does not want any to perish (see 2 Pet 3:9). Hence he gives his Son so **that the world might be saved through him**. The gift of salvation, which the Father offers us all through Jesus, is eternal life: a participation in the divine life of the Trinity. We accept this gift through faith in Jesus. Faith is yielding to the action of the Spirit, who first moves a person to assent to what God has revealed and to commit one's whole life to God.[11] As Jesus will later tell a crowd, faith is our consenting to and cooperating with God's work in us: "No one can come to me unless the Father who sent me draw him" (6:44).

3:18 The human response to this transaction has the most serious of consequences, for the decision for belief or unbelief in the Son is directly linked to eternal life or condemnation: **Whoever believes in him will not be condemned, but whoever does not believe has already been condemned, because he has not believed in the name of the only Son of God**. One either accepts this witness of God and believes in "the name," meaning the reality, of the Son of God, or one refuses the witness and remains under condemnation and in the darkness of sin.

3:19–21 The Evangelist explores the inner dynamics of belief or unbelief through a contrast between coming to the light or staying in the darkness. In doing so, he summarizes an important theological theme in the Gospel: judgment.

And this is the verdict, that the light came into the world. The Father sent his Son into the world out of love. As the spiritual light, the Son comes into the fallen world, which is enshrouded in the darkness of sin (1:5; 8:12; 9:5). As the light shining in darkness, the presence and work of the Son in the world necessarily provokes a response: people respond to the light with either faith

11. Catechism 150, 153.

or unbelief. Thus the Son's appearance is a situation of judgment. It is a crisis in the deepest sense: *krisis* is the Greek word translated as "verdict." Ultimately, there are only two options: either people receive the light or they reject him.

John makes clear the dynamics of faith in ways that are both honest and familiar: **but people preferred darkness to light, because their works were evil. For everyone who does wicked things hates the light and does not come toward the light, so that his works might not be exposed**. The decision for faith or unbelief is not simply an intellectual matter: it also has moral dimensions. John unmasks our reluctance to break off from our evil ways and come into the light of truth as a consequence of our attachment to our evil acts. We hesitate to embrace the truth because it means having to give up all those sinful behaviors. Pointing to the same dynamic, St. Paul speaks of the willful refusal of God's revelation by those who "in their wickedness suppress the truth" (Rom 1:18, our translation). As St. Augustine comments, people "love the truth for the light it sheds, but hate it when it shows them up as being wrong."[12]

But whoever lives the truth comes to the light. Coming to Christ in faith requires that people turn away from sin and embrace a way of life marked by love, in imitation of Jesus (13:34–35). If we are animated and empowered by God's own action, the divine light ultimately reveals the true character of our lives: **so that** our **works may be clearly seen as done in God**.

Reflection and Application (3:1–21)

This passage teaches us two fundamental truths. First, what God offers us is the pure gift of a life that exceeds anything we could realize by ourselves: we must be born again from above. Second, the action by which we receive this gift is to believe in Jesus Christ and his redeeming act of love on the cross (3:14–15). In this process, it is God, not us, who seizes the initiative. God takes the first step by moving us to faith; our role is to cooperate and consent. As the Catechism (153) puts it,

> *Faith is a gift of God, a supernatural virtue infused by him.* "Before this faith can be exercised, man must have the grace of God to move and assist him; he must have the interior helps of the Holy Spirit, who moves the heart and converts it to God, who opens the eyes of the mind and 'makes it easy for all to accept and believe the truth'" (*Dei Verbum* 5; cf. DS 377; 3010).

12. St. Augustine, *Confessions* 10.23.34.

To bring home this biblical truth, St. Bernard of Clairvaux, in his treatise *On Grace and Free Will*, utilizes the refrain: "To consent is to be saved."[13] We must consent to God's action in us, and we must "think along with God"—the second meaning of Bernard's Latin word *consentire*. That is, intellectually and personally, we must accept the divine teaching concerning the gift of salvation and its source in Jesus. Many practicing Christians have only a habitual consent to this truth, and such lukewarm faith can fail them in moments of trial or opposition. This gospel passage calls us to a more consistent, profound life of prayer, in which we consent to the Holy Spirit's teaching and action within us: "This is how we know that we remain in him and he in us, that he has given us of his Spirit" (1 John 4:13).

The Baptist's Final Testimony and John's Reflection (3:22–36)

[22]After this, Jesus and his disciples went into the region of Judea, where he spent some time with them baptizing. [23]John was also baptizing in Aenon near Salim, because there was an abundance of water there, and people came to be baptized, [24]for John had not yet been imprisoned. [25]Now a dispute arose between the disciples of John and a Jew about ceremonial washings. [26]So they came to John and said to him, "Rabbi, the one who was with you across the Jordan, to whom you testified, here he is baptizing and everyone is coming to him." [27]John answered and said, "No one can receive anything except what has been given him from heaven. [28]You yourselves can testify that I said [that] I am not the Messiah, but that I was sent before him. [29]The one who has the bride is the bridegroom; the best man, who stands and listens for him, rejoices greatly at the bridegroom's voice. So this joy of mine has been made complete. [30]He must increase; I must decrease."

[31]The one who comes from above is above all. The one who is of the earth is earthly and speaks of earthly things. But the one who comes from heaven [is above all]. [32]He testifies to what he has seen and heard, but no one accepts his testimony. [33]Whoever does accept his testimony certifies that God is trustworthy. [34]For the one whom God sent speaks the words of God. He does not ration his gift of the Spirit. [35]The Father loves the Son and has given everything over to him. [36]Whoever believes in the Son has eternal life, but whoever disobeys the Son will not see life, but the wrath of God remains upon him.

13. Bernard of Clairvaux, *On Grace and Free Will* 1.1.2 (PL 182:1002).

NT: Mark 6:17–29; Acts 19:1–7; 1 Thess 5:1–11
Catechism: faith, 150–55; mysteries of Jesus' hidden life, 523–24

3:22–24 The Evangelist gives us a final word from John the Baptist. **Jesus and his disciples** leave Jerusalem but stay in **Judea**, where they conduct a **baptizing** ministry. It seems that Jesus continues the Baptist's conversion rite of baptism, but without the theme of preparing for the one to come, for he is now present. Jesus likely connects this action to his baptizing "with the holy Spirit" (1:33) and to the people's embracing the kingdom as they are "being born of water and Spirit" (3:5).[14] However, John 4:2 clarifies that Jesus himself was not baptizing, only his disciples. While Jesus is in Judea, John the Baptist is farther north in Samaria, where he continues his ministry: **people came to be baptized, for John had not yet been imprisoned**. While the Fourth Gospel does not discuss the Baptist's imprisonment, we learn from the †Synoptics that he was arrested and executed by Herod Antipas, Rome's client-king of Galilee (Mark 6:17–29).

3:25–26 The setting for the Baptist's final testimony to Jesus is **a dispute** over **ceremonial washings** between **the disciples of John and a Jew**. The dispute must have something to do with the baptizing activity of Jesus and his disciples, because the Baptist's disciples come to him with the report: **Rabbi, the one who was with you across the Jordan, . . . here he is baptizing and everyone is coming to him**. The Baptist takes the opportunity to clarify once and for all the nature of the relationship between Jesus and himself.

3:27–30 The Baptist first states a basic theological principle: **No one can receive anything except what has been given him from heaven**. The Baptist can do only what he has received from heaven: he is not **the †Messiah**, but he **was sent before him** (1:20–23). He then gives a poetic testimony to Jesus: **The one who has the bride is the bridegroom; the best man, who stands and listens for him, rejoices greatly at the bridegroom's voice. So this joy of mine has been made complete**. The scene in the Baptist's witness is a wedding procession in the evening. Everyone is waiting at the bride's house for the bridegroom to come and lead his bride back to his own house, accompanied by her bridesmaids, family, and friends. Then the celebration can begin. The best man listens for the bridegroom's voice, which will tell him that the wedding rejoicing is about to begin and that his own task has been completed. The Baptist's purpose has been to make Jesus "known to Israel," the Lord's †covenantal bride (1:31), and

14. Acts of the Apostles likewise distinguishes between John's baptism and Christian baptism: the former was a sign of repentance, while the latter forgives sins and imparts the Holy Spirit (Acts 2:38; 19:1–7).

now that Jesus has arrived, the messianic nuptials can begin (2:1–11).[15] The Baptist ends by voicing sentiments shared by every friend of the bridegroom throughout the centuries: **He must increase; I must decrease.**[16]

3:31 It is not clear whether 3:31–36 continues the Baptist's testimony. More likely, it is a reflection offered by the Evangelist, which brings together certain teachings in this chapter. In 3:1–15, we learn of the heavenly gift that Jesus brings: eternal life. Then in 3:16–21, the Evangelist reflects on the gift of faith, its relation to Jesus' passion and resurrection, and the darkness that will tempt us to stay attached to our sins rather than come to the light. After a change of scene (3:22–30), we learn the true greatness of the Baptist and his role in God's saving plan as a witness "to the light" (1:8). Finally, in these concluding verses (3:31–36), the Evangelist returns to consider Jesus himself, the one from heaven who testifies to what he knows because from all eternity he is the Son who is always with the Father.

The one who comes from above is above all. The term "from above" (*anōthen*) recalls the dialogue with Nicodemus, where Jesus spoke of the need to be born again from above (*anōthen*, 3:3, 7) and also of himself as the †Son of Man "who has come down from heaven" (3:13). Jesus distinguished between "earthly things" and "heavenly things" (3:12) and between going up and coming down from heaven (3:13). The Evangelist develops this contrast between **the one who is of the earth** and **the one who comes from heaven**. A person who is of the earth is someone who has refused to accept the testimony of the one who comes from heaven. Implied here is a call for people not to remain in the mode of merely earthly life but to be elevated by God and be "above."

3:32 The heartrending fact is that Jesus, "who comes from heaven" (3:31), **testifies to what he has seen and heard**—he reveals the Father—**but no one accepts his testimony** (as in 1:11). There are other witnesses who testify to Jesus, such as the Baptist, Jesus' own works, and the Scriptures (5:31–40; 14:11).

3:33–34 However, **whoever does accept his testimony certifies**—that is, confirms—**that God is trustworthy**, for the act of faith always includes an element of trust.[17] As the one sent **from God**, Jesus **speaks the words of God**, who holds nothing back: **He does not ration his gift of the Spirit**. The Spirit remains upon Jesus, and Jesus baptizes "with the holy Spirit" (1:33). As Jesus has received the Spirit entirely from the Father, he can pour out the Spirit upon others (7:37–39), an outpouring that will occur after Jesus is glorified.

15. Raymond E. Brown, SS, *The Gospel according to John*, AB 29 (New York: Doubleday, 1966), 1:156.
16. Catechism 523–24.
17. Catechism 154.

3:35–36 As evidenced in the complete anointing of Jesus' humanity with the Spirit, **the Father loves the Son and has given everything over to him**. The Evangelist speaks here of the divine life that the Father without reserve pours into the Son (5:26). Since the Son possesses in himself the fullness of divinity, **whoever believes in the Son has eternal life.** Belief here is not just intellectual assent to a proposition or fidelity to a practice. Rather, it is the personal acceptance of Jesus by which we accept his offer of eternal life (3:15–18). Faith yields to Jesus as the gift and revealer of the Father. Our act of faith is the Father's work within us, the crown of his many actions to which we have yielded: "Everyone who listens to my Father and learns from him comes to me" (6:45). Since faith is a personal act of yielding and obedience, Jesus can contrast belief with disobedience: **whoever disobeys the Son will not see life**. By refusing the Son, one turns down God's invitation to eternal life, thus choosing to remain in spiritual darkness under the condemnation of sin. Hence, **the wrath of God**, the punishment due to sin, **remains upon him** (see 1 Thess 1:10; 5:9).

Reflection and Application (3:22–36)

A principal teaching here concerns faith as an inner dynamic principle, whose effective power we can experience. As Pope Benedict XVI has said: "The Risen Christ needs witnesses who have met him, people who have known him intimately through the power of the Holy Spirit; those who have, so to speak, actually touched him, can witness to him."[18] Such faith is an active principle of life and becomes the force that changes the way a family lives, the way a parish lives, the way each one of us lives. Similarly, Pope St. John Paul II has taught, "A faith which does not become culture is a faith which has not been fully received, not thoroughly thought about, not faithfully lived out."[19] Jesus has just said, "Whoever believes in the Son has eternal life, but whoever disobeys the Son will not see life, but the wrath of God remains upon him" (3:36). Jesus contrasts belief not only with unbelief, a different way of thinking, but also with *disobedience*, a different way of acting as well as thinking. Faith becomes a way of life when it is active in a life of prayer and obedience. It is then that we are among those who have come to know the risen Christ intimately and can bear witness to him (Catechism 150–52).

18. Pope Benedict XVI, "Homily," May 7, 2005.

19. John Paul II, "Letter Founding the Pontifical Council for Culture," May 20, 1982; our translation of the French.

Encounters with Jesus in Samaria and Galilee

John 4:1–54

John 4 continues the theme of faith with two stories about non-Jews coming to believe in Jesus. In the first story, Jesus begins a journey from Judea back north to Galilee, a walk of about two and a half days, and he decides to go through Samaria. Along the way, as he is resting at Jacob's well, a Samaritan woman comes at midday to draw water. Jesus initiates a conversation with her—a very countercultural thing to do—and leads her on a journey of faith to recognize him. The Samaritan woman, whose name we never learn, then becomes the evangelist to her fellow villagers who, through her, come to believe that Jesus is the savior of the world. The second story takes place after Jesus arrives in Galilee. A Gentile royal official asks Jesus to heal his son. Upon learning that Jesus has cured his boy, the official arrives at a genuine faith in Jesus and spreads the word to his household. In both cases we see non-Jews coming to faith in Jesus and sharing that faith with others. Through these accounts, John leads us on the same journey taken by these individuals, moving us to a deeper understanding and experience of faith in Jesus.

A Samaritan Woman's Faith Journey I: Gift of Living Water (4:1–15)

---

[1]Now when Jesus learned that the Pharisees had heard that Jesus was making and baptizing more disciples than John [2](although Jesus himself

was not baptizing, just his disciples), [3]he left Judea and returned to Galilee.

[4]He had to pass through Samaria. [5]So he came to a town of Samaria called Sychar, near the plot of land that Jacob had given to his son Joseph. [6]Jacob's well was there. Jesus, tired from his journey, sat down there at the well. It was about noon.

[7]A woman of Samaria came to draw water. Jesus said to her, "Give me a drink." [8]His disciples had gone into the town to buy food. [9]The Samaritan woman said to him, "How can you, a Jew, ask me, a Samaritan woman, for a drink?" (For Jews use nothing in common with Samaritans.) [10]Jesus answered and said to her, "If you knew the gift of God and who is saying to you, 'Give me a drink,' you would have asked him and he would have given you living water." [11][The woman] said to him, "Sir, you do not even have a bucket and the cistern is deep; where then can you get this living water? [12]Are you greater than our father Jacob, who gave us this cistern and drank from it himself with his children and his flocks?" [13]Jesus answered and said to her, "Everyone who drinks this water will be thirsty again; [14]but whoever drinks the water I shall give will never thirst; the water I shall give will become in him a spring of water welling up to eternal life." [15]The woman said to him, "Sir, give me this water, so that I may not be thirsty or have to keep coming here to draw water."

OT: Gen 29:1–14; 2 Kings 17

NT: Acts 8:4–25

Catechism: Jesus' human nature, 470–78; symbols of the Holy Spirit, 694; Jesus reveals the Spirit, 728

Lectionary: Third Sunday of Lent (Year A; optional Years B and C); Common of Dedication of a Church; Baptism of Children

4:1–3

Jesus **left Judea and** headed north **to Galilee** because **the †Pharisees had heard that Jesus was making and baptizing more disciples than John**. The Evangelist further specifies that **Jesus himself was not baptizing**, but only **his disciples** (see 3:22).[1]

4:4

While other routes were available for Jews to take in order to avoid Samaria, Jesus **had to pass through Samaria**. John often uses the expression "had to" to indicate a necessity due to the Father's will.[2] He thus hints that the ensuing dialogue with a woman and conversion of a Samaritan town were part of the Father's saving plan.

1. Scholars often point to this shift from 3:22 as evidence that the Gospel underwent revisions in the course of its composition.

2. As in John 3:7, 14, 30; 9:4; 10:16; 12:34; 20:9.

Samaritans

BIBLICAL BACKGROUND

Jews and Samaritans were ethnic and religious rivals in antiquity, and the history of their relationship was marked by dislike and occasional persecutions.[a] Samaria is the central part of Palestine, situated between Galilee to the north and Judea to the south. It takes its name from the capital city of the northern kingdom of Israel, which broke away from the Davidic monarchy in Jerusalem in 922 BC (1 Kings 12:16–20). In 721 BC, this kingdom was conquered by the Assyrian Empire. The Assyrians, in keeping with their occupation policy, deported some Israelites and resettled foreigners in those lands. The intermarriage between the Israelites and those foreign peoples became a source of ethnic tension with Jews.

Samaritans worshiped the God of Israel but did so in a way different from Jews. The major point of religious contention between Samaritans and Jews was the place where God was to be worshiped. Jews worshiped at the Jerusalem temple, the reconstruction of which Samaritans had obstructed (see Ezra 4); the Samaritans worshiped at a temple built on Mount Gerizim, which was illegitimate in Jewish eyes and was destroyed by the Jewish king John Hyrcanus in about 129 BC. For their part, Jewish readers of Scripture would have regarded Samaritan worship as contaminated by paganism. According to 2 Kings 17, the Assyrians brought in five foreign peoples to resettle the Samaritan region (17:24), and each group brought their gods (17:29–34).

John 4 is one of several indications in the New Testament of a mutual openness between the Samaritans and the first Christians (Luke 17:16; Acts 8:4–25).

a. See John P. Meier, *A Marginal Jew*, ABRL (New York: Doubleday; New Haven: Yale University, 2001), 3:532–42.

4:5–6 Jesus arrived at a Samaritan **town** named **Sychar**. The most likely candidate for this place is the modern town of Askar, about a mile northeast of **Jacob's well**. The well is so named because it was presumed that **Jacob** gave **his son Joseph** the land near Shechem (Gen 48:21–22).

Jesus, tired from his journey, sat down. The divine Word has taken on a genuine human nature and thus truly suffers thirst and fatigue from his journey.[3] The comment that Jesus stopped to rest **at** a **well** evokes a familiar scene in the Bible: a meeting at a well that leads to marriage. In Gen 24:10–53, Abraham's servant, who was sent to find a wife for Isaac, meets Rebekah at a well, and she, having been thus identified by divine sign, agrees to become Isaac's wife. Similarly, Isaac's son Jacob meets Rachel, the love of his life, at a well (Gen

3. Catechism 470–78.

29:1–14). Exodus 2:15–21 tells of Moses, who protects the daughters of "the priest of Midian" at a well, and this event leads to the priest giving his daughter Zipporah in marriage to Moses.

The timing of this episode at **noon** is significant. In addition to the reasons discussed below, it establishes a contrast with the previous dialogue with Nicodemus, who came to Jesus at night (3:2).

4:7–9 The remark that a Samaritan woman **came to draw water** at noon introduces another important motif in this story: conduct that transgresses cultural and social expectations.[4] The woman probably has something to hide because she goes to the well both at the wrong time of day for drawing water (not morning or evening) and by herself (not accompanied by other women of the village).[5] The departure from cultural norms continues when Jesus initiates a conversation in a public place with the **woman** and says, **Give me a drink**. Although it is in a public place, Jesus goes against the custom of his day because men would not address women who are not family members in one-on-one conversation, especially when they are alone—a condition underlined here by the remark that the **disciples** are absent. The Samaritan woman points out Jesus' breach of religious convention: he, **a Jew**, is asking **a Samaritan woman for a drink**. On account of dietary and purity laws, the **Jews use nothing in common with Samaritans**.

4:10 Jesus responds to the woman's recognition of his breach of convention: **If you knew the gift of God and who is saying to you, "Give me a drink," you would have asked him and he would have given you living water**. The conversation began with literal talk about drinking water, but now Jesus shifts to a spiritual level with his reference to "living water," which refers spiritually to the water of eternal life. Jesus is thirsting for more than drinking water. He wants the Samaritan woman's faith commitment to him. Jesus thirsts to give her the living water, the Holy Spirit, who is frequently referred to as "gift" in the New Testament (e.g., Acts 2:38; 8:20; 10:45) and symbolized by water (John 3:5; 7:37–39).[6] But the expression "living water" is also a Semitic idiom that means "running water" (Lev 14:5–6 NJB).[7] The woman, like Nicodemus, thinks here in earthly terms and thus does not understand Jesus' meaning.

4:11–12 The Samaritan woman challenges Jesus with two questions. The first displays her misunderstanding: **Sir, you do not even have a bucket and the cistern is**

4. See Jerome H. Neyrey, SJ, "What's Wrong with This Picture? John 4, Cultural Stereotypes of Women, and Public and Private Space," *Biblical Theology Bulletin* 24 (1994): 77–91.

5. Ibid., 82.

6. Catechism 694.

7. Rendered "fresh water" in NABRE.

Pope Francis on the Holy Spirit, the "Living Water"

LIVING TRADITION

The Creed tells us that the Spirit is "Lord," fully God, the Third Person of the Blessed Trinity. He is the gift of the risen Christ, who draws us, through faith, into communion with the Triune God. The Creed also tells us that the Spirit is the "Giver of Life." How greatly we desire true life and the fullness of beauty, love, and peace! The Holy Spirit, dwelling in our hearts, is the pure source of "living water, springing up to eternal life" which Jesus promised to the Samaritan woman. Sent by Jesus from the Father, the Spirit purifies, renews, and transforms us; he grants us his sevenfold gifts and makes us children of God our Father. Even now the Holy Spirit invites us to see all things with the eyes of Christ, to recognize God's immense love for us, and to share that love with all our brothers and sisters.[a]

a. Pope Francis, "General Audience," May 8, 2013.

deep; where then can you get this living water?[8] Where can this man obtain running water, much less give some to her, when he plainly has no vessel to get it or carry it? Jesus is speaking on a spiritual level, but the woman is thinking in earthly terms. The second question raises the important issue of Jesus' identity: **Are you greater than our father Jacob, who gave us this cistern and drank from it himself with his children and his flocks?** The Greek phrasing of the woman's question indicates that she expects no for an answer. Her questions, in their †irony, entertain the possibility that Jesus might in fact be greater than Jacob.

4:13–14 Jesus answers her questions in a way that forces her to search more deeply. He first contrasts physical water with the spiritual water of which he speaks: **Everyone who drinks this water will be thirsty again; but whoever drinks the water I shall give will never thirst**. The water he gives is not physical water, which slakes thirst only for a time, but spiritual water that satisfies completely and forever. Jesus then promises, **The water I shall give will become in him a spring of water welling up to eternal life**. This water from Jesus is the Holy Spirit, an interior source of blessing and refreshment. The Holy Spirit imparts a participation in the divine life, lifting human existence to a level far beyond natural life and giving a person an eternal existence that begins now.

4:15 The woman realizes that Jesus' water is not like the water in the well: **Sir, give me this water, so that I may not be thirsty or have to keep coming here**

8. The Greek word *kyrios* means "Lord" and "master" as well as "Sir." The woman is not only being more polite but is also moving closer to faith.

to draw water. But while she mistakenly thinks that Jesus' water will satisfy physical thirst, there is irony in her speech, because the water Jesus gives will indeed satisfy thirst permanently. While she is still thinking mostly on an earthly level, she is growing in her openness to Jesus and his gift.

A Samaritan Woman's Faith Journey II: Worship in Spirit and Truth (4:16–26)

[16]Jesus said to her, "Go call your husband and come back." [17]The woman answered and said to him, "I do not have a husband." Jesus answered her, "You are right in saying, 'I do not have a husband.' [18]For you have had five husbands, and the one you have now is not your husband. What you have said is true." [19]The woman said to him, "Sir, I can see that you are a prophet. [20]Our ancestors worshiped on this mountain; but you people say that the place to worship is in Jerusalem." [21]Jesus said to her, "Believe me, woman, the hour is coming when you will worship the Father neither on this mountain nor in Jerusalem. [22]You people worship what you do not understand; we worship what we understand, because salvation is from the Jews. [23]But the hour is coming, and is now here, when true worshipers will worship the Father in Spirit and truth; and indeed the Father seeks such people to worship him. [24]God is Spirit, and those who worship him must worship in Spirit and truth." [25]The woman said to him, "I know that the Messiah is coming, the one called the Anointed; when he comes, he will tell us everything." [26]Jesus said to her, "I am he, the one who is speaking with you."

OT: Gen 12:1–3; Exod 3:13–15; Deut 18:15–18; Isa 49:1–6

NT: Rom 8:14–17; Gal 4:1–7

Catechism: the Lord's name, 446, 590; worship in Spirit and truth, 1104–9, 1179

Lectionary: Third Sunday of Lent (Year A; optional Years B and C); Common of Dedication of a Church; Baptism of Children

4:16–18

The dialogue takes a significant turn when Jesus tells the woman, **Go call your husband and come back**, and she replies, **I do not have a husband**. Jesus, however, already knows about the woman's present state: **You are right in saying, "I do not have a husband." For you have had five husbands, and the one you have now is not your husband**. At the ordinary level, the woman's relationship history is highly irregular and suspicious. But the biblical background of this story suggests a deeper dimension. The location at the well recalls biblical stories featuring Isaac, Jacob, and Moses where encounters at wells lead to marriages.

Moreover, the biblical account of Samaritan religious history includes the imported gods (see sidebar on p. 82), which lingered in Jewish memory. In this light, when Jesus speaks of the woman's husbands, he is concerned not only with her relationship history but, even more, with the Samaritans' relationship with God: the woman's five husbands symbolize the pagan gods of five nations mentioned in 2 Kings 17. Jesus thirsts not only for water but, more important, for a permanent union between the Samaritans and the Father.

4:19–20 The Samaritan woman expresses no misunderstanding this time: **Sir, I can see that you are a prophet**. She has progressed in her understanding of Jesus, as shown in the development of her addressing him from "Sir" (4:15) to "prophet." Realizing Jesus' prophetic insight, she asks his opinion on one of the most controversial aspects of Samaritan-Jewish relations: the place of worship: **Our ancestors worshiped on this mountain; but you people say that the place to worship is in Jerusalem**. Samaritans did not worship in the temple in Jerusalem but at a temple on Mount Gerizim. The Jewish king John Hyrcanus destroyed this Samaritan temple in about 129 BC, and it was never forgotten in Samaria. Perhaps this prophet can settle the dispute over where God should be worshiped.

4:21–22a Jesus opens her mind to new possibilities: **Believe me, woman, the †hour is coming when you will worship the Father neither on this mountain nor in Jerusalem.** He foretells a future when Jews, Samaritans, and indeed the whole world will come to know the Father and worship him in a new way (see 4:23–24). He then contrasts the Jews' knowledge of God with that of the Samaritans: **You people worship what you do not understand; we worship what we understand.** The word translated by the NABRE as "understand" is the Greek word for "know."[9] In the biblical sense, knowing involves not just intellectual apprehension but also a kind of union between the knower and the known. Origen describes this deeper dimension of knowing: Scripture says that "those who have been made one with and united with something *know* that with which they have been made one and have been involved."[10] By virtue of their †covenant, the †Jews know the one God in a way that the Samaritans do not.

4:22b Jesus explains the significance of the fact that his people, the Jews, know God in this way: **Salvation is from the Jews**. Jesus, the savior of the world, is a Jew. Distinguishing the Samaritans ("you people") from the Jews, Jesus identifies himself as a Jew and aligns himself with his people ("we"). The Scriptures attest

9. This verb, *oida*, is rendered as "know" in NIV, NJB, NRSV, RSV.

10. Origen, *Commentary on the Gospel according to John: Books 13–32*, trans. Ronald E. Heine, FC 89 (Washington, DC: Catholic University of America Press, 1993), 19:22. This principle illustrates why "to know" is a biblical idiom for the sexual union of husband and wife: "Adam knew his wife Eve, and she conceived" (Gen 4:1, our translation).

Fig. 3. Mount Gerizim

that God chose Israel, also called Jacob, and entered into covenant with them, so that the people Israel might show forth his holiness and serve his purposes, bringing blessing and salvation to the whole world. God promised Abraham, Isaac, and Jacob that "in your descendants all the nations of the earth will find blessing" (Gen 26:4; see 12:3; 28:14). In Isa 49, when the Lord speaks of his future act of salvation, he declares to his Servant, the personification of his people Israel: "I will make you a light to the nations [Gentiles, or non-Jews], / that my salvation may reach to the ends of the earth" (Isa 49:6). After a long time of preparation, "when the fullness of time had come, God sent his Son, born of a woman" (Gal 4:4), a Jewish woman, and thus the salvation of the entire world comes in Jesus, a descendant of Abraham and child of Israel. Through Jesus, God fulfills his covenantal promises of salvation to Israel and brings the Gentiles to himself, giving them access to the salvation and blessing promised "to Abraham and to his descendants forever" (Luke 1:55; see Gal 3:26–29).

4:23 While the woman cited events from her people's past (4:12, 20), Jesus now redirects her attention to the present—**the hour is coming, and is now here**—and lifts her mind to his **Father**. In verse 21 Jesus has hinted at a new kind of worship that is confined neither to Mount Gerizim nor to the Jerusalem temple.[11]

11. Catechism 1179.

Now he teaches that this new mode of worship that the Father desires is worship **in Spirit and truth**. Indeed, those who worship in this mode are **true worshipers**—true in the sense of being †eschatologically complete.

4:24 Jesus says that **God is Spirit** and, accordingly, **those who worship him must worship in Spirit and truth**. He explained to Nicodemus that to see and enter God's kingdom, one must be "born of water and Spirit" (3:5), receive a new heavenly life through the Spirit in baptism. As the †incarnate Word, Jesus himself is "the truth" (14:6), the revelation of God, and he "came into the world, to testify to the truth" (18:37; see 8:40). To worship in Spirit and truth means to worship God as revealed in Jesus, who is the Truth, and animated by the Holy Spirit, who imparts new heavenly life and understanding of Jesus' revelation. "Spirit and truth" does not imply that this worship is only interior or immaterial. Jesus has already explained to Nicodemus that a person must be born anew by "*water* and Spirit" (3:5, emphasis added), and he will instruct his disciples to eat his body and drink his blood in the Eucharist (6:53).

St. Paul describes such prayer to the Father as a gift of the Spirit: "God has sent the spirit of his Son into our hearts, crying out, 'Abba, Father!'" (Gal 4:6; see Rom 8:15–16). The Letter of Jude also urges us: "build yourselves up in your most holy faith; pray in the holy Spirit" (20). To worship in Spirit and truth, our prayer must be animated by the Holy Spirit in response to Jesus' revelation of the Father.[12]

4:25 The woman's response is searching: perhaps this man is **the Messiah**, for, she reasons, **when he comes, he will tell us everything**. The Samaritans awaited a †messianic figure whom they called the *Taheb* and whom they associated with the promised †Prophet-like-Moses (Deut 18:15). Although we cannot know the exact nature of this expectation, the phrase "he will tell us everything" probably refers to this promised prophet, who was regarded as an authoritative messianic teacher. The woman is obliquely asking if Jesus is the Prophet-like-Moses.

4:26 In response, Jesus openly declares his identity, revealing not only his messianic vocation but much more: **I am he, the one who is speaking with you**. The expression "I am he" renders a Greek phrase (*egō eimi*) that is literally "I am." Jesus is not only acknowledging his messiahship; he is also identifying himself with the divine name.

12. Worship "in Spirit and truth" is the Trinitarian worship of God. For instance, the Order of the Mass is directed to the Father, and many of its prayers are prayed "through Christ our Lord." The Holy Spirit "makes the unique mystery [of Christ] present" in liturgy (Catechism 1104), and the priest invokes the Holy Spirit to sanctify the bread and wine before the consecration at the Epiclesis (see Catechism 1105–9).

Names and the Divine Name

BIBLICAL BACKGROUND

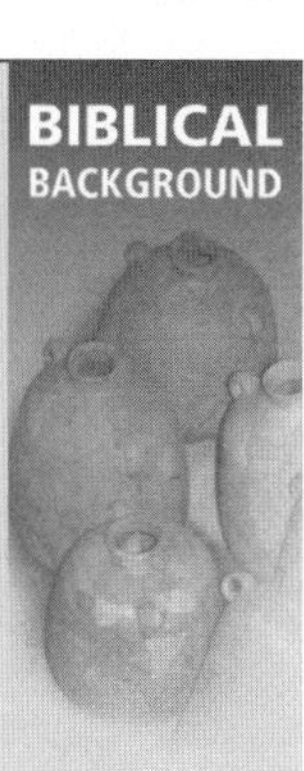

Throughout the Bible, a person's name was more than a means of reference. It expressed a person's identity and role in a profound way. When God revealed his name to Moses on Mount Sinai, it was a profound, personal revelation of himself.[a] God reveals his name to be "I am who I am" (Exod 3:14), which is linguistically related to the proper name "Yahweh" (or †YHWH).[b] There are cases where God identifies himself as "I am YHWH," and these are usually translated as "I am the LORD" (Exod 6:2–8; Lev 19:10). There are places in Isaiah where God identifies himself with the simple Hebrew formula *'ani hu'* ("I am he" or "I am") as a title (Isa 43:10; 52:6).

When the Greek translation called the †Septuagint was produced around 200 BC, the Hebrew name YHWH was rendered into Greek as *kyrios* ("Lord"), and God's words in reference to himself in Exod 3:14 ("I am who I am") and the title *'ani hu'* were both rendered as *egō eimi* ("I am"). Several times in John's Gospel, Jesus identifies himself with this simple formula "I AM" (*egō eimi*).[c] When Jesus identifies himself as "I am" or when Christians call him "Lord" (*kyrios*), there is an identification made between Jesus and YHWH, the God of Israel.[d]

a. Catechism 446.
b. Both "I am who I am" and †YHWH are based in the Hebrew verb *hayah*, meaning "to be."
c. As in John 4:26; 6:20; 8:24, 28, 58; 13:19; 18:5–6, 8. NABRE sometimes capitalizes "AM" in these "I am" statements of Jesus to indicate that he is employing a divine self-reference by allusion to the divine "I am" statements in the Old Testament. Similarly, English translations traditionally render Hebrew †YHWH as LORD in capital letters. For discussion, see Rudolf Schnackenburg, *The Gospel according to St. John*, vol. 2, *Commentary on Chapters 5–12*, trans. Cecily Hastings, Francis McDonagh, David Smith, and Richard Foley, SJ (New York: Seabury, 1980), 79–89.
d. Catechism 590.

A Samaritan Woman's Faith Journey III: Reaping the Fruit of Evangelization (4:27–42)

[27]At that moment his disciples returned, and were amazed that he was talking with a woman, but still no one said, "What are you looking for?" or "Why are you talking with her?" [28]The woman left her water jar and went into the town and said to the people, [29]"Come see a man who told me everything I have done. Could he possibly be the Messiah?" [30]They went out of the town and came to him. [31]Meanwhile, the disciples urged him, "Rabbi, eat." [32]But he said to them, "I have food to eat of which you do not know." [33]So the disciples said to one another, "Could someone have

brought him something to eat?" [34]Jesus said to them, "My food is to do the will of the one who sent me and to finish his work. [35]Do you not say, 'In four months the harvest will be here'? I tell you, look up and see the fields ripe for the harvest. [36]The reaper is already receiving his payment and gathering crops for eternal life, so that the sower and reaper can rejoice together. [37]For here the saying is verified that 'One sows and another reaps.' [38]I sent you to reap what you have not worked for; others have done the work, and you are sharing the fruits of their work."

[39]Many of the Samaritans of that town began to believe in him because of the word of the woman who testified, "He told me everything I have done." [40]When the Samaritans came to him, they invited him to stay with them; and he stayed there two days. [41]Many more began to believe in him because of his word, [42]and they said to the woman, "We no longer believe because of your word; for we have heard for ourselves, and we know that this is truly the savior of the world."

OT: Isa 49:1–6; Joel 4:13

NT: Matt 9:37–38; 13:24–43; 1 Cor 1:25–31

Catechism: evangelization flows from knowing Jesus, 426–29, 850; Jesus does the Father's will, 2824

Lectionary: Third Sunday of Lent (Year A; optional Years B and C); Common of Dedication of a Church; Baptism of Children

4:27 The **disciples** now return with food. Since Jesus' conversation with the Samaritan woman transgressed cultural conventions, they are **amazed that he was talking with a woman**.

4:28–30 At this point, the Gospel narrative splits into two scenes: one with the Samaritan woman in the town, the other with Jesus and the disciples at the well. First, the narrative follows the Samaritan woman. She had come to the well to draw water (4:7), but now she **left her water jar**, the whole reason for her trip to the well (or so she thought). Her encounter with Jesus has so moved her that he becomes her new concern. She **went into the town** to tell her neighbors about her encounter with Jesus—the very definition of "evangelization." The woman brought the good news to the people of her town and invited them to know Jesus themselves: **Come see a man who told me everything I have done. Could he possibly be the Messiah?** She speaks from experience, not hesitating to mention her own past and Jesus' prophetic knowledge (4:18–19). Upon hearing her testimony, the Samaritan townspeople **went out of the town and came to him**. Like Andrew and Philip in John 1, the Samaritan woman becomes a witness whose testimony leads others to Jesus.[13]

13. Catechism 428–29, 850.

4:31–34

The disciples, meanwhile, are concerned with providing food for Jesus and ask him to **eat**. But Jesus responds, **I have food to eat of which you do not know**. The disciples do not understand and wonder who has provided him with food. Like the temple authorities, Nicodemus, and the Samaritan woman, Jesus' disciples do not realize that he is speaking of spiritual realities. **Jesus**, who has had nothing to eat, or presumably to drink, reveals the true source of his sustenance: **My food is to do the will of the one who sent me and to finish his work**. Doing the Father's will is the source of his strength, and Jesus has found this sustenance in winning over the Samaritan woman to whom the Father had sent him. Jesus' response also foreshadows that moment when he completes the Father's will and declares from the cross: "It is finished" (19:30).[14]

4:35–38

Jesus continues with an ambiguous figure of speech about harvesting. The proverb probably has nothing to do with the actual time of these events, because, given that Jesus was just in Jerusalem for Passover (2:13), the actual harvest would be much closer than four months away. Rather, the harvest is a biblical image for God's †eschatological judgment (Hosea 6:11; Joel 4:13; Matt 13:24–43). Here and elsewhere, Jesus refers to the work to be done in the Father's plan as the harvest, which continues up to "the end of the age" (Matt 9:37–38; 28:19–20).

The proverb, **In four months the harvest will be here**, must mean something like, "We have plenty of time." But on the contrary, Jesus insists that the time is urgent: **I tell you, look up and see the fields ripe for the harvest. The reaper is already receiving his payment and gathering crops for eternal life, so that the sower and reaper can rejoice together. For here the saying is verified that "One sows and another reaps." I sent you to reap what you have not worked for; others have done the work, and you are sharing the fruits of their work**. In effect, Jesus claims the following: "Open the eyes of your heart and see how urgent the times are. We must preach the gospel and gather in the harvest already prepared by my Father. You are being sent to reap the fruit of the labor of many prophets, patriarchs, and saints who have gone before you. People must be prepared to understand the meaning of my coming death and resurrection." Jesus thus expresses his deep desire to do for the whole world, through his disciples, what he has been doing for the Samaritan woman.

4:39–42

The focus shifts back to **the Samaritans, many of** whom **began to believe in** Jesus **because of** the woman's testimony. They are the firstfruits of the "harvest" (4:35) gathered in by the woman. These Samaritans **came to** Jesus and **invited him to stay with them**. Jesus accepted their welcome and **stayed there two days** (see 1:39). While Jesus stays with them, they experience his reality for

14. Catechism 2824.

themselves (**we have heard for ourselves**), not simply on account of the **word** of another. Accordingly, they acknowledge him to be **the savior of the world**. With this title, these good people manifest not only an openness of spirit but also a willingness to accept that Jesus is savior of all, not only of Jews or Samaritans. His saving power is destined to "reach to the ends of the earth" (Isa 49:6).

Reflection and Application (4:1–42)

A woman with an irregular past comes to a well to draw ordinary drinking water, but encounters an offer of divine life instead. In its own way, this incident of the Samaritan woman and Jesus teaches something that St. Paul often insisted upon: our knowledge of Jesus the Savior is itself a gift from God. God's call, his grace, and our own relationship with him are pure, undeserved gifts. Saint Paul reminds the Corinthian Christians and us too: "Consider your own calling, brothers. Not many of you were wise by human standards, not many were powerful, not many were of noble birth. Rather, God chose the foolish of the world to shame the wise, and God chose the weak of the world to shame the strong. . . . It is due to him that you are in Christ Jesus, who became for us wisdom from God, as well as righteousness, sanctification, and redemption" (1 Cor 1:26–27, 30).

As the Holy Spirit impresses upon us the utter giftness of God's grace, two things begin to happen. First, we are overcome with awe and gratitude, and our trust in God grows into genuine freedom. We have nothing to fear from experiencing our need for God's mercy. Second, we discover in ourselves a zeal to bring this good news to others. Like the Samaritan woman we want everyone to know Jesus, and we want to share with them what he has done for us.

A Galilean Gentile's Faith Journey: Jesus Heals an Official's Son (4:43–54)

[43]After the two days, he left there for Galilee. [44]For Jesus himself testified that a prophet has no honor in his native place. [45]When he came into Galilee, the Galileans welcomed him, since they had seen all he had done in Jerusalem at the feast; for they themselves had gone to the feast.

[46]Then he returned to Cana in Galilee, where he had made the water wine. Now there was a royal official whose son was ill in Capernaum. [47]When he heard that Jesus had arrived in Galilee from Judea, he went to him and asked him to come down and heal his son, who was near death.

[48]Jesus said to him, "Unless you people see signs and wonders, you will not believe." [49]The royal official said to him, "Sir, come down before my child dies." [50]Jesus said to him, "You may go; your son will live." The man believed what Jesus said to him and left. [51]While he was on his way back, his slaves met him and told him that his boy would live. [52]He asked them when he began to recover. They told him, "The fever left him yesterday, about one in the afternoon." [53]The father realized that just at that time Jesus had said to him, "Your son will live," and he and his whole household came to believe. [54] [Now] this was the second sign Jesus did when he came to Galilee from Judea.

OT: 1 Kings 17:17–24; 2 Kings 5:1, 8–14
NT: Matt 8:5–13; Mark 7:24–30
Catechism: Christ the physician, 1503–5

4:43–44 **After the two days,** Jesus **left** Samaria, where he had met with a warm reception. Then he went to **Galilee**, saying **a prophet has no honor in his native place**. These two statements create a puzzling situation. In the †Synoptics, the same statement about "a prophet . . . without honor" is linked to Jesus' being rejected in Galilee (Mark 6:4), whereas John suggests that this lack of honor is his very reason for leaving Judea and going to Galilee.

4:45–46 Jesus **returned to Cana**, where he had performed his first miraculous †sign (2:1–11). The **Galileans welcomed him**, but we are also alerted that the Galilean enthusiasm was on shaky footing, for it was because **they had seen all he had done in Jerusalem at the feast**. In 2:23–25, we learned that Jesus was untrusting of those drawn to him simply as a miracle worker. Jesus' miracles are to be seen as signs that reveal spiritual truths, not simply as impressive spectacles. Perhaps the best way to understand Jesus' statement in 4:44 about a prophet without honor is as an anticipation of the superficiality he was going to meet in Galilee.

We are next introduced to **a royal official whose son was ill in Capernaum**, about a day's journey from Cana. The term for "royal official" indicates that this man was probably an official of Herod Antipas, Rome's client-king of Galilee. The official could be either Jewish or Gentile, but for several reasons, the likelihood is that he was Gentile. First, this episode follows on the account of the faith of the Samaritans, who are non-Jews. Second, this episode resembles two other Gospel accounts where Jesus heals a Gentile's child at a distance (the centurion's boy in Matt 8:5–13; Luke 7:1–10; the Syrophoenician woman's daughter in Mark 7:24–30).[15] So understood, John 4 portrays Jesus' response to genuine faith

15. The prophets Elijah (1 Kings 17:17–24) and Elisha (2 Kings 5:1, 8–14) are also reported to have cured Gentiles by a prophetic word.

Saint Cyril of Alexandria on the Healings of the Royal Official and His Boy

LIVING TRADITION

The one command of the Savior heals two souls. In the official, the Savior's command brings about unexpected faith even as it also rescues the child from bodily death. It is difficult to say which one is healed first. Both, I suppose, are healed simultaneously. The disease left at the command of the Savior. The official's servants meet him and tell him of the healing of the child. This shows at the same time the swiftness of the divine commands and how wisely Christ ordered all of this. They speedily confirmed the hope of their master, who was weak in faith. . . . When the official learned that the sick child's recovery coincided exactly with Jesus' command, he is saved with "his whole house." He attributes the power of the miracle to the Savior Christ and he is brought to a firmer faith.[a]

a. Cyril of Alexandria, *Commentary on John* 2.5, in ACCS 4a:176.

wherever he finds it, even if the person is outside of the †covenant community (e.g., Samaritans) and seems to be far from knowing God (e.g., Gentiles).

4:47–48 Upon hearing that Jesus was **in Galilee**, the royal official **went to** Jesus and **asked him to come down and heal his son, who was near death**. Jesus, however, challenges the official: **Unless you people see signs and wonders, you will not believe.** Jesus criticizes the superficial enthusiasm of the Galileans and induces the man to manifest genuine faith through this challenge.

4:49–50 The royal official passes the test. He presses on and appeals to Jesus personally in an initial movement of faith: **Sir, come down before my child dies**. Like the Samaritan woman (4:11, 15), the official addresses Jesus as "Sir" (*kyrios*). Jesus answers, **You may go; your son will live**. Thus he encourages the official to believe, and the royal official takes a further step: he **believed what Jesus said to him and left**. While he has not yet arrived at mature faith in Jesus, this fledgling Gentile believer begins the journey back to Capernaum.

4:51–54 As he was heading home, **his slaves met him and told him that his boy would live**. The royal official learned that this happened exactly when **Jesus had said, "Your son will live."** The word of the Lord proves itself true. By heading for home, the royal official has shown that he believed the word that Jesus spoke to him; now he rejoices to see Jesus' faithfulness. He takes the last step of faith and, like the Samaritan woman, becomes an evangelist by declaring his faith: **he and his whole household came to believe**. This **second sign** reveals that faith in Jesus must rise above being superficially impressed with him as a religious teacher or miracle worker and must mature to a genuine, personal faith in him.

Reflection and Application (4:43–54)

Having completed the first part of the Book of Signs (1:18–4:54; see "Structure and Literary Features" in the introduction), we can reflect on how to read the Gospel narratives in faith. Unlike any other story about a past figure, the Gospels tell us about someone who is *alive* and *present*. The Gospels are a means of revelation that puts us in actual contact with their protagonist, the living Jesus Christ. For centuries the individual events of Jesus' life have been called "mysteries" (Catechism 512–18). In the New Testament, the Greek word *mystērion* ("mystery") can refer to some aspect of God's plan of salvation in Christ that is being made known in and through the Church's preaching, liturgy, and faith (1 Cor 2:7–8; Eph 3:3–6). A mystery is an act of God in history, and to truly understand this historical action is to understand the divine mystery, which it bears. As St. Augustine remarks in a sermon on Mary's anointing of Jesus' feet with ointment (John 12:3), "We have heard the fact, now let us search after the mystery."[16]

When reading the Gospels in faith, we should try to open ourselves up to the living Christ, who forever exists as the healer of the royal official's son. When we read the biblical text with a faithful, receptive heart, we encounter the very same mystery of Christ that his disciples encountered in Jesus' turning water into wine and the Gentile official encountered in the healing of his child. That same healing power of Jesus is available to us through the Holy Spirit, to work in our lives both physically and spiritually. Speaking of the mysteries of the liturgical year, Blessed Columba Marmion made a statement that applies also to the Scriptures:

> Although it is always the same Savior, the same Jesus, pursuing the same work of our sanctification, each mystery [of his life], however, is a fresh manifestation of Christ for us; each has its own special beauty, its particular splendor, and likewise its own grace. . . . The Fathers of the Church speak more than once of what they call the *vis mysterii*, the virtue and signification of the mystery which is being celebrated. . . . Each of Christ's mysteries, representing a state of his Sacred Humanity, thus brings us a special participation in his Divinity.[17]

By reading this Gospel in faith, we are invited to experience Jesus putting us to the test and challenging our faith and willingness to trust him, as he tested the royal official. If we, like the royal official, put our trust in Jesus' word, we will see him working in our lives, in our families, and in the world.

16. St. Augustine, *Tractates on John* 50.6 (PL 35:1760), our translation.
17. Blessed Columba Marmion, *Christ in His Mysteries*, 7th ed. (London: Sands, 1939), 22–24.

The Obedient Son, Lord of the Sabbath

John 5:1–47

The Gospel again shifts from Galilee to Jerusalem, where Jesus goes for a liturgical festival. With this journey, the Book of †Signs opens a new subsection (5:1–10:42), which treats Jesus' relation to some major Jewish liturgical feasts: sabbath (5:1–47), Passover (6:1–71), Tabernacles (7:1–10:21), and Dedication (10:22–42).

John 5 begins with Jesus healing a paralyzed man on the sabbath (5:1–9), and this event becomes the cause of controversy (5:10–18). Like Jesus' other miracles in John, this healing is a sign, and Jesus teaches that this sign reveals his unique relationship with the Father and the divine power with which he acts (5:19–47). These events mark the beginning of open hostility to Jesus from the Jerusalem religious authorities, whom John calls the †Jews.

Jesus Heals on the Sabbath (5:1–9)

[1]After this, there was a feast of the Jews, and Jesus went up to Jerusalem. [2]Now there is in Jerusalem at the Sheep [Gate] a pool called in Hebrew Bethesda, with five porticoes. [3]In these lay a large number of ill, blind, lame, and crippled. [[4†]] [5]One man was there who had been ill for thirty-eight years. [6]When Jesus saw him lying there and knew that he had been ill for a long time, he said to him, "Do you want to be well?" [7]The sick man answered him, "Sir, I have no one to put me into the pool when the water is stirred up; while I am on my way, someone else gets down there before

Fig. 4. Model of the pools of Bethesda

me." [8]Jesus said to him, "Rise, take up your mat, and walk." [9]Immediately the man became well, took up his mat, and walked.

Now that day was a sabbath.

OT: Isa 35:1–10

NT: Mark 2:1–12

Catechism: Anointing of the Sick, 1502–5

5:1–2 **Jesus went up to Jerusalem** for an unspecified **feast**. By **the Sheep [Gate]**, there was **a pool called in Hebrew Bethesda, with five porticoes**. Archaeological evidence shows that this site consisted of two adjoining pools that shared a wall, and each pool was enclosed by colonnaded porticoes. As this story suggests, the waters were thought to have curative powers.

5:3–9 Assembled around in porticoes were **a large number of ill, blind, lame, and crippled** people, hoping for healings.[1] One man in particular **had been ill for thirty-eight years**, and based on the description of his cure (5:8), he is paralyzed. Knowing of the man's long-term illness, Jesus approached him and asked, **Do you want to be well?** The man replied with desperation that this

1. John 5:4, not printed in the text of the NABRE but included in the footnotes, reads: "For [from time to time] an angel of the Lord used to come down into the pool; and the water was stirred up, so the first one to get in [after the stirring of the water] was healed of whatever disease afflicted him." This verse was inserted by an early scribe to provide background for the man's reply in 5:7.

seemed impossible: he could never enter the pool in time to take advantage of the opportunity for healing. Then, in words similar to other accounts of Jesus healing the paralyzed (Mark 2:11), Jesus tells him, **Rise, take up your mat, and walk**. The man did exactly that: **Immediately the man became well, took up his mat, and walked**. Jesus healed this very sick man who longed to be made well but was unable to help himself. The healing of the paralyzed man shows that in Jesus, God is fulfilling his promises to bring salvation to his people.[2] Concerning this time, Isaiah said, "The eyes of the blind shall see, / and the ears of the deaf be opened; / Then the lame shall leap like a stag" (Isa 35:5–6).

The closing comment, **That day was a sabbath**, sets up both the controversy (5:10–18) and the discourse (5:19–47) in which Jesus will set forth what this miraculous †sign reveals: namely, he possesses the unique divine power that works on the sabbath because he shares the identity of God.

The Controversy Begins: Working on the Sabbath (5:10–18)

[10]So the Jews said to the man who was cured, "It is the sabbath, and it is not lawful for you to carry your mat." [11]He answered them, "The man who made me well told me, 'Take up your mat and walk.'" [12]They asked him, "Who is the man who told you, 'Take it up and walk'?" [13]The man who was healed did not know who it was, for Jesus had slipped away, since there was a crowd there. [14]After this Jesus found him in the temple area and said to him, "Look, you are well; do not sin any more, so that nothing worse may happen to you." [15]The man went and told the Jews that Jesus was the one who had made him well. [16]Therefore, the Jews began to persecute Jesus because he did this on a sabbath. [17]But Jesus answered them, "My Father is at work until now, so I am at work." [18]For this reason the Jews tried all the more to kill him, because he not only broke the sabbath but he also called God his own father, making himself equal to God.

OT: Exod 20:8–11; 31:12–17; Lev 24:10–23; Deut 5:12–15; Jer 17:21–22
NT: Matt 12:1–8; Luke 6:6–11
Catechism: the sabbath day, 345–49, 2168–73; Jesus and Israel, 574–76

5:10–13 Jesus instructs the healed man to "take up your mat, and walk" (5:9). When **the Jews** see this, they object: **It is the sabbath, and it is not lawful for you to**

2. Catechism 1503.

The Sabbath

BIBLICAL BACKGROUND

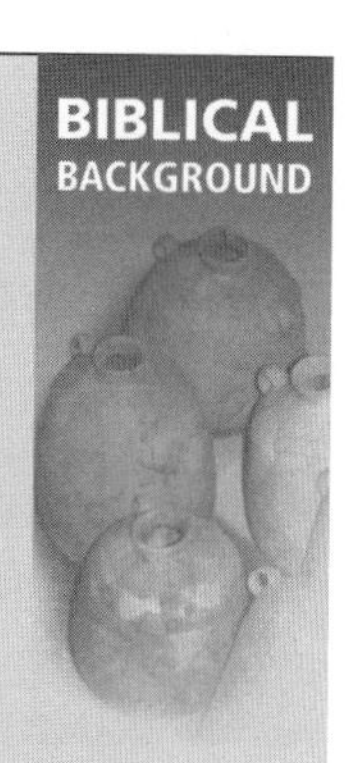

The sabbath day is the seventh day of the week, from sundown on Friday to sundown on Saturday, on which Israel was to rest from work as part of their †covenant with God (Exod 31:12–17).[a] The Old Testament gives two principal motives for keeping the sabbath. First, in Exod 20:8–11, the motive is God's rest on the seventh day of creation, which he blessed and set apart from other days (Gen 2:3). Observing the sabbath is thus a recognition of God's sovereignty over all creation as its creator. Second, in Deut 5:12–15, the sabbath rest is a commemoration of the exodus, when God freed the Israelites from slavery. For Israel, the sabbath involves an imitation of God not only in his rest but also in his loving-kindness: "Your male and female slave may rest as you do. Remember that you too were once slaves in the land of Egypt, and the Lord, your God, brought you out from there with a strong hand and outstretched arm. That is why the Lord, your God, has commanded you to observe the sabbath day" (Deut 5:14–15).

While sabbath observance is a key component of Jewish life, the specifics of what exactly constituted the work to be avoided on the sabbath was the topic of lively disputes among Jewish thinkers throughout antiquity. Different Jewish groups had different opinions on these matters.[b]

a. Catechism 348, 2168–73.

b. For discussion of sabbath law around Jesus' time, see John P. Meier, *A Marginal Jew*, ABRL (New York: Doubleday; New Haven: Yale University, 2009), 4:235–52.

carry your mat. The context suggests that "the †Jews" here are Jewish authorities in Jerusalem.[3] Their objection to the man's carrying his mat seems grounded in the prohibition of carrying burdens from one's house or through the city gates on the sabbath (Jer 17:21–22).[4] The healed man responds that the **man who made** him **well** so ordered him. The authorities want to know who this man is, for in light of their interpretation of sabbath law, it seems that he has asked the healed man to do something in violation of the sabbath. But the healed man **did not know who it was, for Jesus had slipped away** into the **crowd**.

5:14 **Jesus** later **found** the healed man **in the temple area** and warned him: **Do not sin any more, so that nothing worse may happen to you**. The

3. First, the reprimand implies their authority to adjudicate matters of legal observance. Second, Jesus mentions (5:33) that the same group sent a delegation to John the Baptist (1:19), a group of "priests and Levites." The power to send a formal delegation of priests likewise suggests authority. For discussion of John's use of the term "the Jews," see sidebar on p. 101.

4. See *Jubilees* 2:30; *Mishnah Shabbat* 7:2.

connection between sin and sickness anticipates the disciples' question in 9:2 about whose sin caused a man to be born blind. There, Jesus clarifies for his disciples that the man's blindness was not due to anyone's sin (9:3). Accordingly, Jesus' remark here can mean that sin causes something worse to a person than physical illness: spiritual illness that can be eternally fatal.

5:15–16 After this encounter, the healed **man went and told the Jews that Jesus was** his healer. The authorities then **began to persecute Jesus because he did this on a sabbath**. This marks the beginning of conflict between Jesus and the Jewish authorities in the Gospel. It begins over a question of legal observance, and the †Synoptics likewise report that Jesus' actions and self-understanding with regard to the sabbath were a source of controversy with religious leaders (Matt 12:1–14; Luke 6:1–11). The verb translated as "persecute"[5] also has the resonance of "prosecute" in a judicial sense, and this dimension of meaning fits with the legal question of sabbath observance. It is †ironic that the Jewish authorities should be trying to bring Jesus to judgment, since his coming into the world has the effect of bringing divine judgment to people. In 3:19–21, the Evangelist teaches that Jesus' coming into the world and people's responses to him are the occasion for judgment. While various people sit in judgment over Jesus, they are the ones who, through their responses to Jesus, are really being judged. The Gospel develops this teaching about judgment in its narrative, where the encounter between Jesus and others appears as a great cosmic lawsuit, a trial complete with witnesses and evidence.

5:17–18 Jesus responds to the authorities' charge with an even stronger claim: **My Father is at work until now, so I am at work**. Jewish reflection on the nature of God's sabbath rest (Gen 2:2–3) led to the conclusion that God continued to perform two major activities on the sabbath: giving life and passing judgment on the dead, as seemed evident from the fact that people are born and die on the sabbath. This background sheds light on Jesus' response. Jesus has healed a paralyzed man and declares that he can work on the sabbath, in this case, to give life. Jesus is thus exercising a power that belongs only to God and does not cease on the sabbath. The authorities understand the seriousness of this claim: **He also called God his own father, making himself equal to God**. In the authorities' eyes, Jesus is a mere man who is claiming to be God, a claim they regard as blasphemy. Since blasphemy is a capital crime (Lev 24:10–23), **the Jews tried all the more to kill him**.

5. Greek *diōkō*.

John and the Jews

BIBLICAL BACKGROUND

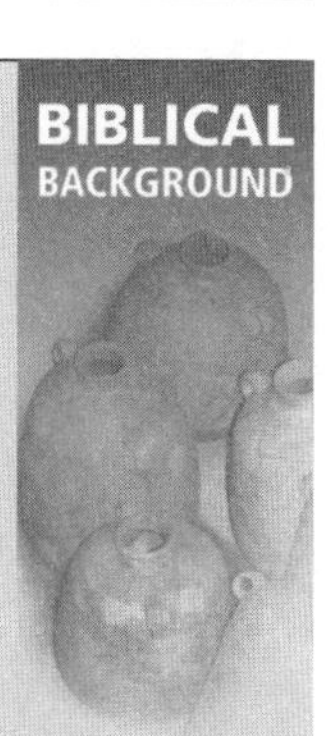

The polemic toward the †Jews is one of the most difficult topics in the interpretation of John. The Gospel frequently uses the general category "the Jews" to designate the religious authorities in Jerusalem who oppose Jesus and take hostile action against him, culminating in his death. In this Gospel, "the Jews" are said to "persecute Jesus" and seek "to kill him" (5:16, 18). In the course of a heated exchange, Jesus declares to them that they belong to their "father the devil" (8:44).

In keeping with the teachings of the Second Vatican Council, we need to keep several things in mind as we seek to interpret John's language about "the Jews."

First, the Gospel depicts a variety of Jewish persons and groups. Jesus does things that display his own Jewishness. He goes to Jerusalem to celebrate the holy days (2:13; 7:14) and to the †synagogue, where he interprets Scripture (6:31–59). He declares to the Samaritan woman that "salvation is from the Jews" (4:22). The Gospel depicts a variety of responses to Jesus from different Jewish groups. Some are positive and welcoming toward Jesus (e.g., the Bethany family in John 11), others are ambivalent (e.g., the crowd in John 7, some †Pharisees in 9:16), still others are hostile (e.g., Caiaphas in John 11:49–50; the group in 5:16–18).

Second, John does not use the term "the Jews" with a consistent tone or to designate a single group. Some uses of the category are positive (11:19, 31, 36), others are neutral (2:13), and the majority are negative. John 7:13 illustrates the complexity of John's use of the term "the Jews." The narrator says that the festival crowd, which is Jewish, is "afraid of the Jews": thus Jews are afraid of "the Jews." Such instances suggest that when John uses "the Jews" negatively, he does not have in mind all Jewish people but those Jerusalem religious authorities who aggressively oppose Jesus and work for his death.

Third, it is generally thought that John's Gospel has been shaped by later first-century conflicts between Jews who did not believe in Jesus as the †Messiah and those who did. The Christ-believing Jews were the newer, smaller group and were struggling to articulate their faith over and against a long-standing Jewish tradition, most of whose custodians disagreed with their claims about Jesus. In this challenging situation, the language and tone of the Christ-believing group toward its opponents was quite sharp, and some of this tone is reflected in John's Gospel, which was completed at the end of the first century.

This commentary will consider the Jews as a special glossary item and indicate when the Gospel seems to be using the category as shorthand for a specific group.

The Catholic Church and the Jews

The Catholic Church's relationship with Jews and Judaism has taken on new life since the Second Vatican Council, prominently in the pontificate of Pope St. John Paul II. These positive initiatives were preceded by a sad, painful history between Jews and Christians in which the marginalization and persecution of Jews by Christians were justified by appeal to biblical texts. Since Vatican II, the Church has been very explicit in condemning anti-Semitism: the Church "decries hatred, persecutions, displays of anti-Semitism, directed against Jews at any time and by anyone."[a] The Church teaches that Jewish people should not be uniquely blamed for Jesus' death.[b] All sinners, ourselves included, are responsible for Jesus' death (Catechism 598). The Church also teaches that God's covenant with the Jews, the family of Abraham, endures and "has never been revoked" (Catechism 121). Consequently, Jews should never be thought of "as rejected or accursed by God," for they are part of the people of God, and the Church has a unique spiritual bond with them.[c]

There are many ways in which Catholics and Jews can work together and grow in mutual understanding and respect for each other's faith. While there are areas of shared belief and interest, there are also fundamental differences between the two faiths, especially the Christian belief that Jesus of Nazareth is the †incarnation of God, the fulfillment of God's covenantal promises, and the savior of the world. Without ignoring the past or the fundamental differences of belief, Jews and Christians can live peacefully with each other and learn from each other as we move toward the end of days, when Jews look for the glorious appearance of the Messiah and Christians look for the public manifestation of the risen Christ in glory. On that day, St. Paul teaches, the whole people of God, "all Israel will be saved" (Rom 11:26).

a. Second Vatican Council, *Nostra Aetate* (Declaration on the Relation of the Church to Non-Christian Religions) 4. All citations of Church documents will be taken from the English text at www.vatican.va.

b. Second Vatican Council, *Nostra Aetate*.

c. Second Vatican Council, *Lumen Gentium* (The Dogmatic Constitution on the Church) 16; *Nostra Aetate* 4.

The Work of the Father and the Son (5:19–30)

[19]Jesus answered and said to them, "Amen, amen, I say to you, a son cannot do anything on his own, but only what he sees his father doing; for what he does, his son will do also. [20]For the Father loves his Son and shows him everything that he himself does, and he will show him greater works than these, so that you may be amazed. [21]For just as the Father raises the

dead and gives life, so also does the Son give life to whomever he wishes. [22]Nor does the Father judge anyone, but he has given all judgment to his Son, [23]so that all may honor the Son just as they honor the Father. Whoever does not honor the Son does not honor the Father who sent him. [24]Amen, amen, I say to you, whoever hears my word and believes in the one who sent me has eternal life and will not come to condemnation, but has passed from death to life. [25]Amen, amen, I say to you, the hour is coming and is now here when the dead will hear the voice of the Son of God, and those who hear will live. [26]For just as the Father has life in himself, so also he gave to his Son the possession of life in himself. [27]And he gave him power to exercise judgment, because he is the Son of Man. [28]Do not be amazed at this, because the hour is coming in which all who are in the tombs will hear his voice [29]and will come out, those who have done good deeds to the resurrection of life, but those who have done wicked deeds to the resurrection of condemnation.

[30]"I cannot do anything on my own; I judge as I hear, and my judgment is just, because I do not seek my own will but the will of the one who sent me."

OT: Ps 29; Ezek 37:1–14; Dan 7:9–14; 12:2–3

NT: Matt 25:31–46; Rev 20:11–15

Catechism: God is love, 221; the Holy Trinity, 253–56; risen with Christ, 1002–4; final judgment, 1021–22, 1038–41

Jesus' actions on the sabbath have provoked a legal controversy. The authorities think Jesus has violated the sabbath and blasphemed, and the atmosphere is that of a courtroom. Jesus responds to these charges with a discourse (5:19–47), defending his words and deeds on the basis of his identity as the Son. Jesus explains that his healing the paralyzed man on the sabbath is a †sign, which reveals that he possesses the unique divine powers to give life and judge—the two powers that God does not cease to exercise on the sabbath.

5:19–20a Jesus has spoken of his single-minded devotion to the Father's will (4:34) and now he continues: **Amen, Amen, I say to you, a son cannot do anything on his own, but only what he sees his father doing; for what he does, his son will do also**. The NABRE understands this saying as a proverb.[6] Jesus' words can also be taken as a response to some implicit thinking in the authorities' objection to his claim: "My Father is at work, . . . so I am at work" (5:17). The Jewish authorities might understand that claim to mean that there are two separate workers (the Father and Jesus). So understood, Jesus would be a second worker who is

6. On the so-called parable of the apprenticed son; see C. H. Dodd, "A Hidden Parable in the Fourth Gospel," in *More New Testament Studies* (Grand Rapids: Eerdmans, 1968), 30–40.

"equal to God" (5:18) but whose powers are distinct from God's—a separate competitor on the same level with God, a rival deity. But Jesus is affirming that he is not the Father's competitor but his obedient Son. **For the Father loves his Son and shows him everything that he himself does**. The terms "Father" and "Son" are relational and affectionate, and here the †incarnate Word unveils a glimpse of God's inner life.[7] From all eternity, the Father loves and begets the Son (1:1, 18). Beloved by the Father, the Son receives from the Father his life and mission, which he obediently carries out in love. As **the Father loves his Son and shows him everything**, so will Jesus tell his disciples whom he loves, "I have told you everything I have heard from my Father" (15:15).

5:20b–23 From eternity the Father shows all his works to the Son, and **he will show him greater works than these, so that you may be amazed**. The Son has the unique divine powers to raise **the dead** and **give life** and to **judge**. The "greater works" are these divine actions, which the Son sees from all eternity and which he now performs in his humanity. This is the mystery revealed by Jesus' healing the paralytic on the sabbath: Jesus is the Father's obedient Son, who receives everything from the Father and possesses in himself the divine powers over life, death, and judgment.

Since the Father **has given all judgment to his Son**, the criterion of judgment consists in whether one believes in the Son. Since the Son is constituted wholly by his relationship with the Father, a response to the Son is the same as a response to the Father. Jesus' words here also reflect the Jewish legal understanding of sender and envoy.[8] According to this understanding, when a sender gives a mission to an envoy and empowers him to act on his behalf, the envoy's actions on behalf of the sender are legally binding because they are, in effect, the sender's actions. As the one sent by the Father, Jesus is the perfect envoy who obediently carries out the Father's work, and a response to the envoy, the Son, has the same force as a response to the sender, the Father. Consequently, Jesus says, **Whoever does not honor the Son does not honor the Father who sent him.**

5:24 An essential aspect of honoring the Son is hearing his word, which is the Father's word: **Amen, amen, I say to you, whoever hears my word and believes in the one who sent me has eternal life**. Belief in the Father, who sent Jesus, takes place by a genuine hearing of Jesus' word, which means yielding to his word and taking it in. As we see in John 6, this belief is enabled by the Father's

7. Catechism 221, 240, 255.

8. Peder Borgen, "God's Agent in the Fourth Gospel," in *Religions in Antiquity: Essays in Memory of Erwin Ramsdell Goodenough*, ed. Jacob Neusner (Leiden: Brill, 1968), 137–48; repr. in *The Interpretation of John*, 2nd ed., ed. John Ashton (Edinburgh: T&T Clark, 1997), 83–95.

work in the believer, and it results in eternal life. The one who hears and believes in the Son **will not come to condemnation, but has passed from death to life**. This hearing, believing, and having eternal life all take place *now*, in the present moment, as does the passing from death to life, and it has future effects.[9] One's present response in yielding faith to Jesus leads to a future freedom from condemnation. We must still pass through bodily death, but we will do so as those already possessing eternal life.

5:25 Jesus further discusses his divine power to give life and judge: **The †hour is coming and is now here when the dead will hear the voice of the Son of God, and those who hear will live**. These dead are the ones who are spiritually dead in sin and who are awakened to faith and eternal life by the voice of God's Son. "The voice of the LORD is power" (Ps 29:4), and the power of God's Word, by whom all things were created (John 1:3), will be demonstrated visibly when Jesus calls the dead man Lazarus out of the tomb (11:43).

5:26 The Son has the power to give life to the dead because of his relationship with the Father: **For just as Father has life in himself, so also he gave to his Son the possession of life in himself**. The Father—whom later tradition calls *Principium Deitatis*, meaning the coeternal source of the Deity—has no priority of time or dignity within the Godhead.[10] All that the Father is, including his being the one who has life in himself, he gives to the Son in that one eternal act, without beginning or end, by which he is Father and the Son is Son (1:1–2).

5:27–29 The Father has given the Son **power to exercise judgment, because he is the Son of Man**. The judgment effected by the †Son of Man (see sidebar on p. 52) has both present and future aspects. People's response to Jesus in the present determines their eternal fate. In the future, at the end of days, there will be a resurrection of all the dead **in which all who are in the tombs will hear** the Son's **voice** and arise.[11] Those **who have done good deeds** will go **to the resurrection of life**, and **those who have done wicked deeds to the resurrection of condemnation** (see Dan 12:2–3; Rev 20:13). One's conduct and response to Jesus in the present time determines one's eternity (see Matt 25:31–46).

5:30 The first part of Jesus' discourse ends with the same theme with which it began (5:19): Jesus' faithful obedience to the Father's will. **I cannot do anything on my own; I judge as I hear, and my judgment is just, because I do not seek my own will but the will of the one who sent me**. Jesus is the faithful, obedient Son, who does everything given him by the Father. Having been

9. Catechism 1002.

10. The Father, the Son, and the Holy Spirit have existed from all eternity as coequal persons of the one divine nature (Catechism 253).

11. Catechism 1038.

confronted with the charges of sabbath violation and blasphemy (5:16–18), Jesus defends himself by teaching that he is the Father's perfectly obedient Son. Everything about the Son—his life, words, deeds—comes from the Father, and as the obedient Son, he possesses the unique divine powers to do the Father's works on the sabbath.

Reflection and Application (5:19–30)

The Church's teaching about the Blessed Trinity—there is one God, who is three persons—articulates the central mystery of Christian faith. Although this mystery lies beyond human comprehension and the doctrines that define this mystery are quite technical, the Trinity is of enormous importance for human life. Human beings were created to share God's own life, and since God's life is the eternal communion of love between Father, Son, and Holy Spirit, it is this eternal, Trinitarian communion of life and love that human beings were created to share. As the Catechism (221) puts it, "God himself is an eternal exchange of love, Father, Son, and Holy Spirit, and he has destined us to share in that exchange." The Trinity is the goal of human life, and it gives meaning to our entire existence. Only the full participation in God's Trinitarian life will permanently and completely satisfy us as human beings. The Trinity is the answer we seek, the fulfillment of our hopes, and the satisfaction of our hearts. And only Jesus, the Word made flesh, is the "gate" (10:9) and the "way" (14:6) to share in the Trinitarian communion.

Witnesses to Jesus (5:31–40)

[31]"If I testify on my own behalf, my testimony cannot be verified. [32]But there is another who testifies on my behalf, and I know that the testimony he gives on my behalf is true. [33]You sent emissaries to John, and he testified to the truth. [34]I do not accept testimony from a human being, but I say this so that you may be saved. [35]He was a burning and shining lamp, and for a while you were content to rejoice in his light. [36]But I have testimony greater than John's. The works that the Father gave me to accomplish, these works that I perform testify on my behalf that the Father has sent me. [37]Moreover, the Father who sent me has testified on my behalf. But you have never heard his voice nor seen his form, [38]and you do not have his word remaining in you, because you do not believe in the one whom he has sent. [39]You search the scriptures, because you think you have

eternal life through them; even they testify on my behalf. [40]But you do not want to come to me to have life."

OT: Deut 4:9–14; Ezek 33:30–33
NT: Phil 2:6–11; Col 1:15–20; 1 John 5:6–12
Catechism: signs of the kingdom, 547–50; God's Spirit and Word in Israel, 702, 707

Thus far, Jesus has been refuting the charges of sabbath violation and blasphemy on the basis of his identity as the obedient Son who does only what he receives from the Father. In doing so, Jesus has explained that the healing of the paralytic is a †sign revealing him to be the Son, who has uniquely divine power to do the Father's work. Jesus continues his defense by calling witnesses who testify to his identity: John the Baptist, his own works, the Father, and the Scriptures.

5:31–32 Jesus' identity as the Son is the basis on which he has been refuting the charges brought against him. For the sake of argument, he grants the Jewish legal principle that forbids self-testimony in a judicial proceeding: **If I testify on my own behalf, my testimony cannot be verified.**[12] Accordingly, Jesus begins to call witnesses to testify **on** his **behalf**. He mentions **another who testifies**, and this is the Father, the ultimate witness behind the others whom Jesus will call.

5:33–35 The first witness is **John** the Baptist, to whom the same Jewish authorities Jesus now debates had **sent emissaries**. The Baptist **testified to the truth**, meaning to Jesus. He declared that he was preparing for the Lord's coming and bore witness that Jesus was "the Lamb of God" (1:29), "the Son of God" (1:34), anointed with the Holy Spirit. Since the Baptist "was not the light, but came to testify to the light" (1:8), Jesus says that he **was a burning and shining lamp**. While Jesus does not need or **accept testimony from a human being**, he cites the Baptist as a witness for their sake: **so that you may be saved**. Jesus does not need the Baptist's testimony to give him legitimacy, but he cites it as a help for others to believe in him.

During the short time that the Baptist conducted his ministry, the authorities sought him out: **You were content to rejoice in his light**. But they did not accept the Baptist's witness about Jesus. In Ezekiel, the Lord himself described this phenomenon, telling the prophet, "For them you are only a singer of love

12. As noted by Raymond E. Brown, SS, *The Gospel according to John*, AB 29 (New York: Doubleday, 1966), 1:223, the invalidity of self-testimony in a legal proceeding is attested in *Mishnah Ketuboth* 2:9: "None may be believed when he testifies of himself. . . . None may testify of himself"; in *The Mishnah*, trans. Herbert Danby (London: Oxford University, 1933), 247. All quotations of the Mishnah are from Danby.

songs, with a pleasant voice and a clever touch. They listen to your words, but they do not obey them" (Ezek 33:32). The Baptist may have been a fascinating person with interesting things to say, but the authorities were not really affected by his testimony.

5:36 The second witness is **the works that the Father gave** him, and this **testimony** is **greater than John's**. As Lucien Cerfaux puts it, "The miracles of the Son, his 'works,' are in reality the work of the Father, his essential activity of creating and giving life. As we look upon these, we see in one and the same regard the Son and the Father whom he makes known."[13] Jesus' signs bear witness **that the Father has sent** him. The healing of the paralytic on the sabbath reveals that Jesus is the Son, who possesses in himself divine power and obediently does the Father's work.

5:37 Third, Jesus appeals to the direct testimony of **the Father**, whose word Jesus speaks and whose works he performs. The qualifying statement, **But you have never heard his voice nor seen his form**, probably alludes to a traditional description of God's appearance at Mount Sinai. Moses tells the Israelites, "The LORD spoke to you from the midst of the fire. You heard the sound of the words, but saw no form; there was only a voice" (Deut 4:12). If Deuteronomy says that the Israelites heard the Lord's voice at Sinai and Jesus specifies that they have never heard the *Father's* voice, then whose voice did the Israelites hear speaking at Sinai? The implication seems to be that the Sinai †theophany was a manifestation of the divine Word, God the Son. The Prologue states, "No one has ever seen God. The only Son, God, who is at the Father's side, has revealed him" (1:18). Similarly, Jesus later says, "Not that anyone has seen the Father except the one who is from God," that is, the Son (6:46). Only the divine Word, the Son existing with the Father from all eternity, can reveal the Father. Similarly, other New Testament passages speak of the Son as the Father's expression, his "image" (Col 1:15).

5:38 Although the Father bears witness, Jesus says that his opponents do not **have his word remaining** within them. This is so, Jesus says, **because you do not believe in the one whom he has sent**. Jesus is the Father's Word. Jesus' opponents do not have the Father's Word dwelling within them because they do not receive Jesus, whom the Father sent to reveal the truth.

At this point, Jesus shifts from being the accused to being the accuser. From refuting his opponents' charges, he goes on the offensive to countercharge his

13. Lucien Cerfaux, "Les miracles, signes messianiques de Jésus et oeuvres de Dieu, selon l'Évangile de saint Jean," in *Recueil Lucien Cerfaux: Études d'exégèse et d'histoire religieuse de Monseigneur Cerfaux* (Gembloux: Éditions J. Duculot, 1954), 2:48, our translation.

LIVING TRADITION

"O Come, O Come, Emmanuel" and the Son at Sinai

Since only the Son reveals the Father, many early Christians interpreted some appearances of God (†theophanies) in the Old Testament as appearances of the divine Word. This interpretation appears in the famous Advent hymn, "O Come, O Come, Emmanuel":

> O come, O come, great Lord of might,
> Who to your tribes on Sinai's height
> In ancient times did give the law
> In cloud and majesty and awe.[a]

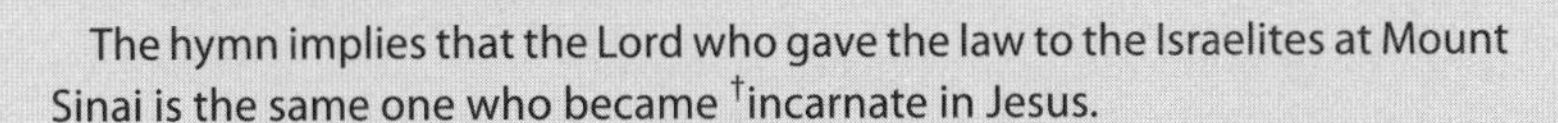

The hymn implies that the Lord who gave the law to the Israelites at Mount Sinai is the same one who became †incarnate in Jesus.

a. John D. Witvliet and David Vroege, eds., *Proclaiming the Christmas Gospel: Ancient Sermons and Hymns for Contemporary Christian Inspiration* (Grand Rapids: Baker Books, 2004), 82; repr. of English trans. by John Mason Neale (1851). Catechism 707.

opponents. †Ironically, while the authorities have never seen the Father's form nor heard his voice, he is right there in their midst (5:37). They do not recognize this because they do not believe in Jesus.

5:39 The last witness Jesus calls is **the scriptures**. His opponents **search** and study Scripture as the source and path to **eternal life**, and they have objected to Jesus' words and deeds on the basis of their interpretation of Scripture (5:10–18). Now Jesus cites the Scriptures as bearing witness **on** his **behalf**, not against him. The Old Testament bears witness to Jesus as the fulfillment of God's promises to save, and this witness comes to light only through faith in Jesus and the interior action of the Holy Spirit in the believer (12:16; 14:26). Jesus' opponents, who do not believe in him, prefer their own understanding of Scripture to the living, personal presence of that Word before them. By resisting him, they fail to have the Father's testimony impressed on their hearts. As 1 John 5:9–10 states: "Now the testimony of God is this, that he has testified on behalf of his Son. Whoever believes in the Son of God has this testimony within himself."

5:40 Jesus then links the inability of his accusers to receive this testimony with a willful decision on their part: **But you do not want to come to me to have life**. Jesus' opponents look upon the Scriptures as the means for receiving eternal life, but they refuse to approach the one through whom the Father gives eternal life (3:16).

Reflection and Application (5:31–40)

God speaks to people through his Word in Scripture, and to receive this Word, certain dispositions are required on our part as readers. First, faith is a matter of receiving God's action, which moves us to the reality revealed by its light. Also, we need to be humble and receptive to the Holy Spirit's action within us, so that we may be taught by him. When we read Scripture prayerfully, we should realize that we are reading God's Word, addressing us powerfully in the present moment. As the Letter to the Hebrews teaches, "The word of God is living and effective, sharper than any two-edged sword, penetrating even between soul and spirit, joints and marrow, and able to discern reflections and thoughts of the heart" (4:12). Let us approach the Scripture as God's Word to us in the present moment with a spirit of faith, humility, and receptivity to the Spirit working within us.

The Accusers Accused (5:41–47)

41"I do not accept human praise; 42moreover, I know that you do not have the love of God in you. 43I came in the name of my Father, but you do not accept me; yet if another comes in his own name, you will accept him. 44How can you believe, when you accept praise from one another and do not seek the praise that comes from the only God? 45Do not think that I will accuse you before the Father: the one who will accuse you is Moses, in whom you have placed your hope. 46For if you had believed Moses, you would have believed me, because he wrote about me. 47But if you do not believe his writings, how will you believe my words?"

OT: Deut 18:15–22; Jer 29:24–32; Sir 10:19–11:6
NT: Luke 4:1–13; 1 Cor 1:18–31
Catechism: Christian beatitude, 1720–24

5:41 Jesus continues his countercharge by repudiating **human praise** and honor (compare Mark 12:14). Even though honor was the major social value in Jesus' day (see sidebar on p. 111), such human esteem is empty, especially if those giving it refuse God (Sir 10:19–25).

5:42–43 The statement, **I know that you do not have the love of God in you**, resembles Jesus' words in 5:38. In both cases, the refusal to receive Jesus is a refusal to receive the Father's Word and the love given through him. As Rudolf Schnackenburg observes, the expression, **I came in the name of my Father**,

Honor and Shame

BIBLICAL BACKGROUND

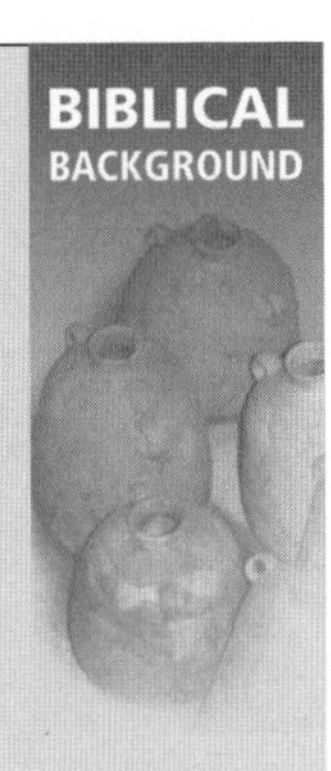

The Greek word translated here as "praise" (*doxa*) can also mean "glory" or "honor." Jesus' words about praise in 5:41–47 evoke the ancient categories of honor and shame. In Greco-Roman society, honor was the most important cultural value. Honor was the public recognition and praise given to a person for great achievement or simply for being associated with the right people, such as belonging to an upper-class family (see 1 Cor 1:26–27). Examples of public honor were the massive monuments built throughout the Roman world to glorify the emperors. Shame, the opposite of honor, was public disapproval and scorn directed at a person for disgraceful actions. In this honor-shame culture, people might go to great lengths to gain honor and to avoid shame.

draws on Jewish understandings of an officially sent envoy (see comments on 5:20b–23) and of a true prophet, one who speaks in the Lord's name (see Deut 18:19).[14] As the one who is sent by the Father and does his will perfectly, Jesus has no greater credentials, yet his opponents **do not accept** him. Since Jesus is the Father's only Son and perfect envoy, "all others who claim to have a mission of salvation from God . . . are 'thieves and robbers'" (10:8).[15] Salvation comes only through Jesus, and anyone who **comes in his own name** (see Jer 29:25), whom Jesus' unbelieving opponents would prefer to **accept**, is a false prophet or pretender.

5:44 Jesus connects his opponents' refusal to **believe** in him with their preference for **praise** from other people instead of **praise** from **God** (see 12:43). This valuing of human honor is a source of human blindness to God's action. If we are too concerned with winning praise and recognition from others, we can be dulled in mind and heart to God's Word. While Jesus' opponents seek after fleeting praise from other people, they neglect the only thing of lasting consequence: the praise, or approval, that God gives.

5:45–47 This discourse started with Jesus as the one accused by his opponents. It now ends with his opponents as the ones to be accused **before the Father**. The authorities appealed to the authority of Moses (**in whom you have placed your hope**) and the †Torah to accuse Jesus (see 5:11–18). Yet since the Scriptures are a

14. Rudolf Schnackenburg, *The Gospel according to St. John*, vol. 2, *Commentary on Chapters 5–12*, trans. Cecily Hastings, Francis McDonagh, David Smith, and Richard Foley, SJ (New York: Seabury, 1980), 127–28.

15. Ibid., 127.

witness to Jesus (Moses **wrote about me**), both the Scriptures and Moses stand on Jesus' side against his accusers. Scripture bears witness to Jesus, and faith in Jesus opens the way to see this testimony. But on account of their unbelief, the authorities do not fully understand **Moses** and the Scriptures because they do not see how they bear witness to Jesus. Thus Jesus concludes, **If you do not believe his writings, how will you believe my words?**

Reflection and Application (5:41–47)

Jesus contrasts seeking praise from other people with seeking praise from God (5:44). When a person does something truly good, it is appropriate that praise be given to that one. But as St. Thomas Aquinas writes, "Glory, in the sense of fame, is the least permanent of things; in fact, nothing is more variable than opinion and human praise."[16] The desire for fame and praise from people can be a powerful temptation to sin (Luke 4:5–8; John 7:1–10). At one level, it can lead us to do bad things so that others may approve of us. At a deeper level, the desire for fame can make us so self-absorbed that we lose sight of what is good and important in life: love of God and love of neighbor. †Ironically, by seeking self-exaltation, we can make ourselves the slaves of others because we allow their opinions to determine how we should live. This temptation to seek human rather than divine approval is especially strong for those in leadership positions of any kind—occupational, political, religious, and so forth. Since the success of such leaders is often measured by how much people like them, it is easy for them to forget that they are accountable first of all to God and that their true value is the approval given by God. Jesus calls us to keep our priorities in order and to live life according to God, who is truth and goodness itself.

16. St. Thomas Aquinas, *Summa contra gentiles* 3.29.7, in *Summa contra Gentiles*, trans. Anton C. Pegis, FRSC, James F. Anderson, Vernon J. Bourke, and Charles J. O'Neil (Notre Dame, IN: University of Notre Dame, 1975), 3:116. Catechism 1723.

Jesus and Passover: Food for Eternal Life

John 6:1–71

Continuing the motif of this subsection of the Gospel (5:1–10:42), John presents Jesus in relation to another Jewish liturgical feast: Passover. John 6 is composed of several interrelated scenes. First, Jesus performs a miraculous †sign near Passover time: he multiplies loaves and fish to feed a great multitude, a miracle that recalls God feeding Israel with manna in the wilderness (6:1–15). Then Jesus begins to reveal the meaning of this sign by walking upon the stormy sea and declaring "I am" (6:16–21). After a brief introduction (6:22–31), Jesus delivers a discourse on himself as the bread of life in which he teaches what the true bread provided by God is and what it means to feed on this bread (6:32–59). Last, Jesus' radical teaching causes some disciples to fall away, while others reaffirm their faith in him (6:60–71).

John 6 is one of the most theologically complex chapters in the Gospel. There is deep reflection on Jewish liturgical traditions and on many biblical themes: the tree of life in Eden, the manna in the wilderness, Wisdom's invitation to share in her food. These Old Testament realities help us to understand Jesus and the gift of his body and blood on the cross and in the Eucharist. Through many allusions, we are led to appreciate Jesus' gift of himself to the Father and to us. Jesus' self-gift was actualized in his passion and is made present as our nourishment in the Eucharist, our foretaste of the heavenly banquet.

Jesus Provides Bread for a Multitude (6:1–15)

---

[1]After this, Jesus went across the Sea of Galilee [of Tiberias]. [2]A large crowd followed him, because they saw the signs he was performing on the

sick. [3]Jesus went up on the mountain, and there he sat down with his disciples. [4]The Jewish feast of Passover was near. [5]When Jesus raised his eyes and saw that a large crowd was coming to him, he said to Philip, "Where can we buy enough food for them to eat?" [6]He said this to test him, because he himself knew what he was going to do. [7]Philip answered him, "Two hundred days' wages worth of food would not be enough for each of them to have a little [bit]." [8]One of his disciples, Andrew, the brother of Simon Peter, said to him, [9]"There is a boy here who has five barley loaves and two fish; but what good are these for so many?" [10]Jesus said, "Have the people recline." Now there was a great deal of grass in that place. So the men reclined, about five thousand in number. [11]Then Jesus took the loaves, gave thanks, and distributed them to those who were reclining, and also as much of the fish as they wanted. [12]When they had had their fill, he said to his disciples, "Gather the fragments left over, so that nothing will be wasted." [13]So they collected them, and filled twelve wicker baskets with fragments from the five barley loaves that had been more than they could eat. [14]When the people saw the sign he had done, they said, "This is truly the Prophet, the one who is to come into the world." [15]Since Jesus knew that they were going to come and carry him off to make him king, he withdrew again to the mountain alone.

OT: Exod 16; Num 11:4–8; 2 Kings 4:42–44
NT: Mark 6:34–44; 14:22–25
Catechism: the Eucharist as thanksgiving, 1328–32
Lectionary: 17th Sunday of the Year (Year B); the Holy Eucharist

6:1–4 The Gospel implies that **after** the sabbath controversy in Jerusalem in chapter 5, Jesus traveled north to Galilee, for as this chapter begins, **Jesus went across the Sea of Galilee**. Three notices set the scene for the feeding †sign that is about to occur. First, **a large crowd followed** Jesus **because they saw the signs he was performing on the sick**. The Gospel has shown that those who come to Jesus on account of his miracles often possess a shallow interest in him because they see him only as a wonder-worker (2:23–25; 4:48). The crowd, drawn as it is to Jesus by his miracles, probably fits this category. Second, **Jesus went up on the mountain**. This detail echoes the action of Moses, who likewise went up on Mount Sinai to receive the †Torah. Third, the **Jewish feast of Passover was near**. This notice indicates John's concern to unfold the spiritual relationship between Jesus and the exodus, the origin of Passover, in God's plan, especially God's loving-kindness for his people as shown in his providing them with food in the wilderness.

6:4–7 Upon seeing **a large crowd** approaching, Jesus asks **Philip**, **"Where can we buy enough food for them to eat?"** Jesus does not ask this question out of ignorance but **to test** Philip. By doing so, he invites Philip to grow in his faith in him. Instead, Philip thinks in terms of money: it would take an enormous sum, the better part of a year's **wages**, to feed such a large crowd—and only **for each of them to have a little**.

6:8–9

Andrew intervenes in the conversation by calling attention to a young **boy** with **five barley loaves and two fish**. His mention of barley loaves recalls the incident in 2 Kings 4:42–44, where the prophet Elisha fed more than one hundred men with twenty barley loaves. But like Philip, Andrew contrasts the enormity of the crowd with the small means at hand: **What good are these for so many?**

6:10

Jesus acts on his intention to feed the crowd. He first tells the disciples, **Have the people recline**: get them ready to eat. The comment about **grass** recalls Ps 23:2, where the psalmist says of †YHWH his shepherd, "In green pastures he makes me lie down." The disciples obey Jesus' instruction, and **the men reclined, about five thousand in number**. With the presence of women and children, the crowd would have been even larger.

6:11

Jesus' gestures resemble accounts of the Last Supper in the †Synoptics: he **took the loaves, gave thanks, and distributed them**.[1] While John's Gospel does not narrate the institution of the Eucharist at the Last Supper, it underlies Jesus' teaching on the gift of his body and blood throughout chapter 6. Another important detail concerns the one who feeds the crowd. In the Synoptics, Jesus gives the bread to the disciples, who then feed the crowds (Matt 14:19; Mark 6:41; 8:7; Luke 9:16). But John does not mention any role of the disciples; Jesus feeds the crowd directly. John thus underscores that Jesus is the ultimate source of the bread for the crowd. Philip and Andrew stressed the scant means to feed such a huge crowd, but Jesus miraculously produces a superabundance of bread. The entire crowd was completely satisfied, for all had **as much** bread and **fish as they wanted**.

6:12–13

After the crowd has eaten, Jesus orders **his disciples** to **gather the fragments left over, so that nothing will be wasted**. Of the four Gospel accounts of this miracle, only John records Jesus' command and the reason for gathering the fragments.[2] In doing so, John draws out the comparisons between Jesus' gift of bread and the gift of manna to the Israelites in the wilderness. Each morning the Israelites were to gather only enough manna for the day, and a double amount before the sabbath (Exod 16:16–24). If any manna was kept for the following day, it would spoil. But

1. The Greek verb for "give thanks" is *eucharisteō*. In the †Synoptic accounts, the similar fourfold gesture—took, blessed, broke, gave—is mentioned at both the multiplication of the loaves and the Last Supper, establishing a connection between the two events (compare Mark 8:6 and 14:22). The same pattern likewise appears immediately before the words of consecration in the Mass.

2. See Francis Moloney, *Signs and Shadows: Reading in John 5–12* (Minneapolis: Fortress, 1996), 58–59.

Fig. 5. Sea of Galilee at sunset

unlike the manna, Jesus orders his disciples to gather the bread fragments so that they will not perish. The bread that Jesus gives is both like and unlike the manna. The mention of the **twelve wicker baskets** suggests completeness, and it may imply the number of apostles to whom the **fragments** are confided.[3]

6:14–15 Having experienced the feeding miracle, the crowd immediately concludes, **This is truly the Prophet, the one who is to come into the world**. The crowd believes that Jesus is the messianic †Prophet-like-Moses (Deut 18:15; see John 1:21; 4:19). They recognize a connection between Jesus' feeding miracle and the giving of the manna, and some Jewish circles were expecting manna to return in the time of the †messiah.[4] Thus they conclude that Jesus is this promised messiah figure. However, Jesus does not go along with the crowd's reaction. Instead, he **withdrew again to the mountain alone** in order to evade their plans **to come and carry him off to make him king**.[5]

3. At the end of this chapter, the Twelve are mentioned for the first time in John (6:67, 70–71).

4. For instance, *2 Baruch* 29:8; *Ecclesiastes Rabbah* 1.9. See G. K. Beale and D. A. Carson, eds., *Commentary on the New Testament Use of the Old Testament* (Grand Rapids: Baker Academic, 2007), 444.

5. Wayne Meeks has shown that the roles of prophet and king were both applied to Moses in some ancient Jewish circles. See his *The Prophet-King: Moses Traditions and the Johannine Christology* (Leiden: Brill, 1967).

Reflection and Application (6:1–15)

In various ways, the Gospels present Jesus as confronting and resisting the temptation to be a messiah other than the one willed by the Father. Matthew and Luke tell us of his temptation by Satan in the desert, who tested and challenged him to prove that he was the Son of God by doing as Satan said (Matt 4:1–11; Luke 4:1–13). In other places, †Pharisees challenged him to produce a †sign to prove his messiahship (Mark 8:11–13). Jesus even called Peter "Satan" when Peter had rebuked him after hearing that his messiahship would involve suffering and death (Mark 8:32–33). Here in John 6:15, Jesus resists the crowd's designs to make him king *on their terms*. We might imagine them thinking, "How wonderful it would be if he was the kind of messiah that we want and who followed our instructions about how things should be!"

The Church faces the same temptation today: the temptation to be a Church other than the one willed by the Father by accepting people's criteria of what a proper church should be. How often is the Church advised to modernize its teaching about sexual morality, abortion, same-sex marriage, the education of children, and many other issues? Many in the world offer acceptance to the Church if the Church does as they say. Yet the Church must always be the Church willed by the Father and, when necessary, suffer ridicule and even rejection as its Lord did. Only then can the Church be the faithful witness that ultimately leads people to salvation in Christ.

Theophany upon the Sea (6:16–21)

[16]When it was evening, his disciples went down to the sea, [17]embarked in a boat, and went across the sea to Capernaum. It had already grown dark, and Jesus had not yet come to them. [18]The sea was stirred up because a strong wind was blowing. [19]When they had rowed about three or four miles, they saw Jesus walking on the sea and coming near the boat, and they began to be afraid. [20]But he said to them, "It is I. Do not be afraid." [21]They wanted to take him into the boat, but the boat immediately arrived at the shore to which they were heading.

OT: Gen 15:1; Ps 89:6–15; 93; 107:23–32

NT: Mark 6:45–52; Rev 1:12–18

Catechism: the divine name, 446–51

6:16–18 Matthew, Mark, and John all report Jesus walking upon the sea after multiplying the loaves, but John narrates this event in his own unique manner. Jesus has been away on the mountain for some time. In his absence, the **disciples went down to the sea, embarked in a boat, and went across the sea to Capernaum**. This description introduces a series of allusions to Ps 107, which recounts a variety of distressing situations in which God helped his people. One of these situations is a sea voyage, and among those in distress are those who "go down to the sea in ships" (Ps 107:23 †LXX, our translation). The description puts the disciples, who **went down to the sea**, in the same position as those who were to be helped by God in Ps 107.

John devotes much attention to the sea conditions. It was **evening** and **had already grown dark**. The **sea was stirred up** and **a strong wind was blowing**. The disciples are on a boat in the dark of night, on a violent, stormy sea, and they are alone: **Jesus had not yet come to them**.

6:19 Furthermore, the disciples **had rowed about three or four miles**. Not only are the conditions difficult, but the disciples are in deep water, far from shore. While the disciples are in a dangerous situation, they do not become **afraid** until they see **Jesus walking on the sea and coming near the boat**. Whereas in the †Synoptics the disciples are frightened because they think they see "a ghost" (Matt 14:26; Mark 6:49), in John there is no such suggestion. The disciples know exactly who and what they see, and this sight provokes fear.

6:20 The reason why the sight of Jesus walking upon the sea provokes fear is found in Jesus' words: **It is I**—literally, "I am." Jesus' use of "I am" here probably has the same strong meaning as it does elsewhere in John where Jesus identifies himself with the divine name (see sidebar on p. 89). By identifying himself as "I am," Jesus reveals himself to the disciples as the Lord.[6] His walking on the sea is a †theophany. That the scene is to be understood as a theophany is corroborated by several details. First, the disciples' response to seeing Jesus is fear, and biblical theophanies often provoke fear because people behold God's awesome, overwhelming magnificence (Exod 3:6; 20:18). Second, Jesus exhorts them, **Do not be afraid**, and the reassurance not to fear is often the first thing spoken to human beings in a theophany (see Gen 15:1; 26:24; Dan 10:11–12; Rev 1:17). Third, in addition to identifying himself as the Lord with the "I am," Jesus is "walking on the sea"—an allusion to Job, which describes †YHWH, "who walks upon the sea" (Job 9:8 LXX, our translation).[7]

6. Catechism 446.
7. See also Ps 89:9–11; 93.

6:21

The disciples **wanted to take him**—literally, receive him—**into the boat**, and this receiving implies growth in faith (see 1:12). The concluding notice—**the boat immediately arrived at the shore to which they were heading**—again alludes to God's rescue of the distressed sailors in Ps 107:30: "God brought them to the harbor they longed for."

Before the boat crossing, the crowd hailed Jesus as the †Prophet-like-Moses and wanted "to make him king" (6:14–15). But to avoid them, Jesus withdrew to the mountain. Although Jesus is the promised prophet and king, he does not fulfill these roles in the way that the crowd thinks. In multiplying bread and fish and in crossing the sea, he reveals himself as the Lord, who says and does the things attributed to YHWH in Scripture. Jesus is prophet and king, but these titles will not suffice: most important, Jesus is the Lord himself, who feeds his people and walks upon the sea. In both the feeding miracle and the walking on the sea, Jesus displays his power over creation. His words and actions undergird the authority of his claims in the discourse he is about to deliver and dispose us to listen to him.

Setting Up the Discourse: Context, the Basic Principle, and God's Work (6:22–29)

[22]The next day, the crowd that remained across the sea saw that there had been only one boat there, and that Jesus had not gone along with his disciples in the boat, but only his disciples had left. [23]Other boats came from Tiberias near the place where they had eaten the bread when the Lord gave thanks. [24]When the crowd saw that neither Jesus nor his disciples were there, they themselves got into boats and came to Capernaum looking for Jesus. [25]And when they found him across the sea they said to him, "Rabbi, when did you get here?" [26]Jesus answered them and said, "Amen, amen, I say to you, you are looking for me not because you saw signs but because you ate the loaves and were filled. [27]Do not work for food that perishes but for the food that endures for eternal life, which the Son of Man will give you. For on him the Father, God, has set his seal." [28]So they said to him, "What can we do to accomplish the works of God?" [29]Jesus answered and said to them, "This is the work of God, that you believe in the one he sent."

OT: Ps 119:97–104; Prov 9:1–10; Sir 14:20–15:8

NT: 2 Cor 1:21–22; Eph 1:11–14

Catechism: symbols of the Holy Spirit, 698

Lectionary: 18th Sunday of the Year (Year B); the Holy Eucharist

This section connects the feeding miracle (6:1–15) and the sea crossing (6:16–21) with the Bread of Life Discourse (6:32–58). In this discourse, Jesus will teach that he is the life-giving bread that God gives from heaven. Here in 6:22–29 Jesus prepares his hearers for this teaching in several ways. First, he instructs them that they need to elevate their minds above physical bread, which sustains earthly life, to heavenly bread, which gives eternal life (6:26–27). Second, Jesus establishes the discourse's basic principle: people should work to obtain the bread that lasts for eternal life, which he provides (6:27). Third, Jesus introduces the theme of God's work, which leads to faith in Jesus and the reception of the life-giving bread (6:28–29).

6:22–25 On the **next day, the crowd** is mystified by Jesus' absence. They know that **there had only been one boat there** on the previous day and that **Jesus** did not leave in that boat; **only his disciples** did. It seems that some **boats** came **from Tiberias** to a location **near the place** where **the Lord gave thanks.**[8] The people hailed the **boats and came to Capernaum looking for Jesus**. Upon finding him there, they voice their wonderment, **Rabbi, when did you get here?**

6:26 Jesus gets right to the point. The real reason why the crowd, initially drawn to him because he worked healing miracles (6:2), is **looking for** him is **because** they want more food: **you ate the loaves and were filled**. Although they witnessed the healings and ate their fill, they did **not** recognize these miracles as †**signs**. They do not see spiritually what the feeding miracle revealed about Jesus and his work. Hence Jesus withdrew to the mountain to evade their attempt to make him king (6:14–15).

6:27 Jesus exhorts them to elevate their thinking above **food that perishes** to **the food that endures for eternal life**. He establishes the basic principle for the discourse: people should **work** to obtain **the food that endures for eternal life**, which **the** †**Son of Man will give** (compare 4:14).

These words about food enduring for eternal life run throughout the discourse and reflect biblical traditions in which God's wisdom and word, meaning the †Torah or the Mosaic law, were likened to food and drink. The psalmist prays, "How sweet to my palate are your words, / sweeter than honey to my mouth" (Ps 119:103, our translation). Proverbs depicts God's Wisdom as inviting people to understand her as a woman making a dinner invitation: "Come, eat of my food, / and drink of the wine I have mixed!" (Prov 9:5). Sirach likewise uses the imagery of food and eating to describe learning from God's wisdom and law: "Whoever fears the Lord / [and] . . . is practiced in the Law will come to

8. The Greek verb is *eucharisteō*, from which comes the English word "Eucharist."

Wisdom. . . . / She will feed him with the bread of learning, / and give him the water of understanding to drink" (Sir 15:1, 3).[9]

As **the Son of Man** who came down from heaven, Jesus is the one on whom **the Father, God, has set his seal.** The language of sealing designates ownership, and the New Testament often describes the indwelling of the Holy Spirit as a sealing, impressing a permanent mark (2 Cor 1:22; Eph 1:13; 4:30).[10] The Baptist reported that the Holy Spirit descended and remained upon Jesus (1:32); thus Jesus has been revealed as the Father's representative and accredited envoy.

6:28–29 Responding to Jesus' exhortation to "work" for imperishable food (6:27), the crowd asks what they need to do in order **to accomplish the works of God,** possibly understanding them in terms of pious works prescribed by Torah. Jesus responds in the singular: **This is the work of God, that you believe in the one he sent.** God's work is the act that the Father performs in believers' hearts, which enables faith in Jesus. As we will see developed in the discourse, this work has two aspects. Not only does "the work of God" refer to the work that *God* does in *us*, leading us to faith in Jesus (6:37, 39, 44–45, 65); it also applies to *our* work of yielding to God's action in us. Our work is to yield to the Father's work within us and so believe in his Son and receive him as the source of our eternal life.

The Bread of Life I: God Is Giving the Bread of Life (6:30–34)

[30]So they said to him, "What sign can you do, that we may see and believe in you? What can you do? [31]Our ancestors ate manna in the desert, as it is written:

> **'He gave them bread from heaven to eat.'"**

[32]So Jesus said to them, "Amen, amen, I say to you, it was not Moses who gave the bread from heaven; my Father gives you the true bread from heaven. [33]For the bread of God is that which comes down from heaven and gives life to the world."

[34]So they said to him. "Sir, give us this bread always."

OT: Exod 16; Ps 78:17–31

NT: Matt 16:1–4

Catechism: Christ prefigured by the manna, 1094

Lectionary: 18th Sunday of the Year (Year B); the Holy Eucharist

9. God's Word is also likened to the manna in Philo, *Allegorical Interpretations* 3.162. Compare *Genesis Rabbah* 70.5.

10. Catechism 698.

Jesus' audience suspects that he is claiming to be even greater than Moses. They challenge Jesus to demonstrate this claim by doing something even greater than Moses did, and they cite the scriptural example of the manna (6:30–31). Jesus redirects the crowd's attention from God's action in their ancestral past to God's action in the present moment (6:32). He says that the Father is *now* providing bread from heaven, which gives life to the whole world (6:33)

6:30–31 Earlier the crowd thought that Jesus was the promised †Prophet-like-Moses (6:14–15). Now they realize that he is claiming to be even greater than this promised prophet, indeed, greater than Moses himself. They ask him for another †**sign** so that they **may see and believe in** him (compare Matt 16:1–4). If Jesus is greater than Moses, they reason, he should do something even greater than the signs and wonders Moses did. They cite Scripture and appeal to a great act associated with Moses: **Our ancestors ate manna in the desert, as it is written: "He gave them bread from heaven to eat."** Their citation does not exactly match any biblical text, but it is closest to Exod 16:4, which recounts the Lord's gift of manna to the Israelites (see also Ps 78:24; Neh 9:15). This scriptural text about the manna is at the center of the whole ensuing discourse.

6:32 Presented with this text, Jesus begins the Bread of Life Discourse. The discourse follows an established manner of Jewish preaching, which elaborates on the elements mentioned in a biblical quotation, in this case, Exod 16:4, referenced in John 6:31.[11]

Jesus begins his response to the crowd's challenge with the assertion that **it was not Moses who gave** you **the bread from heaven**. As with the Samaritan woman (4:20–21), Jesus redirects the crowd's attention from their ancestral past to the present moment: **My Father gives you the true bread from heaven**. Moses was not the source of the manna: it was the Lord. The Lord provided Israel with manna, and he continues his providential care by now providing true bread from heaven. The modifier "true" should not be taken to imply that the manna was false, but rather that it was incomplete or less than perfect.[12] The manna was a genuine gift from God, and it also foreshadows the even greater care that God provides in Jesus.[13]

11. The classic study analyzing this discourse in terms of common Jewish modes of homiletic exegesis is Peder Borgen, *Bread from Heaven: An Exegetical Study of the Concept of Manna in the Gospel of John and the Writings of Philo* (Leiden: Brill, 1965). With a few exceptions, we follow Borgen's general division of the discourse.

12. See Cardinal Henri de Lubac, SJ, *Corpus Mysticum: The Eucharist and the Church in the Middle Ages*, ed. Laurence Paul Hemming and Susan Frank Parsons, trans. Gemma Simmonds, CJ, Richard Price, and Christopher Stephens (Notre Dame, IN: University of Notre Dame, 2007), 188.

13. Catechism 1094.

Saint Ignatius of Antioch on Hungering for the Bread of God

The Apostolic Fathers are a group of ancient Christian authors whose writings are very close in time to the New Testament but not included in the biblical †canon. Among them are seven letters written by St. Ignatius of Antioch while he was being transported to Rome to be martyred around the year AD 110. In his *Letter to the Romans*, St. Ignatius speaks of his desire for the Eucharist and how he prefers it to all earthly things:

> Do not talk about Jesus Christ while you desire the world. Do not let envy dwell among you. . . . There is no fire of material longing within me, but only water living and speaking in me, saying within me, "Come to the Father." I take no pleasure in corruptible food or the pleasures of this life. I want the bread of God, which is the flesh of Christ who is of the seed of David; and for drink I want his blood, which is incorruptible love.[a]

a. Ignatius of Antioch, *Letter to the Romans* 7.1–3, in *The Apostolic Fathers: Greek Texts and English Translations*, 3rd ed., ed. and trans. Michael W. Holmes (Grand Rapids: Baker Academic, 2007), 233.

6:33–34 The description that this bread **comes down from heaven** connects this bread with Jesus, who, as the †Son of Man, came down from heaven (3:13, 31). This heavenly bread **gives life to the world**. Like the Samaritan woman who asked for water that would quench all thirst, the crowd says, **Sir, give us this bread always** (see 4:15). As he has done before, Jesus will now raise the discussion to a whole new level.

The Bread of Life II: The Father's Gift (6:35–40)

[35]Jesus said to them, "I am the bread of life; whoever comes to me will never hunger, and whoever believes in me will never thirst. [36]But I told you that although you have seen [me], you do not believe. [37]Everything that the Father gives me will come to me, and I will not reject anyone who comes to me, [38]because I came down from heaven not to do my own will but the will of the one who sent me. [39]And this is the will of the one who sent me, that I should not lose anything of what he gave me, but that I should raise it [on] the last day. [40]For this is the will of my Father, that everyone who sees the Son and believes in him may have eternal life, and I shall raise him [on] the last day."

OT: Gen 3:21–24; Isa 49:8–12; 55:1–5
NT: 1 Cor 15:20–28
Catechism: necessity of faith, 161; how the dead rise, 997–1001
Lectionary: For the Dead; Burial of Baptized Children

After teaching that God is now providing life-giving bread from heaven, Jesus identifies himself as this bread of life in whom God makes good on his promises of end-time salvation (6:35). The Father works to bring people to Jesus and give them eternal life through him. As the obedient Son, Jesus accepts all who come to him, moved as they are by the Father (6:37). Jesus does the Father's will by giving believers a share in the end-time resurrection and eternal life (6:38–40).

6:35 Jesus identifies himself as the true, life-giving bread from the Father: **I am the bread of life**. This is the first of seven "I am + predicate" titles in John's Gospel in which Jesus says "I am" and then includes another term.[14] Through these seven titles, Jesus reveals different aspects of himself and his saving work. As the bread of life, Jesus is the Father's gift, who gives sustenance and eternal life to believers.

Jesus' identification of himself as bread from God develops biblical imagery for God's wisdom and law, which were likened to food and drink (see comments on 6:27). In this symbolism, to feed on God's wisdom or †Torah means to take it in, to learn from it and allow it to transform one's life. Starting from this foundation, Jesus will lead his hearers to an altogether new level of meaning in which they are invited to feed on him as God's gift.

As the bread of life, Jesus is God's wisdom, who has come down from heaven and become flesh. This is why Jesus can make an extraordinary claim: **Whoever comes to me will never hunger, and whoever believes in me will never thirst**. In Isaiah, the Lord declares that when he brings about his people's end-time salvation, they would never again know hunger or thirst (Isa 49:10; 48:21). The Lord invites his people: "Only listen to me, and you shall eat well. . . . / Pay attention and come to me; / listen, that you may have life" (Isa 55:2–3). Jesus combines allusions to God's wisdom with Isaiah's prophecies of salvation and points to himself as the one who makes these prophetic promises a reality. When we come to, or believe in, Jesus, we recognize him as God's wisdom, as the one who teaches God's ways and in whom God fulfills his promises to save.

14. The seven "I am + predicate" titles in John are the bread of life (6:35, 51), the light of the world (8:12; 9:5), the gate (10:9), the good shepherd (10:11, 14), the resurrection and the life (11:25), the way and the truth and the life (14:6), and the true vine (15:1, 5).

6:36–37 After revealing this, Jesus laments that his hearers **do not believe**. Through the feeding miracle and his own speech, the crowd seems to realize that Christ is something more than Moses. But they do not accept him for who he is.

Jesus now develops the discourse's basic principle—work to obtain this life-giving bread (6:27)—and in doing so, he explains why believing in him is work done by the Father, "the work of God, that you believe in the one he sent" (6:29). Jesus first says all **that the Father gives** to him **will come to** him. The Father works on people's hearts and moves them to faith in Jesus; in this way he "gives" people to Jesus (see 6:44).

Perfectly obedient to the Father, Jesus says, **I will not reject anyone who comes to me**. The Greek word translated here as "reject" (*ekballō*) literally means "to throw out." One can detect an allusion to God throwing Adam and Eve out of Eden: "And he cast Adam out [*ekballō*] and settled him opposite the garden of delight" (Gen 3:24 †LXX). This subtle hint anticipates another allusion to Eden when Jesus talks about food that gives eternal life (6:51). These allusions to Eden signal that what was lost by Adam and Eve's sin will be restored by Jesus.

6:38–40 Jesus will never drive away those given him by the Father because he does only the Father's **will**. He specifies two things as the Father's will: first, **that I should not lose anything of what he gave me**; and second, **that I should raise [it] on the last day**, that is, give **eternal life** to all who believe **in him** and **raise him [on] the last day**. The Father's will is the salvation of all humanity through Jesus. The work of salvation, which includes a share in the end-time resurrection (see 5:25, 28; 1 Cor 15:20–23), is the revelation of the Father's love (3:16). By doing the work of salvation, Jesus reveals the Father's love for humanity—and his own desire to draw us to share in his relationship with the Father.

The Bread of Life III: Yielding to the Father (6:41–47)

[41]The Jews murmured about him because he said, "I am the bread that came down from heaven," [42]and they said, "Is this not Jesus, the son of Joseph? Do we not know his father and mother? Then how can he say, 'I have come down from heaven'?" [43]Jesus answered and said to them, "Stop murmuring among yourselves. [44]No one can come to me unless the Father who sent me draw him, and I will raise him on the last day. [45]It is written in the prophets:

'They shall all be taught by God.'

Everyone who listens to my Father and learns from him comes to me. [46]Not that anyone has seen the Father except the one who is from God; he has seen the Father. [47]Amen, amen, I say to you, whoever believes has eternal life."

OT: Exod 16; Num 14:26–35; Isa 54:11–17
NT: Matt 11:25–27
Catechism: faith, 153–55
Lectionary: 19th Sunday of the Year (Year B); For the Dead; Burial of Baptized Children

Some of Jesus' listeners object to his claim to be the bread from heaven because they know his earthly family (6:41–42). With an allusion to the book of Exodus, Jesus treats their response as rebellious grumbling (6:43) and then develops the theme of God's working. The Father works within people by teaching them and drawing them to faith in Jesus (6:44–45). Jesus exhorts his hearers to yield to the work that God is doing and so come to the Son, the only one who knows and reveals the Father. By believing in Jesus and receiving him, one receives the gift of eternal life that he offers (6:46–47).

6:41–42 John identifies some within Jesus' audience as the †**Jews** (see sidebar on p. 101). They challenge Jesus' claim to have come **down from heaven**, because they **know his father and mother**. They are thinking primarily in earthly terms and not the heavenly terms to which Jesus has summoned them (6:27).

6:43 Jesus does not regard this as innocent questioning but as **murmuring** (*gongyzō*). This Greek word describes the rebellious grumbling of the Israelites against the Lord and Moses in the wilderness (Exod 17:3; Num 14:26–35). In effect, Jesus is telling his listeners that their hearts are as hard as those who murmured in the desert, to whom Moses declared, "Your grumbling [*gongysmos*] is not against us, but against the Lord" (Exod 16:8 LXX).

6:44 Jesus again points to the truth: **No one can come to me unless the Father who sent me draw him, and I will raise him on the last day**. Developing his earlier remarks about God's work in 6:29, 37, Jesus speaks of the Father as working to bring people to faith in him. He instructs them to yield to this "work of God" and so receive the gift of eternal life through faith in him.[15]

6:45–46 Jesus supports this claim with **the prophets**, freely citing Isa 54:13: **They shall all be taught by God**. Being taught by God involves listening to the Father, yielding to him, and thus being brought to Jesus. The Father's action is secret and hidden, but it has an attracting power to bring us to the Son, **the one who**

15. Catechism 153–54.

is from God and who alone **has seen the Father**. Only the "Son, God, who is at the Father's side" (1:18) can truly reveal the Father (see Matt 11:25–27).

6:47 Jesus reiterates the connection between receiving him in faith and receiving the gift of eternal life: **Amen, amen, I say to you, whoever believes has eternal life.** All people have access to God's gift of eternal life through Jesus, and we receive this gift already in the present through faith in him.

The Bread of Life IV: The Bread Is Jesus' Flesh (6:48–59)

[48]I am the bread of life. [49]Your ancestors ate the manna in the desert, but they died; [50]this is the bread that comes down from heaven so that one may eat it and not die. [51]I am the living bread that came down from heaven; whoever eats this bread will live forever; and the bread that I will give is my flesh for the life of the world."

[52]The Jews quarreled among themselves, saying, "How can this man give us [his] flesh to eat?" [53]Jesus said to them, "Amen, amen, I say to you, unless you eat the flesh of the Son of Man and drink his blood, you do not have life within you. [54]Whoever eats my flesh and drinks my blood has eternal life, and I will raise him on the last day. [55]For my flesh is true food, and my blood is true drink. [56]Whoever eats my flesh and drinks my blood remains in me and I in him. [57]Just as the living Father sent me and I have life because of the Father, so also the one who feeds on me will have life because of me. [58]This is the bread that came down from heaven. Unlike your ancestors who ate and still died, whoever eats this bread will live forever." [59]These things he said while teaching in the synagogue in Capernaum.

OT: Gen 3:21–24; Lev 17:8–14; Deut 12:20–28

NT: Mark 14:22–26; 1 Cor 10:16–17; 11:23–32

Catechism: signs and institution of the Eucharist, 1333–40; the Eucharist as sacrificial memorial and Christ's presence, 1362–78; fruits of Holy Communion, 1391–98

Lectionary: Corpus Christi (Year A); 20th Sunday of the Year (Year B); For the Dead; Burial of Baptized Children; Holy Eucharist

Jesus spoke of "food that endures for eternal life" (6:27) and then was challenged by the crowd to perform a †sign greater than the manna (6:30–31). Jesus went on to speak of "the bread of God . . . which comes down from heaven" (6:33) and identified himself as this heavenly "bread of life" (6:35). Jesus now returns to the manna, and his discourse crescendos in the revelation that the bread from heaven that gives eternal life is the crucified and glorified flesh of Jesus himself (6:48–51). With strong realism, Jesus teaches that he gives this very same flesh as nourishment to believers in the Eucharist, the sacrament of his body and blood (6:53–58).

6:48–51 Returning to the themes of manna and life-giving bread, Jesus compares himself as **the bread of life** with **the manna**. The manna was a providential gift from the Lord to sustain the Israelites in the wilderness. But despite its wondrous nature, the manna did not give eternal life: **Your ancestors ate the manna in the desert, but they died**. However, the bread of life **from heaven** does what the manna could not: it gives eternal life, so that **whoever eats this bread will live forever**. The food that gives immortality is an allusion to the tree of life in the garden of Eden. According to Genesis, the tree of life's fruit could give immortality. After their sin, God expelled Adam and Eve from Eden to keep them from eating this food (Gen 3:22–23). Now Jesus says that anyone who eats the bread he gives will live forever. Jesus opens the way to paradise and offers the food that gives immortality.

Then Jesus explains what it means to *eat* **the living bread that came down from heaven**.[16] At one level, in light of the biblical imagery for God's wisdom and †Torah, eating this bread means taking Jesus in as spiritual nourishment and wisdom. But there is a much greater depth to his words. Jesus now specifies that this **bread** that gives eternal life is his own **flesh**. He gives his flesh **for the life of the world** in his perfect act of love and obedience on the cross.[17] Once crucified and transformed by the resurrection, Jesus' human flesh becomes the source of eternal life for the whole world. It is Jesus' own flesh that people must eat.

6:52 **The †Jews** react more strongly than before. They **quarreled** (literally, "fought") **among themselves** over Jesus' statement about eating his **flesh**. Jesus' command to eat his flesh, and later to drink his blood, is appalling to his hearers. The Torah expressly forbade the eating of blood or of flesh with any blood left in it (Lev 17:14; 19:26; Deut 12:23); eating human flesh would be unthinkable.

6:53 With his audience in shock, Jesus increases the boldness of his teaching. Eating the bread of life cannot be understood only as a metaphor for the believer taking in God's wisdom, for Jesus speaks of his flesh as the direct object of eating (6:51). The eucharistic reference is unmistakable because Jesus speaks not only of his flesh but also of his blood: **Amen, amen, I say to you, unless you eat the flesh of the Son of Man and drink his blood, you do not have life within you.**

6:54–55 The divine Word has assumed a human nature in Jesus, and as the bread of life, Jesus has come down from heaven to give eternal life to those who receive

16. Borgen, *Bread from Heaven*, 34–38, 86–98.

17. In John 6:51, Jesus says, I "give . . . my flesh for [*hyper*] the life of the world" (6:51). This is verbally connected to the Last Supper accounts, where Jesus speaks of his body "given for [*hyper*] you" (Luke 22:19; see Mark 14:24).

Panis Angelicus

At the request of Pope Urban IV, St. Thomas Aquinas composed a series of prayers and hymns for the newly established Feast of the Body and Blood of Christ (*Corpus Christi*). Saint Thomas's hymns for this feast reveal his deep love for Jesus in the Holy Eucharist. Among these is a hymn known as *Panis Angelicus* or "The Bread of Angels." Saint Thomas derives this phrase from Wis 16:20, which speaks of the manna as "food of angels and . . . bread from heaven." Following John's Gospel, St. Thomas interprets the manna as a sign foreshadowing the Eucharist:

> The Bread of Angels now is Bread of man.
> Heavenly Bread fulfills what prophecies foreshow.
> O wondrous thing! God is consumed
> By the poor, the humble, and the low.
> You, threefold God and one, we pray:
> Be present as we worship well.
> Lead us on Your pathways
> To live in glory where You dwell.[a]

a. St. Thomas Aquinas, *The Aquinas Prayer Book: The Prayers and Hymns of St. Thomas Aquinas*, ed. and trans. Robert Anderson and Johann Moser (Manchester, NH: Sophia Institute Press, 2000), 95.

him. This life becomes available through the sacrifice of the †Son of Man on the cross, where Jesus gives his flesh and blood. The same flesh and blood offered by Christ to the Father on the cross and then resurrected to glory is given to us in the Eucharist.[18] By consuming Christ's glorified **flesh** and **blood** in the Eucharist, we receive **eternal life** and will also share in his resurrection: **I will raise him on the last day**.

Jesus' words about his flesh and blood have a strong realism. The verb used for "eat" in 6:54–58 is different from the verb used in the preceding conversation and is very graphic. In other Greek literature, it designates how animals eat.[19] While obedient listening and faith are means of ingesting God's Word and wisdom, the change to a more concrete verb for eating accents the fact that Christ's offer of his body and blood entails something even more radical: consuming his **flesh** and **blood** in the Eucharist. All the material food and drink in the world, including the manna and the multiplied loaves, are gifts from God

18. Catechism 1367.

19. Greek *trōgō*. See BDAG 1019; Francis J. Moloney, SDB, *The Gospel of John* (Collegeville, MN: Liturgical Press, 1998), 221–22.

to sustain mortal life. They are also imperfect foreshadowings of the **true food** and **true drink** by which God gives us eternal life.

6:56–57 Jesus explains the Eucharist as the food of eternal life by linking it to participation in the divine communion: **Whoever eats my flesh and drinks my blood remains in me and I in him.** In John, the verb "remain" (*menō*) designates the mutual indwelling of Father and Son, the eternal relationship between them in which Jesus invites his disciples to share (see 1:39; 14:10; 15:4–10). By our consuming Christ's body and blood in the Eucharist, he dwells within us, and we in turn share in his divine life. The Eucharist is truly "holy communion" (Catechism 1391). As St. Paul writes to the Corinthians, "The cup of blessing that we bless, is it not a participation [Greek *koinōnia*, literally, "fellowship, communion"] in the blood of Christ? The bread that we break, is it not a participation in the body of Christ?" (1 Cor 10:16).

Jesus continues, **Just as the living Father sent me and I have life because of the Father, so also the one who feeds on me will have life because of me**. In 5:26, Jesus spoke of his own possession of the divine life, which is the Father's eternal gift to the Son. As the bread of life, Jesus came down from heaven to give "life to the world" (6:33). Jesus' divine life is given to those who receive Jesus in faith as God's wisdom and, even more profoundly, consume his eucharistic body and blood. This mutuality between the Father, Jesus, and the disciples is a mystery of love: Jesus prays to the Father, "I made known to them your name . . . that the love with which you loved me may be in them and I in them" (17:26).

6:58–59 Jesus closes the discourse by returning to the opening scriptural text (6:31) and summarizing his teaching.[20] Jesus again identifies himself as **the bread that came down from heaven** to give eternal life, in contrast to the manna that sustained physical life and foreshadowed him: **Unlike your ancestors who ate and still died, whoever eats this bread will live forever**. John concludes by reporting that this discourse was given **in the †synagogue at Capernaum**.

Reflection and Application (6:48–59)

The Holy Eucharist is "the source and summit of the Christian life" (Catechism 1324).[21] It is the real, substantial presence of Christ among us: "the body and blood, together with the soul and divinity, of our Lord Jesus Christ and, therefore, *the whole Christ is truly, really, and substantially* contained" (Catechism 1374, quoting the Council of Trent). At every Mass, Jesus' gift of himself

20. Borgen, *Bread from Heaven*, 20–27.
21. Quoting *Lumen Gentium* 11.

to the Father on the cross is made present again sacramentally in the Eucharist and offered to us as our food for eternal life. Not only does the Eucharist unite believers to Christ; it also unites us to one another. As Henri de Lubac writes, "The Eucharist makes the Church" (adopted into the Catechism 1396).[22] If the Holy Spirit is the soul of the Church, the Eucharist is its beating heart, pumping Christ's blood through the members of his body, the Church. If we are to grow in holiness and love, we must make the Eucharist the center of our lives, because in doing so we make Christ the center of our lives. If we receive Christ worthily in the Eucharist and worship him in Eucharistic adoration, he will fill us with his grace and enlarge our hearts to love and serve more perfectly. Eucharistic worship and adoration does not detract from works of love. On the contrary, it is what enables us to do them in the first place. Consider these words of Blessed Mother Teresa of Calcutta: "If we truly understand the Eucharist; if we make the Eucharist the central focus of our lives; if we feed our lives with the Eucharist, we will not find it difficult to discover Christ, to love him, and to serve him in the poor."[23]

Rebellion among Jesus' Followers (6:60–71)

[60]Then many of his disciples who were listening said, "This saying is hard; who can accept it?" [61]Since Jesus knew that his disciples were murmuring about this, he said to them, "Does this shock you? [62]What if you were to see the Son of Man ascending to where he was before? [63]It is the spirit that gives life, while the flesh is of no avail. The words I have spoken to you are spirit and life. [64]But there are some of you who do not believe." Jesus knew from the beginning the ones who would not believe and the one who would betray him. [65]And he said, "For this reason I have told you that no one can come to me unless it is granted him by my Father."

[66]As a result of this, many [of] his disciples returned to their former way of life and no longer accompanied him. [67]Jesus then said to the Twelve, "Do you also want to leave?" [68]Simon Peter answered him, "Master, to whom shall we go? You have the words of eternal life. [69]We have come to believe and are convinced that you are the Holy One of God." [70]Jesus answered them, "Did I not choose you twelve? Yet is not one of you a devil?" [71]He was referring to Judas, son of Simon the Iscariot; it was he who would betray him, one of the Twelve.

22. De Lubac, *Corpus Mysticum*, 88.

23. Mother Teresa, *In My Own Words*, ed. José Luis González-Balado (Liguori, MO: Liguori Publications, 1996), 97.

OT: Isa 41:13–20
NT: Matt 16:13–20; 19:16–26
Catechism: signs of bread and wine, 1336; the Lord's Prayer, 2765–66
Lectionary: 21st Sunday of the Year (Year B)

6:60–61a Some of Jesus' **disciples** refuse his words about his body and blood. They describe his **saying** as **hard**, as unacceptable. Now they are **murmuring** like the Israelites in the wilderness and the †Jews who objected to Jesus' teaching (6:41–42).

6:61b–62 Instead of watering down his teaching, Jesus challenges them: **Does this shock you? What if you were to see the Son of Man ascending to where he was before?** Jesus, the †Son of Man and bread of life, has come down from heaven and will offer his flesh and blood as eternal food. If these disciples cannot accept that Jesus came down from heaven, took flesh, and commands his followers to eat his flesh and drink his blood, how will they accept his returning to the Father by means of his death on the cross and resurrection?[24] Jesus must offer his flesh for the world's salvation on the cross, displaying his love for the Father and the Father's love for the world (14:31; 3:16). After being gloriously transformed in the resurrection, Jesus' flesh will be apt for heavenly existence and having ascended to glory, become spiritual food for believers.

6:63 The remedy for these disciples is to be more spiritual—that is, to believe with a deep faith, born of the Spirit: **It is the spirit that gives life, while the flesh is of no avail** (compare 3:6). These disciples should not make Jesus conform to their human standards ("the flesh") but should conform themselves to his Spirit-filled, life-giving teachings: the **words** of **spirit and life**. As St. Cyril of Alexandria comments: "It is not the nature of the flesh that renders the Spirit life-giving, but the might of the Spirit that makes the body life-giving. The words that I have spoken to you are spirit, that is, both spiritual and of the Spirit, and they are life."[25]

6:64–65 With some of his disciples now rebelling, Jesus, who knows all things pertaining to his mission, **knew from the beginning the ones who would not believe and the one who would betray him**. The power to believe is found in love. The light of divine truth exceeds our mind's power; it cannot be mastered by us (3:8). Although far beyond our mind's power, the divine truth is attractive, and those who yield to its light yield to its lovableness. On our part, this yielding to the divine light is an act of the will. Conversely, those who love themselves to the point that they are unwilling to risk surrendering to the light will never know

24. Raymond E. Brown, SS, *The Gospel according to John*, AB 29 (New York: Doubleday, 1966), 1:299.
25. Cyril of Alexandria, *Commentary on John* 4.3, in ACCS 4a:246.

Saint Augustine on Being Drawn by the Father

LIVING TRADITION

Do not think that you are drawn unwillingly; the mind is also drawn by love.... [It] may be said to us, "How do I believe by will, if I am drawn?" I say, it is not enough by will; you are also drawn by pleasure. What does it mean to be drawn by pleasure? "Take delight in the Lord, and he will grant you your heart's requests" [Ps 36:4]. There is a certain pleasure of the heart to which that heavenly [bread] is sweet bread. Moreover, if it was allowed a poet to say, "His own pleasure draws each man" [Virgil, *Eclogues* 2.65], not need but pleasure, not obligation but delight, how much more forcefully ought we to say that a man is drawn to Christ who delights in truth, delights in happiness, delights in justice, delights in eternal life—and all this is Christ? . . .

Give me one who loves, and he feels what I am saying. Give me one who desires, give me one who hungers, give me one traveling and thirsting in this solitude and sighing for the fountain of an eternal homeland, give me such a one, and he knows what I am saying....

Therefore, if those things which amid earthly delights and pleasures are revealed to those who love them draw them, because it is true that "his own pleasure draws every man" [Virgil], does not Christ, revealed by the Father, draw? For what does the soul desire more strongly than the truth? . . .

[Jesus adds] "And I will raise him up on the last day." I deliver to him what he loves, I deliver what he hopes for; he will see what he has believed in while still not seeing. He will eat what he hungers for; he will be filled with that for which he thirsts. Where? In the resurrection of the dead, for "I will raise him up on the last day."[a]

a. St. Augustine, *Tractates on John* 26.4–6.

what it is to believe. They resist the Father's work; hence Jesus reaffirms, **For this reason I have told you that no one can come to me unless it is granted him by my Father** (see 6:29, 37, 44).

6:66–69 Jesus' words are too much for these disciples. Like the rich young man who cannot accept Jesus' teachings on wealth and discipleship (Matt 19:16–22), **many disciples** left him because of these teachings.[26] Jesus then turns to his inner circle, **the Twelve**, and asks them if they **also want to leave**. We hear Peter's famous confession of faith in Jesus (compare Matt 16:16–19). By asking, **To whom shall we go?**, he affirms that apart from Jesus there is nothing truly worthwhile. Jesus' teachings are **the words of eternal life**. And Peter continues, **We have come to believe and are convinced that you are the Holy One of**

26. Catechism 1336.

God. In the Scriptures, holiness is *the* attribute proper to God, "the Holy One" (Isa 41:14). Similarly, in John's Gospel only the Father (17:11), the Holy Spirit (1:33; 14:26; 20:22), and (here) Jesus are called "holy." By calling Jesus "the Holy One of God," Peter professes Jesus' divinity. He has yielded in love to the beauty of the light and has experienced its truth.

6:70–71 While Peter speaks as leader of the Twelve ("*We* have come to believe"), Jesus knows that not all of the Twelve agree. Jesus speaks figuratively of **a devil** in their midst, referring to **Judas**, one of Jesus' closest disciples, a member of **the Twelve**.

Reflection and Application (6:60–71)

John 6 integrates Jesus' gift of his body and blood in the Eucharist with his identity as God's Word and Wisdom. It is fair to say that since the Reformation, Catholics, despite recent papal exhortations, have not fed on the Word of God in Scripture as they have frequented the Eucharist. Vatican II has offered us a reminder of the relation of these two foods given to us by and as God's Word: "The Church has always venerated the divine Scriptures just as she venerates the body of the Lord, since, especially in the sacred liturgy, she unceasingly receives and offers to the faithful the bread of life from the table both of God's word and of Christ's body."[27]

While Scripture is not a sacrament in the technical sense, it is a privileged, divinely inspired means by which faithful readers can truly encounter the Lord Jesus. Our challenge is to recognize the Word of God speaking in the Scriptures and present substantially in the Eucharist. We should strive to avoid approaching these two gifts with a sense of routine, which can keep us from experiencing their transforming effect. From the Scriptures we learn how to experience the attractiveness of God's Word and to come to the Eucharist with a hunger and thirst to take him in as our light, our joy, our life-sustaining food. Pope Benedict XVI quotes St. Jerome: "We are reading the sacred Scriptures. For me, the Gospel is the Body of Christ; for me, the holy Scriptures are his teaching."[28]

27. *Dei Verbum* (Word of God) 21.
28. Pope Benedict XVI, *Verbum Domini* (Word of the Lord) 56, quoting Jerome, *On the Psalms* 147.

Jesus at the Festival of Tabernacles I

John 7:1–52

In chapter 7, Jesus makes his third trip to Jerusalem. Consistent with his interest in this section of the Gospel (5:1–10:42), John presents Jesus in relation to another Jewish liturgy: the weeklong Festival of Tabernacles. All of John 7:10–10:21 takes place within the general context of this festival. When Jesus was last in Judea, conflict broke out between him and the Jerusalem religious authorities over his activities on the sabbath and his claim to be "equal to God" (5:18). During this visit, the conflict escalates and intensifies. The question of Jesus' identity, especially in terms of where he came from, is central in John 7.

Jesus Goes to the Festival on His Own Terms (7:1–13)

---

[1]After this, Jesus moved about within Galilee; but he did not wish to travel in Judea, because the Jews were trying to kill him. [2]But the Jewish feast of Tabernacles was near. [3]So his brothers said to him, "Leave here and go to Judea, so that your disciples also may see the works you are doing. [4]No one works in secret if he wants to be known publicly. If you do these things, manifest yourself to the world." [5]For his brothers did not believe in him. [6]So Jesus said to them, "My time is not yet here, but the time is always right for you. [7]The world cannot hate you, but it hates me, because I testify to it that its works are evil. [8]You go up to the feast. I am not going up to this feast, because my time has not yet been fulfilled." [9]After he had said this, he stayed on in Galilee.

[10]But when his brothers had gone up to the feast, he himself also went up, not openly but [as it were] in secret. [11]The Jews were looking for him at the feast and saying, "Where is he?" [12]And there was considerable murmuring about him in the crowds. Some said, "He is a good man," [while] others said, "No; on the contrary, he misleads the crowd." [13]Still, no one spoke openly about him because they were afraid of the Jews.

OT: Lev 23:33–43; Deut 13:2–6; 16:13–17
NT: Mark 3:31–35; 6:1–6; Luke 4:9–12
Catechism: Mary ever virgin, 499–501

7:1 Jesus remained in **Galilee**, where the events of John 6 took place, because **the Jews** in **Judea were trying to kill him**. The open hostility of the Jerusalem authorities ("the †Jews") toward Jesus started in Judea after he healed a paralyzed man on the sabbath (5:16) and grew into a desire by some to kill him following his claim to be "equal to God" (5:18).

7:2 The **Jewish feast of Tabernacles was near**. Tabernacles was one of three annual religious festivals for which Jewish men were required to make a pilgrimage to Jerusalem.[1] As an observant Jew, Jesus will go up to this feast, and there he will employ elements of the festival liturgy—water and light—to reveal aspects of himself and his work. The Jewish feast provides the context for understanding Jesus, as Jesus reveals how the festival liturgy foreshadows his own mission.

7:3–5 Before going to Jerusalem, Jesus has an encounter with his **brothers**. New Testament writings refer to a group known as "the brothers of the Lord" (see Mark 6:1–3; 1 Cor 9:5), among whom was James, a leader of the early Jerusalem church (Gal 1:19). The New Testament does not say that the "brothers" of Jesus are the biological children of Mary. Consistent with testimony from the early Church, Catholics believe that Jesus' mother, Mary, remained a virgin throughout her entire life (Catechism 499–500). Tradition has offered two explanations for the identity of Jesus' brothers: they are Joseph's children from a previous marriage or brothers in the broad sense of kin.[2]

As in the †Synoptics, Jesus' **brothers** do not think favorably of him during his ministry: they **did not believe** (see Mark 3:21). They challenge Jesus to go to Judea **so that your disciples also may see the works you are doing**. If Jesus

1. The other two pilgrim festivals were Passover with Unleavened Bread (Exod 12:1–20; Deut 16:1–8) and Pentecost (Lev 23:15–21; Deut 16:9–12).

2. Early Christian witnesses for belief in the perpetual virginity of Mary include Jerome, *Against Helvidius*; Athanasius, *Against the Arians* 2.70; Didymus, *On the Trinity* 3.4; Epiphanius, *Agkurotos* 120; and *Panacea against Heresies* 78.6; St. Augustine, *Sermon* 186.1; and *On Holy Virginity* 4.4; Peter Chrysologos, *Sermon* 117; Pope Leo I, *Letter* 28.2. The *Proto-Evangelium of James* 9 (mid-second century AD) affirms that at the time of his marriage to Mary, St. Joseph was an older man who had children of his own.

Festival of Tabernacles

BIBLICAL BACKGROUND

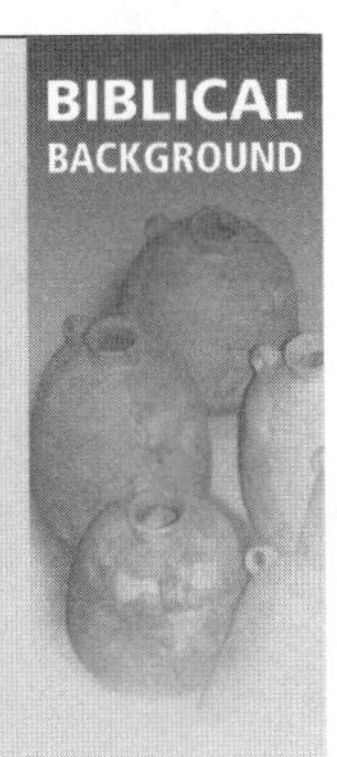

The Festival of Tabernacles (also known as Booths; Hebrew *Sukkoth*) was an eight-day liturgical festival held in the autumn. The festival celebrated God's providential care for his people both in giving them the fall harvest each year (Deut 16:13–15) and during their time in the wilderness after the exodus (Lev 23:42–43). The festival involved the building of huts, or booths, in which Jews lived to commemorate their ancestors' time in the wilderness. Also at the festival, the faithful would assemble bundles of branches that would be waved during parts of the celebration. According to the †Mishnah, the Tabernacles liturgy featured the daily praying of the Hallel Psalms (113–118), lots of music and dancing, and ceremonies involving water and light—ceremonies of particular significance for John. Tabernacles was an extremely joyous festival. As the Mishnah puts it, "He that never has seen the joy [during a Tabernacles celebration] has never in his life seen joy."[a]

a. *Mishnah Sukkah* 5:1.

does great **things** and **wants to be known publicly**, then he should not work **in secret**. Instead, he should **manifest** himself **to the world**. The brothers want Jesus to make a grand public display of himself at the festival so that people will come to know him. The brothers' challenge resembles the temptation in which Satan asks Jesus to throw himself off the parapet of the temple and make a spectacle of his divine sonship—a temptation to seek honor and praise for himself (see Matt 4:5–7; Luke 4:9–12). But Jesus acts according to the Father's will and does not conduct himself to win the praise of others (5:41). His miracles are not meant to impress but to lead people to faith (2:23–25).

7:6 Jesus rejects his brothers' wishes. His **time** corresponds to his †hour (2:4; 7:30; 8:20): the divinely appointed time of his cross and resurrection, through which he will preeminently reveal the Father's love and accomplish his work. Jesus contrasts his time, which **is not yet here** and **has not yet been fulfilled** (7:8), with that of his brothers: **the time is always right for you**. The brothers want Jesus to conform to their wishes regarding how he should act, but Jesus acts only according to the Father's will.

7:7 Jesus adds that the **world hates** him. Here, "the world" refers to human beings and their world as they are in rebellion against God and consequently under the power of sin (see sidebar on p. 37). The world hates Jesus because he testifies that the world's ways and **works are evil**. He testifies to the world simply by his presence. As the Evangelist teaches, "The light came into the world, but people preferred darkness to light, because their works were evil" (3:19). By coming into the world as its Light, Jesus lays bare the two basic alternatives in human existence: the godly way or the ungodly ways of the world, the light or the darkness. The **world cannot hate** Jesus' brothers because they are conformed to its ways and standards, such as the self-centered desire for honor. Jesus does not act according to the world's ways and refuses to conform to its standards. His life is perfectly attuned to the Father's will.

7:8–9 By refusing to go to **this feast**, Jesus refuses his brothers' request that he manifest himself in the way they want: a grand display for human praise. Instead of going up to Jerusalem with his brothers, Jesus **stayed on in Galilee**.

7:10 After saying that he was not going up to the festival, Jesus **himself also went up**. This statement can give the impression that Jesus deceived his brothers in saying that he would not be going to the festival. The key to a correct interpretation is to compare what Jesus does with what his brothers want him to do. John repeats much of the language from the brothers' challenge (7:4) but uses it to show that Jesus does the opposite of what the brothers want. The brothers suggest that Jesus stop acting "in secret" (7:4), but Jesus goes to the festival **in secret**. The brothers want Jesus to "manifest" (*phaneroō*) himself "to the world" (7:4), but Jesus goes to the festival **not openly** (*ou phanerōs*). The issue is not attendance at the festival, but when and how Jesus will manifest himself publicly.

7:11 John sets the stage for Jesus' appearance by describing the situation in Jerusalem. The **Jews were looking for him at the feast**, an action recalling the earlier remark that some were looking to kill Jesus (7:1). However, others kept quiet about Jesus because **they were afraid of the Jews**, most likely the Jerusalem religious authorities. The festival crowd in Jerusalem would be made up of Jews, and for John to say that "they were afraid of the Jews" signals that here the term "the †Jews" refers to a particular group and not to Jewish people in general.

7:12–13 Among the festival crowd, there are different opinions about Jesus. Some think that he is **a good man**. But others think **he misleads the crowd**. The term "misleads" (*planaō*) connotes leading people away from God by teaching bad doctrine. Deuteronomy 13:6 †LXX uses this same verb for the actions of a false prophet who leads Israel away from the Lord: "that prophet . . . shall die for he spoke in order to lead you astray [*planaō*] from the Lord, your God." Perhaps some think that Jesus is a false prophet because he calls God his Father and claims equality with God (5:18).

Who Is Jesus That He Can Say and Do These Things? (7:14–30)

[14]When the feast was already half over, Jesus went up into the temple area and began to teach. [15]The Jews were amazed and said, "How does he know scripture without having studied?" [16]Jesus answered them and said, "My teaching is not my own but is from the one who sent me. [17]Whoever chooses to do his will shall know whether my teaching is from God or whether I speak on my own. [18]Whoever speaks on his own seeks his own glory, but whoever seeks the glory of the one who sent him is truthful, and there is no wrong in him. [19]Did not Moses give you the law? Yet none of you keeps the law. Why are you trying to kill me?" [20]The crowd answered, "You are possessed! Who is trying to kill you?" [21]Jesus answered and said to them, "I performed one work and all of you are amazed [22]because of it. Moses gave you circumcision—not that it came from Moses but rather from the patriarchs—and you circumcise a man on the sabbath. [23]If a man can receive circumcision on a sabbath so that the law of Moses may not be broken, are you angry with me because I made a whole person well on a sabbath? [24]Stop judging by appearances, but judge justly."

[25]So some of the inhabitants of Jerusalem said, "Is he not the one they are trying to kill? [26]And look, he is speaking openly and they say nothing to him. Could the authorities have realized that he is the Messiah? [27]But we know where he is from. When the Messiah comes, no one will know where he is from." [28]So Jesus cried out in the temple area as he was teaching and said, "You know me and also know where I am from. Yet I did not come on my own, but the one who sent me, whom you do not know, is true. [29]I know him, because I am from him, and he sent me." [30]So they tried to arrest him, but no one laid a hand upon him, because his hour had not yet come.

OT: Gen 17:1–14

NT: Matt 12:9–14, 22–32

Catechism: Jesus reveals the Father, 238–42; Christ at the heart of catechesis, 426–29; Jesus and the law, 577–82

7:14–15 During the weeklong Festival of Booths, Jesus goes **into the temple** precincts **to teach**. His audience is **amazed** at his knowledge of Scripture and ponders his source: **How does he know scripture without having studied?** They contrast what they know about Jesus—that he did not receive formal education in scriptural interpretation—and his impressive teaching. In effect, they ask, "Where did he get all this, since he didn't get it from school?"

7:16–18 Jesus answers with three statements. First, he declares that the Father is the source of his teaching: **My teaching is not my own but is from the one who sent me**. Everything about Jesus—his words, his deeds, his very self—is constituted by his relationship with the Father, and all that he says and does was given him by the Father (5:19–20, 36–37).

Second, Jesus sets forth a condition for knowing that the Father is the source of his teaching: **Whoever chooses to do his will shall know whether my teaching is from God or whether I speak on my own**. God's will is to give all people salvation, to draw them into eternal communion with himself through Jesus (3:16–17; 6:39–40), whose words and deeds were given him by the Father for this purpose. As previously discussed, God's work in the world is directed toward this goal: "This is the work of God, that you believe in the one he sent" (6:29). Cooperating with God's work means yielding to his action within us, which leads to faith in Jesus. This yielding involves a choice, a grace-assisted act of the will, on our part, which opens us up to God's action in Jesus. The more we do God's will and yield to his action in us, the more clearly we shall perceive the truth revealed by Jesus. As St. Augustine writes, "The more ardently we love God, so much the more certainly and calmly do we see Him."[3]

Third, resuming topics from 5:41–47, Jesus contrasts one who **speaks on his own**—that is, teaches his own ideas—with one who **seeks the glory of the one who sent him**. The first kind of person acts out of self-interest: he **seeks his own glory** (see 5:43). Jesus does not seek glory for himself (5:41) but aims only at doing the will of the Father who sent him (4:34). The faithful, obedient envoy **is truthful, and there is no wrong in him**. In this way, Jesus defends himself against the charge of being a false, misleading prophet, suggested in 7:12.[4] According to the †Torah, a false prophet comes on his own initiative and speaks his own words, not God's (Deut 18:20).

7:19–20 Jesus resumes several other themes from John 5. First, he mentions his relationship to **Moses**, who gave **the law**. Previously Jesus has said, "If you had believed Moses, you would have believed me, because he wrote about me" (5:46). Thus, to understand and believe Moses fully requires that one recognize how his writings, Scripture, testify to Jesus. The efforts of Jesus' opponents to kill him show that they do not fully understand what Moses wrote. Hence Jesus says, **None of you keeps the law**. Jesus, who knows what is in people's hearts

3. St. Augustine, *On the Trinity* 8.9, in *The Trinity*, trans. Stephen McKenna, CSSR, FC 45 (Washington, DC: Catholic University of America Press, 1963), 266.

4. See Wayne Meeks, *The Prophet-King: Moses Traditions and the Johannine Christology* (Leiden: Brill, 1967), 45–57.

(2:24–25), knows about the murderous plotting of some and asks, **Why are you trying to kill me?**

The question is so abrupt that the crowd accuses Jesus of being **possessed** (John 8:48, 52; 10:20–21; see Matt 12:22–32). Their response, **Who is trying to kill you?**, may indicate that some in the crowd are ignorant of the plotting against Jesus.

7:21–23 Jesus answers with a defense of his action that has sparked the opposition to him: his healing a paralyzed man on the sabbath (5:1–18). Jesus defends this action by using a Jewish mode of scriptural argumentation reasoning that if a lesser thing is true, how much more true is a greater, related thing.[5] Jesus compares two actions pertaining to sabbath observance. He begins with circumcision, the lesser term of the argument. Jews **circumcise** their male babies on **the sabbath**, and this is not considered a violation of command in the Torah to cease from work on the sabbath.[6] Jesus, however, healed a **whole person on a sabbath** (the greater term). If it is a legitimate and good thing to circumcise on the sabbath, how much more legitimate and good is it for Jesus to heal an entire person on the sabbath.

7:24 Jesus exhorts his audience, **Stop judging by appearances**. He will use a similar expression in 8:15, where "by appearances" is literally "according to the flesh." His opponents' interpretation of sabbath law keeps them from recognizing what Jesus is implicitly teaching to be the purpose of the sabbath in God's designs: the welfare of human beings.[7] Their judgment is superficial because it keeps them from perceiving Jesus' healing miracle as a †sign. They cannot see that Jesus' healing of the man and ordering him to carry his mat on the sabbath is a revelation of his working with divine power in the world. Thus Jesus encourages his opponents to **judge justly**, to change how they see him and his teaching.

7:25–27 Another debate arises among the festival participants. Unlike "the crowd" in 7:20, **the inhabitants of Jerusalem** seemingly know about the plot **to kill** Jesus. They are surprised that Jesus **is speaking openly** at the festival. In Greco-Roman antiquity, the term for "speaking openly"[8] characterized a true friend, someone who spoke honestly and directly, and it was also the right of a citizen to speak publicly. Before Jesus appeared at the festival, "no one spoke openly about him because they were afraid" (7:13). Jesus' open, bold speech sets him apart from this frightened crowd, and it shows him to be a trustworthy, courageous

5. The argument is called in Hebrew *qal wahomer*, "the less and the great."

6. See *Mishnah Shabbat* 19:1–6.

7. See Deut 5:12–15; Mark 2:27; 3:4. Also John P. Meier, *A Marginal Jew*, ABRL (New York: Doubleday; New Haven: Yale University, 2009), 4:295–97.

8. Greek *parrēsia*. See Plutarch, "How to Tell a Flatterer from a Friend," 29–32.

individual. The Jerusalemites speculate as to whether **the authorities have realized that he is the Messiah**. This remark indicates that it is the Jerusalem religious authorities who **say nothing to him**, who are seeking to kill Jesus.

The festival pilgrims previously wondered about the origin of Jesus' teaching (7:15). Now they discuss his messianic identity in terms of his origins (a recurring topic at Tabernacles: 7:28, 40–42, 52; 8:14; 9:29–30). They question whether Jesus can be the †Messiah because they know where he came from. Some ancient Jewish writings suggest that **the Messiah** would appear out of nowhere, and thus **no one** would **know** where he came from.[9] For the Jerusalemites, their knowledge that Jesus came from Nazareth seems to disqualify him from being the Messiah.

7:28–29 Jesus challenges them to change how they think about him. His response, **You know me and also know where I am from**, can be taken as a statement that reaffirms his previous teaching about being sent by the Father and challenges the Jerusalemites to think about him in these terms. Jesus' response can also be translated as a question: "You know me, and you know where I come from?" (RSV).[10] Taken in this way, Jesus asks a rhetorical question that confronts their disbelief: "You think you know where I come from, but really you don't." Either way, the Jerusalemites draw conclusions about Jesus' identity by thinking on an earthly level in terms of his coming from Nazareth, while Jesus challenges them to elevate their thinking to a higher, spiritual level so as to perceive his origin **from** the Father **who sent** him. The Father, not Nazareth, is the origin of real importance. But since the Jerusalemites are "judging by appearances" (7:24), they do not grasp Jesus' origin with the Father and thus **do not know** the Father, whom he reveals.

7:30 For the first time, some people try **to arrest** Jesus. But the attempt fails **because his †hour had not yet come**. Jesus' life unfolds in accord with the divine plan, and nothing happens to him by accident or without his consent.[11]

Reflection and Application (7:14–30)

"Whoever chooses to do his will shall know whether my teaching is from God or whether I speak on my own" (7:17). Saint John Chrysostom sees in Jesus' words here a spiritual truth about the relationship between doing the

9. See *1 Enoch* 48:6; Raymond E. Brown, SS, *The Gospel according to John*, AB 29 (New York: Doubleday, 1996), 1:52–53.

10. Since ancient Greek texts were written without punctuation, decisions about punctuating the biblical text are made by translators.

11. See St. Augustine, *Tractates on John* 31.5.

good and knowing the truth. He says that living a life of sin and wickedness can obstruct one's perception of the truth, whereas a life of virtue can dispose one to see the truth.[12] Since God is both the Good and the True, doing the good and knowing the truth are intimately related: knowing the truth leads us to act well, and acting well helps us to know the truth.

Jesus Announces His Departure (7:31–36)

[31]But many of the crowd began to believe in him, and said, "When the Messiah comes, will he perform more signs that this man has done?"

[32]The Pharisees heard the crowd murmuring about him to this effect, and the chief priests and the Pharisees sent guards to arrest him. [33]So Jesus said, "I will be with you only a little while longer, and then I will go to the one who sent me. [34]You will look for me but not find [me], and where I am you cannot come." [35]So the Jews said to one another, "Where is he going that we will not find him? Surely he is not going to the dispersion among the Greeks to teach the Greeks, is he? [36]What is the meaning of his saying, 'You will look for me and not find [me], and where I am you cannot come?'"

OT: Exod 7:1–6; Deut 18:15–20; 34:10–12
NT: James 1:1
Catechism: the title "Christ," 436–40

7:31 While some tried to arrest Jesus (7:30), **many of the crowd began to believe in him**, perhaps because of his bold speech (7:26). The ensuing discussion shows that their faith is basic and not very profound. We have seen that faith based on Jesus' miracles is very rudimentary and must mature into a genuine faith in Jesus himself. The crowd wonders, **When the Messiah comes, will he perform more signs that this man has done?** By a †signs-working †messiah, they probably have in mind the †Prophet-like-Moses, through whom God would perform signs and wonders as he did through Moses (see Exod 7:1–6; Deut 34:10–12).

7:32–33 When the †**Pharisees** learn of such speculation, they **and the chief priests** dispatch **guards**, probably the temple police, **to arrest** Jesus. Then Jesus announces for the first time: **I will be with you only a little while longer, and then I will go to the one who sent me**. Jesus' impending return to the Father is an important theme in the remainder of the Gospel. The important point is *where* Jesus is going: to the Father who sent him. Again we see that Jesus'

12. St. John Chrysostom, *Homilies on John* 49.1.

relationship with the Father completely defines his identity, origin, mission, and destination.

7:34 Jesus adds, **You will look for me but not find [me], and where I am you cannot come** (repeated in 8:21–22; 13:33). Jesus is the trailblazer who opens the way to eternal life with the Father. After he has accomplished his saving work and returned to the Father, he will prepare a dwelling place for his people and then return to take us to be with the Father (14:2–3).

7:35–36 Jesus' words prompt another debate over his identity, which again shows the crowd's lack of understanding. Jesus speaks of going to the heavenly Father, but his audience thinks that he is talking about going to another geographical location: **the dispersion among the Greeks**. "The dispersion," or diaspora, refers to Jewish communities that had developed outside the Holy Land for any number of reasons, such as being displaced by conquest or migrating for economic opportunities. Here it designates the geographical regions in which those communities live (see James 1:1). The crowd declares that they do not understand **the meaning of his saying** in 7:34. Since they do not recognize Jesus' divine origin with the Father, they do not understand the spiritual dimension of his speech, that he is going to the Father. Saints John Chrysostom and Augustine rightly notice the †irony in the comment about Jesus going **to teach the Greeks.**[13] The crowd unknowingly anticipates the proclamation of the gospel among Gentiles by the apostles after Jesus' resurrection.

Rivers of Living Water (7:37–39)

[37]On the last and greatest day of the feast, Jesus stood up and exclaimed, "Let anyone who thirsts come to me and drink. [38]Whoever believes in me, as scripture says:

'Rivers of living water will flow from within him.'"

[39]He said this in reference to the Spirit that those who came to believe in him were to receive. There was, of course, no Spirit yet, because Jesus had not yet been glorified.

OT: Gen 2:10–14; Isa 55:1–5; Ezek 47:1–12; Zech 14:6–9

NT: 2 Cor 5:16–21

Catechism: symbols of the Holy Spirit, 694; Jesus and the Spirit, 727–30; grace of baptism, 1262–74; resurrection as new creation, 2174.

Lectionary: Vigil for Pentecost; For the Baptism of Children; For Confirmation

13. St. Augustine, *Tractates on John* 31.10–11; St. John Chrysostom, *Homilies on John* 50.3.

7:37–38

For the first seven days of the Feast of Tabernacles, the priests would carry water from the Pool of Siloam in procession to the temple and pour it out as a libation—a sacrificial offering—and a symbolic prayer for rain.[14] On the eighth day, **the last and greatest day of the feast**, Jesus uses this liturgical use of water to talk about the spiritual life that he gives. Jesus makes the invitation, **Let anyone who thirsts come to me and drink**. His words recall the Lord's invitation in Isa 55:1, "All you who are thirsty, / come to the water!" This Isaiah passage speaks of the gratuitous abundance that God will provide when he works his definitive act of salvation. Jesus previously said that he will give living water, which satisfies forever—an inner "spring of water welling up to eternal life" (4:14). Jesus now elaborates on his gift of living water: it is the Holy Spirit.

Jesus describes his gift by reference to **scripture**. The statement, **Rivers of living water will flow from within him**, is not a direct quotation from any biblical book, but it evokes several biblical texts. It alludes first of all to the garden of Eden, from which a river of life-giving water flows (Gen 2:10–14). Biblical traditions employ the imagery of Eden, the original creation, to depict the perfected, future state of affairs, the new creation, that God's definitive act of salvation will inaugurate (see Isa 65:17–25; 66:22–23). Ezekiel sees God's new temple as the centerpiece of this perfect future world, and that new temple is the source of an Edenic river that gives life, healing, and unending sustenance to the whole world (Ezek 47:1–12). Zechariah says that on the Day of the Lord, when the whole world comes to know that †YHWH is king, "fresh water shall flow from Jerusalem" (Zech 14:8–9). These †eschatological promises provide background for Jesus' teaching about the Holy Spirit as the living water.[15]

7:39

John clarifies that Jesus' words about living water refer to the Holy **Spirit that** believers **were to receive**. Old Testament prophets foretold that God would pour out his Spirit in the end times (see sidebar on p. 47). By speaking about his gift of living water at Tabernacles, Jesus shows that the liturgical outpourings of water during Tabernacles are an anticipation of God's pouring out his Spirit upon believers at the time of salvation. Jesus, the source of the living water, gives the Holy Spirit to believers, and the Spirit then flows from within them.[16] When believers are "born of water and Spirit" (3:5) in baptism, they receive the Holy Spirit, the living water, from Jesus and become a new creation in him (see 2 Cor 5:17; Gal 6:15; Eph 2:15).

14. *Mishnah Sukkah* 4:9–10.

15. Catechism 694, 705.

16. For discussion of how to punctuate these verses (and the different interpretations that follow), see Gail R. O'Day, "The Gospel of John," in *The New Interpreter's Bible*, vol. 9 (Nashville: Abingdon, 1995), 622–23.

John's comment—**There was . . . no Spirit yet, because Jesus had not yet been glorified**—should not be taken to imply that the Holy Spirit did not exist before Jesus' †hour, because the Holy Spirit has already appeared in the Gospel (1:32–33; 3:5, 8, 34). The Spirit, however, is poured out upon believers only after Jesus' glorification (16:7; 19:30; 20:22). John is not talking about the existence of the Holy Spirit as such, but the Spirit's indwelling in believers.

Reflection and Application (7:37–39)

The Fourth Gospel features water symbolism in speaking of the Holy Spirit. The Church receives this symbolism and employs it in the sacrament of baptism. Through the waters of baptism, the Holy Spirit comes to dwell in the Christian, and the "rivers of living water . . . flow from within him" (7:38). The Holy Spirit gives us a share in God's eternal life (Catechism 694). Scripture speaks of life-giving waters and the outpouring of the Holy Spirit as elements of God's new creation. Through the Holy Spirit, we become part of the new creation in Christ (2 Cor 5:17) and truly share in these realities of salvation. Accordingly, the Church proclaims this Gospel text in liturgies associated with the outpouring of the Holy Spirit, for example, the Mass for Confirmation.

Divisions in the Crowd and the Leadership (7:40–52)

[40]Some in the crowd who heard these words said, "This is truly the Prophet." [41]Others said, "This is the Messiah." But others said, "The Messiah will not come from Galilee, will he? [42]Does not scripture say that the Messiah will be of David's family and come from Bethlehem, the village where David lived?" [43]So a division occurred in the crowd because of him. [44]Some of them even wanted to arrest him, but no one laid hands on him.

[45]So the guards went to the chief priests and Pharisees, who asked them, "Why did you not bring him?" [46]The guards answered, "Never before has anyone spoken like this one." [47]So the Pharisees answered them, "Have you also been deceived? [48]Have any of the authorities or the Pharisees believed in him? [49]But this crowd, which does not know the law, is accursed." [50]Nicodemus, one of their members who had come to him earlier, said to them, [51]"Does our law condemn a person before it first hears him and finds out what he is doing?" [52]They answered and said to him, "You are not from Galilee also, are you? Look and see that no prophet arises from Galilee."

OT: Deut 19:15–21; 1 Sam 16:1–3, 10–13; Mic 5:1–3

NT: Luke 2:1–7

Catechism: faith is a grace and a human act, 153–55; divisions among Jewish authorities concerning Jesus, 595–96

7:40–42 Again there is debate over Jesus' identity. Like those in 7:31, **some in the crowd** proclaim, **This is truly the Prophet**, that is, the †Prophet-like-Moses. **Others** think that Jesus is a different †**Messiah** figure, the new Davidic king promised by God.

A third group objects to calling Jesus **Messiah** because they know he came **from** Nazareth in **Galilee** (see 1:45–46). For support, they appeal to **scripture** and its promise that **the Messiah will be of David's family and come from Bethlehem**, David's hometown (1 Sam 16; Mic 5:1–5). This objection implies their belief that Jesus is neither a descendant of David nor born in Bethlehem. While Jesus' Davidic ancestry is attested in many New Testament writings,[17] and his birth in Bethlehem is found in Matthew and Luke (Matt 2:1; Luke 2:4–7), neither point appears in John. If, however, one reads the crowd's statement in 7:42 as †irony, one could detect a subtle affirmation of both Jesus' Davidic ancestry and birth in Bethlehem. That is, the crowd does not realize that Jesus is the Messiah, which he is, and John underscores their ignorance by having them deny Jesus' Davidic ancestry and birth in Bethlehem, both of which are also true. For John, while Jesus is the Messiah and the Prophet-like-Moses, what is really important is that Jesus is the Son sent by the Father. Recognizing that Jesus is from the Father, not knowing his lineage and hometown, is the real key to grasping who he is.

7:43–44 These differences of opinion cause **a division** among **the crowd**, here causing the first split that forms among people on account of Jesus (see 9:16; 10:19). **Some** in the crowd **even wanted to arrest** Jesus, but again, the arrest attempt fails. These divisions illustrate the judgment occasioned by Jesus' presence in the world (3:19–21). His coming into the world prompts a response from all who encounter him.

7:45–46 The **guards** sent to arrest Jesus return to the authorities empty-handed. When **the chief priests and** †**Pharisees** ask the guards why they are returning without Jesus in custody, they reply, **Never before has anyone spoken like this one**. Like the crowds who are "amazed" at Jesus' teaching (7:15) and miracles (7:21), the guards are awed at his teaching: there is something unprecedented about Jesus.

7:47–49 Frustrated with the guards, **the Pharisees** ask them, **Have you also been deceived?** The term for "deceived" (*planaō*) appeared in 7:12, where some said that Jesus "misleads" the crowd; it implies the charge of being a false prophet.

17. Matt 1:1–17; Mark 10:47–48; Luke 1:32; Acts 2:25–33; Rom 1:3; Rev 5:5; 22:16.

The Pharisees ask rhetorically, **Have any of the authorities or the Pharisees believed in him?** The question implies that none of the Jewish authorities believe in Jesus, a claim that readers of the Gospel will learn is false (12:42–43; 19:38–39). The question contrasts the authorities with the people in the crowd who began to believe in Jesus (7:31). The Pharisees denounce the **crowd** as **accursed** because they do not **know the law**. The Pharisees, who are learned and have positions of authority, are convinced that Jesus is a false prophet, in contrast to the ignorant crowd who has started to believe in him.[18]

7:50–52 Among the religious authorities is **Nicodemus**, a Pharisee **who had come to** Jesus **earlier** (3:1–2). His presence shows that not all the Pharisees have the same opinion about Jesus.[19] Nicodemus makes an appeal to judicial procedure: **Does our law condemn a person before it first hears him and finds out what he is doing?** His question, which expects a no, is a reminder that the †Torah requires an investigation before condemning anyone (Deut 19:15–19). The other Pharisees have just condemned the crowd for not knowing the law (7:49), but Nicodemus's question subtly asks whether they know the law themselves.

Nicodemus's insinuation that these Pharisees do not know the law is †ironically confirmed in their response. They sarcastically ask him, **You are not from Galilee also, are you?**, as if being from Galilee makes one sympathetic to Jesus. Then they respond to Nicodemus's appeal to Scripture with their own appeal: **Look and see that no prophet arises from Galilee.**[20] In their view, Jesus cannot be a prophet because of his Galilean origin. And yet the Scriptures do speak of a prophet coming from Galilee: Jonah (2 Kings 14:25). These Pharisees do not know the Scriptures as well as they think.

The debate again revolves around Jesus' identity in terms of his origins. Like others in this chapter, these Pharisees miss the point because they think of Jesus' origins in terms of his hometown. The real issue is Jesus' origin with the Father.

Reflection and Application (7:40–52)

Throughout John 7, various groups wrestle with the question "Who is Jesus?" While the people in the narrative debate this question, the believing reader of the Gospel knows the answer by faith: Jesus is the Son, the one sent by the

18. The Pharisees' remarks may also reflect a disparaging attitude, attested in the †Mishnah, on the part of the learned and pious against the common people, the "people of the land." See *Mishnah Hagigah* 2:7; *Mishnah Tohorot* 8:1–5. Their disparagement may allude to Deut 27:26, "Cursed be anyone whose actions do not uphold the words of this law!"

19. Catechism 595–96.

20. The verb for "look" also appears in 5:39, where Jesus tells his audience to "search" the Scriptures.

Father. The Catechism teaches that faith is a gift from God, which no one can earn or achieve on his or her own, although it does require a graced human acceptance of this gift (Catechism 153–55). Our relationship with God is his gift to us. It is worth pausing to praise God for the gift of faith by which we know him personally. Like the groups in the Gospel, we ourselves and others are at various stages of the spiritual life and have different dispositions to religious faith in general. We should pray for ourselves and for others that God will give all of us his grace to know and love him more deeply. Like the father of the possessed boy, who asked Jesus to help his son, we pray, "I do believe, help my unbelief!" (Mark 9:24).

Jesus at the Festival of Tabernacles II

John 7:53–8:59

Chapter 8 presents a story of Jesus and a woman caught in adultery, who was being used by his enemies in an attempt to trap Jesus. The narrative then resumes its account of Jesus' visit to Jerusalem for Tabernacles. This chapter develops a number of themes that appeared in John 7. Various groups continue to debate the meaning of Jesus' words, often failing to understand that he is speaking at a spiritual level. Jesus continues to receive a mixed response from people: some begin to believe in him while others, especially some religious authorities, are hostile. Their hostility increases over the course of an intense debate. The antagonism reaches a boiling point at the very end when Jesus declares his divine identity and his opponents try to kill him.

Jesus and a Woman Caught in Adultery (7:53–8:11)

[[53]Then each went to his own house, [1]while Jesus went to the Mount of Olives. [2]But early in the morning he arrived again in the temple area, and all the people started coming to him, and he sat down and taught them. [3]Then the scribes and the Pharisees brought a woman who had been caught in adultery and made her stand in the middle. [4]They said to him, "Teacher, this woman was caught in the very act of committing adultery. [5]Now in the law, Moses commanded us to stone such women. So what do you say?" [6]They said this to test him, so that they could have some charge to bring against him. Jesus bent down and began to write on the ground with his finger. [7]But when they continued asking him,

he straightened up and said to them, "Let the one among you who is without sin be the first to throw a stone at her." [8]Again he bent down and wrote on the ground. [9]And in response, they went away one by one, beginning with the elders. So he was left alone with the woman before him. [10]Then Jesus straightened up and said to her, "Woman, where are they? Has no one condemned you?" [11]She replied, "No one, sir." Then Jesus said, "Neither do I condemn you. Go, [and] from now on do not sin any more."]

OT: Num 5:12–31; Deut 22:22–24; Sir 23:22–24; Jer 17:12–13
NT: Matt 7:1–5; Luke 6:41–42
Catechism: mercy and sin, 1846–48; adultery, 2380–81
Lectionary: 5th Sunday of Lent (Year C)

The story of Jesus and the woman caught in adultery (John 7:53–8:11) has a complicated history. It does not appear in any major Greek copy of John before the sixth century, which is why it appears in brackets in the NABRE, although it does appear in earlier Latin manuscripts. In some Greek manuscripts of John, the story appears in places other than its present location. One manuscript group has the account at the end of the Gospel, after 21:25. In addition, it appears in some manuscripts of the Gospel of Luke, after 21:38. The Greek language in this story differs noticeably from that in the rest of John. These factors suggest that the story did not originate with the rest of the Fourth Gospel. Rather, it resembles conflict stories found in the †Synoptics. The Church receives this text as inspired Scripture and proclaims it liturgically on the fifth Sunday of Lent in Year C.

7:53–8:3 **Early in the morning** on the next day, Jesus went into **the temple area**, where he attracted a crowd. While he was teaching, **the scribes and the Pharisees brought a woman who had been caught in adultery**. Although the †Torah prescribed an investigative test for suspected cases of adultery (Num 5:12–31), there is apparently no ambiguity here: this woman is unquestionably guilty. They **made her stand in the middle** as one accused of a capital crime (see Sir 23:22–24).

8:4–6 The woman's accusers address Jesus as **Teacher** and claim, **This woman was caught in the very act of committing adultery**. According to the Torah, adultery is a capital offense, and Deut 22:22–24 prescribes stoning for both the man and woman involved (see also Lev 20:10). Since the woman is unquestionably guilty of a capital crime, the answer should be straightforward: she should be stoned to death. But they ask Jesus, **So what do you say?**, not to administer justice (notice that the adulterous man is nowhere to be found) but to entrap

Jesus. If the scribes and †Pharisees can corner Jesus into taking a stance against the law, then they will **have some charge to bring against him** (see 5:45; Matt 12:10; Acts 24:2).[1]

The meaning of Jesus' nonverbal response—he **bent down and began to write on the ground with his finger**—is unclear. It could simply be a †sign of indifference, showing that he refuses to be drawn into this trap.[2] Another possibility is that Jesus' gesture is a subtle allusion to Jer 17:13, which literally reads, "O Hope of Israel, O †YHWH, all who abandon you will be put to shame, those who turn away will be written in the earth because they have abandoned the Fountain of Living Waters."[3] By writing on the ground, Jesus would be reminding the woman's accusers that they too are sinners subject to God's judgment, sinners who refuse Jesus' invitation to come in faith to him, the "Fountain of Living Waters" (Jer 17:13; John 7:37).

8:7–8 After the scribes **continued asking**, Jesus **straightened up** and said, **Let the one among you who is without sin be the first to throw a stone at her**. According to Deut 17:6–7, the witnesses who testify to the guilt of an accused person in a capital case are the ones who begin the execution. The scribes and Pharisees are the woman's accusers. But Jesus reframes the issue by calling attention to the accusers' own sinfulness. While the particular sins may differ, both the woman and her accusers are sinners and stand guilty before God. Jesus thus exhorts the accusers to reject self-righteousness and embrace genuine humility, which is to recognize the truth about oneself before God and with respect to others (see Matt 7:1–5; Luke 6:41–42). After this pronouncement, Jesus once more **bent down and wrote on the ground**.

8:9 After hearing Jesus' words, the woman's accusers **went away one by one, beginning with the elders**. Their motives in leaving are not clear. Perhaps they realize that their plan to entrap Jesus has failed. Or perhaps Jesus' words touched their hearts: they acknowledge their own sinfulness and have a conversion of heart. After all departed, Jesus was **alone with the woman before him**.

8:10–11 Jesus addresses the woman and calls attention to the fact that all her accusers are gone. The woman acknowledges that **no one** is left to condemn her, and Jesus replies, **Neither do I condemn you**. As he did to the formerly paralyzed man in 5:14, Jesus tells her to change her ways: **Go, [and] from now on do not**

1. Gail R. O'Day, "John 7:53–8:11: A Study in Misreading," *Journal of Biblical Literature* 111 (1992): 631–40.

2. Francis J. Moloney, SDB, *The Gospel of John* (Collegeville, MN: Liturgical Press, 1998), 261.

3. Rudolf Schnackenburg, *The Gospel according to St. John*, vol. 2, *Commentary on Chapters 5–12*, trans. Cecily Hastings, Francis McDonagh, David Smith, and Richard Foley, SJ (New York: Seabury, 1980), 166–67; our translation of Jer 17:13.

Pope Francis on Christ's Mercy

[This] Gospel presents to us the episode of the adulterous woman ([John] 8:1–11), whom Jesus saves from being condemned to death. Jesus' attitude is striking: we do not hear words of scorn, we do not hear words of condemnation, but only words of love, of mercy, which are an invitation to conversion. "Neither do I condemn you; go, and do not sin again" (v. 11). Ah! Brothers and Sisters, God's face is the face of a merciful father who is always patient. Have you thought about God's patience, the patience he has with each one of us? That is his mercy. He always has patience, patience with us, he understands us, he waits for us, he does not tire of forgiving us if we are able to return to him with a contrite heart.[a]

a. Pope Francis, "Angelus," March 17, 2013.

sin any more. Jesus offers this woman a fresh start by turning away from her sins and opening herself to God's infinite mercy.

Reflection and Application (7:53–8:11)

Jesus shows loving-kindness to a person involved in sexual immorality. Many men and women are in a similar situation today. Turning away from such sinful activity can be very difficult. The gentle mercy of Jesus, which is infinitely greater than the worst of our sins, is available to all in the sacrament of reconciliation, through which he pardons all our sins, even the most serious ones. Moreover, Christians who are not involved in such sinful behavior do well to avoid the proud self-righteousness of the woman's accusers and instead imitate Jesus, not condemning but lovingly summoning the sinner to repent and live a better life.

The Light of the World (8:12–20)

[12]Jesus spoke to them again, saying, "I am the light of the world. Whoever follows me will not walk in darkness, but will have the light of life." [13]So the Pharisees said to him, "You testify on your own behalf, so your testimony cannot be verified." [14]Jesus answered and said to them, "Even if I do testify on my own behalf, my testimony can be verified, because I know where I came from and where I am going. But you do not know where I come from or where I am going. [15]You judge by appearances, but I do not

judge anyone. [16]And even if I should judge, my judgment is valid, because I am not alone, but it is I and the Father who sent me. [17]Even in your law it is written that the testimony of two men can be verified. [18]I testify on my behalf and so does the Father who sent me." [19]So they said to him, "Where is your father?" Jesus answered, "You know neither me nor my Father. If you knew me, you would know my Father also." [20]He spoke these words while teaching in the treasury in the temple area. But no one arrested him, because his hour had not yet come.

OT: Deut 17:6–7; 19:15; Isa 8:23–9:6; Zech 14:1–9, 16–19
NT: Matt 5:13–16; 1 John 1:5–10; Rev 4:8–11; 22:1–5
Catechism: Trinity's works in creation, 257–60

Drawing on another element of the Tabernacles liturgy, Jesus identifies himself as the light of the world. The †Pharisees, who emerged as Jesus' opponents in 7:45–52, confront him directly and challenge his claims. Jesus defends himself on the basis of his unique relationship with the Father, a relationship his opponents do not understand.

8:12 In his teaching about the living water, the Holy Spirit (7:37–39), Jesus alluded to the water ceremonies at Tabernacles. Now he uses light, another prominent part of the Tabernacles liturgy, to reveal himself as **the light of the world**. According to the †Mishnah, during the week of Tabernacles giant lampstands were set up in the temple precincts to provide illumination so the festival pilgrims could celebrate at night.[4] The theological symbolism of these lights is not clear. One possibility is that the lights were anticipation of God's end-time salvation described in Zech 14. Zechariah says that on the Day of the Lord, †YHWH will come to save his people and defeat their enemies. Unending daylight will follow, and the Gentile nations will come to Jerusalem annually to celebrate the Festival of Tabernacles (Zech 14:7, 16–19).

As the light of the world, Jesus says, **Whoever follows me,** those who respond positively to him with faith and discipleship, **will not walk in darkness, but will have the light of life** (see Isa 8:23–9:6). The Father sent Jesus into the world, darkened by sin, to be its spiritual light (1:4–5). As the light, Jesus guides us on the way to eternal life with the Father.[5] The presence of Jesus in the world as Light is also the occasion of judgment, because the light provokes a response from people (3:19–21). Those who follow Jesus believe that he illumines the way to the Father, and they live their lives accordingly. A negative response to Jesus is a decision to remain in spiritual darkness.

4. *Mishnah Sukkah* 5:1–4.
5. Catechism 260.

The Easter Vigil Liturgy, Service of Light

The most prominent use of light and darkness symbolism in the Church's liturgy is the beginning of the Easter Vigil. The liturgy begins with the church in darkness. After the blessing of the Easter fire, the priest or deacon processes into the darkened church with the lit Easter candle while singing "Christ, our Light," to signify the risen Christ as the light of the world. Once the participants' candles have been lit by the Easter fire, there is the Easter proclamation, the Exsultet, which proclaims Christ as the light:

> This is the night
> that with a pillar of fire
> banished the darkness of sin. . . .
> Therefore, O Lord,
> we pray you that this candle,
> hallowed to the honor of your name,
> may persevere undimmed,
> to overcome the darkness of this night. . . .
> May this flame be found still burning
> by the Morning Star:
> the one Morning Star who never sets,
> Christ your Son,
> who, coming back from death's domain,
> has shed his peaceful light on humanity.[a]

a. *Daily Roman Missal*, 7th ed. (Woodridge, IL: Midwest Theological Forum, 2011), 273–74.

8:13 For the first time, hostile **Pharisees** speak directly to Jesus. Instead of addressing the content of Jesus' statement in 8:12, they focus on the fact that he makes such claims about himself—not *what* he says, but *that* he says it. By their objection, **You testify on your own behalf, so your testimony cannot be verified**, they protest that these claims are not valid because he makes them all by himself without corroboration (see 5:31–32).[6] Their objection corresponds to the inadmissibility of self-testimony, a principle attested to in the Mishnah and based on prescriptions of the †Torah requiring the testimony of two or three witnesses in capital cases (Deut 17:6; 19:15).[7]

8:14 Jesus responds by stating that his relationship with the Father legitimates his claims. His opening statement, **Even if I do testify on my own behalf, my**

6. The NABRE translates as "verified" the Greek word *alēthēs*, which literally means "true" and can mean "valid" in legal settings (Schnackenburg, *St. John*, 2:468).

7. *Mishnah Ketuboth* 2:9.

testimony can be verified, seems to contradict his previous claim in 5:31, "If I testify on my own behalf, my testimony cannot be verified." Informing both 5:31 and 8:14 is Jesus' relationship with the Father, but this relationship is viewed from different angles.[8] In 5:31, he grants the legal principle about invalid self-testimony in order to teach that the Father does give valid testimony about him (5:32). Here, however, Jesus insists that *his* self-testimony is valid because of his relationship with the Father. Jesus is unique in regard to self-testimony because he alone knows the Father (**I know where I came from and where I am going**), he alone has seen the Father (6:46), and he alone reveals him (1:18). Jesus' union with the Father gives his self-testimony a unique validity. No authority can sit in judgment over it, for there is no greater authority. The Pharisees **do not know** his relationship with the Father and thus do not recognize that his self-testimony is valid.

8:15–16 Jesus shifts from testimony to judgment by saying, **You judge by appearances**, literally, "according to the flesh." His words recall 7:24, "Stop judging by appearances, but judge justly." Like the crowd in 7:25–30, 40–44, the Pharisees do not see beyond the visible and apparent. They do not discern Jesus' relationship with the Father and thus fail to recognize his identity.

Jesus contrasts the Pharisees' kind of judgment with his own by saying, **But I do not judge anyone**. Yet in the very next statement, Jesus says, **And even if I should judge, my judgment is valid, because I am not alone, but it is I and the Father who sent me**. Once again, Jesus' relationship with the Father legitimates his activity. Since the Son does nothing apart from the Father (5:19, 22, 27), Jesus' judgment is valid because it comes to him from the Father. All of Jesus' actions proceed from his union with the Father.

8:17–18 Returning to the issue of testimony, Jesus points out that **in your law it is written that the testimony of two men can be verified**. In 8:13, the Pharisees appealed to legal principle when they objected to Jesus making claims about himself. Turning the tables, Jesus appeals to the †Torah and produces two witnesses: **I testify on my behalf and so does the Father**. Having just cited his union with the Father as legitimating his self-testimony, here Jesus invokes the distinction between Father and Son as providing two distinct witnesses: the Father and the Son. The relationship between Father and Son is thus marked by both unity and distinction.

8:19 Judging "by appearances" (8:15), the Pharisees ask Jesus to produce his **father**, thinking of Joseph as a witness. They do not realize that Jesus is speaking on a different level, about his heavenly Father. Jesus highlights their lack of

8. Schnackenburg, *St. John*, 2:120–21, 192–93.

Fig. 6. Model of the temple sanctuary featuring the Court of Women

understanding: **You know neither me nor my Father. If you knew me, you would know my Father also**. Since these Pharisees do not know that Jesus is the Son, they also do not know the Father whom the Son reveals. These Pharisees are in the dark because they do not understand and believe in the Light.

8:20 This exchange takes place near **the treasury in the temple area**. According to the Mishnah, the massive lampstands used during Tabernacles were located in the Court of the Women, which contained boxes for financial donations.[9] Jesus identifies himself as the light of the world in the very place where the lights of Tabernacles were lit. As the lamps at Tabernacles provided light for the liturgy of God's people Israel, so does Jesus as the light of the world illumine the way to the unending liturgy of heaven (see Rev 4:8–11; 5:9–14; 22:3). Since Jesus' life unfolds according to the divine plan, **no one arrested him, because his †hour had not yet come**.

Reflection and Application (8:12–20)

Jesus identifies himself as the light of the world (8:12). He reveals the truth to a world darkened by sin and error. He also shows us how to live so that

9. *Mishnah Sukkah* 5:2–4; *Mishnah Sheqalim* 6:5.

we may reach our goal of eternal life with the Father. Jesus is the light, and his light shines in and through us when, by faith, we yield to his action in us, follow his teachings, and imitate his love and holiness in our daily lives. Thus he says to us, "You are the light of the world. . . . Your light must shine before others, that they may see your good deeds and glorify your heavenly Father" (Matt 5:14, 16).

The Obedient Son Reveals the Father (8:21–30)

[21]He said to them again, "I am going away and you will look for me, but you will die in your sin. Where I am going you cannot come." [22]So the Jews said, "He is not going to kill himself, is he, because he said, 'Where I am going you cannot come'?" [23]He said to them, "You belong to what is below, I belong to what is above. You belong to this world, but I do not belong to this world. [24]That is why I told you that you will die in your sins. For if you do not believe that I AM, you will die in your sins." [25]So they said to him, "Who are you?" Jesus said to them, "What I told you from the beginning. [26]I have much to say about you in condemnation. But the one who sent me is true, and what I heard from him I tell the world." [27]They did not realize that he was speaking to them of the Father. [28]So Jesus said [to them], "When you lift up the Son of Man, then you will realize that I AM, and that I do nothing on my own, but I say only what the Father taught me. [29]The one who sent me is with me. He has not left me alone, because I always do what is pleasing to him." [30]Because he spoke this way, many came to believe in him.

OT: Gen 2:16–17; Exod 3:13–14; Wis 2:23–24.

NT: Mark 10:32–34; Rom 5:12–14

Catechism: necessity of faith, 161; original sin, 402–9; gravity of sin, 1861; Christ's obedience, 2824–25.

Jesus continues to reveal his relationship with the Father, declaring his divine identity and the deliverance from sin and death that his cross and resurrection will accomplish (8:24, 28). Jesus' audience, seemingly the †Pharisees from 8:12–20, continue to misunderstand him, for he and they are speaking on two different levels (8:23).

8:21–24 A new line of discussion begins with Jesus repeating what he said in 7:33–34 about going away and his audience being unable to follow, but now he adds something new: **You will die in your sin**. Many biblical texts witness to a deep connection between sin and death. In Gen 2:17, God tells Adam that death is the consequence of sin and disobedience. Interpreting Genesis, St. Paul writes that through Adam "sin entered the world, and through sin, death" (Rom 5:12).

In John's Gospel, "sin" refers both to acts of personal wrongdoing (5:14; 9:2–3; 19:11; 20:23) and to the condition of being separated from God, being in a state of sin (1:29; 9:34; 16:8–9; see sidebar on p. 163).[10] When Jesus says, "You will die in your sin," he is talking about dying in a state of separation from God. Jesus came to take "away the sin of the world" (1:29) and offer eternal life with the Father to all. Because Jesus is **I AM**—the divine name (see sidebar on p. 89)—only he can heal humanity of sin and reconcile it with the Father. Those who **believe** in him accept his gift of eternal life with the Father, whereas those who reject him refuse his gift and thus die separated from God.

Jesus' audience again does not understand him. When they hear him say, **Where I am going you cannot come**, they think he is **going to kill himself**. Jesus explains their incomprehension by contrasting their spiritual affiliation with his own. Jesus belongs **to what is above** and not **to this world**, but his uncomprehending audience belongs **to what is below** and **to this world** (see 3:31). In spatial terms, Jesus and his audience are communicating on two different levels. They cannot understand him because they think about him only in their own earthly terms, not in his heavenly terms.

8:25–27 The misunderstanding continues. After Jesus identifies himself as "I AM," his audience asks, **Who are you?**, perhaps expecting Jesus to complete his statement, "I am . . ." Because they are "from below," they do not grasp that he is talking about his divine identity. Jesus calls attention to the fact that he has been speaking constantly about his identity: **What I told you from the beginning.**[11] Since Jesus' audience does not grasp his divine identity, he says, **I have much to say about you in condemnation**: Jesus' interlocutors are mistaken about much. **But** this is not the time for talking about condemnation. Rather, Jesus' mission is to reveal the Father **who sent** him and to do his work. John then clarifies for his readers what Jesus' audience does not understand: **He was speaking to them of the Father**.

8:28 Jesus makes his second statement about the lifting **up** of **the** †**Son of Man** on the cross (see 3:14; 12:32). The first statement, to Nicodemus, reveals the mystery of the cross as salvation (3:14–15). This second statement focuses on the cross as the culmination of Jesus' revelation. The verb "lift up" has a twofold

10. Catechism 405, 408, 1861.

11. The Douay-Rheims version treats "the beginning" as a title for Jesus, similar to the title "the Alpha" in Rev 22:13 (see Col 1:18; Rev 1:8; 21:6). In this translation, Jesus responds to the question "Who are you?" with the statement: "The beginning, who also speak unto you" (8:25).

sense.[12] In a literal way, Jesus will be lifted up physically from the ground after he is nailed to the cross. But in a spiritual way, the lifting up on the cross is also his exaltation. The cross is where God, who is radical and subsisting self-giving love, shines forth most radiantly and gloriously. When the cross is so perceived with eyes of faith, people **will realize** the revelation of Jesus' divine identity (**I AM**) and of **the Father**, to whom Jesus is perfectly obedient and transparent.

8:29–30 As the obedient Son, Jesus affirms that the Father is always **with** him. The phrase **because I always do what is pleasing to him** is more descriptive than causal. That is, the Father is not always with Jesus *because* Jesus is obedient. Rather, Jesus' obedience describes or characterizes his intimate, constant relationship with the Father. Some of the Pharisees are taken with Jesus' manner of speaking, and despite their previous incomprehension, **many** start **to believe in him** (compare 7:31, 45–46).

The Jerusalem Debate I: Jesus Brings True Freedom from Sin (8:31–36)

[31]Jesus then said to those Jews who believed in him, "If you remain in my word, you will truly be my disciples, [32]and you will know the truth, and the truth will set you free." [33]They answered him, "We are descendants of Abraham and have never been enslaved to anyone. How can you say, 'You will become free'?" [34]Jesus answered them, "Amen, amen, I say to you, everyone who commits sin is a slave of sin. [35]A slave does not remain in a household forever, but a son always remains. [36]So if a son frees you, then you will truly be free."

OT: Exod 6:2–8
NT: Rom 6:16–23; Gal 3:7–9; 4:1–7
Catechism: freedom and responsibility, 1731–42

Verse 31 begins a lengthy, difficult argument that runs to the end of the chapter. Readers are urged to consult the explanation of "John and the Jews" (see sidebar on p. 101), since the commentary on this debate presupposes that explanation.

In this opening section of the debate, Jesus invites fledging believers (8:30) to elevate their thinking to his level. He teaches that receiving the truth he reveals imparts true freedom. But again, his audience does not understand.

12. See comments on John 3:14–15.

8:31–32

The debate begins between Jesus and **those Jews who believed in him.**[13] Apparently, these are some of the †Pharisees from 8:12–30, because there has been no indication of a change in audience. Jesus begins to teach them about genuine discipleship and invites them to go deeper in faith. True **disciples** faithfully receive Jesus' **word**, embrace it, and allow it to transform their lives (1 John 2:14; see John 5:38). Those who do so **will know the truth**: to receive Jesus' revelatory word is to know the truth because Jesus, as God's Word, is himself the truth (14:6). Those who receive **the truth** revealed by Jesus and let it take root and mature in them **will** be **set free**. The nature of this freedom will become clearer in 8:34–35. But notice how Jesus says that human freedom follows upon and presupposes knowledge of the truth. In order to be truly free, a person must first know what is true.

8:33

These fledgling believers find Jesus' remarks about being set free very strange. First, they articulate their identity by appealing to their ancestry as **descendants of Abraham**. They do so accurately, for "children of Abraham" is an established title for Israel as the †covenant people of God.[14] But the second claim, We **have never been enslaved to anyone**, is striking and works on multiple levels. The descendants of Abraham had been slaves in Egypt, and God's action to deliver them from slavery in the exodus, along with the Sinai covenant that followed, was of the greatest importance for Jewish self-understanding (Exod 6:2–8). Furthermore, the Jewish people lived under the Gentile domination of the Roman Empire in Jesus' day. Puzzled, they ask, **How can you say, "You will become free"?** As they misunderstood the Scriptures about prophets from Galilee (7:52), these Pharisees now misunderstand their own identity as descendants of Abraham, Jesus himself, and the freedom he offers to those who receive him in faith. However, at a deeper level, Jesus' interlocutors may be expressing a lack of awareness of their spiritual

13. A crucial issue in 8:31–59 is the identity of the †Jews whom Jesus engages in this intense debate. The debate opens with notice that Jesus addresses a group of fledgling believers (8:31). But the tone of the debate shifts so dramatically that it is difficult to see how the latter parts of the debate could be between Jesus and a group of believers.

Some commentators have taken 8:31 as integral to the debate and read it as being between Jesus and a group of incipient Jewish believers. See (with qualifications) Craig S. Keener, *The Gospel of John: A Commentary* (Peabody, MA: Hendrickson, 2003), 1:746–47, 753; Andrew T. Lincoln, *The Gospel according to St. John* (Peabody, MA: Hendrickson, 2005), 269–77. Another major alternative is to take the debate as being between Jesus and hostile Jewish authorities (so Raymond E. Brown, SS, *The Gospel according to John*, AB 29 [New York: Doubleday, 1966], 1:354). This interpretation substantially disregards 8:31 and considers it an editorial addition that connects 8:32–59 with 8:21–30. Our commentary tries to integrate elements from both positions: "the Jews who began to believe in him" (8:31, our translation) are some Pharisees from 8:13 who have been hostile to Jesus, start to believe, but then return to being hostile to him after hearing his words in 8:32–36.

14. See 2 Chron 20:7; Ps 105:6; Gal 3:7–9.

enslavement to the power of sin and the consequent need for the freedom that Jesus offers (compare 9:39–41).

8:34 Jesus redirects them to a more profound kind of slavery and freedom. He clarifies that **everyone who commits sin is a slave of sin**. At the heart of sinful actions is the willful rejection of God, and this rejection of God separates a person from him. This resulting state of separation, that is a "state of sin," is aptly characterized as slavery, because people are powerless to free themselves from it and to reconcile themselves to God.

8:35–36 Jesus elaborates with an example from ancient society. He contrasts a slave with a son in a household: **A slave does not remain in a household forever, but a son always remains**. A slave is unable to free himself from his enslavement, but a son is able to make another **truly free** on account of his authority and permanent status in the household. This example has theological overtones because Jesus is the Son. He did not come to bring political liberation from the Romans, but freedom in the most profound sense: freedom from sin, which alienates us from God. True freedom follows upon receiving the truth that Jesus reveals: "You will know the truth, and the truth will set you free" (8:32). As the Son who remains eternally with the Father, Jesus is able to free all people enslaved to sin, who, as slaves, cannot free themselves.

Reflection and Application (8:31–36)

Jesus' saying, "You will know the truth, and the truth will set you free" (8:32), underscores two important doctrines. First, Catholic teaching strongly affirms that human beings can genuinely know the truth about reality and that this ability is a hallmark of human dignity. This needs to be stressed on account of widespread relativism that says there is no truth, only individual opinions and expressions of power. Second, genuine human freedom depends on our knowing the truth. Jesus reveals the truth about God and also about human beings. As the Second Vatican Council teaches, "Only in the mystery of the †incarnate Word does the mystery of man take on light. . . . [Jesus], by the revelation of the mystery of the Father and His love, fully reveals man to man himself and makes his supreme calling clear."[15]

Knowing the truth involves knowing the truth about human nature, about what is truly good for people and contributes to human flourishing. A truly free person acts in accordance with the moral truth about human nature, because

15. Pastoral Constitution on the Church in the Modern World (*Gaudium et Spes* [Joy and Hope]), 22.

Sin in the Fourth Gospel

BIBLICAL BACKGROUND

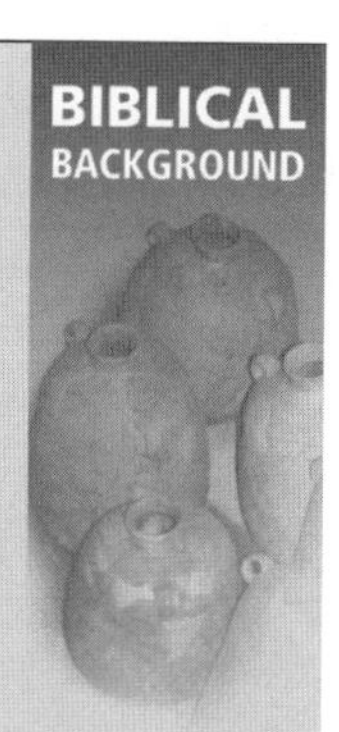

Jesus' saying, "Everyone who commits sin is a slave of sin" (8:34), illustrates how sin is used with both narrow and broad meanings in John's Gospel. Narrowly, sin can refer to a specific evil action, which offends God and breaks his law. When Jesus says, "Everyone who commits *sin* . . . ," he uses "sin" in that narrow sense (see 5:14; 8:46; 9:2–3; 20:23). When he goes on to say that every sinner "is a slave of *sin*," he uses sin in a broader sense. In this sense, sin designates a spiritual condition of separation from God, which oppresses and enslaves the fallen human race (1:29; 8:21; 9:34; see Rom 6:16–23). In John's Gospel, being "in sin" is the condition of those who have willfully separated themselves from God by their sinful actions. John's Gospel teaches that at the heart of sin is the willful rejection of God and his Word. The Prologue speaks of the world's sin as a refusal to "know" or "accept" the Word of God (1:10–11). Similarly, when describing the Holy Spirit's action to convict the world of sin, Jesus defines the world's sin as a refusal of God's Word: "They do not believe in me" (16:9).

human beings cannot be free and good if they act in a way that does not contribute to human flourishing, such as following evil and vice.[16]

The Jerusalem Debate II: Affiliation and Action (8:37–47)

[37]"I know that you are descendants of Abraham. But you are trying to kill me, because my word has no room among you. [38]I tell you what I have seen in the Father's presence; then do what you have heard from the Father."

[39]They answered and said to him, "Our father is Abraham." Jesus said to them, "If you were Abraham's children, you would be doing the works of Abraham. [40]But now you are trying to kill me, a man who has told you the truth that I heard from God; Abraham did not do this. [41]You are doing the works of your father!" [So] they said to him, "We are not illegitimate. We have one Father, God." [42]Jesus said to them, "If God were your Father, you would love me, for I came from God and am here; I did not come on my own but he sent me. [43]Why do you not understand what I am saying? Because you cannot bear to hear my word. [44]You belong to your father the devil and you willingly carry out your father's desires. He was a murderer

16. See Pope John Paul II, *Fides et Ratio* (On the Relationship between Faith and Reason), 25.

from the beginning and does not stand in truth, because there is no truth in him. When he tells a lie, he speaks in character, because he is a liar and the father of lies. [45]But because I speak the truth, you do not believe me. [46]Can any of you charge me with sin? If I am telling the truth, why do you not believe me? [47]Whoever belongs to God hears the words of God; for this reason you do not listen, because you do not belong to God."

OT: Gen 3:1–15; Exod 4:22–23; Wis 2:23–24

NT: Matt 1:18–25; 1 John 3:4–18

Catechism: fall of the angels, 391–95; man's first sin, 397–401; Jews not collectively responsible for Jesus' death, 597–99; the Church and the Jews, 839–40.

Jesus has declared that he offers divine truth and freedom to those who receive his word. These religious authorities question their need for what Jesus offers in light of their being children of Abraham. In this scene, the exchange between Jesus and the authorities becomes increasingly heated. The controversy turns on the relationship between spiritual affiliation (expressed in the family language of "father and son") and action (behaviors characteristic of a particular affiliation).

8:37–38 Jesus agrees that these religious authorities are **descendants of Abraham**. But he contrasts their affiliation with Abraham with their present actions: **You are trying to kill me**. Jesus thus introduces the focal category for this part of the debate: the relationship between affiliation and action. The authorities' present actions contradict their spiritual affiliation.

While the text is not clear, it seems that those who oppose Jesus in this scene are some †Pharisees from 8:13.[17] Pharisees emerged as among the religious authorities who are hostile to Jesus (4:1; 7:25, 32, 45–52), but after encountering Jesus directly, some have started to believe in him (8:30–31). Jesus has then challenged them to go deeper and become genuine disciples who receive and abide in his word (8:31–32). But these Pharisees, perhaps offended at Jesus' suggestion that they need what only he can offer, reject his words (8:33), and their hostility reemerges.

Jesus links their desire to kill him with their not receiving his **word**, their unbelief in him. Jesus' spiritual affiliation is with the Father, and it is demonstrated in his actions: his perfect obedience to the Father in word and deed (8:28–29). Jesus speaks only **what** he has **seen in the Father's presence** and exhorts his audience to receive and act upon this word **from the Father**.

8:39–41a But Jesus' opponents do not realize that he is referring to God when speaking about his "Father" as the source of his teaching and authority. They counter

17. See the sidebar, "John and the Jews," on p. 101.

with a claim about their own parental affiliation: **Our father is Abraham.** Jesus' response has four interconnected parts. (1) Jesus says, **If you were Abraham's children, you would be doing the works of Abraham.** One who has a spiritual affiliation with a particular authority figure should act in a manner consistent with that relationship. Jesus has affirmed that his opponents are "descendants of Abraham" (8:37) in a genetic sense. But (2) their action does not correspond to their affiliation, because they **are trying to kill** Jesus, who is from the Father. By refusing his word and trying to kill him, the opponents place themselves in opposition to **the truth** that he reveals **from God.** (3) **Abraham did not do** what Jesus' opponents are now doing, and this shows the distance between them and Abraham, whom they claim as their father. (4) Jesus then begins to indicate the affiliation their present actions reflect: **You are doing the works of your father!**

8:41b With things becoming more heated, Jesus' opponents respond with a two-part statement about their affiliation. They appeal to their **one Father, God,** in light of the †covenant relationship between God and Israel, whom he calls "my son, my firstborn" (Exod 4:22). The declaration, **We are not illegitimate**—literally, "born from fornication"—makes the same basic point in negative terms, for fornication is a biblical metaphor for idolatry (Jer 2:20–21; Hosea 1:2; 2:4). The illegitimacy remark may also be a subtle attack on Jesus' human origins. As Matt 1:20–23 and Luke 1:26–39 both affirm, Mary conceived Jesus by the power of the Holy Spirit and without a human father prior to the completion of her marriage to Joseph. There arose rumors in antiquity that Mary's pregnancy resulted from some kind of immorality, and the illegitimacy remark might reflect such rumors; his opponents would in effect be saying, *We* are not illegitimate, but *you* are.[18]

8:42 Jesus responds to his opponents' claim to have affiliation with God the Father by returning to the issue of the relationship between affiliation and action: **If God were your Father, you would love me.** Jesus is the Son, who **came from God** as his perfectly obedient envoy. A response to an envoy is a response to the one who sent him (5:20–23; 8:38).[19] If his opponents had spiritual affiliation with God, they would love Jesus because he was sent by the Father as his faithful envoy.

8:43–47 Jesus explains that his opponents **do not understand** him because they **cannot bear to hear** his **word,** his revelation. Their conduct characterizes affiliation not with God but with **the devil,** the very opposite of what they claim,

18. Origen, *Contra Celsus* 1.28.

19. See Peder Borgen, "God's Agent in the Fourth Gospel," in *Religions in Antiquity: Essays in Memory of Erwin Ramsdell Goodenough*, ed. Jacob Neusner (Leiden: Brill, 1968), 137–48; repr. in *The Interpretation of John*, 2nd ed., ed. John Ashton (Edinburgh: T&T Clark, 1997), 83–95.

Rhetoric of Praise and Blame

BIBLICAL BACKGROUND

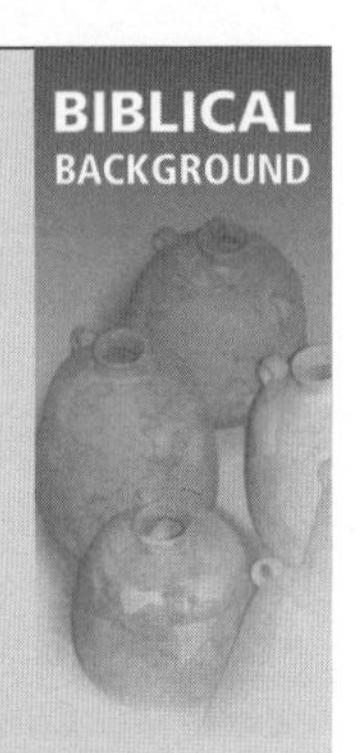

Rhetoric, the art of speaking or writing to persuade, was an extremely important part of public life in Greco-Roman antiquity. It was a highly conventional discipline with specific rules and practices for suiting one's language to a particular purpose or occasion. One form of rhetorical speech was that of praising or shaming another party, known respectively as encomium or invective. The first-century rhetorician Aelius Theon taught that the rhetoric of praise and blame should call attention, either positive or negative, to certain things about another, such as their birth, upbringing, social status, wealth, and conduct.[a] As an author from the Greco-Roman world, John has employed elements of rhetorical invective in his account of the argument between Jesus and his opponents.[b] For instance, Theon cites a person's origins and actions as topics to critique, and the debate between Jesus and his opponents takes up the topics of fathers and conduct. This kind of rhetoric is not so much concerned with making literal claims as it is with criticizing one's opponents or defending oneself against them.

a. See "The Exercises of *Aelius Theon*," in *Progymnasmata: Greek Textbooks of Prose Composition and Rhetoric*, ed. George A. Kennedy (Atlanta: Society of Biblical Literature, 2003), 50–51.
b. See Keener, *Gospel of John*, 1:752–53.

and their behavior reflects this **father's desires**. The devil **was a murderer from the beginning** because through the sin he instigated, death came to humanity (see Gen 3; Wis 2:24; Rom 5:12). Moreover, the connection between murder and being a devil's son may reflect an ancient Jewish interpretation of Cain, who was speculated to be a son of the devil because he committed the first murder (see 1 John 3:11–18).[20] Similarly Jesus' opponents want to kill him (8:37, 40). Jesus asserts that the devil is **a liar and the father of lies**, in whom **there is no truth**. The serpent lied and so deceived Eve, leading her and Adam to commit sin. However, Jesus speaks the truth that he "heard from God" (8:40), and for this reason, his opponents are hostile toward him and **do not believe**. Their antagonism is unwarranted because of Jesus' sinlessness (**Can any of you charge me with sin?**), which supports the truthfulness of his revelation.

This section of argument concludes with the exchange in 8:46–47. Jesus first asks a rhetorical question—**If I am telling the truth, why do you not believe me?**—and follows it with the observation **Whoever belongs to God hears**

20. *Targum Pseudo-Jonathan* on Gen 4:1; 5:3; see Brown, *John*, 1:358; Keener, *Gospel of John*, 1:760–61.

the words of God. Hearing, that is, accepting, God's word spoken by Jesus characterizes affiliation with God, just as remaining in Jesus' word characterizes discipleship (8:31). By contrast, the rejection of Jesus' word and the desire to kill him do not characterize affiliation with God the Father who sent him. Consequently, Jesus' refutes his opponents' claim in 8:41 by asserting here, **You do not belong to God**.

Reflection and Application (8:37–47)

The Gospel refers to Jesus' opponents here as †Jews (8:31, 48, 52, 57). Tragically, biblical passages such as this one have been used in Christian history to promote hatred and persecution of Jews and Judaism. In the aftermath of the Holocaust and in accord with the teachings of the Second Vatican Council, great care must be taken to avoid interpreting biblical texts like John 8 in such a way. The Church condemns anti-Semitism as sinful and teaches that Jews are not to be singled out as uniquely to blame for Jesus' death (Catechism 597–99). Furthermore, the Church teaches that we have a unique spiritual relationship with the Jews (Catechism 839) and that God's covenant with them "has never been revoked" (Catechism 121).

We should not overlook 8:31, which says that Jesus' opponents here had started to believe but later turned on him. The same issue of the relationship between affiliation and action is adapted to a Christian audience in 1 John (e.g., 1 John 4:11–18), and it offers us an opportunity for self-examination. When we consider our own conduct and attitudes in everyday life, does it characterize ties with God or with the devil? Do we seek and embrace the truth or do we resist it? Do we promote and protect the goodness of life or do we depreciate and destroy life? Is our faith and practice consistent with being a child of God or do our actions reveal us as doing the devil's work by sinning?

The Jerusalem Debate III: Greater Than Abraham and the Prophets (8:48–59)

[48]The Jews answered and said to him, "Are we not right in saying that you are a Samaritan and are possessed?" [49]Jesus answered, "I am not possessed; I honor my Father, but you dishonor me. [50]I do not seek my own glory; there is one who seeks it and he is the one who judges. [51]Amen, amen, I say to you, whoever keeps my word will never see death." [52][So] the Jews said to him, "Now we are sure that you are possessed. Abraham

died, as did the prophets, yet you say, 'Whoever keeps my word will never taste death.' [53]Are you greater than our father Abraham, who died? Or the prophets, who died? Who do you make yourself out to be?" [54]Jesus answered, "If I glorify myself, my glory is worth nothing; but it is my Father who glorifies me, of whom you say, 'He is our God.' [55]You do not know him, but I know him. And if I should say that I do not know him, I would be like you a liar. But I do know him and I keep his word. [56]Abraham your father rejoiced to see my day; he saw it and was glad." [57]So the Jews said to him, "You are not yet fifty years old and you have seen Abraham?" [58]Jesus said to them, "Amen, amen, I say to you, before Abraham came to be, I AM." [59]So they picked up stones to throw at him; but Jesus hid and went out of the temple area.

OT: Gen 15; 17:1–22; Lev 24:14–16
NT: Matt 9:32–34; Mark 3:22–30
Catechism: the promised Spirit, 705–6; theophanies and the law, 707–8

The intensity of the Jerusalem debate reaches its peak in this final section. Jesus continues to say things about himself that seem completely unbelievable to his opponents. He claims to have the power to save people from death (8:51) and to be greater than Abraham, who actually saw him (8:56). The debate culminates with Jesus declaring his divine identity (8:58). Because of this, his opponents to try to kill him.

8:48–49 Jesus' opponents make two counterattacks. First, they call him a **Samaritan**, which counts Jesus among the ethnic and religious rivals to the †Jews. Second, they associate Jesus with the devil—he is **possessed**—a charge made against Jesus elsewhere in the Gospels (see 7:20; 10:20; Matt 9:32–34). Jesus rejects the accusation of being **possessed** and demonstrates it with his holy behavior: **I honor my Father.**[21]

8:50–51 Jesus reaffirms that he does **not seek** his **own glory** (see 5:41; 7:18). Instead, the Father will honor him, and it is the Father's judgments, not those of people, that ultimately matter, because **he is the one who judges**. Whereas the Father **seeks** to give honor to Jesus, his opponents **dishonor** him. By contrasting the Father's honoring Jesus and his opponents' dishonoring him, Jesus reiterates his declaration that his opponents have positioned themselves in opposition to the Father. Since Jesus is the Father's envoy, to dishonor Jesus is to dishonor the Father.

Jesus previously claimed to reveal the truth that sets humans free (8:31–32). Now he makes an even stronger claim by saying, **Whoever keeps my word will**

21. Brown, *John*, 1:366.

never see death. Jesus declares that his revelatory word preserves those who embrace it from death.

8:52–53 So implausible is this claim to Jesus' opponents that they say, **Now we are sure that you are possessed**. How can Jesus say that his word saves people from death when the great heroes of the Bible like Abraham and the prophets died? And yet, they correctly identify the root issue in Jesus' claim. If Jesus' word saves people from death, what does that say about who he is? Hence they ask, expecting a no, **Are you greater than our father Abraham, who died? Or the prophets, who died?** But the question also reveals a degree of misunderstanding, because they think Jesus is talking about being saved merely from bodily death. Nevertheless, their last question, **Who do you make yourself out to be?**, points to the central issue (compare 5:18): who is Jesus?

8:54–55 Jesus returns to the honor language and the claim of 8:50: **If I glorify myself, my glory is worth nothing; but it is my Father who glorifies me**. Since only the Son knows the Father from all eternity, only he can reveal the Father (1:18). Jesus' opponents reject him and his word as being from the Father; thus, he says, they **do not know** the Father, **but I know him**. Moreover, if Jesus would deny his relationship with the Father, he would be **a liar** like them (returning to the connection between the opponents' behavior and the devil, who is "a liar and the father of lies"; 8:44). Jesus, however, is the Father's obedient Son: **I do know him and I keep his word**.

8:56 Building on 8:52–53, Jesus elaborates on his relationship with Abraham: **Abraham your father rejoiced to see my day; he saw it and was glad** (see 8:40). Jesus alludes to the †theophanies to Abraham in Gen 15 and 17. In Gen 17:17, Abraham laughed at God's words that he and Sarah would conceive a child in their old age. The verb "rejoiced" in John's Gospel interprets Abraham's laughter as joy rather than astonishment. In Gen 15:13–16, God appeared to Abraham and revealed the future events of the exodus to him. Some ancient Jews interpreted God's revelation of the future to Abraham as containing more than just the exodus, and John 8:56 seems to imply that this revelation to Abraham included the knowledge that the †Messiah would be his descendant.[22]

8:57 Jesus' opponents find this claim absolutely unbelievable, and they point to Jesus' age to show it: **You are not yet fifty years old and you have seen Abraham?** Once again, they think about Jesus in completely earthly terms and do not realize that there is more to him than his human origins, namely, his divinity.

22. So *Jubilees* 15:33–34; *Apocalypse of Abraham* 22–32; *4 Ezra* 13:12–15; see James L. Kugel, *The Bible as It Was* (Cambridge, MA: Belknap, 1997), 168–70; Louis Ginzberg, *The Legends of the Jews*, trans. Henrietta Szold (Philadelphia: Jewish Publication Society of America, 1968), 1:285.

8:58–59 The debate comes to a thunderous end with Jesus' solemn pronouncement: **Amen, amen, I say to you, before Abraham came to be, I AM.** By using the divine name, I AM, Jesus identifies himself with the God of Israel. Jesus can say that he existed before Abraham because he is the divine Word who "was in the beginning with God" (1:2).[23] Jesus' identity as I AM is fundamental to all the claims in the entire debate: his affiliation with the Father, his speaking the Father's words, and his saving people from spiritual death. After much misunderstanding, Jesus' opponents recognize the meaning of this claim. They think he is just a human being and not the God of Israel walking on earth as a man. Thus they think he commits blasphemy by making such a claim. According to Lev 24:16, blasphemy against God's name was a capital crime, which carried the penalty of death by stoning. Consequently, **they picked up stones to throw at him; but Jesus hid and went out of the temple area.**

23. Some ancient Christian interpreters read Gen 17 as †theophany of the divine Word to Abraham; see Irenaeus, *Against Heresies* 4.7.1–4; Tertullian, *Against Praxeas* 22.

The Light of the World: Illumination and Judgment

John 9:1–41

Ever since Jesus arrived in Jerusalem for Tabernacles, he has encountered a mixed response. Some people are sympathetic, while others are hostile. At the end of chapter 8, he has left the temple area after a heated exchange that culminated in an attempt to kill him. John 9 builds upon these contrasts with the account of a blind man. Jesus has previously identified himself as the light of the world (8:12), and John 9 displays in narrative form what it means for Jesus to be the light.[1] Two key aspects of Jesus' identity as the light are on display in this account: first, he is the revealer, who gives spiritual light and life; second, his presence becomes the occasion of judgment.

The Light Illumines One in Darkness (9:1–7)

[1]As he passed by he saw a man blind from birth. [2]His disciples asked him, "Rabbi, who sinned, this man or his parents, that he was born blind?" [3]Jesus answered, "Neither he nor his parents sinned; it is so that the works of God might be made visible through him. [4]We have to do the works of the one who sent me while it is day. Night is coming when no one can work. [5]While I am in the world, I am the light of the world." [6]When he had said this, he spat on the ground and made clay with the saliva, and smeared the

1. The main components of this argument are given in William M. Wright IV, *Rhetoric and Theology: Figural Reading of John 9*, Beihefte zur Zeitschrift für die neutestamentliche Wissenschaft 165 (Berlin: Walter de Gruyter, 2009).

clay on his eyes, [7]and said to him, "Go wash in the Pool of Siloam" (which means Sent). So he went and washed, and came back able to see.

OT: Exod 20:1–6; Deut 28:15–29; Isa 42:1–9

NT: Mark 8:22–26; Luke 13:1–5

Catechism: original sin, 396–406; liturgical signs and symbols, 1145–52; forgiveness of sins, 1229–33; punishments of sin, 1263–64; Christian initiation, 1472–73

Lectionary: 4th Sunday of Lent (Year A; optional Years B and C); For the Baptism of Children

9:1–2 After avoiding the attempt on his life (8:59), Jesus went through Jerusalem and **saw a man blind from birth**. His disciples ask him, **Who sinned, this man or his parents, that he was born blind?** Their question reflects the kind of theological thinking found in Deuteronomy, at an earlier stage of salvation history. According to this theology, God blesses people for their righteousness and punishes people for their sins in this present earthly life.[2] Among the various punishments for breaking the †covenant, Deut 28:28 mentions, "The LORD will strike you with madness, blindness and panic." In Exod 20:5, the Lord declares that he inflicts "punishment for their ancestors' wickedness on the children of those who hate me." Taken together, these texts illuminate the disciples' rationale: the question is not *whether* the man's blindness was caused by sin, but *whose* sin was the cause. The disciples could also be recalling Jesus' words to the formerly paralyzed man—"Look, you are well; do not sin any more, so that nothing worse may happen to you" (5:14)—interpreting them to imply that the man's paralysis was punishment for sin.

9:3 Like the blind man, the disciples' question reveals that they are somewhat in the dark themselves. Jesus first corrects their thinking about the man's blindness: **Neither he nor his parents sinned**. The man's blindness was not God's punishment for any sin. In Luke 13:1–5, Jesus observes that tragedies do occur in life, but this does not necessarily mean that God is directly punishing someone.[3] Instead, the man's blindness serves a larger purpose in God's plan: **so that the works of God might be made visible through him**. Jesus came to do God's work in the world: he reveals the Father and carries out the Father's plan of salvation so that sinners may have eternal life through him. Jesus will use the man's blindness as a means to manifest God's work.

9:4 Jesus stresses the urgency of doing God's work and includes his disciples in it by using the first-person plural: **We have to do the works of the one who sent**

2. Later biblical books (e.g., Job and Daniel) affirm the basic principle—God blesses righteousness and punishes wickedness—but qualify it in different ways (e.g., according to Daniel, these blessings and punishments are ultimately given in the afterlife).

3. Catechism 1472.

me while it is day. After Jesus returns to the Father, he will send the Holy Spirit to dwell within his disciples (14:16–18; 20:22), and the Church will continue his work in the world (see 14:12; 17:18). "The day" is whenever people can encounter the Father and his saving work done by Jesus and, by extension, the Church.[4] But since every life and the world as a whole will come to an end, this day will not go on forever: **Night is coming when no one can work**. Jesus and his disciples must be about the Father's work in the world; people's salvation depends on it.

9:5–7 The healing of the man born blind is a †sign, a perceptible disclosure of "the works of God" (9:3) done by Jesus, **the light of the world**. As in the accounts in Mark (7:31–37; 8:22–26), Jesus **spat on the ground and made clay with the saliva, and smeared the clay on** the blind man's **eyes**, and told him, **Go wash in the Pool of Siloam**.[5] Jesus' use of materials—spit, mud, water—underscores the materiality of this healing sign and subtly connects it with the †incarnation. Just as Jesus' flesh embodies and reveals his divinity, so also his perceptible signs disclose his divine identity and work.[6] Like other biblical figures, who faithfully do what God says without speaking (e.g., Abraham in Gen 22:1–3), the blind man unquestioningly carries out Jesus' instructions: **He went and washed, and came back able to see**.

By delivering this man from the darkness of his blindness, Jesus reveals that he, as the light of the world, delivers all who are in the spiritual darkness of sin and alienation from God. Jesus also shows that the time of salvation announced by Isaiah is present in his ministry, for the Servant of the Lord was called "to open the eyes of the blind" (Isa 42:7; see also 29:18; 35:5).

Reflection and Application (9:1–7)

In the Church's tradition, the healing of the man born blind has frequently been interpreted in terms of conversion, baptism, and spiritual transformation. The blind man signifies humanity afflicted by original sin ("blind from birth"). He receives sight after Jesus smears mud on his eyes (the same verb for "smearing" is used later for sacramental anointing with oil) and washes with water (as in baptism), and as we will see, the man progresses in his understanding of

4. Rudolf Schnackenburg, *The Gospel according to St. John*, vol. 2, *Commentary on Chapters 5–12*, trans. Cecily Hastings, Francis McDonagh, David Smith, and Richard Foley, SJ (New York: Seabury, 1980), 241–42.

5. The Hebrew of Isa 8:6 names Siloam as *shiloakh*. This word is related to the Hebrew verb *sh-l-kh*, which means "send." John connects the etymological meaning of Siloam as "sent" with Jesus, who was sent by the Father and performs the healing through the waters of Siloam.

6. Catechism 1151.

Fig. 7. Remains of the Pool of Siloam

Jesus. Accordingly, from its early centuries up to today, the Church proclaims this Gospel on the fourth Sunday of Lent, when catechumens are preparing for their baptism at the Easter Vigil. Saint Augustine writes,

> This blind man is the human race, for this blindness happened through sin in the first man from whom we all have taken the origin not only of death, but also of wickedness. For . . . the blindness is lack of faith and the enlightenment faith. . . .
>
> [Jesus] besmeared the eyes of the blind man. He was besmeared and yet did not see. He sent him to the pool which is called Siloam, . . . which is interpreted "Who has been sent." You already know who has been sent; for unless he had been sent, no one of us would be sent away from wickedness. Therefore, he washed his eyes in that pool which is interpreted "Who has been sent"; he was baptized in Christ. If then, when in some way he baptized him in himself, he then enlightened him; perhaps when he besmeared him, he made him a catechumen.[7]

The Questioning Begins (9:8–12)

[8]His neighbors and those who had seen him earlier as a beggar said, "Isn't this the one who used to sit and beg?" [9]Some said, "It is," but others said,

7. St. Augustine, *Tractates on John* 44.1–2.

"No, he just looks like him." He said, "I am." [10]So they said to him, "[So] how were your eyes opened?" [11]He replied, "The man called Jesus made clay and anointed my eyes and told me, 'Go to Siloam and wash.' So I went there and washed and was able to see." [12]And they said to him, "Where is he?" He said, "I don't know."

Lectionary: 4th Sunday of Lent (Year A; optional Years B and C)

As the light of the world, Jesus not only brings spiritual illumination and deliverance from darkness; he also effects judgment through people's responses to him. The theme of judgment begins to emerge in 9:8–12 as two courtroom elements appear: the questioning of the formerly blind man and his testimony about Jesus.

9:8–9

Starting in 9:8, the story follows the formerly blind man. Jesus does not reappear until 9:35. Just as the different groups at Tabernacles debated Jesus' identity (chap. 7), the man's **neighbors and those who had seen him earlier as a beggar** debate the man's own identity: **Isn't this the one who used to sit and beg?** Also like the groups at Tabernacles, the neighbors are divided in their conclusions: **Some said, "It is," but others said, "No, he just looks like him."** When the man speaks for the first time, he simply identifies himself: **I am** he.

9:10–12

With the man's identity determined, the neighbors begin another line of questioning: **How were your eyes opened?** The man responds by telling about the healing miracle: **The man called Jesus made clay and anointed my eyes and told me, "Go to Siloam and wash." So I went there and washed and was able to see**. Even though the man has not physically seen Jesus, he is a reliable witness because his telling corresponds to the account of the miracle in 9:6–7. But his affirmations about Jesus, while accurate, are rudimentary. He refers to his healer as **the man called Jesus**, and when asked about Jesus' whereabouts, he responds, **I don't know**.

The Pharisees Debate: Sin or Sign? (9:13–17)

[13]They brought the one who was once blind to the Pharisees. [14]Now Jesus had made clay and opened his eyes on a sabbath. [15]So then the Pharisees also asked him how he was able to see. He said to them, "He put clay on my eyes, and I washed, and now I can see." [16]So some of the Pharisees said, "This man is not from God, because he does not keep the sabbath." [But] others said, "How can a sinful man do such signs?" And there was a division among them. [17]So they said to the blind man again, "What do

you have to say about him, since he opened your eyes?" He said, "He is a prophet."

OT: 1 Kings 17:17–24; 2 Kings 5

NT: Luke 13:10–17

Catechism: the visible world, 346–48; signs of the kingdom, 547–49; divisions among Jewish authorities concerning Jesus, 595–96

Lectionary: 4th Sunday of Lent (Year A; optional Years B and C)

9:13–15 The neighbors bring the healed man **to the Pharisees**, who start to question him. John adds, **Jesus had made clay and opened his eyes on a sabbath.** Jesus' words and actions regarding the sabbath have been a divisive issue between him and his opponents (see 5:1–18; 7:21–24). Controversy over the sabbath reemerges here, and the specific issue seems to be the making of clay, which could qualify as kneading, an activity prohibited on the sabbath in the †Mishnah.[8]

Like the neighbors, **the Pharisees also asked him how he was able to see.** The healed man retells the healing miracle. With the †Pharisees now questioning him, the account looks even more like a judicial process. The man acts as a witness, who gives evidence about what happened to him. At a deeper level, the man is also an evangelist. Often, the Fourth Gospel uses "testify" as a synonym for "evangelize": sharing with others what Jesus has done for oneself.

9:16 After the man presents testimony to the Pharisees, they draw conclusions about Jesus. Even though he does not appear directly, Jesus remains the central topic of this judicial proceeding. The judicial atmosphere contributes to the demonstration of his identity as the light, whose coming effects judgment through the responses people make to him.

The Pharisees divide into two groups in their assessment of the evidence. They disagree over the nature of Jesus' actions and what they imply about him. One group concludes, **This man is not from God, because he does not keep the sabbath.** This group looks at Jesus' actions and sees a sabbath violation. Since they perceive Jesus' actions as a sin, they conclude that he is not from God. They are "judging by appearances" (7:24; 8:15), not perceiving the spiritual reality revealed through him and his perceptible actions. They believe he is just a man and not the Son, who rightfully gives life on the sabbath because he has the unique divine powers that operate even on the sabbath (5:19–21). Another group of Pharisees asks **how** Jesus could be **a sinful man** and still perform **such signs.** Note that this second group calls the healing a "sign," not a sin. While these Pharisees do not make a positive affirmation about Jesus, they are more

8. *Mishnah Shabbat* 7:2.

attuned to the nature of the healing miracle as a †sign, a perceptible disclosure of Jesus' spiritual identity and work.

These differences result in **a division** (Greek *schisma*) **among** the Pharisees. Some Pharisees, like Nicodemus (7:50–51), have been sympathetic to Jesus while others opposed him (7:47–49, 52). Now, like the crowd at Tabernacles (7:43), the Pharisees themselves are formally split over Jesus.[9] The Light of the World is effecting a judgment between people who respond to him in different ways.

9:17 Since the Pharisees do not agree, they ask the healed man what he thinks about Jesus, and he declares, **He is a prophet**. The man may be thinking of prophets like Elijah and Elisha who performed healing miracles through God's power (1 Kings 17:17–24; 2 Kings 5). By calling Jesus a prophet, the man progresses from his first affirmation about his healer, when he spoke only of "the man called Jesus" (9:11).

In the Dark (9:18–23)

[18]Now the Jews did not believe that he had been blind and gained his sight until they summoned the parents of the one who had gained his sight. [19]They asked them, "Is this your son, who you say was born blind? How does he now see?" [20]His parents answered and said, "We know that this is our son and that he was born blind. [21]We do not know how he sees now, nor do we know who opened his eyes. Ask him, he is of age; he can speak for himself." [22]His parents said this because they were afraid of the Jews, for the Jews had already agreed that if anyone acknowledged him as the Messiah, he would be expelled from the synagogue. [23]For this reason his parents said, "He is of age; question him."

NT: Luke 21:12–19; Acts 4:1–22; 2 Cor 11:23–28
Catechism: bearing witness to the truth, 2471–74
Lectionary: 4th Sunday of Lent (Year A; optional Years B and C)

9:18–19 Verses 18–23 play an important role in John's demonstration of Jesus as the light. The healed man, who testifies in Jesus' defense, does not appear at all in this subsection. Only the authorities who **did not believe** and the man's parents, who are afraid, appear. The light of the world effects judgment through peoples' responses to him; this section showcases those in the dark.

Those †Pharisees (whom John now calls **the †Jews**) who have concluded that Jesus is a sinner now take a new approach: they question whether a miracle

9. Catechism 595–96.

happened in the first place. If the man was never blind to begin with, then no †sign took place, and that would end the debate over whether Jesus is a sinner (9:16). They call the man's **parents** as witnesses and ask them, **Is this your son, who you say was born blind? How does he now see?** The phrasing, "who you say was born blind," hints at the Pharisees' skepticism and disbelief. They are trying to discredit both the miracle and the formerly blind man with testimony that he was not blind in the first place.

9:20–21 They ask the man's parents about three matters: first, whether he is their son; second, whether he was born blind; third, how he came to see. The parents address only the first two: **This is our son** and **he was born blind**. Thus the man's blindness is no longer in dispute. But his parents refuse to say anything about the healing or healer: **We do not know how he sees now, nor do we know who opened his eyes**. About these matters, they redirect the Pharisees to their son: **Ask him . . . ; he can speak for himself.**

9:22–23 John explains that the parents did not say anything about Jesus **because they were afraid of the Jews**. The man and his parents are themselves Jews, and like the Jewish crowd at Tabernacles, they are afraid of the Jewish authorities who oppose Jesus (7:11–13, 25). John elaborates: **The Jews had already agreed that if anyone acknowledged him as the Messiah, he would be expelled from the synagogue** (see John 12:42; 16:2; Luke 21:12–16).[10] The man's parents are afraid to say anything about Jesus because they do not want to lose their religious and social ties with their †synagogue community. By explaining the parents' motivation, John reveals a very unsettling dimension of their statement: **He is of age; question him**. By shifting the focus back to their son, his parents put him in jeopardy in order to protect themselves. They act out of fear and self-interest. Throughout John 9, the formerly blind man is the only one who testifies in Jesus' defense. By explaining the parents' motivation, John sets up a contrast between the parents' fearfulness and their son's courage.

Reflection and Application (9:18–23)

Faithfulness to Jesus sometimes comes at a high price. The New Testament gives many examples of people who meet trouble and hostility because of their faith in Jesus.[11] The formerly blind man is a model of bold witness to Christ, a model of evangelization, even in the face of opposition (Catechism 2471). In a world where hostility to religious beliefs and expression is rising, courageous

10. See "Historical Context" in the introduction to this volume.
11. Luke 21:16–19; John 16:1–4; Acts 4:1–22; 2 Cor 11:23–28; Heb 10:32–36.

witness becomes all the more important. The most radical witness to Christ is martyrdom (from the Greek *martyria*, meaning "witness"). While martyrdom may not be asked of all, this kind of radical faithfulness and testimony is the model to which all believers should aspire. As theologian Hans Urs von Balthasar writes, it "does not mean that every single Christian must suffer bloody martyrdom, but he must consider the entire case [i.e., martyrdom] as the external representation of the inner reality out of which he lives."[12] It is of the person with this kind of faithfulness that Jesus says, "I will give the victor the right to sit with me on my throne, as I myself first won the victory and sit with my Father on his throne" (Rev 3:21).

Sight and Blindness (9:24–34)

[24]So a second time they called the man who had been blind and said to him, "Give God the praise! We know that this man is a sinner." [25]He replied, "If he is a sinner, I do not know. One thing I do know is that I was blind and now I see." [26]So they said to him, "What did he do to you? How did he open your eyes?" [27]He answered them, "I told you already and you did not listen. Why do you want to hear it again? Do you want to become his disciples, too?" [28]They ridiculed him and said, "You are that man's disciple; we are disciples of Moses! [29]We know that God spoke to Moses, but we do not know where this one is from." [30]The man answered and said to them, "This is what is so amazing, that you do not know where he is from, yet he opened my eyes. [31]We know that God does not listen to sinners, but if one is devout and does his will, he listens to him. [32]It is unheard of that anyone ever opened the eyes of a person born blind. [33]If this man were not from God, he would not be able to do anything." [34]They answered and said to him, "You were born totally in sin, and are you trying to teach us?" Then they threw him out.

OT: Exod 3:4–10; Tob 2:9–10; 11:9–15
NT: Acts 4:13–22; 1 Cor 10:1–5
Catechism: theophanies and the law, 707–8
Lectionary: 4th Sunday of Lent (Year A; optional Years B and C)

9:24 The parents' testimony confirmed that something extraordinary had occurred. The man was born blind and, as all can observe, he now sees. The

12. Hans Urs von Balthasar, *The Moment of Christian Witness*, trans. Richard Beckley (San Francisco: Ignatius Press, 1994), 22.

authorities again call the man and solemnly command him to tell the truth: **Give God the praise!** (see Josh 7:19). They demand that the man agree with their conclusion: **We know that this man is a sinner** (see 9:16). Despite the man's testimony that Jesus healed him, which has been confirmed, these †Pharisees remain assured of their conclusion that Jesus is a sinner and not from God. The other Pharisees mentioned in 9:16, who were more sympathetic toward Jesus, have dropped out of the account.

9:25 Unlike his questioners, who know and are sure of their conclusion about Jesus, the healed man is less certain: **If he is a sinner, I do not know**. While he does not make a positive affirmation about Jesus, he does not agree with these Pharisees. He simply goes back to the evidence of what happened to him: **One thing I do know is that I was blind and now I see**.

9:26–27 Running out of options, the hostile Pharisees again ask the man to recount what happened to him: **What did he do to you? How did he open your eyes?** Having told the healing miracle twice (9:11, 15), the man does not retell it again but responds with the strong declaration: **I told you already and you did not listen**. He then asks, **Why do you want to hear it again? Do you want to become his disciples, too?** As the questioning goes on, the man becomes bolder in his speech about Jesus, and now, perhaps with a hint of sarcasm, he is questioning the Pharisees! His "sight" into what the miraculous †sign reveals about Jesus is growing.

9:28–29 As the tension between the authorities and the man grows, the contrast between them becomes sharper. The Pharisees **ridiculed him** and set up two issues for contrast. The first is discipleship: **You are that man's disciple; we are disciples of Moses!** In other words, they claim to be good Jews and that the healed man is not.[13] Stung by the man's questions, they do not refer to Jesus by name but only as "that man."

The second point of contrast is religious authority. The Pharisees appeal to Moses as an authoritative teacher: **We know that God spoke to Moses**. In the †Torah, God speaks to Moses on many occasions (e.g., Exod 3:4–10; 33:7–23; 34:27–35). The Torah is the ultimate authority for the Pharisees and the basis on which they justify their conclusions about Jesus. Just as the Pharisees said, "We know that this man is a sinner" (9:24), so now they say, "We know that God spoke to Moses." Their words, however, are full of †irony. They appeal to the authority of Moses, and yet, as Jesus said of Moses, "He wrote about me"

13. This contrast between the discipleship of Moses and the discipleship of Jesus may reflect the experiences of later first-century Jewish and Christian groups, defining themselves against each other over their beliefs about Jesus.

(5:46). God did speak to Moses, and Moses bears witness to Jesus. Moreover, the Fourth Gospel hints that the divine Word was active in the Old Testament (12:41; see 1 Cor 10:1–5; Catechism 707). John implies that when God spoke to Moses, it was the divine Word, later to become †incarnate in Jesus, who spoke to Moses (see comments on 5:37). In this light, the Pharisees' appeal to Moses as their authority is ironic, since they do not recognize that the God who spoke to Moses has become incarnate in Jesus. Furthermore, they contrast their knowledge about God's revelation to Moses with their ignorance about Jesus: **We do not know where this one is from**. This comment recalls the extensive discussion of Jesus' identity in John 7–8, where Jesus has repeatedly taught that his origin is with the Father (7:28–29; 8:28, 38). By professing ignorance of Jesus' origins, the Pharisees show their ignorance of his divine identity and perhaps a refusal to come to an obvious conclusion.

When Jesus first identified himself as the light of the world, he said, "Whoever follows me will not walk in darkness, but will have the light of life" (8:12). This exchange between the Pharisees and the healed man displays this distinction in action. As the questioning unfolds, some Pharisees become increasingly opposed to Jesus: they see his actions as a sin, conclude that he cannot be from God, and affiliate themselves with Moses and against Jesus. The Pharisees show themselves to be blind to Jesus the light.

9:30 By contrast, the formerly blind man has progressed considerably in his affirmation of Jesus from his first remarks in 9:9–12. His speech about Jesus has become more substantial. His boldness toward the Pharisees has also grown. He demonstrates bold, frank speech, an ancient virtue that was previously attributed to Jesus (7:26; see Acts 4:13–22, with the Greek term for "boldness" in 4:13).[14] The bold speech of Jesus and the healed man stands in sharp contrast to the fearful silence of others, such as the Tabernacle pilgrims (7:13) and the man's parents (9:22).

The man responds with astonishment: **This is what is so amazing, that you do not know where he is from, yet he opened my eyes**. He is baffled that the Pharisees do not recognize Jesus on the basis of what he has done. Unlike the Pharisees, the man, who had been blind, "sees" the healing miracle; he recognizes it as a sign revealing Jesus' identity. Consequently, he can see, although not perfectly, that it signifies something extraordinary about Jesus.

9:31–33 The man now formulates an argument in Jesus' defense. He introduces the principle that **God** only **listens** to **one** who **is devout and does his will**. Jesus could not have done this healing if he were a sinner because God would

14. Similarly Origen, *Fragments on the Gospel of John* 71.

Saint Thomas Aquinas on What Causes Faith

Why is it that, while the healed man and the Pharisees are confronted with the same miracle, he believes and they do not? This kind of situation is not uncommon. People encounter the truths of faith, for example, in the teaching or life of a saint. Some people are moved to faith by the saint's example of holiness or miracles but others are not. Why is this so?

Saint Thomas Aquinas explains that both an external cause (e.g., preaching) and an internal cause (the grace of the Holy Spirit) are needed:

> As regards . . . man's assent to the things which are of faith, we may observe a twofold cause, one of external inducement, such as seeing a miracle, or being persuaded by someone to embrace the faith: neither of which is a sufficient cause, since of those who see the same miracle, or who hear the same sermon, some believe, and some do not. Hence we must assert another internal cause, which . . . is from God moving man inwardly by grace. . . . To believe does indeed depend on the will of the believer: but man's will does need to be prepared by God with grace.[a]

Aquinas teaches that faith is a gift from God, and the reception of faith requires both an external and an internal cause. The external cause would be the contents of faith being presented to someone from the outside, such as in a homily or miracle. But that external content needs to be received by a well-disposed heart, which is first prepared by an internal cause. This internal cause is God's grace, which prepares someone to receive faith and can itself be accepted or rejected.

a. St. Thomas Aquinas, *Summa theologica* 2–2, q. 6, a. 1. See also his *Lectures on Romans* 331.

not have listened to him. He strengthens his argument by appealing to the unprecedented character of the miracle: **It is unheard of that anyone ever opened the eyes of a person born blind**. While Scripture contains a report of a blinded person having his sight miraculously restored (Tob 11:9–15), there is no account of sight being given to a person born blind. No one has ever done what Jesus has done. Consequently, the man reaches a conclusion favorable to Jesus: **If this man were not from God, he would not be able to do anything**. The man's conclusion is a double negative, not a robust profession of faith (see 9:35–38 below). He may be very close to faith in Jesus, but he is not quite there yet.

9:34

The Pharisees have had enough of the man and slander him: **You were born totally in sin**. Like the disciples in 9:2, they view the man's congenital blindness as a punishment for sin—an interpretation that Jesus has rejected (9:3). Previously the Pharisees said that the Jewish crowd, "which does not know the law, is accursed" (7:49), and now an ordinary Jewish man, whom they regard as a sinner, has the audacity and arrogance to debate them, the learned religious authorities, on theological matters: **Are you trying to teach us?** With contempt and perhaps exasperation, the Pharisees **threw him out** of their presence.

The Fullness of Sight (9:35–38)

[35]When Jesus heard that they had thrown him out, he found him and said, "Do you believe in the Son of Man?" [36]He answered and said, "Who is he, sir, that I may believe in him?" [37]Jesus said to him, "You have seen him and the one speaking with you is he." [38]He said, "I do believe, Lord," and he worshiped him.

OT: Dan 7:13–14
Catechism: why the word became flesh, 456–60; worshiping God alone, 2084–86
Lectionary: 4th Sunday of Lent (Year A; optional Years B and C)

9:35

Jesus now reappears on the scene. As he took the initiative in 9:1, Jesus seeks the healed man out and asks, **Do you believe in the Son of Man?** In the Gospel, this title designates Jesus as the †incarnate revelation of God, God's presence in the flesh (see sidebar on p. 52). Although the man may not immediately grasp the depths of the question, Jesus is asking whether the man believes that he is the incarnate Word of God.

9:36–37

The man responds with a question of his own: **Who is he, sir, that I may believe in him?** He has become increasingly well-disposed to Jesus over the course of the chapter, as is evident in his improving descriptions of Jesus: "the man called Jesus" (9:11), "a prophet" (9:17), "from God" (9:33). However, he has not yet made a profession of faith. Jesus now reveals himself as the †Son of Man: **You have seen him and the one speaking with you is he**. The incarnation means that God speaks and acts directly in Jesus, and it is fitting that language of sensation is used in Jesus' revelation to the man: the man *sees* Jesus and implicitly *hears* Jesus *speaking* with him.

9:38

Only in this scene does the healed man see Jesus with his own eyes and converse with him. It is this personal interaction with Jesus that enables him to make a profession of faith in him: **I do believe**. The man addresses Jesus as **Lord** and gives him the response that is proper to God alone: the man **worshiped him**.

In this chapter, the man has started in physical blindness, and Jesus, the light, has not only given him physical sight but, what is more important, the spiritual sight of faith. Faith in the incarnation involves spiritual sight, "the eyes of faith," which discern God and his work in material realities, like the flesh of Jesus, the healing miracle, and—in the later context of the Church—the sacraments.

Reflection and Application (9:35–38)

The Christian belief that God became human in Jesus of Nazareth is astounding. Since God is absolutely perfect and complete in himself, God does not need anything, including the created world.[15] God does not owe us anything nor does he get anything out of us. Everything God does for us is an utterly selfless gift of love. Moreover, God did not have to save us once we sinned and turned away from him. But God *chose* to save us, and he did so by becoming one of us and dying as a man on the cross. The incarnation reveals how great is God's love for us.

The Verdict (9:39–41)

[39]Then Jesus said, "I came into this world for judgment, so that those who do not see might see, and those who do see might become blind."

[40]Some of the Pharisees who were with him heard this and said to him, "Surely we are not also blind, are we?" [41]Jesus said to them, "If you were blind, you would have no sin; but now you are saying, 'We see,' so your sin remains."

OT: Isa 43:1–8
Catechism: to judge the living and the dead, 678–82
Lectionary: 4th Sunday of Lent (Year A; optional Years B and C)

9:39 Jesus' concluding pronouncement, **I came into this world for judgment**, reveals what has been taking place all through this chapter. He alludes to his earlier self-identification as "the light of the world" (9:5), because his identity as light is related to judgment (3:19–21). Jesus' presence in the world prompts a response

15. Robert Sokolowski, *The God of Faith and Reason* (Notre Dame, IN: University of Notre Dame, 1981), 1–11, 31–40.

from people and produces a distinction between those who respond positively and those who respond negatively to him. Peoples' responses to Jesus in the present determine the verdict of their end-time judgment (5:24; 12:47–48).[16]

Jesus came **so that those who do not see might see**. On the one hand, to those who recognize their own spiritual blindness, their own sinfulness and need for salvation, and receive him, Jesus imparts the spiritual illumination of faith and "the light of life" (8:12) delivering them from darkness. Jesus gave the blind man physical sight, and led him to the spiritual sight of faith (9:35–38). On the other hand, Jesus' coming means that **those who do see . . . become blind**. Those who reject Jesus, exemplified here by the antagonistic †Pharisees, are rendered spiritually blind, because they do not perceive the light. As the Lord says of those refusing redemption, they are "blind though they have eyes" (Isa 43:8).

Jesus' pronouncement reveals the †irony in the preceding events. John has presented 9:8–34 as a judicial trial, complete with witnesses and conclusions drawn from testimony. However, since Jesus comes into the world as the light and peoples' responses to him constitute judgment on themselves, ironically, the ones who are really on trial here are the Pharisees and the healed man, not Jesus. The responses of the individuals display the judging effect of Jesus as the light, revealing those who walk in light or in darkness, those who see or are blind spiritually.

9:40–41 Hearing Jesus' declaration, **the Pharisees**, who obviously can see physically, want to know if Jesus is including them among the spiritually **blind**. **Jesus** begins, **If you were blind**—that is, if they recognized their own need for Jesus—they would approach him, believe, and receive his gift, to which Jesus is implicitly calling them here. Then, **you would have no sin**, you would not be in the spiritual condition of separation from God, rooted in the willful rejection of his Word (see sidebar on p. 163). But these Pharisees resolutely reject Jesus: **Now you are saying, "We see," so your sin remains**. Since they choose not to believe in Jesus, they are unable to see the light and thus remain in darkness.

16. Catechism 679.

The Good Shepherd and the Festival of Dedication

John 10:1–42

John 10 contains two major sections, both of which take place in Jerusalem. First, the Good Shepherd Discourse (10:1–21) continues the story in John 9. This story features a series of contrasts, including faith and unbelief, sight and blindness, and the relationship between different religious authorities and their disciples. John 9 ended with the formerly blind man professing faith in Jesus and Jesus pronouncing the †Pharisees, the religious authorities, to be spiritually blind on account of their unbelief in him. The Good Shepherd Discourse develops the theme of religious teachers and disciples, but with a different set of images: shepherds and sheep.

The second section (10:22–42) recounts an incident several months later at the Festival of the Dedication (Hanukkah). The two exchanges between Jesus and the Jewish authorities at this festival revolve around Jesus' union with the Father.

The Shepherd Discourse I: Introducing the Imagery (10:1–6)

[1]"Amen, amen, I say to you, whoever does not enter a sheepfold through the gate but climbs over elsewhere is a thief and a robber. [2]But whoever enters through the gate is the shepherd of the sheep. [3]The gatekeeper opens it for him, and the sheep hear his voice, as he calls his own sheep by name and leads them out. [4]When he has driven out all his own, he walks ahead of them, and the sheep follow him, because they recognize his

voice. [5]But they will not follow a stranger; they will run away from him, because they do not recognize the voice of strangers." [6]Although Jesus used this figure of speech, they did not realize what he was trying to tell them.

OT: Ps 23; 95; Ezek 34
NT: Matt 9:35–38
Catechism: the Church as sheepfold, 754
Lectionary: 4th Sunday of Easter (Year A)

The Good Shepherd Discourse divides into two sections (10:1–6, 7–18). In the first section, Jesus gives his teaching in "veiled speech" (10:6, our translation), using the imagery of sheep and shepherds, but he does not indicate what these images mean. After John specifies that Jesus' hearers did not understand him (10:6), Jesus moves to the second section of the discourse (10:7–18), where he interprets the meaning of the shepherd, sheep, gate, and pasture given in the first section.

10:1–2 Still addressing the †Pharisees from John 9, Jesus introduces two opposing parties: **a thief and a robber** against **the shepherd**. He first contrasts them in regard to entering the **sheepfold**, a pen constructed either from natural materials in the countryside or as part of a domestic dwelling space.[1] The thief **does not** go in **through the gate**, but **climbs over elsewhere**. The characterization of such a person as a "thief and a robber" suggests a desire to exploit the sheep for personal benefit. The term for "robber" implies violence, for elsewhere it describes Barabbas the "revolutionary" (John 18:40) and the two criminals crucified with Jesus (Matt 27:38, 44). This imagery also resonates with Ezekiel's indictment of Judah's leadership for their self-serving exploitation of God's people (Ezek 34:2–8). Unlike the thief and robber, the one with proper access to the **sheep**, who **enters through the gate,** is the **shepherd**. The mention of sheep develops the theme of discipleship from John 9:28.

10:3–4 The **gatekeeper opens** the door **for** the shepherd. Although no real clue is given as to what the gatekeeper signifies, a tentative but plausible case can be made for the Father as the gatekeeper. The gatekeeper gives the shepherd access to the sheep, and it is the Father who has given the disciples to Jesus (10:29; see also 6:37; 17:6, 9, 11–12, 24). The gatekeeper opens the gate through which the shepherd leads out his sheep to the pasture of eternal life (see 10:27–28), and it is the Father who has sent Jesus into the world to save it and give eternal life (3:16–17).

1. Craig S. Keener, *The Gospel of John: A Commentary* (Peabody, MA: Hendrickson, 2003), 1:809–12.

Fig. 8. A sheepfold

Here several elements in Jesus' words resonate with the theme of leaders and disciples. First, **walks ahead** and **follow** characterize the relationship of the teacher, who leads, and the disciples, who follow (John 13:36–37; 15:20). Second, the Greek verb for **driven out** was used in 9:34, when the †Pharisees "threw . . . out" the formerly blind man. This creates a contrast between Jesus and the Pharisees as religious leaders. Whereas the Pharisees angrily *ejected* the healed man, Jesus *leads* his sheep out to good pasture, to eternal life (10:9, 28). Third, Jesus says, **The sheep follow him, because they recognize his voice**. A true disciple is one who hears and receives Jesus' revelatory word: "Whoever belongs to God hears the words of God" (8:47). Similarly, Jesus tells Pilate, "Everyone who belongs to the truth listens to my voice" (18:37). Fourth, Jesus **calls his own sheep by name**. In the Gospel, Jesus calls several disciples by name—Peter (1:42), Lazarus (11:43), Mary Magdalene (20:16)—who hear and respond positively to him. Similarly, the formerly blind man became a believer in Jesus after he saw Jesus and heard him "speaking" (9:37) to him.

10:5 The sheep follow the shepherd and **will not follow a stranger . . . because they do not recognize the voice of strangers**. The shepherd and the sheep know each other personally. The sheep have only one shepherd and are single-minded in their devotion and attentiveness to him. They do not listen to any other leader because no other knows them as their shepherd does.

Shepherd Imagery in the Bible

BIBLICAL BACKGROUND

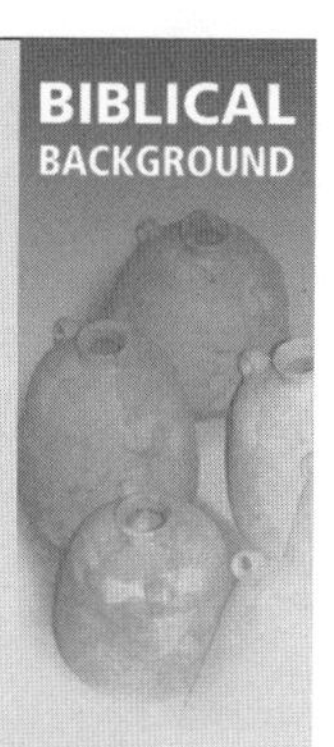

The shepherd is a common image for leadership in the ancient world. Shepherd imagery appears throughout Scripture to depict God's people (the sheep) and their leaders (the shepherds). The primary leader and shepherd of God's people is God himself. Psalm 23 famously begins, "The Lord is my shepherd; / there is nothing I lack," and in Isa 40:11, the prophet characterizes God as redeemer in this way: "Like a shepherd he feeds his flock; / in his arms he gathers the lambs, / Carrying them in his bosom, / leading the ewes with care." The leaders whom God appoints over his people are also called shepherds (2 Sam 5:2; Ps 78:70–72; Jer 3:15; 23:4). As shepherds, these human leaders are to care for God's people; the people are *God's* sheep, not the possession of the appointed leadership. As Ps 95:7 puts it: "He is our God, / we are the people he shepherds, / the sheep in his hands."

When the human leadership fails to care for God's sheep and leads them astray from God, it comes under God's judgment (see Jer 23:1). Ezekiel indicts the authorities in Judah for their self-interest, exploitation of God's people, and failure to care for the sheep (34:2–10). In response to their failures, the Lord declares, "I will . . . put a stop to their shepherding my flock, so that these shepherds will no longer pasture them" (Ezek 34:10). He adds, "I myself will search for my sheep and examine them" (34:11). Other texts speak of God appointing a faithful shepherd, a new king in the lineage of David, to care for his redeemed people (Jer 23:4–5; Ezek 34:23; Mic 5:3).[a] In the New Testament, Jesus uses shepherd imagery in regard to himself and his mission (Matt 9:35–36; 25:32; Luke 15:3–7), and this imagery is also used of the appointed leaders of the Church (John 21:15–19; Acts 20:28–31; Eph 4:11; 1 Pet 5:1–4). The same imagery continues in Church life, where heads of parishes are called "pastors" and bishops carry a crosier, a staff that resembles a shepherd's crook.

a. See the noncanonical *Psalms of Solomon* 17:40.

10:6 Jesus spoke with a **figure of speech**, a term that ordinarily means "proverb" (Prov 1:1 †LXX) or "wise saying" (Sir 6:35; 8:8; 2 Pet 2:22). In John, it designates figurative or veiled speech, which is not immediately understood (16:25, 29). Once again, Jesus' audience does not understand **what he was trying to tell them**.

Reflection and Application (10:1–6)

The relationship between Jesus and his disciples, like a shepherd to his sheep, is worth pondering. As the shepherd knows his sheep by name, the Lord Jesus knows each one of his disciples intimately and personally. The psalmist describes this personal knowing: "LORD, you have probed me, you know me . . . / Even before a word is on my tongue, / LORD, you know it all. / Behind and before you encircle me / and rest your hand upon me" (139:1, 4–5). This relationship starts with God's initiative, for he first calls each by name just as with Abraham (Gen 22:1), Moses (Exod 3:4), and Samuel (1 Sam 3:10). When the disciple hears the shepherd's voice, he responds with attentiveness and obedience. This response arises from the personal commitment and relationship to Jesus, who first knew and called each one. Jesus calls his disciples to follow him to the good pasture of eternal life, which he shares with the Father and the Holy Spirit.

The Shepherd Discourse II: Interpreting the Imagery (10:7–21)

[7]So Jesus said again, "Amen, amen, I say to you, I am the gate for the sheep. [8]All who came [before me] are thieves and robbers, but the sheep did not listen to them. [9]I am the gate. Whoever enters through me will be saved, and will come in and go out and find pasture. [10]A thief comes only to steal and slaughter and destroy; I came so that they might have life and have it more abundantly. [11]I am the good shepherd. A good shepherd lays down his life for the sheep. [12]A hired man, who is not a shepherd and whose sheep are not his own, sees a wolf coming and leaves the sheep and runs away, and the wolf catches and scatters them. [13]This is because he works for pay and has no concern for the sheep. [14]I am the good shepherd, and I know mine and mine know me, [15]just as the Father knows me and I know the Father; and I will lay down my life for the sheep. [16]I have other sheep that do not belong to this fold. These also I must lead, and they will hear my voice, and there will be one flock, one shepherd. [17]This is why the Father loves me, because I lay down my life in order to take it up again. [18]No one takes it from me, but I lay it down on my own. I have power to lay it down, and power to take it up again. This command I have received from my Father."

[19]Again there was a division among the Jews because of these words. [20]Many of them said, "He is possessed and out of his mind; why listen to him?" [21]Others said, "These are not the words of one possessed; surely a demon cannot open the eyes of the blind, can he?"

OT: Jer 23:1–8; Ezek 34

NT: Matt 11:25–27; 1 Tim 2:3–6; Heb 13:20–21; 1 Pet 5:1–4

Catechism: Jesus' self-offering, 606–9; Church as sheepfold, 754

Lectionary: 4th Sunday of Easter (Year B); Common of Pastors; Holy Orders; For the Dead; For Unity of Christians; Sacred Heart

Jesus now interprets the shepherd imagery introduced in 10:1–5 to teach about his identity as the good shepherd who was sent by the Father to lay down his life for the good of his sheep.

10:7 Beginning with another **Amen, amen, I say to you** (see 10:1), Jesus makes his third "I am + predicate" statement in the Gospel: **I am the gate for the sheep**. In the first part of the discourse, Jesus spoke of the opened gate as the way by which the shepherd leads his sheep out (10:2–4). Now he develops this image: **Whoever enters through me will be saved, and will come in and go out and find pasture.** Jesus is the open door through which we enter into salvation and good pasture, which he later identifies as "eternal life" (10:28). His claim to be the gate is very similar to his self-identification in 14:6, "I am the way. . . . No one comes to the Father except through me." By leading his sheep to the pasture of eternal life, Jesus performs the actions of the Lord in Ezek 34. Since the leadership of Judah failed his people, the Lord says, "I myself will search for my sheep. . . . In good pastures I will pasture them" (Ezek 34:11, 14).

10:8–9 Jesus also develops the imagery of the thief and robber, who do not enter through the gate (10:1): **All who came [before me] are thieves and robbers.**[2] This verse created some interpretive difficulty for the early Church, because, as St. Augustine points out, Jesus is surely not indicting the great biblical heroes and the faithful leadership of Israel who came before him as thieves.[3] Most likely, Jesus is criticizing any religious authority who rivals or challenges him as leader of the sheep, and in the Gospel's immediate context, it would apply to the †Pharisees of John 9. The remark, **The sheep did not listen to them**, links the thief and robber to the "stranger" (10:5), reinforcing their status as opponents of Jesus the shepherd.

10:10 Jesus develops the contrast between the thief and the shepherd in regard to their actions toward the flock. The activities of the **thief** are harmful to the sheep: he **comes only to steal and slaughter and destroy** (the Greek word translated as "destroy" is *apollymi*). By contrast, Jesus' mission is life-giving: **I came so that they might have life** (Greek *zōē*) **and have it more abundantly**. This contrast illustrates the Evangelist's teaching about why Jesus came into the world: "God so loved the world that he gave his only Son, so that everyone who believes in him might not perish [*apollymi*] but might have eternal life [*zōē*]" (3:16). The Father offers an infinity of life and love to humanity through Jesus.

2. The words "before me" are bracketed in the NABRE because they are absent in some early Greek manuscripts of John but present in others.

3. St. Augustine, *Tractates on John* 45.8–9.

10:11 With his fourth "I am + predicate" title, Jesus declares, **I am the good shepherd**, and he reveals how he makes this life available in overflowing abundance: **A good shepherd lays down his life for the sheep**. We should appreciate how startling this statement is. What shepherd would sacrifice his own life for his livestock? He can acquire more sheep, but he has only one life. And yet this is precisely what Jesus says that he does for his sheep, for us. Whereas the thief seeks personal gain at the sheep's expense (see Jer 23:1–8; Ezek 34), the good shepherd does the opposite: he allows himself to be harmed for the sheep's gain. This is precisely what makes the shepherd "good." The Greek more literally reads "noble shepherd."[4] This expression captures the heroic and praiseworthy dimensions of Jesus' actions. Jesus makes a free, voluntary gift of his life on the cross, through which his sheep come to receive life in abundance (see Heb 13:20–21). His self-gift on the cross is a perfect act of love, the perfect example of his teaching that laying down one's life for another is the greatest expression of love (15:13).[5] Self-sacrificial love is the defining standard for all disciples of Jesus (15:12–14, 17), and especially for those appointed to be shepherds of his flock (21:15–19).

10:12–13 Jesus contrasts the good shepherd and the **hired man**.[6] Unlike the good shepherd, who "calls his own sheep by name" (10:3), the hired man **is not a shepherd and** his **sheep are not his own**. His relationship to the flock is mercenary. Thus the good shepherd and the hired man act differently in face of danger to the flock. The danger comes from the **wolf**, the typical threat to sheep (Sir 13:16; Matt 7:15; 10:16). The principal opponent of Jesus is the devil; he is "the ruler of this world [who] will be driven out" (12:31) when Jesus lays down his life. Christian tradition has likewise interpreted the wolf in 10:12 as the devil, the enemy who seeks the complete ruin of humanity.[7] When confronted with the threat, the hired man abandons **the sheep**, and **the wolf catches and scatters them**. The hired man is a self-interested coward: he **works for pay and has no concern for the sheep**. The good shepherd, however, is selfless and courageous because he lays down his life for his own sheep.

10:14–15 The personal relationship between **the good shepherd** and his sheep has mystical depths. Jesus compares the mutual knowing of shepherd and sheep (**I know mine and mine know me**) to the mutual knowing within God (**just**

4. Jerome H. Neyrey, SJ, "The 'Noble' Shepherd in John 10: Cultural and Rhetorical Background," *Journal of Biblical Literature* 120 (2001): 267–91.

5. Catechism 606–9.

6. On this contrast, see Neyrey, "'Noble' Shepherd," 281–83, to which we are indebted.

7. Augustine, *Tractates on John* 46.8–9; Cyril of Alexandria, *Commentary on John* 6; Gregory the Great, *Homily on the Gospels* 15; Thomas Aquinas, *Commentary on John* 10.3, section 1405.

as the Father knows me and I know the Father). From all eternity, the Father gives all that he is to the Son (5:26) and "shows him everything" (5:20). The Son, who alone has seen and knows the Father, reveals the Father and does his work in the world (1:18; 8:38; see Matt 11:25–27). The relationship of Father and Son is one of unity (10:30) and eternal love (5:20; 17:24), which is the most radical self-giving (3:35; 17:10). Similarly, Jesus knows his disciples in the most personal and intimate way. He **will lay down** his **life for the sheep** in an act of perfect love and draw them into communion with himself and thus with the Father (15:1–8; 17:22–23).

10:16 The sum total of Jesus' disciples will include more than his present band. These are **other sheep that do not belong to this fold**. "Other sheep" refers in a general way to later generations of believers (20:29–31), who are in great measure Gentiles, gathered to the God of Israel through faith in Jesus (see sidebar on p. 213). Jesus will **lead** these sheep and, just like the present flock, which listens and follows (10:4), these future believers will **hear** his **voice**. Before his passion begins, Jesus prays for these future believers: "those who will believe in me through their word, so that they may all be one" (17:20–21). In both John 10 and 17, the end result is the same: the unity of believers gathered together with Jesus the shepherd (**one shepherd**) and with each other (**one flock**).

10:17 Jesus says, **This is why the Father loves me, because I lay down my life**. The point is not that the Father's love for Jesus is the consequence of Jesus' giving his life, as if the Father would not love him if he did not give his life. Rather, the self-giving love of Jesus, manifested in his laying down his life for the sheep, *illustrates* the Father's love (see 3:16–17). But the cross, in itself, does not constitute the totality of his saving work. Jesus lays down his life **in order to take it up again**. His self-gift does not end in death but in the glorified life of the resurrection, of which he gives believers a share (6:39–40).

10:18 Jesus' giving of his life on the cross is a perfect gift: **I lay it down on my own**. No one forces Jesus onto the cross or **takes** his life **from** him. His statement, **I have power to lay it down, and power to take it up again**, refers to God's sovereign power over life and death, which the Father and the Son both have (5:21–22, 26). Since Jesus has the power of God, he has the power to overcome his own death in the resurrection.

The **Father** has given Jesus the **command** to lay down his life for the sheep and take it up again. Underlying this command is the Father's love for the world: God "wills everyone to be saved and to come to knowledge of the truth" (1 Tim 2:4). By laying down his life and rising from the dead, Jesus obediently fulfills the Father's command and reveals to the world his love and his desire to save it (3:16–17).

10:19–21 For the third time, **there was a division among the Jews** (see 7:43; 9:16). When some hear Jesus claiming this power to take up his life after laying it down, they make a familiar charge: he is **possessed and out of his mind** (see 7:20; 8:48, 52). Others disagree, because Jesus opened **the eyes of the blind**. These people are thinking about Jesus in light of his miraculous †signs, as did the formerly blind man: "It is unheard of that anyone ever opened the eyes of a person born blind. If this man were not from God, he would not be able to do anything" (9:32–33).

Reflection and Application (10:7–21)

The shepherd's heart must be one of self-sacrificing love and service, and the sheep must be faithful, trusting, docile, and obedient. Preaching on this text, Pope St. Gregory the Great holds up the different figures as models for his audience's self-examination. He urges clergy to follow the example of Christ in his total devotion to the sheep: "We are to devote our external goods to his sheep in mercy; then, if it should be necessary, we are to offer even our death for these same sheep." Moreover, he warns clergy to avoid being a hireling who "is eager for earthly advantages, rejoices in the honor of preferment, feeds on temporal gain, and enjoys the deference offered him by other people" and, when the wolf appears, remains "silent" (see 1 Pet 5:1–5). Christ's sheep must be obedient in faith and love and must long for heaven more than all worldly things. Thus he exhorts us: "Let us enkindle our hearts, my friends, let our faith grow warm again for what it believes, let our desire for heavenly things take fire. To love thus is to be already on the way."[8]

At the Festival of Hanukkah (10:22–30)

[22]The feast of the Dedication was then taking place in Jerusalem. It was winter. [23]And Jesus walked about in the temple area on the Portico of Solomon. [24]So the Jews gathered around him and said to him, "How long are you going to keep us in suspense? If you are the Messiah, tell us plainly." [25]Jesus answered them, "I told you and you do not believe. The works I do

8. Gregory the Great, *Homilies on the Gospels* 15, in *Forty Gospel Homilies*, trans. Dom David Hurst (Kalamazoo, MI: Cistercian Publications, 1990), 107.

Festival of the Dedication

BIBLICAL BACKGROUND

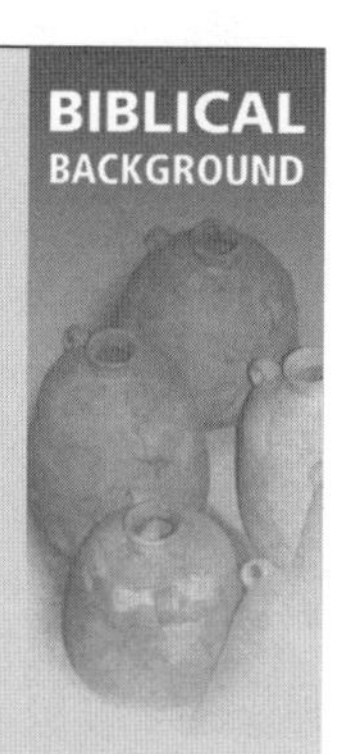

The Festival of the Dedication is more commonly known by its Hebrew name *Hanukkah* ("Dedication"). In 168 BC, the land of Judah was ruled over by the Greco-Syrian king Antiochus IV "Epiphanes." He started a massive persecution of the Jews, outlawing Jewish religious practices under pain of death and desecrating the temple by setting up in it a blasphemous statue of a pagan god. This sparked outrage among some Jews, leading to an armed Jewish rebellion called the Maccabean revolt, after the leader of the rebellion, a man named Judas, who was nicknamed Maccabeus, or "the Hammer." A few years into the rebellion, the Jewish fighters recaptured the temple. They purified and rededicated it, making it suitable for worship once again. A joyous eight-day festival, similar to Tabernacles, was instituted to celebrate the temple's rededication and to praise God for victory and the restoration of worship (1 Macc 4:55–56, 59; 2 Macc 1:9, 18). A custom of lighting candles developed in Jewish tradition in connection with the relighting of the temple lamps.[a]

a. Josephus, *Jewish Antiquities* 12.7.7; *b. Shabbat* 21b; Lawrence H. Schiffman, *Texts and Traditions: A Source Reader for the Study of Second Temple and Rabbinic Judaism* (Hoboken, NJ: Ktav, 1998), 711–12.

in my Father's name testify to me. [26]But you do not believe, because you are not among my sheep. [27]My sheep hear my voice; I know them, and they follow me. [28]I give them eternal life, and they shall never perish. No one can take them out of my hand. [29]My Father, who has given them to me, is greater than all, and no one can take them out of the Father's hand. [30]The Father and I are one."

OT: Ps 23; 2 Macc 10:1–8
NT: Luke 22:66–71; Acts 3:1–11
Catechism: Trinity, 253–60
Lectionary: Fourth Sunday of Easter (Year C)

10:22 The narrative jumps forward several months to the Feast of the **Dedication**, which was celebrated in **winter**, roughly during December (the Jewish month of Chislev). Dedication was an eight-day festival, which celebrated the rededication of the temple during the Maccabean revolt. Once again, John connects Jesus to a Jewish liturgical festival.

10:23 During the festival, **Jesus** was walking in the temple's **Portico of Solomon**. Built into the temple's outer walls were long, columned porches that opened up to the temple plaza. The Portico of Solomon was built into the temple's eastern wall and was thought to have been built by King Solomon, who constructed the first Jerusalem temple (see Acts 3:1–11).[9] According to Raymond Brown, this detail about Jesus' location makes historical sense: "At this winter season, when the cold winds sweep in from the east across the great desert, we find Jesus in the east portico of the Temple, the only one of the porticoes whose closed side would protect it from the east wind."[10]

10:24 The †**Jews** encircle Jesus and ask about his identity: **If you are the Messiah, tell us plainly**. The question of whether Jesus was the †Messiah came up repeatedly during Tabernacles (7:26–27, 31, 40–43). The crowds had debated this question among themselves, and now the **Jews**, here perhaps temple authorities, put the question directly to Jesus. Their question, "Are you the Messiah?," is the same one put to Jesus by Caiaphas in the †Synoptic accounts of Jesus' trial before the †Sanhedrin (Matt 26:63–65; Mark 14:61–62; Luke 22:66–67). They ask for an answer in plain speech, unlike the veiled, figurative speech in the Shepherd Discourse.

10:25 Jesus has repeatedly spoken about himself as the one sent by the Father (7:28–29; 8:16, 24–29, 38, 42), but his hearers do not understand: **I told you and you do not believe**. They do not believe because they are trying to understand Jesus on *their* terms, not his terms (8:23). Faith is the necessary condition and key for understanding Jesus and his revelation.

Since his opponents do not believe his words, Jesus appeals to his deeds: **The works I do in my Father's name testify to me**. Jesus' actions bear witness to him (5:36), and the miraculous †signs disclose his identity and work (9:3–5). Between his words and his deeds, Jesus has said much about his identity. But the key to grasping their meaning is faith in Jesus, which his audience lacks.

10:26–27 Jesus explains his listeners' unbelief with the pastoral imagery from the Shepherd Discourse: **You do not believe, because you are not among my sheep**. Jesus' sheep are those who believe in him and live in a personal relationship with him: **My sheep hear my voice; I know them, and they follow me** (10:3–4, 14). Unlike his opponents, Jesus' disciples know that he is the Messiah (the question raised in 10:24) because they know him personally through faith.

10:28 Jesus reveals that the "pasture" (10:9) to which he leads his sheep is **eternal life**. He came to give life in abundant excess (10:10), and his faithful followers **shall never perish** spiritually or, ultimately, in any other way. His remark, **No one can take them out of my hand**, refers to the shepherd's protecting of the sheep from

9. See Josephus, *Jewish War* 5.1.185; and *Jewish Antiquities* 15.11.3.397–402.

10. Raymond E. Brown, SS, *The Gospel according to John*, AB 29 (New York: Doubleday, 1966), 1:405.

the wolf, for the same verb translated "take . . . out" here also refers to the wolf who "catches" the sheep (10:12). As the psalmist prays, "Even when I walk through the valley of the shadow of death, / I will fear no evil, for you are with me" (Ps 23:4).

10:29–30 Jesus can so bless and protect his sheep because of his relationship with the **Father**, who **is greater than all**. The Father draws disciples to Jesus and **has given them to** him as a gift (6:37, 39; 17:6). As the Scriptures present God's sheep as his unique possession, here the sheep are presented as the possession of the Father and of Jesus. Jesus just said, "No one can take them out of my hand" (10:28), and now he adds, **No one can take them out of the Father's hand**. The power and custody that Jesus has with respect to the sheep is the same as the Father's. Accordingly, Jesus says, **The Father and I are one**. In the Gospel context, Jesus' statement means that he and the Father are one in their position and action toward the sheep. In coming to define the doctrine of the Trinity under the Spirit's guidance, the Church discerned that the "oneness" spoken of in the text between the Father and Son refers not only to their actions but also to their very being.[11] That is, the Father and Jesus act with the same divine power because, with the Holy Spirit, they share the one divine nature.[12]

Reflection and Application (10:22–30)

Here and in the next scene (10:31–39), Jesus affirms his unity with the Father. The relationship between the Father and the Son and also the Holy Spirit is the mystery of the Blessed Trinity. The Trinity lies at the heart of Christian life. Through the humanity of Jesus, God enters into a profound relationship of intimacy with his people: God literally becomes one of us. He does this so that human beings might come to share in the eternal exchange of love that is the Trinity. As St. Athanasius famously put it: the Word of God "became man so that we might become God."[13] Sharing in God's Trinitarian life is the pasture to which the good shepherd comes to lead us.

Blasphemy? (10:31–42)

[31]The Jews again picked up rocks to stone him. [32]Jesus answered them, "I have shown you many good works from my Father. For which of these are

11. See Brown, *John*, 1:407.
12. Catechism 236, 253–56, 258.
13. Athanasius, *On the Incarnation* (PG 25b: 192b), our translation. See also Catechism 460.

you trying to stone me?" [33]The Jews answered him, "We are not stoning you for a good work but for blasphemy. You, a man, are making yourself God." [34]Jesus answered them, "Is it not written in your law, 'I said, "You are gods"'? [35]If it calls them gods to whom the word of God came, and scripture cannot be set aside, [36]can you say that the one whom the Father has consecrated and sent into the world blasphemes because I said, 'I am the Son of God'? [37]If I do not perform my Father's works, do not believe me; [38]but if I perform them, even if you do not believe me, believe the works, so that you may realize [and understand] that the Father is in me and I am in the Father." [39][Then] they tried again to arrest him; but he escaped from their power.

[40]He went back across the Jordan to the place where John first baptized, and there he remained. [41]Many came to him and said, "John performed no sign, but everything John said about this man was true." [42]And many there began to believe in him.

OT: Lev 24:10–16; Ps 82

NT: Matt 26:63–68; Rev 21:22–26

Catechism: why the Word became flesh, 456–60; signs of the kingdom, 547–50; Jesus and Israel's faith in the one God, 587–91

10:31 After Jesus claims identity and equality with God (10:30), there is another attempt **to stone** him to death (see 8:59). His opponents see his claim as blasphemy, and, according to Lev 24:16, the punishment for blasphemy is death by stoning.

10:32–33 Jesus' question, **For which of** . . . my **many good works from** the **Father** . . . **are you trying to stone me?**, leads his opponents to spell out their motivations for trying to kill him. Their response makes clear that the driving issue in this episode is whether Jesus' claim, "The Father and I are one" (10:30), constitutes **blasphemy**. They further specify their charge: **You, a man, are making yourself God**. In their eyes, Jesus is just a man who claims to be God, and this constitutes blasphemy (John 5:18; 8:53; see Matt 26:65).

10:34–36 Jesus refutes this accusation by appealing to Scripture. He starts with Ps 82:6: **I said, "You are gods."** In Ps 82, God indicts a subordinate group of authorities for failing to judge and act in a holy way. God refers to these individuals as "gods," but on account of their injustice and corruption, he says, "Like any mortal you shall die" (82:7). As in 7:21–23, Jesus employs a mode of scriptural argumentation known as "the lesser and the greater."[14] If **scripture** can call a lesser group "gods," then how much more fitting is the title **Son of God** for Jesus, **whom the Father has consecrated and sent into the world**.

14. Hebrew *qal wahomer*.

The mention of consecration illumines the relationship between Jesus and the Feast of Dedication.[15] This festival celebrates the reconsecration of the temple, the place of God's special presence among his people. As the †incarnate Word, whose body is the "temple" (2:21), Jesus is the one consecrated by the Father. The rededication of the earthly temple made earthly worship possible again, and Jesus makes possible "worship in Spirit and truth" (4:24).

10:37–39 Jesus' opponents refuse to **believe** his words, but they are somewhat disposed to his **works**, which they seem to acknowledge as "good" (10:32). He encourages them to **believe the works**, which bear witness to him (10:25). If viewed properly, they are a means by which people can come to believe in him. By coming to faith in this way, Jesus says, **you may realize [and understand] that the Father is in me and I am in the Father**. As in 10:30, he concludes with another profound claim about his relationship with the Father, which is one of communion and mutual indwelling. Jesus' teaching again receives a negative response from his listeners, but like the other attempts to **arrest him**, this one fails (7:32; see 8:20).

10:40–42 Jesus leaves Judea and heads east **across the Jordan to the place where John first baptized**. As he did with the Samaritans (4:40; see also 1:39), he **remained** with the people of the Transjordan, allowing them to experience his reality for themselves. The people of the Transjordan reiterate the Baptist's role as witness to Jesus: **Everything John said about this man was true**. On the basis of the Baptist's testimony and their own encounter with Jesus, **many there began to believe in him**. Unlike many of his own people in Judea, who did not believe in him, the people of the Transjordan, like the Samaritans, start to believe in him.

15. See Francis J. Moloney, SDB, *The Gospel of John* (Collegeville, MN: Liturgical Press, 1998), 316–19.

The Resurrection and the Life

John 11:1–54

After the subsection concerning Jesus and the Jewish liturgies (5:1–10:42), we arrive at the last part of the Book of Signs (11:1–12:50). This narrates the final events of Jesus' public ministry and looks forward to the †hour of his passion and resurrection.

Over the course of the Gospel, the magnificence of Jesus' †signs has been increasing: a superabundance of good wine (2:1–11); healing a man paralyzed for thirty-eight years (5:1–9); feeding a crowd of over five thousand (6:1–15); healing a man blind from birth (9:1–7). In John 11, Jesus performs the greatest sign of his public ministry: he brings Lazarus, who has been dead for four days, back to life. This sign reveals Jesus' divine power over life and death, and many come to believe in him as a result. While the sign reveals Jesus' power to give life, it is an important factor leading to his death. John 11 concludes with a decision by a group of Jerusalem religious authorities that Jesus must die.

The One You Love Is Ill (11:1–6)

[1]Now a man was ill, Lazarus from Bethany, the village of Mary and her sister Martha. [2]Mary was the one who had anointed the Lord with perfumed oil and dried his feet with her hair; it was her brother Lazarus who was ill. [3]So the sisters sent word to him, saying, "Master, the one you love is ill." [4]When Jesus heard this he said, "This illness is not to end in death, but is for the glory of God, that the Son of God may be glorified through it."

[5]Now Jesus loved Martha and her sister and Lazarus. [6]So when he heard that he was ill, he remained for two days in the place where he was.

OT: 1 Kings 17:17–24
NT: Mark 11:11–12; 14:3–9; Luke 10:38–42
Catechism: Christ the physician, 1503–5
Lectionary: Fifth Sunday of Lent (Year A; optional Years B and C)

11:1–3 John introduces us to a family of Jesus' friends: **Lazarus** and his sisters **Mary** and **Martha** (see Luke 10:38–42). They live in **Bethany**, a village just to the southeast of Jerusalem, and the †Synoptics report that Jesus stayed there when visiting Judea (Mark 11:11–12). Although John does not narrate it until the next chapter (12:1–8), he mentions the incident of **Mary** anointing Jesus **with perfumed oil and** drying **his feet** to show that this family and Jesus are close friends. The sisters send messengers to inform Jesus that his friend Lazarus is **ill**.

11:4 Jesus' response, **This illness is not to end in death, but is for the glory of God, that the Son of God may be glorified through it**, resembles his words about the purpose of the man's congenital blindness in 9:3. Like the man's blindness, Lazarus's illness and then death is not a meaningless tragedy. Rather, it serves a larger purpose in the Father's plan: the revelation of Jesus' divine glory.

11:5–6 We might expect Jesus to rush to help his sick friend, but instead **he remained for two days in the place where he was.** John heightens the emotional tension by reaffirming that **Jesus loved Martha and her sister and Lazarus**.

Reflection and Application (11:1–6)

Jesus' response to the news about Lazarus can seem really astonishing. His beloved friends have sent word to him. Jesus knows that Lazarus is ill, and he loves him dearly. And yet he waits. When our loved ones are ill, we often ask Jesus for help, and sometimes he seems to delay. John invites us to ponder Jesus' words: "This illness is not to end in death, but is for the glory of God" (11:4). Suffering and death are not meaningless; God can use them for his purposes in the world, even if their role in God's plan remains hidden from us.

Lazarus Has Died (11:7–16)

[7]Then after this he said to his disciples, "Let us go back to Judea." [8]The disciples said to him, "Rabbi, the Jews were just trying to stone you, and you want to go back there?" [9]Jesus answered, "Are there not twelve hours in a

day? If one walks during the day, he does not stumble, because he sees the light of this world. [10]But if one walks at night, he stumbles, because the light is not in him." [11]He said this, and then told them, "Our friend Lazarus is asleep, but I am going to awaken him." [12]So the disciples said to him, "Master, if he is asleep, he will be saved." [13]But Jesus was talking about his death, while they thought that he meant ordinary sleep. [14]So then Jesus said to them clearly, "Lazarus has died. [15]And I am glad for you that I was not there, that you may believe. Let us go to him." [16]So Thomas, called Didymus, said to his fellow disciples, "Let us also go to die with him."

OT: Jon 2:3–10; Dan 12:2–3
NT: Mark 8:31–38; 2 Tim 2:11–13
Catechism: Christ's human knowledge, 471–74
Lectionary: Fifth Sunday of Lent (Year A; optional Years B and C)

11:7–10 Two days later, Jesus invites his disciples, **Let us go back to Judea**. They left Judea because of the attempts to arrest and stone him to death in Jerusalem (10:31, 39). Surprised that he wants **to go back** to Judea, the disciples remind Jesus of the dangers there: **The †Jews were just trying to stone you**. He answers with a figure of speech. When people walk around **during the day**, . . . **the light** of the sun helps them avoid falling or stumbling. So too does Jesus, the light of the world (8:12; 9:5), provide guidance for those who walk in his ways. Jesus exhorts his disciples to follow him as the light, for the failure to do so (i.e., **one who walks at night**) will result in greater problems than the threats in Judea. Schnackenburg paraphrases Jesus' statement thus: "If you refuse to walk with me, . . . you run into darkness and are in danger of a much worse sort of fall, failing to attain salvation."[1]

11:11 Just as the "good shepherd lays down his life for the sheep" (10:11) and confronts the danger to his sheep head-on (10:10–14), Jesus now courageously heads into danger to help Lazarus. These actions foreshadow what he will do on the cross: lay down his life and embrace death so that his own will receive life.

Jesus says **Lazarus is asleep**, a biblical metaphor for death,[2] and he is **going to awaken him**. Consistent with the sleeping metaphor, "awakening" or "getting up" can refer to those whom God delivers from the brink of death (Jon 2:7) or whom God will resurrect from death (Dan 12:2–3).

11:12–14 Although **Jesus was talking about** Lazarus's **death**, the **disciples** thought he **meant ordinary sleep** and say, **Master, if he is asleep, he will be saved**.

1. Rudolf Schnackenburg, *The Gospel according to St. John*, vol. 2, *Commentary on Chapters 5–12*, trans. Cecily Hastings, Francis McDonagh, David Smith, and Richard Foley, SJ (New York: Seabury, 1980), 325.
2. Gen 47:28–30; Deut 31:16; 2 Sam 7:12; Acts 7:60; 1 Cor 15:6; 1 Thess 4:13–18.

If Lazarus can get some rest, then he will recover his health—for "saved" can also mean "healed" (see Matt 9:21–22 and Mark 6:56, where the same Greek word is variously translated "cured," "healed," and "saved"). Since the disciples do not understand, **Jesus** tells them plainly, **Lazarus has died**. No one told him that Lazarus had died or even that his sickness was very serious. However, Jesus is the †incarnate Word, who knows everything pertinent to his mission.[3]

11:15–16

Jesus continues, **I am glad for you that I was not there, that you may believe**. He already said that he will use Lazarus's death to manifest his glory (11:4). The raising of Lazarus will be a †sign that reveals the mystery of Jesus and provides an opportunity for others to **believe** in him. Accordingly, Jesus gives the order, **Let us go to him**.

Since they are heading back into danger in Judea, **Thomas**, one of the Twelve, says to the others, **Let us also go to die with him**. By faithfully following Jesus, the disciples head into the same situation with their master (see Mark 8:34–35; 2 Tim 3:10–12).

The Resurrection and the Life (11:17–27)

[17]When Jesus arrived, he found that Lazarus had already been in the tomb for four days. [18]Now Bethany was near Jerusalem, only about two miles away. [19]And many of the Jews had come to Martha and Mary to comfort them about their brother. [20]When Martha heard that Jesus was coming, she went to meet him; but Mary sat at home. [21]Martha said to Jesus, "Lord, if you had been here, my brother would not have died. [22][But] even now I know that whatever you ask of God, God will give you." [23]Jesus said to her, "Your brother will rise." [24]Martha said to him, "I know he will rise, in the resurrection on the last day." [25]Jesus told her, "I am the resurrection and the life; whoever believes in me, even if he dies, will live, [26]and everyone who lives and believes in me will never die. Do you believe this?" [27]She said to him, "Yes, Lord. I have come to believe that you are the Messiah, the Son of God, the one who is coming into the world."

OT: 2 Macc 7; Ezek 37:1–14; Dan 12:1–3; Jon 2:3–11
NT: Luke 10:38–42; 1 Cor 15:21–28; Rev 20:11–15
Catechism: the resurrection, 992–1004
Lectionary: Fifth Sunday of Lent (Year A; optional Years B and C); Feast of St. Martha

3. Catechism 471–74.

Jewish Burial Practices

BIBLICAL BACKGROUND

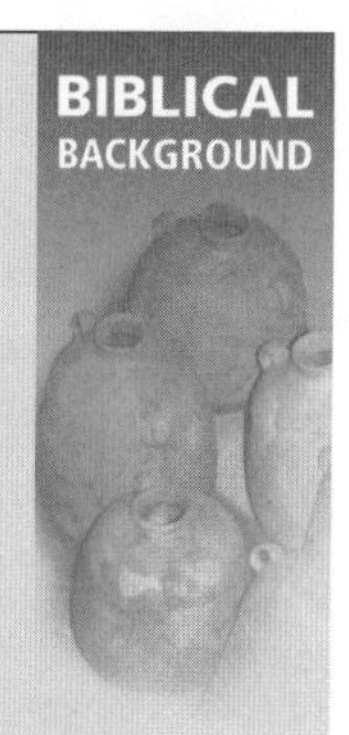

Many details in John 11:1–44 coincide with what is known of ancient Jewish burial practices. The person who died would be buried on the same day. The body was washed and wrapped in burial cloths (see 11:44), and there was a public procession to the burial place, often a cave tomb, with displays of mourning (see Luke 7:12–14). Starting with the day of death, there was a seven-day period of mourning for the deceased. During this time, the bereaved stayed at home (11:20) and neighbors would visit and attend to them (11:19). The mourning could continue for another thirty days and then in a lesser way for a year. At the end of the year, after decomposition of the flesh, the bones would be collected and, for those with the financial means, would be stored in a burial box, called an ossuary.[a]

a. Everett Ferguson, *Backgrounds of Early Christianity*, rev. ed. (Grand Rapids: Eerdmans, 1993), 228–34; Craig S. Keener, *The Gospel of John: A Commentary* (Peabody, MA: Hendrickson, 2003), 2:842–48; Samuel Sandmel, *Judaism and Christian Beginnings* (New York: Oxford: Oxford University Press, 1978), 200–202.

11:17–19 Nearing the outskirts of Bethany, Jesus **found that Lazarus had already been in the tomb for four days.** Some ancient Jewish speculation held that the spirit of the deceased left the burial area after three days, and thus there is no question here: Lazarus is definitely dead.[4]

The notice that **Bethany was near Jerusalem** reminds us of the dangers for Jesus in this area (11:8–10, 16). Some in Jerusalem tried to stone him to death (8:59; 10:31), and here **many of the Jews had come to Martha and Mary to comfort them about their brother**. In this episode, however, the response of these †Jews will be quite different, because of the great †sign that Jesus works in raising Lazarus from the dead (11:45).

11:20 As John 11 unfolds, Jesus moves closer and closer to Lazarus's tomb.[5] He starts in the Transjordan (10:40), enters Judea (11:7), and now he reaches the outskirts of Bethany (11:17, 30). This slow movement toward the tomb builds tension until Jesus finally reaches Lazarus's tomb and confronts an enemy he has come to overthrow: death.

Martha and Mary appear in the same roles that they do in Luke 10:38–42. Upon hearing **that Jesus was coming**, Martha immediately ran out **to meet**

4. *Mishnah Yebamot* 16:3; so Craig S. Keener, *The Gospel of John: A Commentary* (Peabody, MA: Hendrickson, 2003), 2:848n123.

5. Mark W. G. Stibbe, "A Tomb with a View: John 11.1–44 in Narrative-Critical Perspective," *New Testament Studies* 40 (1994): 42–43.

Jesus before he even reaches Bethany proper (11:20, 30). However, **Mary sat at home**, mourning for her brother.

11:21–22 Martha meets Jesus and says, **Lord, if you had been here, my brother would not have died**. When Lazarus was sick, Martha and Mary had sent messengers to Jesus with the implied request that he come and heal him (11:3–4). Even though Lazarus has died and the situation seems impossible, Martha expresses the same confidence in Jesus' power to heal: **Even now I know that whatever you ask of God, God will give you**.

11:23–24 Jesus' response, **Your brother will rise**, refers to the resurrection of the dead, an established Jewish belief in the first century. **Martha**, who believes in the resurrection, agrees: **I know he will rise, in the resurrection on the last day** (see sidebar on p. 206).

11:25–26 Jesus responds to Martha with his fifth "I am + predicate" title, **I am the resurrection and the life**.[6] Jesus is the resurrection because **whoever believes in** him, **even if he dies, will live**. Jesus has promised to "raise up" on the last day those who believe in him and consume his eucharistic flesh and blood (6:40, 44, 54).[7] He is the "life" because through baptism he gives a new spiritual life, the living water of the Holy Spirit, to those who believe in him (3:5). This new life is a participation in the divine communion, and it is enjoyed by believers in the present.[8] As C. H. Dodd succinctly puts it, "Whether the gift of eternal life is conceived as a present and continuing possession . . . or as a recovery of life after the death of the body and the end of the world, . . . the thing that matters is that life is the gift of Christ . . . [which] is Himself."[9]

As he did with the formerly blind man (9:35), Jesus puts the question of faith directly to Martha: **Do you believe this?** Does Martha believe in Jesus as the one who does the things only God can do, and not simply the acts of a healer or prophet?

11:27 Similar to Peter's confession (Matt 16:16), Martha responds with a series of faith-filled affirmations: **Yes, Lord. I have come to believe that you are the †Messiah, the Son of God, the one who is coming into the world**. All of these titles have been confessed previously in the Gospel by Jesus' disciples or others (1:34, 41, 49; 6:14). Martha has a great deal of faith in Jesus, but like the other disciples thus far, hers is not yet fully mature (see 11:39–40).

6. Our interpretation follows C. H. Dodd, *Interpretation of the Fourth Gospel* (1953; repr., New York: Cambridge University, 1998), 364–65.

7. Catechism 994, 1001; 1 Cor 15:21–28; Rev 20:11–15.

8. Catechism 1002–4.

9. Dodd, *Interpretation*, 364.

The Resurrection of the Dead

BIBLICAL BACKGROUND

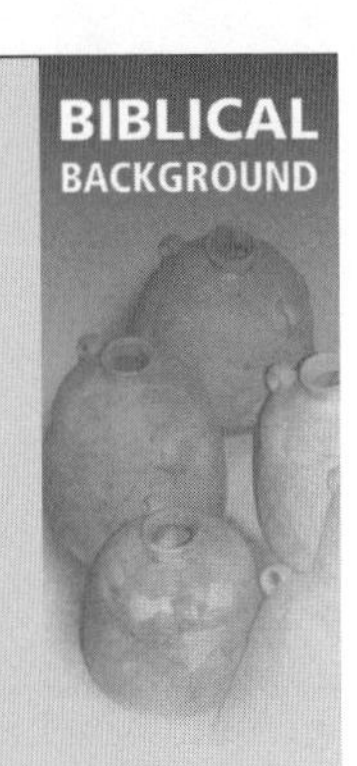

Before the time of Jesus, many Jews believed in the resurrection of the dead, especially †Pharisees. The belief that at the end of the present age of suffering and evil God will raise up and transform those who have died was anticipated in the figurative language of Ezek 37:1–14 and Jon 2:3–11 and articulated in texts like Dan 12:2–3 and 2 Macc 7. God would raise the faithful and righteous to a glorified, perfected mode of life, and they would live forever with God. In the cases where resurrection of the wicked is spoken of, they would be raised up to an everlasting state of punishment, in hell (Dan 12:2). Two aspects of resurrection stand out. First, it is God's ultimate victory over sin and death, the spiritual and physical corruption of God's people. By raising the dead, God overcomes all that harms and corrupts his people. Second, resurrection is about God's justice. Since God is just, he rewards the good and punishes the wicked. Resurrection to glory is God's vindication of those who have suffered and died unjustly. Through the resurrection of the dead, God establishes the fullness of his justice in the world.[a]

a. For a good discussion of resurrection from a Jewish perspective, see Jon D. Levenson, *Resurrection and the Restoration of Israel: The Ultimate Victory of the God of Life* (New Haven: Yale University Press, 2006). From a Christian perspective, see N. T. Wright, *The Resurrection of the Son of God* (Minneapolis: Augsburg Fortress, 2003).

Reflection and Application (11:17–27)

At Sunday Mass we profess in the Nicene Creed, "I believe in the resurrection of the body." Consistent with his words to Martha, when Jesus returns in glory on the last day, he will resurrect and judge the dead (Catechism 997–1001, 1038). Commenting on this article of the creed, St. Thomas Aquinas identifies four ways in which our belief in the resurrection helps us, and these are worth reflecting on:

1. By removing the sadness occasioned by the death of others, . . . [for] inasmuch as [the bereaved] hopes that his dear one will rise again, his sorrow for his death is much alleviated.
2. By removing the fear of death. . . . Since we believe that there is another, better life to which we shall come after death, it is evident that no one should fear death or do anything wrong through fear of death.
3. By making us . . . diligent to perform good works. . . . Because we believe that in return for what we do now we shall receive eternal reward at the resurrection, we apply ourselves to doing good.

4. By drawing us away from evil, . . . [for] fear of punishment (which we believe to be reserved for the wicked) is a motive for avoiding evil deeds.[10]

The Grief of the Son of God (11:28–37)

[28]When she had said this, she went and called her sister Mary secretly, saying, "The teacher is here and is asking for you." [29]As soon as she heard this, she rose quickly and went to him. [30]For Jesus had not yet come into the village, but was still where Martha had met him. [31]So when the Jews who were with her in the house comforting her saw Mary get up quickly and go out, they followed her, presuming that she was going to the tomb to weep there. [32]When Mary came to where Jesus was and saw him, she fell at his feet and said to him, "Lord, if you had been here, my brother would not have died." [33]When Jesus saw her weeping and the Jews who had come with her weeping, he became perturbed and deeply troubled, [34]and said, "Where have you laid him?" They said to him, "Sir, come and see." [35]And Jesus wept. [36]So the Jews said, "See how he loved him." [37]But some of them said, "Could not the one who opened the eyes of the blind man have done something so that this man would not have died?"

OT: Ps 56
NT: 1 Cor 15:20–28; Heb 4:14–16; 5:7–9
Catechism: Jesus' heart, 478; dying in Christ, 1005–14
Lectionary: Fifth Sunday of Lent (Year A; optional Years B and C); Burial of Baptized Children

11:28–32

With Jesus outside **the village**, Martha **secretly** sent word to **her sister Mary**, who had remained at home: **The teacher is here and is asking for you.**[11] When Mary **heard this, she rose quickly and went to him**. As reported in 11:19, the family's friends and neighbors, here called the †**Jews**, had come to console them. When these who were consoling Mary saw her leave, **they followed her, presuming that she was going to the tomb to weep**. When **Mary** met **Jesus** outside of Bethany, **she fell at his feet** and said the exact same words as Martha did (see 11:21). Like Martha, Mary expresses her belief that Jesus has the power to heal.

10. St. Thomas Aquinas, *The Three Greatest Prayers: Commentaries on the Lord's Prayer, the Hail Mary, and the Apostles' Creed*, trans. Laurence Shapcote, OP (Manchester, NH: Sophia Institute Press, 1990), 87–88.

11. The secrecy may reflect the threat posed to Jesus in Judea; so Raymond E. Brown, SS, *The Gospel according to John*, AB 29 (New York: Doubleday, 1966), 1:425; Keener, *Gospel of John*, 2:845.

Saint John Eudes on the Sacred Heart of Jesus

LIVING TRADITION

We see Jesus' very human sorrow over the death of his beloved friend Lazarus. An important expression in Catholic spirituality that celebrates the humanity and love of Jesus is the devotion to his Sacred Heart. A great, but not widely known, advocate of this devotion was St. John Eudes (1601–80), who wrote the following:

> The loving Heart of Jesus loves us with a boundless love. The divine and uncreated love which possesses that adorable Heart, is nothing else but God Himself. Now, since God is unlimited, His love is also unlimited. Since God is everywhere, His love is everywhere, in all places and in all things. Therefore, the Sacred Heart of Jesus loves us not only in heaven, but He also loves us on earth.[a]

a. St. John Eudes, *The Sacred Heart of Jesus*, trans. Dom R. Flower, OSB (New York: P. J. Kennedy & Sons, 1946), 121.

11:33 Jesus loves this family dearly (11:3, 5, 11), and as he sees **her weeping and the Jews who had come with her weeping**, the anguish caused by Lazarus's death moves Jesus also: **he became perturbed and deeply troubled**. The word translated as "perturbed" connotes sternness (see Mark 1:43; 14:5), and when Jesus later arrives at Lazarus's tomb, he is again "perturbed" (11:38). The word translated as "deeply troubled" has the sense of being "worked up." Jesus experiences the same troubling when the †hour of his own death arrives (12:27) and when he announces that one of his disciples will betray him (13:21). In all these occasions, Jesus becomes stirred up because he confronts death itself, which, Paul says in 1 Cor 15:26, is "the last enemy to be destroyed" by God.[12]

11:34–35 When Jesus asks about the location of the tomb, the mourners bid him, **Come and see**, and he starts out toward it. As he approaches his friend's tomb, moved by the mourners' sorrow, **Jesus** himself **wept** over Lazarus's death.

11:36–37 The Jewish mourners can see from Jesus' grief that he truly cares for his loved ones: **See how he loved him**. Others wonder, **Could not the one who opened the eyes of the blind man have done something so that this man would not have died?** The Greek phrasing of this question expects yes for an answer. The mourners know that Jesus did something completely unprecedented in healing the man born blind (see 9:32–33). Their question implies the belief that Jesus indeed has the power to have kept Lazarus from dying.

12. Brown, *John*, 1:435.

Reflection and Application (11:28–37)

The loss of a loved one is one of life's most painful and traumatic experiences. Here we see that Jesus himself experienced the pain of loss caused by death. Jesus grieves and weeps over the death of his friend. He gets angry at death, which destroys life and causes pain. When we feel the pain, sorrow, and anger at the death of a loved one, we should remember that God is there with us in those experiences. The psalmist says that God remembers every tear we shed: "Are my tears not stored in your flask, / recorded in your book" (56:9). By the †incarnation, God has entered into solidarity with humanity; he himself has felt grief and sorrow. This can give us reassurance that "we do not have a high priest who is unable to sympathize with our weaknesses, but one who has similarly been tested in every way, yet without sin" (Heb 4:15).

The Dead Hear the Voice of the Son of God (11:38–44)

[38]So Jesus, perturbed again, came to the tomb. It was a cave, and a stone lay across it. [39]Jesus said, "Take away the stone." Martha, the dead man's sister, said to him, "Lord, by now there will be a stench; he has been dead for four days." [40]Jesus said to her, "Did I not tell you that if you believe you will see the glory of God?" [41]So they took away the stone. And Jesus raised his eyes and said, "Father, I thank you for hearing me. [42]I know that you always hear me; but because of the crowd here I have said this, that they may believe that you sent me." [43]And when he had said this, he cried out in a loud voice, "Lazarus, come out!" [44]The dead man came out, tied hand and foot with burial bands, and his face was wrapped in a cloth. So Jesus said to them, "Untie him and let him go."

OT: 1 Kings 17:7–24; 2 Kings 4:18–37

NT: Mark 5:21–24, 35–43; Luke 7:11–17; Rom 6:3–11; Phil 3:20–21

Catechism: signs of the kingdom, 547–50; Christ's risen humanity, 645–46; Jesus' prayer, 2599–2606

Lectionary: Fifth Sunday of Lent (Year A; optional Years B and C); For the Dead

11:38–39 Jesus finally arrives at the tomb and becomes **perturbed again** (see 11:33). The description of the tomb as a **cave** with a **stone** covering the entrance corresponds to descriptions of Jesus' own tomb in the †Synoptics.[13] Jesus gives the command: **Take away the stone**. But **Martha** protests: **Lord, by now there will be a stench; he has been dead for four days**. Lazarus is indisputably dead,

13. Matt 27:60; 28:2; Mark 15:46; 16:3–4; Luke 23:53; 24:2.

and his body has started to decompose (Gen 3:19). Martha had made a strong profession of faith in Jesus (11:27), but her protest indicates that she does not yet fully understand Jesus' identity as "the resurrection and the life" (11:25).[14] She may believe that Jesus has the divine power to resurrect the dead on the last day, but she does not realize he can revive the dead now.

11:40 Jesus reaffirms that Lazarus's illness and death is for revealing **the glory of God** (see 11:4). He will transform Lazarus's death into a †sign revealing his divine glory as the Son who leads people to the Father. We again meet the Gospel's teaching that faith confers spiritual sight or understanding: **If you believe**, then **you will see**. Faith enables believers to see God manifested in Jesus and his signs. As St. Augustine, inspired by Isa 7:9 †LXX, put it, "Believe in order to understand."[15]

11:41–42 Those present obeyed Jesus and **took away the stone**. Then **Jesus raised his eyes** in prayer to the Father. Through this prayer Jesus gives us insight into his relationship with the Father.[16] He begins, **Father, I thank you for hearing me**. Jesus is the divine Word, who was "with God" (1:1) from eternity, and the Father is always with him (8:29). Since the Father and the Son are in this perpetual relationship, the Father constantly listens to Jesus: **I know that you always hear me**. Previously Jesus said, "Just as the Father raises the dead and gives life, so also does the Son give life to whomever he wishes" (5:21). By bringing Lazarus back to life, Jesus will reveal that he possesses the same divine power to give life and raise the dead as the Father. Before he performs this revelatory sign, Jesus offers this prayer for **the crowd that they may believe that** the Father **sent** him.

11:43–44 After finishing his prayer, Jesus **cried** loudly, **Lazarus, come out!** Regarding his power to raise the dead, Jesus had said, "The †hour is coming in which all who are in the tombs will hear [my] voice and will come out . . . to the resurrection" (5:28–29). Now **the dead man** heard the Son's voice and **came out** of the tomb. Lazarus did not come back to life on his own, for he is still bound **with burial bands, and his face was wrapped in a cloth**. Accordingly, **Jesus** gives the order: **Untie him and let him go**.

These details indicate that the raising of Lazarus is not resurrection, but resuscitation.[17] Jesus brings Lazarus back to mortal life, and consequently Lazarus will die again. The same applies to Jairus's daughter (Mark 5:35–43)

14. Brown, *John*, 1:435.

15. St. Augustine, *Sermon* 43.4, in *Sermons II: On the Old Testament*, trans. Edmund Hill, OP (Brooklyn, NY: New City, 1990), 240.

16. On the importance of Jesus' prayer, see Joseph Ratzinger (Pope Benedict XVI), *Jesus of Nazareth: From the Baptism in the Jordan to the Transfiguration*, trans. Adrian J. Walker (New York: Doubleday, 2007), 1:7–8, 128–68, 170–71, 344.

17. See comments on John 20:6–7.

and the son of the widow of Nain (Luke 7:11–17), and to those revived by God's power through the prophets Elijah (1 Kings 17:7–24) and Elisha (2 Kings 4:8–37). Resurrection is categorically different because it is the raising to a glorified, perfected, and embodied existence, not a return to ordinary mortal life. Those resurrected to glory will never die again. As St. Paul writes, "Christ, raised from the dead, dies no more; death no longer has power over him" (Rom 6:9).

Plans and Prophecies (11:45–54)

[45]Now many of the Jews who had come to Mary and seen what he had done began to believe in him. [46]But some of them went to the Pharisees and told them what Jesus had done. [47]So the chief priests and the Pharisees convened the Sanhedrin and said, "What are we going to do? This man is performing many signs. [48]If we leave him alone, all will believe in him, and the Romans will come and take away both our land and our nation." [49]But one of them, Caiaphas, who was high priest that year, said to them, "You know nothing, [50]nor do you consider that it is better for you that one man should die instead of the people, so that the whole nation may not perish." [51]He did not say this on his own, but since he was high priest for that year, he prophesied that Jesus was going to die for the nation, [52]and not only for the nation, but also to gather into one the dispersed children of God. [53]So from that day on they planned to kill him.

[54]So Jesus no longer walked about in public among the Jews, but he left for the region near the desert, to a town called Ephraim, and there he remained with his disciples.

OT: Deut 12:11–12; 1 Kings 8:22–30; Isa 43:1–8; Jer 31:7–14

NT: Matt 26:1–5, 57–68; Acts 4:5–22; 5:33–40

Catechism: God chooses Abraham to gather scattered humanity, 59–61; the Church: universal sacrament of salvation, 774–76

Lectionary: For the Unity of Christians; For the Spread of the Gospel

11:45–46 The raising of Lazarus is the preeminent †sign in Jesus' public ministry, and like Jesus himself, it prompts different responses from people. **Many of the †Jews who had come to Mary** saw the sign and **began to believe in** him—the outcome for which Jesus prayed before raising Lazarus (11:42). However, others **went to the †Pharisees and told them what Jesus had done**. This report prompts a meeting of the Jerusalem religious authorities, where they decide to seek Jesus' death (11:53). The †irony is striking: Jesus' giving life to Lazarus leads to his own death. This is the dynamic that Jesus expressed in speaking about himself as the good shepherd: the good shepherd freely sacrifices his life (10:11, 15) so that his sheep may receive life (10:10).

11:47 After hearing about Jesus' mighty deed, **the chief priests and the Pharisees convened the †Sanhedrin**, a council of high-ranking priests, aristocrats, and religious experts, which had religious and political authority in Jerusalem. The council deliberates over how to respond to Jesus' **signs** (see Acts 4:16–17).

11:48 The authorities face a problem: **If we leave him alone, all will believe in him, and the Romans will come and take away both our land and our nation**. Their thinking reflects the sociopolitical situation of first-century Judea. Before and even more so after Jesus' earthly ministry, a number of †messianic movements took shape in Palestine, seeking to cast off the Roman occupation in various ways (Acts 5:34–39).[18] The Romans violently crushed these movements. The Jewish authorities now express their fear that Jesus' ministry will either develop into or be perceived as a messianic liberation movement and will become another occasion for Roman violence and destruction. Specifically, the authorities fear that the Romans will take away both "our land and our nation" (11:48). The word translated as "land" (*topos*) literally means "place" and is often a synonym for the temple.[19]

11:49 At the head of the Sanhedrin was **Caiaphas** the **high priest**. Born into a well-established priestly family, Joseph Caiaphas was the high priest in Jerusalem from AD 18–36. Although the †Synoptics narrate Jesus' interrogation by the high priest after his arrest (Matt 26:57–68), John focuses on the role of Caiaphas and the deliberations of the Sanhedrin here.

11:50 Caiaphas rebukes his fellow councillors on the Sanhedrin: **You know nothing, nor do you consider that it is better for you that one man should die instead of the people, so that the whole nation may not perish**. As the high priest, Caiaphas held political and religious authority in Jerusalem, but he was subject to the Roman prefect, who lived at Caesarea Maritima, on the Mediterranean coast. Local authorities like Caiaphas had to keep order, and so he speaks here for political and social stability. Jesus is becoming more and more popular as a †messianic figure. Caiaphas argues that it is better if one person, Jesus, dies so that many will be saved from a violent Roman suppression.[20]

18. L. Michael White counts fifteen such movements. See his helpful chart in *From Jesus to Christianity* (New York: HarperCollins, 2004), 37–39. See also Acts 5:36–37; 21:38.

19. See Deut 12:11; 1 Kings 8:29; 2 Macc 2:8; 5:19–20; Dan 3:38.

20. Caiaphas's moral reasoning resembles trends in contemporary moral theology known as consequentialism or proportionalism, in which the morality of an action is determined by the agent's intentions and the outcomes of the action, but not by the action itself. Pope St. John Paul II strongly criticized these trends in his encyclical *Veritatis Splendor* (Splendor of the Truth) 75–82.

Prophetic Restoration Eschatology

BIBLICAL BACKGROUND

†Eschatology is a theological term referring to the teaching about the last things or ultimate things. In biblical studies, this term often refers to God's actions that are expected to occur at the end of time and to the permanent state of affairs that those actions will bring about. The last things can be understood as the conclusion of the biblical story.

At Mount Sinai, God chose the twelve tribes of Israel and formed them into a nation as his "treasured possession" (Exod 19:5). He entered into a †covenant with them and brought them to live in land he had promised to their ancestors, Canaan. As generations passed, the Israelites forgot the Lord and repeatedly sinned against him. God then meted out the covenantal punishment of exile and scattering (Deut 28:63–64). The twelve tribes were broken up by conquests, exiled from the promised land, and scattered among the Gentile nations (2 Kings 17:6–23; 24:1–4).

Many biblical prophets foretold that God, out of love and covenant faithfulness, would one day bring his people back out of exile in a new act of salvation—a new exodus—and forgive their sins (Jer 31:7–14, 31–34; Isa 43:1–8). He would regather all twelve tribes, bring them back to a bounteous homeland, restore the Davidic monarchy, and purify the temple. When God performs this saving action, he will reveal to all people on earth that he is the one Creator and King of all. Some prophets teach that the Gentiles will be drawn to the restored Israel and come to know God (Isa 2:1–5; 49:1–7; 66:23). Prophetic restoration eschatology was part of the background for Jewish hope for a †messiah and for Jesus' proclamation of the kingdom of God.

11:51–52 John comments that Caiaphas unwittingly admits a spiritual truth: **He did not say this on his own, but since he was high priest for that year, he prophesied that Jesus was going to die for the nation**. Some Jewish traditions held that the gift of prophecy attended the high priesthood (see Exod 28:30; Num 27:21).[21] Caiaphas is thinking in earthly, political terms, reckoning that Jesus' death will save people from Roman destruction. But he speaks prophetically because his words are true in a spiritual sense: Jesus will die "for the nation" of Israel, and **not only for the nation, but also to gather into one the dispersed children of God**.

Throughout the Gospel, Jesus states that his death will gather people together and unite them (10:16; 12:32). This language of gathering "the dispersed children

21. C. H. Dodd, "The Prophecy of Caiaphas: John xi 47–53," in *Neotestamentica et patristica: Eine Freundesgabe, Oscar Cullmann zu seinem 60 Geburtstag*, ed. A. N. Wilder et al. (Leiden: Brill, 1962), 134–43.

of God" recalls the prophetic announcement of a future saving act of God that will regather his people and draw the Gentile nations to himself. John teaches that Jesus' death is this great saving action of God, through which he forms his redeemed community: "There will be one flock, one shepherd" (10:16).

John interprets the life of Jesus in retrospect, and by the time he wrote, the very thing the Jewish authorities in the Gospel narrative tried to prevent had actually occurred. In AD 70, the Romans violently suppressed an armed Jewish rebellion in Palestine and destroyed the temple, putting an end to the priesthood, the sacrifices, and the Jewish leadership in Jerusalem. Ironically, while Jesus' death did not prevent Roman destruction on the earthly level, it does bring about salvation and eternal life. This justifies John's remark about Caiaphas's words as prophecy: Jesus died on behalf of "the nation, and . . . to gather into one the dispersed children of God."

11:53–54 Persuaded by Caiaphas's reasoning, the Jerusalem religious authorities **planned to kill him**. There have been plots and attempts on Jesus' life before (5:18; 7:25; 8:59; 10:31, 39), but only now does the Sanhedrin decide that Jesus must go. Aware of this threat, **Jesus no longer walked about in public among the Jews**. Instead, **he left for** a remote **town called Ephraim**, where **he remained with his disciples**.

Jesus Goes to Jerusalem for His Passover

John 11:55–12:50

Even though we are only at the end of John 11 and ten chapters remain, we have arrived at the end of Jesus' public ministry. Many themes established in the first half of the Gospel are continued here: Jesus' obedience to the Father, who sent him (12:27–28); his †hour (12:20–26); his being "lifted up" on the cross (12:31–36); his relationship with Jewish liturgies (11:55–57; 12:12); his †messianic identity (12:12–19); the mixed responses to him by different groups (12:9–16, 34). A summary of many key teachings in John 1–12 is given in 12:44–50.

The events of John 12 also look toward Jesus' death and resurrection. Mary, the sister of Lazarus, anoints Jesus at a dinner, and this gesture anticipates his approaching burial. Jesus makes his final trip to Jerusalem, where he is welcomed as the messianic king. He announces that the hour of his passion has come, and he explains the significance of what he will accomplish in it. This section, and the first half of the Gospel, comes to a close with Jesus departing the public scene.

Setting the Stage for Jesus' Arrival (11:55–57)

[55]Now the Passover of the Jews was near, and many went up from the country to Jerusalem before the Passover to purify themselves. [56]They looked for Jesus and said to one another as they were in the temple area, "What do you think? That he will not come to the feast?" [57]For the chief priests and the Pharisees had given orders that if anyone knew where he was, he should inform them, so that they might arrest him.

OT: Num 9:1–13; 2 Chron 30:14–20

NT: Matt 26:1–5

Fig. 9. Remains of a mikveh at Qumran

11:55 The third **Passover** in the Gospel draws **near** (see 2:13; 6:4), and John describes the situation in Jerusalem as he looks ahead to Jesus' crucifixion. Participation in the festival required one to be in a state of ritual purity (Num 9:1–13; 2 Chron 30:14–20). **To purify themselves**, the Jewish pilgrims would arrive several days before the festival and wash in pools known as *miqva'ot* (singular *miqveh*). Remains of these pools have survived to today.

11:56–57 The situation in Jerusalem resembles that before Jesus' arrival at the Feast of Tabernacles (7:11–13): the crowd **looked for** Jesus and discussed his whereabouts. And as at Tabernacles, their discussion is overshadowed by a threat from the authorities: **For the chief priests and the †Pharisees had given orders that if anyone knew where he was, he should inform them, so that they might arrest him**. The stage has been set for Jesus' arrival in Jerusalem for Passover, when he will accomplish his saving work.

Mary Anoints Jesus for Burial (12:1–11)

[1]Six days before Passover Jesus came to Bethany, where Lazarus was, whom Jesus had raised from the dead. [2]They gave a dinner for him there, and Martha served, while Lazarus was one of those reclining at table with

him. [3]Mary took a liter of costly perfumed oil made from genuine aromatic nard and anointed the feet of Jesus and dried them with her hair; the house was filled with the fragrance of the oil. [4]Then Judas the Iscariot, one [of] his disciples, and the one who would betray him, said, [5]"Why was this oil not sold for three hundred days' wages and given to the poor?" [6]He said this not because he cared about the poor but because he was a thief and held the money bag and used to steal the contributions. [7]So Jesus said, "Leave her alone. Let her keep this for the day of my burial. [8]You always have the poor with you, but you do not always have me."

[9][The] large crowd of the Jews found out that he was there and came, not only because of Jesus, but also to see Lazarus, whom he had raised from the dead. [10]And the chief priests plotted to kill Lazarus too, [11]because many of the Jews were turning away and believing in Jesus because of him.

OT: Lev 2:1–3; Deut 15:1–11
NT: Mark 14:3–9; Luke 7:36–50; 10:38–42
Catechism: love for the poor, 2443–49

12:1–2

Six days before Passover Jesus again **came to Bethany**. The Gospel puts Jesus' death on Friday afternoon, with the Passover and sabbath starting that evening (19:14, 31). When six days are counted backward, this episode would take place on the preceding Saturday evening. Jesus' friends in Bethany **gave a dinner for him**. Once again taking the active role, **Martha served** the dinner (see 11:20; Luke 10:40). **Lazarus** is very much alive since he is **at table with** Jesus.

The reminder that **Jesus had raised Lazarus** simultaneously looks backward to the miraculous †sign and ahead to Jesus' death—for the raising of Lazarus was the catalyst in the authorities' decision to seek his execution (11:46–53). While readers know that Jesus' death is very close, the persons in the Gospel do not. As O'Day has shown, this scene contains many hints that anticipate the Last Supper and Jesus' passion, and in this way Mary's anointing, as Jesus interprets it, is a symbolic signal that his death is imminent.[1]

12:3

Mary, the sister of Lazarus, does some extravagant things for Jesus.[2] She **anointed the feet of Jesus** with a large amount of very **costly perfumed oil**, an act that anticipates Nicodemus's bringing a huge amount of ointment for Jesus' burial (19:39). Moreover, in another anticipation of Jesus' self-gift, John

1. Gail R. O'Day, "The Gospel of John," in *The New Interpreter's Bible*, vol. 9 (Nashville: Abingdon, 1995), 700–702.

2. See Matt 26:6–13; Mark 14:3–9; Luke 7:36–50. John's account reflects elements from two †Synoptic traditions: Matthew (26:6–13) and Mark (14:3–9) recount an unnamed woman anointing Jesus with oil shortly before his death; Luke (7:36–50) has an account of a sinful woman crying at Jesus' feet and drying them with her hair.

uses the same verb to describe both Mary's action of drying Jesus' feet **with her hair** and Jesus' action of drying his disciples' feet at the footwashing at the Last Supper (13:5).[3] John adds that **the house was filled with the fragrance of the oil**. The scent of the perfumed oil, which fills the whole house, signifies Mary's overflowing generosity in this gesture for Jesus. Also, the word for "fragrance" most often occurs in the †Septuagint in reference to the odor of liturgical sacrifices offered to God (e.g., Lev 2:2). Taken in this light, the fragrance of the oil may anticipate Jesus' sacrificial gift of his own life, which he offers to the Father on the cross.

12:4–6 Mary's use of expensive ointment seems like a waste. **Judas the Iscariot** protests, **Why was this oil not sold for three hundred days' wages and given to the poor?** On the surface, Judas seems to speak out of a righteous concern for the poor. But John tells us the truth: Judas **said this not because he cared about the poor but because he was a thief**, who **used to steal** from the group's **money bag**. This description links Judas to the opponents of the good shepherd: the thief (10:1, 8) and the hired man, who "has no concern for the sheep" (10:13).[4] The comments that Judas **would betray** Jesus and **held the money bag** look ahead to the Last Supper, where mention is made of Judas being the group's treasurer when he leaves to betray Jesus (13:21–30).

12:7–8 **Jesus** defends Mary against Judas's objection: **Leave her alone**. The decision has been made to seek Jesus' execution (11:53), and word is out that the authorities want to arrest Jesus (11:57). By saying, **Let her keep this for the day of my burial**, Jesus reveals to those present that his death and burial are close at hand (see Mark 14:8).

Jesus also responds to Judas's hollow protest about wasting the ointment and not helping the poor: **You always have the poor with you, but you do not always have me**. His words recall Deut 15:11, "The land will never lack for needy persons; that is why I command you: 'Open your hand freely to your poor and to your needy kin in your land.'" There will always be an opportunity to help the poor, and Jesus certainly does not discourage it with these words.[5] However, Jesus takes priority over every other concern—and little time remains before his mortal life ends.

12:9–11 Since Jesus is not appearing "in public" (11:54), when the news gets out that he is in Bethany, a **large crowd of the †Jews** flock to see him and **Lazarus** as well. The raising of Lazarus led many of the witnesses to a basic level of faith in

3. O'Day, "Gospel of John," 701.
4. Ibid., 702.
5. Catechism 2449.

Jesus (11:45). Now a larger crowd comes to see for themselves both Jesus and Lazarus, **whom he had raised from the dead.**

The raising of Lazarus has prompted the †Sanhedrin to seek Jesus' death (11:46–53), and now **the chief priests plotted to kill Lazarus too**. They want Lazarus dead **because many of the Jews** were coming to faith **in Jesus** on account **of him**. This course of action fits with the authorities' fears, voiced at the Sanhedrin meeting, that Jesus is attracting too many followers, who might develop into a political †messianic movement, provoking the Romans to violent repression (11:48). Accordingly, they regard it as necessary to take action before things get out of hand.

The King of Israel (12:12–19)

[12]On the next day, when the great crowd that had come to the feast heard that Jesus was coming to Jerusalem, [13]they took palm branches and went out to meet him, and cried out:

> **"Hosanna!**
> **Blessed is he who comes in the name of the Lord,**
> **[even] the king of Israel."**

[14]Jesus found an ass and sat upon it, as is written:

> **[15]"Fear no more, O daughter Zion;**
> **see, your king comes, seated upon an ass's colt."**

[16]His disciples did not understand this at first, but when Jesus had been glorified they remembered that these things were written about him and that they had done this for him. [17]So the crowd that was with him when he called Lazarus from the tomb and raised him from death continued to testify. [18]This was [also] why the crowd went to meet him, because they heard that he had done this sign. [19]So the Pharisees said to one another, "You see that you are gaining nothing. Look, the whole world has gone after him."

OT: 2 Macc 10:1–8; Ps 118; Zeph 3; Zech 9:9–17

NT: Luke 19:28–40

Catechism: Jesus' entrance into Jerusalem, 559–60; a priestly, prophetic, and royal people, 783–86

Lectionary: Passion Sunday (Year B)

12:12–13

When **the great crowd**, which went to see Jesus in Bethany (12:9), **heard that Jesus was coming to Jerusalem**, they literally gave him the royal welcome.

Many aspects of Jesus' entry into Jerusalem have kingly, †messianic allusions. During the Maccabean revolt, the †Jews waved palm branches in celebration of key victories won against their Gentile oppressors (1 Macc 13:51; 2 Macc 10:7). The crowd welcomes Jesus with **palm branches**, a symbol of Jewish nationalism and liberation, because they receive him as a messianic deliverer who will liberate them from Roman occupation.

The crowd also **cried out** an acclamation composed of several Scripture texts. Their cry, **Hosanna! / Blessed is he who comes in the name of the Lord**, is a quotation of Ps 118:25–26, which praises God for saving his people and depicts a celebratory procession to the temple with "leafy branches" (118:27). The word "hosanna" is a Hebrew phrase (*hoshi'ah na'*) that means "Save [us] please!"[6]

The crowd also hails Jesus as **the king of Israel**. Scripture applies this title to both God (Isa 44:6) and Israel's earthly kings (1 Kings 15:9; Isa 7:1). The *Psalms of Solomon* (not †canonical) likewise refers to both God and the Davidic Messiah as "king" over Israel (17:1, 32–34, 42, 46). The Messiah in *Psalms of Solomon* 17 is a new Davidic warrior-king, who will liberate the Jews from Gentile control and lead them in righteousness. The crowd's use of this title also echoes Zephaniah. After God's wrath purifies people on the "day of the LORD," God will restore and build up his faithful remnant and dwell among them: "The King of Israel, the LORD, is in your midst, / you have no further misfortune to fear" (Zeph 3:15). Through their words and symbolic actions, the crowd welcomes Jesus as a messianic, Davidic king, understood as God's instrument of salvation to throw off Roman oppression and to rule Israel in righteousness.

12:14–15 Jesus responds to the crowd's welcome with a prophetic gesture of his own: he **found an ass and sat upon it**. John gives the proper interpretation of Jesus as king by quoting Scripture. First, the command, **Fear no more**, is common in Scripture and often appears in connection with the coming of God to save his people (Isa 40:9; 41:10; 43:1, 5). Second, the statement, **O daughter Zion; / See, your king comes, seated upon an ass's colt**, comes from Zech 9:9. As discussed previously (see comments on John 2:2), daughter Zion refers to God's faithful people, who are often personified throughout Scripture in feminine terms. So Zech 9:9–17 announces the arrival of a new messianic king. This king, who will establish peace and a great kingdom, is part of God's saving action to restore his people. By sitting on the donkey, prophetically enacting the scenario in Zech 9, Jesus identifies himself as this messiah-king, a humble bringer of †eschatological peace and reconciliation.

6. The NABRE translates it as "LORD, grant salvation!" (Ps 118:25).

We should appreciate the juxtaposition of the crowd's understanding of Jesus as king alongside Jesus' own display of kingship in light of Zech 9:9.[7] The crowd is correct to hail Jesus as king. But his kingship is not exactly what they think. Jesus does not come riding a war horse as a conquering warrior-king. He comes as a king who lays down his life and rides atop a lowly beast of burden. Jesus has not come to defeat the Romans and win political freedom but to defeat Satan, "the ruler of this world" (12:31), and win freedom from the more serious slavery of sin (8:34–36). He has come to "proclaim peace to the nations" (Zech 9:10). This peace comes not through military conquest but through participation in the divine communion, which Jesus' cross and resurrection make possible (John 14:27; 20:21).

12:16 At the time, Jesus' **disciples did not understand** the spiritual meaning of these events. As in 2:17, 20–22, the disciples witnessed an event in Jesus' life but came to understand its meaning only when **they remembered** it after **Jesus had been glorified**. The disciples' remembering is brought about by the Holy Spirit after Jesus' resurrection, for Jesus says that the Spirit, who comes after his glorification, will "remind you of all that [I] told you" (14:26) and "guide you to all truth" (16:13). The full spiritual understanding of Jesus, his work, and the Scriptures comes only after his resurrection and through the interior working of the Holy Spirit.

12:17–19 Jesus' arrival meets with a mixed response. **The crowd**, who witnessed the raising of **Lazarus, . . . continued to testify**. The raising of Lazarus led many to a rudimentary faith in Jesus and motivated the festival crowd to acclaim Jesus as king. But their misunderstanding of Jesus' kingship demonstrates their immature faith. While it may be a starting point, Jesus desires to lead people to a more genuine faith in him. By contrast, **the Pharisees** do not look favorably on the royal welcome given to Jesus. Their initiative to stop people from coming to Jesus is not working: **You see that you are gaining nothing**. Indeed, the very opposite is happening: **The whole world has gone after him**. Like the chief priests in 12:10–11, the †Pharisees recognize the messianic overtones in the crowd's welcome of Jesus. Their fear that people will rally around Jesus as a messianic conqueror seems to be materializing.

Reflection and Application (12:12–19)

The crowd welcomes Jesus into Jerusalem as a warrior-king who will liberate the Jews from Roman oppression. But he is not this kind of kingly deliverer. The

7. Compare John 6:1–21.

more profound freedom that Jesus brings is freedom from sin and the power of Satan. Jesus refuses to fit into the mold that human beings try to create for him. He defies our expectations and often does not act the way we want him to act. As the Lord says in Isaiah, "My thoughts are not your thoughts, / nor are your ways my ways" (55:8). Instead of trying to get Jesus to conform to our expectations, we might ask ourselves how we can open our minds to his thoughts and conform ourselves to his ways.

The Hour Has Come (12:20–26)

[20]Now there were some Greeks among those who had come up to worship at the feast. [21]They came to Philip, who was from Bethsaida in Galilee, and asked him, "Sir, we would like to see Jesus." [22]Philip went and told Andrew; then Andrew and Philip went and told Jesus. [23]Jesus answered them, "The hour has come for the Son of Man to be glorified. [24]Amen, amen, I say to you, unless a grain of wheat falls to the ground and dies, it remains just a grain of wheat; but if it dies, it produces much fruit. [25]Whoever loves his life loses it, and whoever hates his life in this world will preserve it for eternal life. [26]Whoever serves me must follow me, and where I am, there also will my servant be. The Father will honor whoever serves me."

OT: Tob 14:5–7; Isa 2:1–4; 60:1–7; 66:18–23

NT: Matt 2:1–12; Mark 8:31–38; 1 Cor 15:35–38, 42–44

Catechism: why the Word became flesh, 459; our participation in Christ's sacrifice, 618

Lectionary: Fifth Sunday of Lent (Year B); For the Dead; Feast of St. Lawrence; Feast of St. Ignatius of Antioch; Common of Martyrs; Holy Orders; Consecration of Virgins and Religious Profession

12:20–22 Immediately after the †Pharisees' remark, "the whole world has gone after him" (12:19), **some Greeks** appear. They are Gentiles, and it seems that they are well disposed to Judaism or in the process of converting because they have come **to worship at the feast** (see Acts 10:1–2). They approach **Philip** and make a request: **Sir, we would like to see Jesus. Philip** tells **Andrew**, and then both disciples go and tell **Jesus**.

12:23 Upon hearing that Gentiles have come to see him, **Jesus** announces that the moment has arrived **for the †Son of Man to be glorified**. What is it about the arrival of the Greeks that marks the arrival of Jesus' †**hour**? Jesus spoke of his mission to unite all his sheep, including those who "do not belong to this fold," into "one flock" under his leadership (10:16). John has also told us that Jesus would die "not only for the nation, but also to gather into one the dispersed children of God" (11:51–52). Jesus' work has a universal scope: he aims to gather all people, Jews and Gentiles, to the one God through himself. This aim resonates with prophetic texts in which God, after he works his definitive saving action for his people Israel, will be made known to the Gentiles (see sidebar on p. 213). The Gentiles will then make a pilgrimage to Zion to worship the one true God (see Tob 14:6; Isa 60:1–7).[8] John 12 depicts both Jews (12:9–19) and Gentiles (12:20–21) coming together around Jesus. These events illustrate the beginning of the ingathering of all people to God, which Jesus' death on the cross makes possible (12:32). Thus **the hour has come**.

12:24 Jesus now elaborates on the mystery of his hour, beginning with a parable-like saying: **Unless a grain of wheat falls to the ground and dies, it remains just a grain of wheat; but if it dies, it produces much fruit**. Seed imagery is common in Jesus' parables (Mark 4:1–9; Luke 13:18–19), and Paul uses it to give insight into the mystery of the resurrected body (1 Cor 15:35–38, 42–44). Because a seed can grow into a plant only after being buried in the ground, Jesus makes use of it to talk about his death and its benefits. He, the "grain of wheat, . . . dies" on the cross, and his death "produces much fruit," the "crops [literally, "fruit"] for eternal life" (4:36). His death and resurrection make eternal life in communion with God available to all.

12:25 Jesus' movement from death to resurrected life provides the basic pattern for the Christian life. Jesus gives his life for others' good on the cross, and his disciples participate in this saving dynamic by replicating this pattern of loving self-sacrifice: **Whoever loves his life loses it, and whoever hates his life in this world will preserve it for eternal life** (see Mark 8:34–36; John 15:11–17).[9] Here the term "world" means human beings and their world as they are in rebellion against God and under the spiritual powers of sin (see sidebar on p. 37). To hate life in this world does not mean that we should hate our earthly existence as such. Rather, it means detachment from sin and all the things in life that lead us away from and cause us to rebel against God. If we embrace the attitudes that Jesus prescribes and put them into practice, we **will preserve** our lives **for eternal life**.

12:26 Jesus is going to his cross and resurrection, and he has that path in mind when he says, **Whoever serves me must follow me, and where I am, there also will my servant be**. The way of the cross, with the self-sacrificial love and the dying to self-centeredness it entails, is the only way for discipleship. This

8. The Greeks serve a theological function similar to the magi in Matt 2:1–12. Both groups are Gentiles who travel to Jerusalem and seek Jesus the king.

9. Catechism 618.

way is not optional. By following Jesus to the cross, we also follow him to the resurrection, for just as the Father glorifies Jesus in the resurrection, Jesus says, **the Father will honor whoever serves me.**

Reflection and Application (12:20–26)

Jesus' words recall those to his disciples in Mark 8:34–38. His saving work centers on the cross, and any would-be disciple has to "take up his cross, and follow" (Mark 8:34). To follow Jesus means to embrace the cross, because the cross is obedience to God and loving, total self-sacrifice for others. The cross is the common denominator for all modes of Christian life. Like all disciples, single people are called to die to self-centeredness and live a life of love and obedience to God and service for others. This passage from John is proclaimed in liturgies for Holy Orders, the profession of vows by religious, and also on the feasts of some martyrs. Priests, who participate in Christ's spiritual marriage to the Church, give up their lives in loving service just as Christ "loved the church and handed himself over for her" (Eph 5:25). Consecrated religious give themselves to Christ in an exclusive relationship. Similarly, a married person sacrifices one's life out of love for spouse and children. All walks of Christian life take the shape of the cross, and when faithfully and lovingly lived out, lead to the glory of the resurrection and the honor given by the Father.[10]

The Hour of God's Triumph and Glory (12:27–36)

[27]"I am troubled now. Yet what should I say? 'Father, save me from this hour'? But it was for this purpose that I came to this hour. [28]Father, glorify your name." Then a voice came from heaven, "I have glorified it and will glorify it again." [29]The crowd there heard it and said it was thunder; but others said, "An angel has spoken to him." [30]Jesus answered and said, "This voice did not come for my sake but for yours. [31]Now is the time of judgment on this world; now the ruler of this world will be driven out. [32]And when I am lifted up from the earth, I will draw everyone to myself." [33]He said this indicating the kind of death he would die. [34]So the crowd answered him, "We have heard from the law that the Messiah remains forever. Then how can you say that the Son of Man must be lifted up? Who is this Son of Man?" [35]Jesus said to them, "The light will be among you only a little while. Walk while you have the light, so that darkness may

10. See Catechism 1612–1617 (on Christian marriage), 1618–1620 (on consecrated virginity).

not overcome you. Whoever walks in the dark does not know where he is going. [36]While you have the light, believe in the light, so that you may become children of the light."

After he had said this, Jesus left and hid from them.

OT: Ps 6; 89

NT: Mark 14:32–42; Rom 8:14–17; Heb 2:14–18; 5:7–10

Catechism: Christ gathers us into God's kingdom, 541–42; Christ offers his life to the Father, 606–7; agony in Gethsemane, 612; deliver us from evil, 2850–54

Lectionary: Fifth Sunday of Lent (Year B); For the Dead; Triumph of the Holy Cross

12:27–28

Jesus' words here resemble the †Synoptic accounts of his agony in Gethsemane (Mark 14:32–42; see also Ps 6:3–4). After speaking figuratively of his approaching death, Jesus declares, **I am troubled now**. Similarly, Mark states that after arriving in Gethsemane, Jesus "began to be troubled and distressed" (Mark 14:33). Amid this distress, Jesus rhetorically asks, **Yet what should I say? "Father, save me from this †hour"?** Likewise, he prays in Gethsemane, "Abba, Father. . . . Take this cup away from me" (Mark 14:36; see Heb 5:7–10). Rather, Jesus says, **It was for this purpose that I came to this hour**. As in his prayer in Gethsemane—"Not what I will but what you will" (Mark 14:36)—Jesus here fully consents to the work given him by the Father: to reveal the glory of God through his cross and resurrection: **Father, glorify your name.**[11] Jesus reveals God most luminously in the cross, for in this perfect act of self-giving, Jesus reveals that God is radical, self-giving love (see 1 John 4:8).

A heavenly **voice** responds to Jesus, **I have glorified it and will glorify it again**. The Father hears Jesus' prayer and confirms that the divine glory, the infinite exchange of love that is the divine communion, *will* be revealed in the cross. The first part of the response, "I have glorified it," is open to various interpretations. It may be a confirmation that Jesus has been revealing the divine glory throughout his ministry, especially in his †signs (2:11; 11:4; 17:4).

12:29–30

People hear this noise but are unsure what to make of it. Some think it is **thunder**, while **others** think it is an **angel**. Both interpretations have scriptural associations, for God's voice is likened to thunder (2 Sam 22:14; Ps 68:34) and is mediated through angels (Exod 3:2, 4; Judg 2:1–3). **Jesus** explains that the Father's **voice** was for their sake, not his. He himself does not learn anything new from the Father's response. Rather, the Father's voice is a help for others to believe, like the testimony of Jesus' signs and witnesses (5:36; 11:41–45; 12:9–10).

11. On "name," see sidebar on p. 89.

12:31 Jesus reveals more of what he will accomplish in his hour with his third saying about being **lifted up from the earth** on the cross (see 3:14; 8:28).[12] Jesus' death on the cross is the defeat of Satan, **the ruler of this world**, who has been given power over the fallen world on account of humanity's willful rebellion against God (14:30; 16:11). By obediently entering into death and rising from the dead, Jesus destroys death and the fear of death by which Satan keeps the human race enslaved (Heb 2:14–15). Through the cross, Jesus destroys the power of sin (brings **judgment on this world**) by taking away "the sin of the world" (John 1:29) and reconciling sinners to the Father (2 Cor 5:19).

12:32–33 The power of Jesus' death and resurrection is communicated to believers through faith and baptism, by which we receive a share in Christ's life as the Son and become God's children (1:12–13; 8:31–36). This participation in the divine communion, which Jesus' cross makes possible, is reflected in his words: **When I am lifted up from the earth, I will draw everyone to myself.** Previously Jesus said that his being "lifted up" will reveal his identity as "I AM" (8:28) and that by gazing on the cross in faith people will receive "eternal life" (3:14–15). The crucified and exalted Jesus, through whom the Father's glorious love shines forth, is the central point to which all will be gathered from their dispersal in sin and shepherded into the divine communion, eternal life in the "Father's house" (14:2).

12:34 The **crowd**, who welcomed Jesus as †messianic king, does not understand how the king can talk about his death: **How can you say that the †Son of Man must be lifted up?** They support their claims with a generic appeal to **the law** and the belief that **the Messiah remains forever**.[13] They likely refer to expectations that the Davidic messiah-king would drive out the Romans and restore the monarchy, which would then continue permanently, remain forever, in an age of righteousness and peace (Ps 89:21, 29–30, 37–38).

As discussed at 12:12–15, Jesus is the messianic king, but not in the sense that the crowd thinks or wants. A messiah-king whose throne is a cross and who conquers by dying is unheard of and boggles the mind. It is, as St. Paul says, "a stumbling block . . . and foolishness, . . . but to those who are called, . . . the power of God and the wisdom of God" (1 Cor 1:23–24).

12:35 **Jesus** issues a final exhortation to the crowd to receive him in faith. Jesus' hour is at hand, and he will soon be leaving the world: **The light will be among you only a little while**. People do not have an indefinite amount of time in which to receive the Word and his gift. Therefore, Jesus exhorts his hearers to follow him

12. Recall that, for John, "lifted up" has a twofold meaning: Jesus is lifted up physically on the cross, and the same action is his exaltation.

13. W. C. van Unnik, "The Quotation from the Old Testament in John 12:34," *Novum Testamentum* 3 (1959): 174–79.

as **the light, so that darkness may not overcome** them. **Whoever walks in the dark does not know where he is going**, but Jesus, the light of the world, reveals the Father and illumines the way to him amid a dark and sinful world (8:12).

12:36 As long as Jesus is present in the world (and he continues to be present through the Church; see 9:4), people have the opportunity to respond to him. He encourages people to **believe in the light** (in him), **so that** they **may become children of the light**. The Greek expression translated as "children of the light" is literally "sons of light," and we can see a connection between becoming "sons of light" and Jesus, who is both the Son and the light. Jesus gives believers a share in his own divine life and relationship with the Father as the Son (see Rom 8:14–17). By sharing in the Son's own life, believers share in his communion with the Father. The relation between faith and becoming "children" recalls the Prologue: "To those who did accept him he gave power to become children of God, to those who believe in his name" (1:12).

With this final exhortation, **Jesus left and hid from them**. His public ministry comes to a close. The next time Jesus will appear publicly is when Pilate presents him as king, bloodied and crowned with thorns (19:5).

Reflection and Application (12:27–36)

The eternal life that Jesus gives to those who respond positively to him with faith and discipleship is not simply life after death. Eternal life, becoming "children of the light," is a participation in the Trinitarian life of God: the eternal communion between the Father, the Son, and the Holy Spirit. God's love for humanity is so great that he wants to share his own eternal life and love, his very being, with us. Sharing in the life of the Trinity is the ultimate goal and meaning of human life. This is why we were created and the end to which every good thing in life should be directed. God gives us this gift of eternal life through baptism, and believers already possess it. Our challenge is to remain faithful to Jesus and "walk in the light as he is in the light" (1 John 1:7), and not turn our backs on this unimaginable gift, which gives meaning to our entire existence.

Foretold in the Scriptures (12:37–43)

[37]Although he had performed so many signs in their presence they did not believe in him, [38]in order that the word which Isaiah the prophet spoke might be fulfilled:

"Lord, who has believed our preaching,
to whom has the might of the Lord been revealed?"

[39]For this reason they could not believe, because again Isaiah said:

[40]"He blinded their eyes
and hardened their heart,
so that they might not see with their eyes
and understand with their heart and be converted,
and I would heal them."

[41]Isaiah said this because he saw his glory and spoke about him. [42]Nevertheless, many, even among the authorities, believed in him, but because of the Pharisees they did not acknowledge it openly in order not to be expelled from the synagogue. [43]For they preferred human praise to the glory of God.

OT: Isa 6:1–13; 52:13–53:12

NT: Matt 13:10–15; Acts 28:23–31; Rom 11:11–36

Catechism: characteristics of faith, 153–55, 160; divisions among the Jewish authorities concerning Jesus, 595–96; theophanies, 707–8

12:37–38 The evangelist now reflects on the fact that many †Jews **did not believe in** Jesus, even though **he had performed so many †signs in their presence**. John teaches that this disbelief was not because Jesus had failed in his mission. Rather, the people's disbelief in Jesus fulfills Scripture, was known in advance by God, and has been incorporated into his plan. John offers two texts from **Isaiah** as foreseeing the fact that Jesus' revelation to the world would be met with disbelief.

The first text is Isa 53:1, in its form in the †LXX: **Lord, who has believed our preaching, to whom has the might of the Lord been revealed?** This text belongs to the fourth Suffering Servant Song (Isa 52:13–53:12), which depicts the Lord's Servant as suffering and dying to obtain forgiveness for others' sins and also being vindicated by God.[14] Here in John 12:38 the phrase "might of the Lord" literally reads "the arm of the Lord," and Scripture often uses God's "arm" as a figure for his powerful actions, such as the signs worked during the exodus (Deut 4:34; 11:2–3; Ps 98:1). Jesus' ministry has featured both **preaching** and miraculous signs, through which he has **revealed** the Father. And yet many have not believed.

12:39–40 Many did not believe because **they could not believe**—they were prevented from doing so. John appeals to another **Isaiah** text: **He blinded their eyes**

14. This Isaiah text lies behind the identification of Jesus as "the Lamb of God" and his being "lifted up" on the cross.

and hardened their heart, so that they might not see with their eyes and understand with their heart and be converted, and I would heal them. This text, Isa 6:10, is cited often by New Testament writers to explain why many of Jesus' Jewish contemporaries did not believe in him (Matt 13:14–15; Acts 28:26–27; Rom 11:8). John teaches that a person's faith-filled response to Jesus involves both the initiative of God (6:44) and the person's own free response to God (12:42–43). But as Raymond Brown points out, we should not over-read this text in terms of technical theological and philosophical distinctions concerning human free will.[15] Scripture teaches that God is all-powerful and nothing can happen in the world without his willing it. But the biblical writers did not make an explicit distinction between what God deliberately wills and what God permits. If something happens in the world, it is because God has in some respect willed or, we might say, permitted it. These words about God blinding eyes and hardening hearts can be taken in this sense. Furthermore, it is possible to read the Isaiah text as hinting at future changes. God may blind eyes and harden hearts in the present, but his action may ultimately lead to people's conversion and healing.[16]

12:41 These texts from **Isaiah** speak about Jesus' ministry because the prophet **saw his glory and spoke about him**. John refers to the call of Isaiah in which the prophet received a vision of †YHWH and declared, "My eyes have seen, the King, the LORD of hosts" (Isa 6:5). When John says that Isaiah saw "his glory," "his" refers to the divine Word, who possessed divine glory with the Father "before the world began" (John 17:5). As the Prologue teaches, the divine Word was present and working in biblical history before his †incarnation in Jesus (1:9–13).[17] Thus Isaiah saw the divine Word at his call and spoke prophetically about him.

12:42–43 John gives another reason for the response of disbelief during Jesus' ministry. **Many** others, **even among the authorities, believed in him** (7:26, 48–52; see 3:1; 19:38–39), however, they kept their faith secret to avoid being **expelled from the †synagogue** (see 9:22). A severing of these community relations would be a cause of hardship and public shame, and to avoid it, they stay quiet about their faith in Jesus. John's explanatory remark, **They preferred human praise to the glory of God**, plays on the twofold meaning of the Greek word *doxa* as "praise," meaning public honor (see sidebar on p. 111), and "glory." The secret believers value public honor more than the glory that is given to God and received from God through faith in Jesus (12:26).

15. Raymond E. Brown, SS, *The Gospel according to John*, AB 29 (New York: Doubleday, 1966), 1:485.
16. So St. Thomas Aquinas, *Commentary on John* 12.7, section 1702.
17. Catechism 707–8.

Summary of the Book of Signs (12:44–50)

[44]Jesus cried out and said, "Whoever believes in me believes not only in me but also in the one who sent me, [45]and whoever sees me sees the one who sent me. [46]I came into the world as light, so that everyone who believes in me might not remain in darkness. [47]And if anyone hears my words and does not observe them, I do not condemn him, for I did not come to condemn the world but to save the world. [48]Whoever rejects me and does not accept my words has something to judge him: the word that I spoke, it will condemn him on the last day, [49]because I did not speak on my own, but the Father who sent me commanded me what to say and speak. [50]And I know that his commandment is eternal life. So what I say, I say as the Father told me."

NT: Eph 5:6–20; Rev 20:11–15

Catechism: faith, 160–61; last judgment, 1038–41

Lectionary: Preparation and Baptism of Adults—Presentation of the Creed; Christian Initiation apart from Easter Vigil

These verses summarize Jesus' teaching during his public ministry in the first part of the Gospel (chaps. 1–12).

12:44–45 **Whoever believes in me believes not only in me but also in the one who sent me**. Throughout his ministry Jesus has constantly spoken about his identity and work in terms of his relationship with the Father. The divine Word, who was with the Father from all eternity (1:1), has come down from heaven (3:13) and become †incarnate in Jesus. Jesus is the Son of the Father (5:19–23; 11:4), and he and the Father "are one" (10:30), as they both possess the divine power over life and death and the power to judge (5:21–23). Jesus is the Father's perfect envoy, and thus a response to Jesus is a response to the Father (5:30, 36–37). Since he perfectly reveals the Father and does his saving work, Jesus can say, **Whoever sees me sees the one who sent me**. He and the Father are so united that to believe in Jesus means recognizing him as the Son, sent by the Father to do his saving work.

12:46 **I came into the world as light, so that everyone who believes in me might not remain in darkness**. Twice Jesus has referred to himself as the light of the world (8:12; 9:5). Having been sent by the Father, Jesus comes into a world that is fallen and in the spiritual darkness of sin. Jesus is the shining light of divine truth amid the darkness of sin, and "the darkness has not overcome it" (1:5). Jesus invites all people to believe in him and receive the gift of eternal life, which the Father offers through him (3:16–17). Those who believe and receive this gift "will not walk in darkness, but will have the light of life" (8:12).

12:47

Jesus' presence in the world provokes people to respond. Those who respond positively will "not remain in darkness" (12:46). But a negative response is possible: one **hears** his **words and does not observe them**. Regarding such a person, Jesus says, **I do not condemn him**. Jesus has been sent **to save** a sinful **world**, not **condemn** it (3:17). He makes the offer of salvation, but this offer must be freely accepted.[18]

12:48–49

Jesus continues, **Whoever rejects me and does not accept my words has something to judge him: the word that I spoke, it will condemn him on the last day**. Jesus' work is to save, and he does not damn anyone. Rather, people condemn themselves by their own actions and their failure to receive God's Word. Since "the Father . . . has given all judgment to his Son" (5:22), the criterion of judgment consists in whether someone receives the Son and "bears fruit" in works of love (15:1–7). A person's final judgment and eternal destiny is being determined by their present response to Jesus.[19] Peoples' responses to Jesus carry such weight **because** of his relationship to the Father as his obedient Son and perfect envoy: **I did not speak on my own, but the Father who sent me commanded me what to say and speak**.

12:50

During his ministry, Jesus has faithfully carried out the mission he received from the Father: **What I say, I say as the Father told me**. As the obedient Son, he will faithfully complete the Father's saving work in his passion and resurrection. At that †hour, as Jesus said, "I lay down my life in order to take it up again" (10:17), for "this command I have received from my Father" (10:18). The Father's **commandment is eternal life**. The Father's saving work, which Jesus does in loving obedience, saves people from sin and hell and draws them into the infinite exchange of love that is the divine communion.

18. Catechism 160.
19. Catechism 161.

On the Night before He Died

John 13:1–30

John 13–21 comprises the second major part of the Gospel. These chapters are often called the Book of Glory because they focus on the revelation of God's glory in Jesus' passion and resurrection. After Jesus departs from the public scene at the end of John 12, the Gospel narrative slows dramatically. All of John 13–17 takes place during the Last Supper. Like the †Synoptics, John's account of the Last Supper features the announcement of Judas's betrayal and of Peter's denials. But unlike the Synoptics, John does not narrate the institution of the Eucharist. Instead, he presents Jesus prophetically †signifying his death by washing his disciples' feet.

The Footwashing (13:1–11)

[1]Before the feast of Passover, Jesus knew that his hour had come to pass from this world to the Father. He loved his own in the world and he loved them to the end. [2]The devil had already induced Judas, son of Simon the Iscariot, to hand him over. So, during supper, [3]fully aware that the Father had put everything into his power and that he had come from God and was returning to God, [4]he rose from supper and took off his outer garments. He took a towel and tied it around his waist. [5]Then he poured water into a basin and began to wash the disciples' feet and dry them with the towel around his waist. [6]He came to Simon Peter, who said to him, "Master, are you going to wash my feet?" [7]Jesus answered and said to him, "What I am doing, you do not understand now, but you will understand later." [8]Peter said to him, "You will never wash my feet." Jesus answered him, "Unless I

wash you, you will have no inheritance with me." [9]Simon Peter said to him, "Master, then not only my feet, but my hands and head as well." [10]Jesus said to him, "Whoever has bathed has no need except to have his feet washed, for he is clean all over; so you are clean, but not all." [11]For he knew who would betray him; for this reason, he said, "Not all of you are clean."

OT: Gen 18:1–5

NT: Matt 16:21–23; Phil 2:5–11

Catechism: Jesus embraces the Father's love, 609; sacraments of salvation, 1127–29

Lectionary: Holy Thursday; For the Unity of Christians

13:1 As **Passover** approaches, **Jesus knew that his hour**, when he will accomplish the Father's saving work and reveal his love, **had come**. The events of Jesus' †hour are his new Passover and exodus, the great act of salvation in which God's love defeats the power of sin and ransoms those enslaved to it (8:34–36). Jesus approaches his hour filled with love for his disciples, **his own in the world**. John expresses the intensity and extent of Jesus' love through the phrase: **he loved them to the end**. The Greek word for "end" (*telos*) has several dimensions of meaning. Here it means that Jesus loves **to the end** of his own mortal life. "End" here also means the maximum: Jesus loves to the greatest extent possible by giving his life on the cross. And "end" means the goal or that which completes something. Jesus' perfect love on the cross brings the Father's work of salvation to its goal.[1]

13:2 In contrast to Jesus' love stand the powers of evil. **The devil** is his principal opponent in the Gospel, and he seeks to defeat Jesus by destroying him. Sometime before the **supper**, the devil had persuaded **Judas** to betray Jesus and thus bring about his death. Jesus' hour is the showdown between the powers of evil and the love of God that will conquer them in Jesus' cross and resurrection.

13:3 Having emphasized Jesus' love in 13:1, John also emphasizes his knowledge, sovereign power, and divine identity. Jesus was **fully aware that the Father had put everything into his power**. Thus Jesus is completely sovereign over the events of his passion: they happen because he permits them to happen. John also reminds us of Jesus' divine identity by referring to his origin (**He had come from God**) and destiny (**and was returning to God**) with the Father (see 7:28; 8:14).

13:4–5 During the **supper**, Jesus interprets the meaning of his cross with a symbolic action. After removing **his outer garments** and wrapping a **towel around** himself, Jesus **poured water into a basin and began to wash the disciples' feet and dry them**. This is a parabolic action, which displays the Passion in anticipation. In Jesus' day, people most often traveled by foot, walking either barefoot or

1. Catechism 609.

Fig. 10. The Church of the Upper Room, the traditional location of the Last Supper

with open sandals. Travelers' feet would become extremely dirty, and it was an act of hospitality to offer guests water for washing their feet (Gen 18:4; Luke 7:44). Culturally, the underside of the foot was considered a dishonorable part of the body. The washing of another's feet was performed by a slave or person of lower status (1 Sam 25:41).

The footwashing here has several theological meanings. Most fundamentally, it is a symbol of Jesus' death. By washing his disciples' feet, Jesus, "the master and teacher" (13:14), performs the degrading work of a slave. Similarly, by dying on the cross, Jesus, the divine Word through whom "all things came to be" (1:3), will descend to the most miserable depths to which creaturely existence can be reduced for others' sake. Jesus' gesture is a parabolic enactment of Paul's statement in Philippians: "Though he was in the form of God, . . . taking the form of a slave . . . he humbled himself, / becoming obedient to death. . . . Because of this, God greatly exalted him" (2:6–9).

13:6–7 Peter recognizes how inappropriate it is for Jesus, the **Master**, to do a slave's work and asks, **Are you going to wash my feet?** But Peter does **not understand** the meaning of the footwashing, although Jesus says that Peter **will understand later**. Running throughout the Farewell Discourse (13:31–16:33) is a contrast between the present misunderstanding of the disciples and a future time when they will understand the meaning of Jesus and his work. This future understanding will be a gift of the Holy Spirit, who after the resurrection will bring the disciples to understand Jesus' words and deeds (16:13–14).

13:8–9 Not understanding Jesus' action, Peter vehemently refuses to let Jesus **wash** his **feet**. While his objection is well-intentioned, a recognition of Jesus' superiority, Peter showcases his lack of understanding. His protest resembles his objection to Jesus' prophecy that he would suffer and die as the †Messiah: "God forbid. Lord! No such thing shall ever happen to you" (Matt 16:22).

But **Jesus** must wash Peter's feet, and Peter must yield to Jesus' action in order to benefit from it: **Unless I wash you, you will have no inheritance with me**. This statement highlights the relationship between the footwashing and the cross. The footwashing †signifies Jesus' loving action on the cross, and Peter must yield to Jesus' loving action in order to share in Jesus' life, which the cross makes possible.

While Peter agrees to let Jesus wash his feet, he again misunderstands Jesus because he thinks that Jesus is talking about the literal washing of different body parts. Again well-intentioned but not understanding, Peter suggests that Jesus wash more of his body, **my hands and head as well**.

13:10–11 The point is not how much of the body Jesus physically washes at the Last Supper, but what the humble gesture of the footwashing signifies: the cross. Jesus' action on the cross suffices to make one **clean all over**: it cleanses from sin and incorporates people into his divine life (see 15:3). The necessity of a washing by which Jesus cleanses a person is also an allusion to baptism. Jesus spoke of the need to receive new heavenly life through a new birth of "water and Spirit" (3:5; see also Acts 22:16; Titus 3:5). Jesus' cross brings cleansing from sin, and this cleansing power is communicated to believers through baptism. Thus St. Thomas Aquinas teaches, "The sacraments of the Church derive their power specially from Christ's Passion,"[2] and the risen Jesus acts in the Church's sacraments to communicate the saving power of his passion.[3]

But Jesus indicates that some are **not clean**, some will not receive the benefits of the cross. John clarifies that Jesus refers to Judas the betrayer. Since Judas rejects Jesus and yields instead to the devil's suggestions, he will not receive the spiritual purification that proceeds from Jesus' cross.

Reflection and Application (13:1–11)

We see that Peter must yield to Jesus' action to wash his feet, the prophetic, anticipatory gesture, which displays his saving work on the cross. Christ has

2. St. Thomas Aquinas, *Summa theologica* 3, q. 62, a. 6.
3. Catechism 1127.

accomplished this work of salvation for us and offers it to us as a gift. The right response is to receive this gift and yield to his action in our lives, to say yes to him and the transforming power of his grace. Some people resist Christ because they do not consider themselves sinful enough to require him to wash them in baptism or the sacrament of reconciliation. Others have the opposite problem: they stay away because they are ashamed of their lives or secret sins. To both, Jesus speaks gently but firmly as he did to Peter, "Come, for unless I wash you, you cannot share in my inheritance."

An Example for the Disciples (13:12–20)

[12]So when he had washed their feet [and] put his garments back on and reclined at table again, he said to them, "Do you realize what I have done for you? [13]You call me 'teacher' and 'master,' and rightly so, for indeed I am. [14]If I, therefore, the master and teacher, have washed your feet, you ought to wash one another's feet. [15]I have given you a model to follow, so that as I have done for you, you should also do. [16]Amen, amen, I say to you, no slave is greater than his master nor any messenger greater than the one who sent him. [17]If you understand this, blessed are you if you do it. [18]I am not speaking of all of you. I know those whom I have chosen. But so that the scripture might be fulfilled, 'The one who ate my food has raised his heel against me.' [19]From now on I am telling you before it happens, so that when it happens you may believe that I AM. [20]Amen, amen, I say to you, whoever receives the one I send, receives me, and whoever receives me receives the one who sent me."

OT: Ps 41; Isa 43:9–13
NT: Matt 10:40–42; 1 John 3:16–18
Catechism: imitation of Christ, 1693–96; charity, 1823
Lectionary: Holy Thursday; For the Unity of Christians

13:12 We have seen that the footwashing †signifies Jesus' loving self-gift on the cross and the power of the cross communicated to disciples through the sacramental washing of baptism. Having finished the footwashing, Jesus returns to his place **at table** and teaches that the footwashing is also a model for how his disciples should live.

13:13–15 To understand the footwashing as a moral example, we need to remember the difference in status between Jesus and his disciples. Jesus is their **teacher and master**, their superior both as their earthly teacher and as the †incarnate Word (1:14–15, 30). Jesus contrasts his superior status with the humble action he has performed for those subordinate to him: **I, . . . the master and teacher, have washed your feet**. Jesus has performed a humiliating action out of love for his disciples, an action that, culturally, would be beneath even them to do for each other. Jesus holds up the footwashing as their **model to follow** and instructs them to imitate it: **You ought to wash one another's feet**. Since the footwashing signifies the cross, Jesus commands the disciples to practice the same kind of self-emptying humility and love that he will show them on the cross.[4] As 1 John 3:16 teaches, "The way we came to know love was that he laid down his life for us; so we ought to lay down our lives for our brothers." Jesus' command to the disciples to wash one another's feet is substantially the same as his command "Love one another as I love you" (15:12).

13:16–17 Jesus declares that **no slave is greater than his master** (see Matt 10:24; Luke 6:40) and adds the distinctively Johannine language of "sending," **nor any messenger greater than the one who sent him** (see John 14:28). If such selfless, humble service was good enough for Jesus, it is good enough for the disciples. Jesus concludes with the first of two beatitudes in the Fourth Gospel (the other is in 20:29). He pronounces the disciples **blessed** if they **understand** his teaching about the footwashing and **do it**.

13:18 Much as he declared, "Not all of you are clean" (13:11), Jesus clarifies that his remarks about the disciples being "blessed" (13:17) do not apply to **all of** them, namely, not to Judas. Jesus knows the innermost truth about **those whom** he has **chosen**, including Judas's plans to betray him (6:70–71). To show that Judas's presence among the Twelve is part of God's plan, Jesus connects his betrayal by Judas with Ps 41:10, **The one who ate my food has raised his heel against me**. The psalmist speaks of the suffering he experiences from the hostility of close friends, a pattern that anticipates Jesus' passion.

13:19 Jesus informs the disciples of this treachery **before it happens, so that when it happens**, it might confirm, and not undermine, their faith. John has emphasized that Jesus "knew that his †hour" had come (13:1) and was "fully aware" of his power over these events (13:3). By hinting at Judas's impending betrayal, Jesus demonstrates his divine knowledge both of his disciples and of God's plan given in Scripture. Elsewhere in the Farewell Discourse, Jesus similarly predicts bad things that will happen to the disciples (14:29; 16:1–4), but again the very fact that he predicts these things is meant to increase their faith and confidence in him. By revealing that he has knowledge that only God can have, Jesus invites his disciples to **believe that I AM**, that he is the God of Israel. Jesus' words here recall those of the Lord in Isa 43:9–10 †LXX: "Who announces these things or

4. Catechism 1823.

who announces to you the things from the beginning? . . . Be my witnesses, as I am a witness, . . . that you may know and believe and understand that I AM."[5]

13:20 Having instructed his disciples to yield to his saving action and obey his command to love, Jesus concludes by making the disciples his envoys, as he is the Father's envoy. The Father **sent** Jesus into the world to reveal him and do his work, and now Jesus positions himself as the one who will **send** the disciples (see 20:21). The disciples, through whom Jesus' revelation of God's love shines, become witnesses and bearers of his revelation, so that people's response to these holy disciples constitutes a response to Jesus and the Father.[6]

Judas's Betrayal (13:21–30)

[21]When he had said this, Jesus was deeply troubled and testified, "Amen, amen, I say to you, one of you will betray me." [22]The disciples looked at one another, at a loss as to whom he meant. [23]One of his disciples, the one whom Jesus loved, was reclining at Jesus' side. [24]So Simon Peter nodded to him to find out whom he meant. [25]He leaned back against Jesus' chest and said to him, "Master, who is it?" [26]Jesus answered, "It is the one to whom I hand the morsel after I have dipped it." So he dipped the morsel and [took it and] handed it to Judas, son of Simon the Iscariot. [27]After he took the morsel, Satan entered him. So Jesus said to him, "What you are going to do, do quickly." [28][Now] none of those reclining at table realized why he said this to him. [29]Some thought that since Judas kept the money bag, Jesus had told him, "Buy what we need for the feast," or to give something to the poor. [30]So he took the morsel and left at once. And it was night.

NT: Matt 26:20–25
Catechism: definition of sin, 1849–51

13:21 Having already hinted at his impending betrayal, **Jesus** again becomes **deeply troubled** (see 11:33) and openly announces, **One of you will betray me** (see Matt 26:21).[7] As with the Scripture quotation in 13:18, Jesus **testified** about his betrayal to reveal it as part of God's plan, for Jesus' mission is "to testify to the truth" (18:37).

13:22–23 With the **disciples** befuddled over the betrayer's identity, one disciple begins to stand out: the anonymous disciple, **whom Jesus loved**. This so-called Beloved

5. Our translation of LXX.
6. Catechism 1693–94.
7. Catechism 1851.

Disciple has a privileged status with Jesus.[8] The detail that he **was reclining at Jesus' side** means several things. Culturally, the place of the Beloved Disciple at Jesus' side suggests that he serves as the host of the dinner with Jesus, the guest of honor, seated at his left. Also, the Greek phrase for "at the side of" (*en tō kolpō*) also appears in 1:18, where the Son is said to be "at the Father's side" (*eis ton kolpon*) and to have "revealed him." As Jesus is uniquely able to reveal the Father by virtue of his being "at the Father's side," the Beloved Disciple is analogously in a unique position to testify to the spiritual meaning of Jesus by being "at Jesus' side."

13:24–27 **Peter** gestures to the Beloved Disciple, who is both physically and spiritually close to Jesus, to get more information. After he **leaned back against Jesus' chest** and asked, the disciple is given a sign from Jesus that will identify the betrayer: **The one to whom I hand the morsel after I have dipped it**. Recalling the scriptural quote in 13:18, Jesus **dipped the morsel** and **handed it to Judas**. In doing so, Jesus reveals to the Beloved Disciple what he had known "from the beginning" (6:64).

The chapter began with the report that Judas has yielded to demonic suggestions (13:2); when he actively takes **the morsel**, his interior consent to the devil opens the door to outright possession: **Satan entered him** (see Luke 22:3). **Jesus** then instructs Judas and, in a sense, Satan, **What you are going to do, do quickly**. Jesus, who has "everything [in] his power" (13:3), gives permission for the events of his passion to unfold (see 18:8).

13:28–29 Only the Beloved Disciple knew that the morsel identified the betrayer, and thus **none** of the other disciples understand Jesus' words and actions toward Judas. Both mistaken interpretations (**buy** provisions for Passover and **give something to the poor**) recall 12:4–6, where John's audience has learned that Judas is a "thief" and does not care "about the poor." The disciples not only misunderstand the meaning of Jesus' words and actions here; they also do not see the truth of Judas's character.

13:30 Judas, possessed by Satan, **took the morsel and left at once**. John adds that **it was night**. The **night** here refers both to the time of day and the spiritual darkness into which Judas has entered. He has turned away from the light and chosen the darkness. When Judas next appears, we will see him leading those hostile to Jesus, who walk in darkness (18:3).

8. See "Authorship" in the introduction to this volume.

Farewell Discourse I

John 13:31–14:31

John 13:31–16:33 is known as the Farewell Discourse, the departing words of Jesus to his disciples before he leaves them and goes to the Father. The central concern of these chapters is the disciples' life after Jesus' resurrection and ascension. Accordingly, the Church places the liturgical reading of these chapters in the Easter season, after Jesus' resurrection and looking forward to Pentecost.

The Evangelist has composed this material according to the literary genre known as a "testament."[1] Exemplified in biblical texts such as Jacob's last words to his sons in Gen 49, a testament is the farewell address of a teacher or father figure to those whom he leaves behind. Jesus' testament has many standard features: announcement of departure (13:33), words of consolation (14:1, 27), final instructions (13:34; 15:13, 17), warnings about hardships to come (15:18, 21; 16:1–4), securing the group's future needs (14:16, 23, 26; 15:26; 16:7, 13).

Glory Revealed in Love (13:31–38)

[31]When he had left, Jesus said, "Now is the Son of Man glorified, and God is glorified in him. [32][If God is glorified in him,] God will also glorify him in himself, and he will glorify him at once. [33]My children, I will be with you only a little while longer. You will look for me, and as I told the Jews, 'Where I go you cannot come,' so now I say it to you. [34]I give you a

1. See William S. Kurz, SJ, *Farewell Addresses in the New Testament* (Collegeville, MN: Liturgical Press, 1990).

new commandment: love one another. As I have loved you, so you also should love one another. [35]This is how all will know that you are my disciples, if you have love for one another."

[36]Simon Peter said to him, "Master, where are you going?" Jesus answered [him], "Where I am going, you cannot follow me now, though you will follow later." [37]Peter said to him, "Master, why can't I follow you now? I will lay down my life for you." [38]Jesus answered, "Will you lay down your life for me? Amen, amen, I say to you, the cock will not crow before you deny me three times."

OT: Exod 24:16–17

NT: Matt 5:14–16; Mark 14:27–31; Luke 22:31–34; Rom 13:8–10; 1 John 4:7–11

Catechism: characteristics of the people of God, 782; charity, 1822–29; petitions in the Our Father, 2822, 2842

Lectionary: Fifth Sunday of Easter (Year C)

13:31–32 With the departure of Judas, the sequence of events leading to Jesus' †hour has begun. The focus shifts to Jesus and his faithful disciples, and the Farewell Discourse proper begins.

Several important theological themes in the Gospel come together in the statement: **Now is the Son of Man glorified, and God is glorified in him**. The language of "glory" recalls the scriptural background in which the Lord's glory is a sensible manifestation of his awesome presence (see sidebar on p. 39). This motif of revelation connects with John's use of the title †**Son of Man**, which designates Jesus as the one who came down from heaven to reveal the Father (3:12–13) and is lifted up on the cross for the world's salvation (3:14–15; 8:28; 12:32–34). The cross is the moment of glorification because in the cross God is definitively revealed as self-giving love (1 John 4:8–10). The Father loves the Son and gives him for the world's salvation (John 3:16–17), and the Son in turn makes of his life a perfect gift of love and obedience to the Father (10:17–18). Since the love between the Father and the Son is revealed in the cross, **God is glorified in** Jesus' loving obedience, and the Father will further **glorify** Jesus, reveal Jesus' deity, in his resurrected, glorified humanity (8:28; 20:28).

13:33 As he did with the festival crowd and †Pharisees (7:33–34; 8:21; 12:35), Jesus **now** tells the disciples that he will be leaving them in **a little while**, and they **cannot come**, at least not yet. Thus Jesus will now give his disciples instructions for the time when he will be physically absent.

13:34 First and foremost is Jesus' **new commandment** to **love one another** (see 15:12, 17; 1 John 4:7, 11).[2] Jesus' love is the gift of himself in obedience to

2. Catechism 1822–29.

the Father's will for the salvation of the world. He has already shown this love symbolically in the footwashing, and he will enact it on the cross. Just as the disciples are to "wash one another's feet" (13:14) as Jesus washed their feet, so also are they to **love one another** as Jesus has **loved** them. This is the "law of love" (Rom 13:8–10; James 2:8), which summarizes the Father's will and must guide the Church.[3]

13:35 Jesus designates this radical self-giving **love** as the defining characteristic of his **disciples**. This kind of loving practice is revelatory. Just as Jesus' works reveal the Father and himself as the Son (5:36), so will the disciples' **love for one another** make known to **all** that they belong to Jesus. Similarly, Jesus says in Matt 5:16, "Your light must shine before others, that they may see your good deeds and glorify your heavenly Father."

The love of Jesus on the cross is not only the example but also the indispensable source for the disciples' love. The Catechism states, "It is impossible to keep the Lord's commandment by imitating the divine model from outside; there has to be a vital participation, coming from the depths of the heart, in the holiness and the mercy and the love of our God" (2842). Through their loving actions, animated by Jesus' own love for them, the disciples become living testimony to the Father's love, revealed in the cross of Jesus and active in them.

13:36 Running throughout John 13–14 is a pattern in which a disciple questions Jesus and Jesus responds with clarification and further teaching (13:25, 36; 14:5, 8, 22). The Beloved Disciple asked Jesus about the betrayer (13:25), and now **Peter** asks Jesus, **Where are you going?**, not knowing that Jesus is going to the Father. Jesus responds that Peter **cannot follow** him **now** but adds that Peter **will follow later** (compare 13:7). Jesus must go to the Father first to enable others to go to the Father through him.

13:37–38 In the †Synoptics, Peter insists that he will not fail Jesus like the other disciples (Mark 14:27–31; Luke 22:31–34). Here, Peter, who does not even know where Jesus is going, insists that he will **follow** Jesus **now**. He even professes his willingness to **lay down** his **life for** Jesus (Matt 26:35; Mark 14:31), using language that recalls the good shepherd (John 10:15, 17–18).

Jesus' rhetorical question casts doubt on Peter's well-intentioned but naive overconfidence: **Will you lay down your life for me?** Rather, Jesus solemnly declares, **The cock will not crow before you deny me three times**. Peter cannot follow Jesus now, and before the next morning, he will explicitly refuse to do so.

3. Catechism 782, 2822.

Going to the Father (14:1–7)

[1]"Do not let your hearts be troubled. You have faith in God; have faith also in me. [2]In my Father's house there are many dwelling places. If there were not, would I have told you that I am going to prepare a place for you? [3]And if I go and prepare a place for you, I will come back again and take you to myself, so that where I am you also may be. [4]Where [I] am going you know the way." [5]Thomas said to him, "Master, we do not know where you are going; how can we know the way?" [6]Jesus said to him, "I am the way and the truth and the life. No one comes to the Father except through me. [7]If you know me, then you will also know my Father. From now on you do know him and have seen him."

OT: Exod 25:8–9

NT: Acts 4:5–12; 1 Tim 2:1–6; Rev 7:13–17

Catechism: Christ the mediator and fullness, 65–66, 846; believing in Jesus, 151; heaven, 1025–27

Lectionary: Fourth Sunday of Easter (Year A); For the Dead

14:1

Jesus has announced his imminent departure (13:33), but he reassures his disciples: **Do not let your hearts be troubled**. In John, the Greek verb behind "troubled" connotes the distress experienced from the proximity of death (11:33; 12:27; 13:21). Instead, Jesus tells the disciples, to **have faith**, to trust in **God** the Father and in him. As the Father's Son and perfect envoy, Jesus is absolutely reliable and trustworthy, and a faith response to him is a faith response to the Father who sent him (12:44).[4]

14:2–3

Jesus refers to his destination as **my Father's house** in which **there are many dwelling places**. Jesus goes to the Father **to prepare a place** for his disciples with the Father in heavenly glory. Having already promised that his disciples will follow him later (13:36), Jesus now promises to **come back again and take** them to be with him in the Father's glory (see 12:26).

Biblical texts often present God's heavenly dwelling as a temple (e.g., Ps 11:4; Rev 7:15). The earthly sanctuary, a replica of the heavenly one (Exod 25:8–9), was regarded as God's dwelling place among his people. Jesus referred to the Jerusalem temple as "my Father's house" and spoke of its destruction, three days after which a new temple would be built (John 2:16, 19). John reveals that this new temple was to be Jesus' own resurrected body (2:21). The glorified humanity of Jesus is the point where all humanity comes to dwell with the Father. Heaven, "the Father's house," is not so much a place as the divine communion of life and

4. Catechism 151.

LIVING TRADITION

Pope St. John Paul II on Jesus Christ as One Mediator of Salvation for All Humanity

No one, therefore, can enter into communion with God except through Christ, by the working of the Holy Spirit. Christ's one, universal mediation . . . is the way established by God himself. . . .

The universality of salvation means that it is granted not only to those who explicitly believe in Christ and have entered the Church. Since salvation is offered to all, it must be made concretely available to all. But it is clear that today, as in the past, many people do not have an opportunity to come to know or accept the gospel revelation or enter the Church. The social and cultural conditions in which they live do not permit this, and frequently they have been brought up in other religious traditions. For such people salvation in Christ is accessible by virtue of a grace which, while having a mysterious relationship to the Church, does not make them formally part of the Church but enlightens them in a way which is accommodated to their spiritual and material situation. This grace comes from Christ; it is the result of his Sacrifice and is communicated by the Holy Spirit. . . .

The Church offers mankind the Gospel, that prophetic message which responds to the needs and aspirations of the human heart and always remains "Good News." The Church cannot fail to proclaim that Jesus came to reveal the face of God and to merit salvation for all humanity by his cross and resurrection.[a]

a. John Paul II, *Redemptoris Missio* (On the Permanent Validity of the Church's Missionary Mandate) 5, 10, 11, respectively.

love in which we share through the glorified humanity of Jesus.[5] As we shall see, the disciples' sharing in this heavenly communion with the Father through Jesus begins in this life through faith and the indwelling Holy Spirit (14:17, 23).

14:4–7 The disciples do not understand what Jesus is telling them. **Thomas** confesses that the disciples **do not know where you are going**, much less **the way** to get there. **Jesus** responds with the sixth "I am + predicate" title in the Gospel: **I am the way and the truth and the life**. Jesus is **the way** because it is only through him that humanity has access to the Father (see 10:7, 9). Humanity can have access to the Father through Jesus because he is **the truth**, the †incarnate Word, "who has come down from heaven" (3:13) to reveal the Father, accomplish his saving work, and draw people to share in the divine communion. By following Jesus as **the way**, disciples come to know **the truth**, that is, his revelation of the

5. Catechism 1025–27; Benedict XVI, "Homily for the Holy Mass on the Solemnity of the Assumption of the Blessed Virgin Mary," August 15, 2010.

Father: **If you know me, then you will also know my Father.**[6] Jesus is **the life** because only he has come down from heaven and only he can lift humanity up to share in the divine communion, which he as the Son has enjoyed from all eternity. Jesus thus declares, **No one comes to the Father except through me.** Jesus is the "narrow gate" (Matt 7:13–14; Luke 13:24), the "one mediator between God and the human race" (1 Tim 2:5), and "There is no salvation through anyone else, nor is there any other name under heaven given to the human race by which we are to be saved" (Acts 4:12).[7]

Reflection and Application (14:1–7)

The Church has selected this Gospel text as one to be read at liturgies for the dead. We are invited to hear Jesus speaking to us personally, "I will come back again and take you to myself, so that where I am you also may be" (14:3). Jesus has gone to the Father's house and entered into heavenly glory. He promises to come back at the hour of our death and take us to be with him and the Father forever (12:26). Hence, St. Thomas Aquinas comments on John 14:3, "The statement 'I will come again and take you to myself,' can be understood as that spiritual coming with which Christ always visits the Church of the faithful and vivifies each of the faithful at death. . . . [He] will strengthen you in faith and love for [him]."[8] This is the good news of our salvation: through his death and resurrection, Jesus promises to take us to be with the Father in heavenly glory. Consequently, as St. Paul writes, do "not grieve like the rest, who have no hope" (1 Thess 4:13), but rather "have faith in God" and in what Jesus promises (John 14:1). The promises of the Lord are rock-solid because God is faithful: "I have spoken; I will do it" (Ezek 37:14).

Seeing the Father (14:8–14)

[8]Philip said to him, "Master, show us the Father, and that will be enough for us." [9]Jesus said to him, "Have I been with you for so long a time and you still do not know me, Philip? Whoever has seen me has seen the Father. How can you say, 'Show us the Father'? [10]Do you not believe that I

6. Catechism 65–66.

7. Catechism 480, 846–48.

8. St. Thomas Aquinas, *Commentary on John* 14.1, section 1861, in *Commentary on the Gospel of John*, trans. Fabian Larcher, OP, and James A. Weisheipl, OP, introduction and notes by Daniel Keating and Matthew Levering (Washington, DC: Catholic University of America Press, 2010), 2:53.

am in the Father and the Father is in me? The words that I speak to you I do not speak on my own. The Father who dwells in me is doing his works. [11]Believe me that I am in the Father and the Father is in me, or else, believe because of the works themselves. [12]Amen, amen, I say to you, whoever believes in me will do the works that I do, and will do greater ones than these, because I am going to the Father. [13]And whatever you ask in my name, I will do, so that the Father may be glorified in the Son. [14]If you ask anything of me in my name, I will do it."

OT: Exod 33:18–23
NT: Matt 6:9–13; 26:36–46
Catechism: Jesus' mysteries, 516; Jesus teaches us how to pray, 2614, 2825
Lectionary: Fourth Sunday of Easter (Year A); Holy Name of Jesus

14:8 **Philip** does not understand Jesus' words about knowing and seeing the Father in Jesus. He might be looking for a grand †theophany, because his request of Jesus, **Show us the Father**, recalls Moses' request of the Lord at Mount Sinai: "Let me see your glory!" (Exod 33:18).

14:9–11 Philip was among the first disciples called (1:43), and **Jesus** laments his lack of understanding: **You still do not know me, Philip?** To know Jesus is to know that he reveals **the Father**. All the **words** that Jesus speaks are given him by the Father (8:38, 40), and all the **works** he does are performed by the **Father who dwells in** him. The Father is not to be seen anywhere apart from the Son who "has revealed him" (1:18). Thus Jesus declares, **Whoever has seen me has seen the Father**. All of Jesus' words and **works** serve to lead people to **believe** and see the relationship between the Father and the Son revealed in them.[9]

14:12 After speaking about the Father's works performed in Jesus' humanity, Jesus then declares, **Whoever believes in me will do the works that I do, and will do greater ones than these**. These words recall Jesus' earlier teaching in 5:20, where he spoke of the divine actions of God now being performed in the humanity of the †incarnate Son as "greater works." They are "greater" because they are properly divine works now being performed through Jesus' human nature. Enabling the performance of these works is the spiritual union between the Father and Jesus (14:11). With respect to 14:12, a key to Jesus' promise is his explanation, **because I am going to the Father**. When Jesus goes to the Father, his humanity will be glorified and become "greater." The glorified Jesus will send the Holy Spirit to dwell in his disciples (14:16–17) and draw them into spiritual union with himself. Then the properly divine works of God, performed in Jesus' humanity, will be performed by the disciples in

9. Catechism 516.

communion with the risen Jesus. Thus it is in this respect, as the works of God will be performed by the disciples spiritually united to the risen Jesus, that the disciples' works will be "greater." Their works will reveal who Jesus is and thus be revealing of the Father.

14:13–14

Related to these "greater works" and the disciples' communion with Jesus is the petitionary prayer that Jesus invites his disciples to make: **Whatever you ask in my name, I will do** (see 15:7, 16).[10] In the Bible, a person's name expressed their identity or role (see sidebar on p. 89). The name of Jesus similarly expresses the reality of his person, which is complete love and obedience to the Father. Prayers offered in Jesus' name—that is, in union with him—are offered in perfect obedience to the Father's will, for Jesus is perfectly obedient to the Father. Such prayer resembles the petition in the Our Father: "Your will be done, / on earth as in heaven" (Matt 6:10; see 26:39).

Since Jesus is going to the Father and the divine glory will transform his humanity, Jesus will be in the position to hear and answer prayers. Like these "greater works," the granting of these petitions asked by the disciples in communion with Jesus reveals the glorified humanity of the Son existing with the Father, **so that the Father may be glorified in the Son**.

God Will Dwell in the Disciples (14:15–24)

[15]"If you love me, you will keep my commandments. [16]And I will ask the Father, and he will give you another Advocate to be with you always, [17]the Spirit of truth, which the world cannot accept, because it neither sees nor knows it. But you know it, because it remains with you, and will be in you. [18]I will not leave you orphans; I will come to you. [19]In a little while the world will no longer see me, but you will see me, because I live and you will live. [20]On that day you will realize that I am in my Father and you are in me and I in you. [21]Whoever has my commandments and observes them is the one who loves me. And whoever loves me will be loved by my Father, and I will love him and reveal myself to him." [22]Judas, not the Iscariot, said to him, "Master, [then] what happened that you will reveal yourself to us and not to the world?" [23]Jesus answered and said to him, "Whoever loves me will keep my word, and my Father will love him, and we will come to him and make our dwelling with him. [24]Whoever does not love me does not keep my words; yet the word you hear is not mine but that of the Father who sent me."

10. Catechism 2614, 2825.

OT: Ezek 37:23–28

NT: 1 John 2:1–6; Rev 3:20–21

Catechism: titles of the Holy Spirit, 692; promise of the Spirit, 729; Church as communion with Jesus, 788–89

Lectionary: Sixth Sunday of Easter (Years A and C); Confirmation; Pastoral or Spiritual Meetings; For Peace and Justice

14:15 Jesus introduces an important teaching in the Farewell Discourse: **If you love me, you will keep my commandments**. Love and obedience go together. The disciples' personal love for Jesus leads them to obey his commandments, and his most basic commandment—to love—arises from the love he shows them: "As I have loved you, so you also should love one another" (13:34; see sidebar on p. 259).

The disciples' relationship to Jesus mirrors Jesus' own relationship with the Father (15:10). Just as the Son loves the Father and obeys his will, so too must the disciples love Jesus and obey his will, which is the same as the Father's will. Through lives of love and obedience to Jesus, the disciples are conformed to the Father, and the divine love will shine forth radiantly through them.

14:16–17 Jesus promises that once he has entered into heavenly glory, **I will ask the Father, and he will give you another Advocate to be with you always**. This is the first of five promises about the Holy Spirit—the Advocate or Paraclete—made by Jesus in the Farewell Discourse. The Spirit is **another Advocate** because Jesus is also "an Advocate with the Father" (1 John 2:1).[11] The Paraclete is **the Spirit of truth** because he is the Spirit of Jesus, who is "the truth" (14:6), the revelation of God. While distinct from Jesus, the Spirit does not operate independently of him (16:13–15). Since the world does not receive Jesus (see sidebar on p. 37), **the world cannot accept** or receive the Spirit, who abides with Jesus (1:33). The world **neither sees nor knows** the Spirit because the world does not see or know the truth about Jesus by faith. The disciples, however, have some openness to Jesus in faith, which in turn disposes them to the Spirit.[12] Jesus promises that the Spirit **remains with** and **will be in** his disciples.[13] Through the Spirit, God comes to dwell in the hearts of Jesus' disciples, much as the Father dwells in Jesus and Jesus dwells in the Father (14:11).

14:18–20 Jesus goes to the Father, but he promises to **come** back **to** the disciples. After Jesus leaves the world in death, **the world will no longer see** him. But the disciples **will see** Jesus again after the resurrection. The risen Jesus

11. Catechism 692.

12. So Stanislas Lyonnet, SJ, "The Paraclete," in Ignace de la Potterie, SJ, and Stanislas Lyonnet, SJ, *The Christian Lives by the Spirit*, trans. John Morriss (Staten Island, NY: Alba House, 1971), 59–61.

13. This remark specifies that all the Paraclete's actions described in the Farewell Discourse will take place *within* the disciples.

The Holy Spirit, Advocate and Paraclete

BIBLICAL BACKGROUND

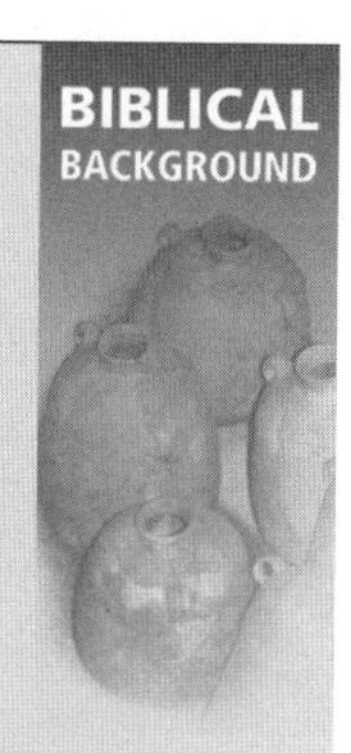

The word translated in the NABRE as "Advocate" is the Greek word *paraklētos*, represented in English as Paraclete.[a] The term comes from a verb meaning "to call to one's side," as with the Latin term *advocatus*, hence "Advocate." The background for this term is the Greco-Roman courtroom. A paraclete was someone who could provide help and assistance to a person in a trial setting: give counsel, plead that person's cause, intercede with the judge. The courtroom background for this term fits with the Gospel's running themes of trial and judgment (see comments on 3:19–21; 9:39). As the Paraclete, the Holy Spirit serves as a counselor for the disciples. He will give comfort and help to the disciples when the hostile, unbelieving world persecutes them (14:16–17; 15:26). Dwelling in the disciples, he will lead them to a deeper understanding of Jesus (14:26; 16:12–15) and enable them to bear witness to him (15:26–27). The Spirit also serves as a prosecutor against the world, for he will prove to the disciples that the world is wrong about "sin and righteousness and condemnation" (16:8).[b]

a. "Advocate" reflects St. Jerome's translation of the Greek *paraklētos* in the Latin Vulgate as *advocatus* in 1 John 2:1. For discussion, see Raymond E. Brown, SS, *The Gospel according to John*, AB 29A (New York: Doubleday, 1970), 2:1135–44; Rudolf Schnackenburg, *The Gospel according to St. John*, vol. 3, *Commentary on Chapters 13–21*, trans. David Smith and G. A. Kon (New York: Crossroad, 1982), 138–54.

b. Catechism 729.

lives forever (**I live**), and he will enable the disciples to share in his eternal, resurrected life (**You will live**). The **day** of the resurrection will be a great moment of revelation, when the disciples will both **realize** who Jesus is and be incorporated into the divine communion. The relationship between the Father and Son—**I am in my Father**—will be revealed to the disciples in the glorified humanity of Jesus. Moreover, a new relationship of communion and indwelling will be created between the risen Jesus and the disciples: **You are in me and I in you.**

14:21

These divine realities will be revealed to the disciples, who love and obey Jesus. As Jesus already said in 14:15, the disciples' love for him is manifested in obedience to his **commandments**. Obedience is the lifestyle of loving God. The disciples' response of love and obedience to Jesus leads into a deeper intimacy with the Father: **Whoever loves me will be loved by my Father**. By loving and obeying Jesus, disciples are given to know more deeply his reality as the risen Lord and the divine love given in him: **I will love him and reveal myself to him.**

14:22 Since Jesus had said that he will reveal himself to the disciples, another disciple, **Judas**, wants to know what has changed in Jesus' plans: **What happened that you will reveal yourself to us and not to the world?** His question recalls the demand of Jesus' "brothers" that he reveal himself in a grand public display to the whole world (see 7:3–5).[14]

14:23–24 Jesus answers by repeating what he has said in 14:15, 21. If the disciples want to know Jesus, they must love him and **keep** his **word**. After the resurrection, the **Father** and the Son will dwell in these disciples through the Holy Spirit, and through him, they will come to know and participate in the divine communion (14:17, 20).[15] In this way, Jesus' commands and his interior prompting through the Holy Spirit lead believers to an inner place where Jesus can reveal himself. This is his promise.

Ezekiel foretold a time when God would dwell with the redeemed people of the new †covenant community: "My dwelling shall be with them; I will be their God, and they will be my people" (Ezek 37:27). This promise of divine indwelling is fulfilled in the gift of the Holy Spirit by which God dwells in Jesus' disciples. God's dwelling in the disciples makes them into a temple (see 1 Cor 3:16; 2 Cor 6:16). The word for **dwelling** (*monē*) also appears in 14:2 for the many "dwelling places" in the Father's house. God's dwelling in Jesus' disciples after the resurrection is a genuine, present sharing in heavenly life that is the Father's house.

Jesus then expresses the relationship between love, obedience, and divine indwelling in negative terms. Disobedience to him is a sign of lack of love for him. Consequently, it is a lack of love for the Father, for Jesus' word **is not** his **but that of the Father**. Love and obedience toward Jesus opens the door for God to dwell in the disciples (see Rev 3:20–21).

Knowing Jesus' Love for the Father (14:25–31)

[25]"I have told you this while I am with you. [26]The Advocate, the holy Spirit that the Father will send in my name—he will teach you everything and remind you of all that [I] told you. [27]Peace I leave with you; my peace I give to you. Not as the world gives do I give it to you. Do not let your hearts be troubled or afraid. [28]You heard me tell you, 'I am going away and I will come back to you.' If you loved me, you would rejoice that I am

14. Gail R. O'Day, "The Gospel of John," in *The New Interpreter's Bible*, vol. 9 (Nashville: Abingdon, 1995), 748.

15. Catechism 788–89.

Saint Teresa of Avila on the Soul as the Father's House

LIVING TRADITION

Saint Teresa of Avila is one of the Church's greatest teachers, especially regarding the spiritual life. In *The Interior Castle*, she develops the image of the Father's many-roomed house (John 14:2, 23) to speak about the soul in which God dwells.

> We consider our soul to be like a castle made entirely out of a diamond or of very clear crystal, in which there are many rooms, just as in heaven there are many dwelling places. For in reflecting upon it carefully, Sisters, we realize that the soul of the just person is nothing else but a paradise where the Lord says He finds His delight. So then, what do you think that abode will be like where a King so powerful, so wise, so pure, so full of all good things takes His delight? I don't find anything comparable to the magnificent beauty of a soul and its marvelous capacity.[a]

a. St. Teresa of Avila, *The Interior Castle*, in *The Collected Works of St. Teresa of Avila*, trans. Kieran Kavanaugh, OCD, and Otilio Rodriguez, OCD (Washington, DC: ICS Publications, 1980), 2:283.

going to the Father; for the Father is greater than I. [29]And now I have told you this before it happens, so that when it happens you may believe. [30]I will no longer speak much with you, for the ruler of the world is coming. He has no power over me, [31]but the world must know that I love the Father and that I do just as the Father has commanded me. Get up, let us go."

OT: Isa 52:7–10; 54:10–13; Jer 33:6–9

NT: Col 3:12–17; 1 John 4:16–21

Catechism: the Spirit reveals the Father and the Son, 243–44; Christ's life as an offering to the Father, 606; the Holy Spirit and the Church, 737

Lectionary: Sixth Sunday of Easter (Year C); Pastoral or Spiritual Meetings; For Peace and Justice

14:25–26 Throughout the Farewell Discourse, Jesus announces beforehand many things that will happen to the disciples (13:19; 14:29; 16:1, 4). Jesus has just **told** the disciples about the realities to be revealed at his resurrection, and he includes the future teaching activity of the **holy Spirit**. As the Father has sent Jesus, upon whom the Spirit descended (1:32–33), **the Father will** also **send** the Spirit in Jesus' **name** and at his request (14:16). The Holy Spirit, who will dwell in Jesus' disciples, **will teach you everything and remind you of all that [I] told you**. There are several instances in the Gospel where disciples are said to remember episodes in Jesus' ministry after his glorification (2:17, 22; 12:16). As this verse suggests, their remembering of Jesus' ministry will be caused by the Spirit. It is not a simple recollection of the past but also a deeper understanding of Jesus and his work given by the Spirit—a spiritual understanding. The Spirit leads disciples into a greater understanding of the mystery of Jesus and makes it come alive for us.[16]

14:27 Among his promises (14:18–24), Jesus includes the promise of his **peace**. Behind this mention of "peace" is the biblical promise of *shalom* (peace, well-being, everything is right), a blessing of reconciliation that God promised to bestow upon his people in his †eschatological act of salvation (Isa 52:7; 54:10–13; Jer 33:6–9; Zech 9:10). Jesus' peace is a fruit of his relationship with the Father, into which he will bring his disciples. It is a supernatural peace that arises from a total love for the Father and therefore is unlike the peace of **the world**, which rejects God. Repeating his words of reassurance (14:1), Jesus calls the disciples to a confident, trusting faith and promises them the peace that comes from obeying the Father and knowing his love. We shall see this promise fulfilled in the Gospel account of Easter Sunday evening, when the risen Jesus gives the disciples his peace, which drives out their fear (20:19; see 20:26; 1 John 4:18). Paul similarly exhorts his readers, "Let the peace of Christ control your hearts" (Col 3:15).

14:28–29 Jesus continues to console his distressed disciples with the promise **I will come back to you**. He will return to them not only after his resurrection, not only at the †Parousia, but also during the present time through the Holy Spirit. While it may be very hard for them to grasp, the disciples should **rejoice** that Jesus is **going to the Father**. The Father is **greater** than Jesus in his mortal humanity, but at his resurrection and ascension, Jesus' humanity will be glorified by the Father and become "greater" (see 14:12). Jesus' entrance into heavenly glory opens up salvation and life with the Father, salvation and life for humanity (see Acts 2:33). Jesus has prophesied these things ahead of time, **so that** when they happen, the disciples **may believe** in him, believe that he is present to the Father and "has revealed him" (1:18).

14:30 Little time remains for Jesus to be with his disciples in an earthly way, because **the ruler of the world**, the devil, **is coming**. Satan has taken possession of Judas, who has gone out into the darkness (13:30) and will next appear leading a band representing all of sinful humanity against Jesus. But Satan, being a creature, **has no power over** Jesus, the †incarnate Word through whom all creation came to be (1:3), who is sinless (8:46), and who has sovereign control over his passion (13:1–3).

14:31 With his passion at hand, Jesus declares, **The world must know that I love the Father and that I do just as the Father has commanded me**. The cross

16. Catechism 243–44, 737.

reveals the depths of Jesus' love for the Father, which is so intense that he willingly embraces the horrible death of the cross to accomplish the Father's work of salvation. Just as the disciples' love for Jesus reveals itself in their obedience to his commands (14:15, 21), so also Jesus' love for the Father reveals itself in his laying down his life for the world's salvation in obedience to the Father's command (10:17–18).[17] Therefore Jesus bids his disciples, **Get up, let us go**—that is, let us go to the cross, where Jesus' love will be on display for the whole world to see.

17. Catechism 606.

Farewell Discourse II

John 15:1–16:4a

The second part of the Farewell Discourse (15:1–16:4a) concerns the Church. Jesus continues teaching about the disciples' communion with himself and with the Father, their present sharing in heavenly life. This participation in the divine communion constitutes the Church's inner, spiritual reality. Jesus communicates this teaching through the image of a vine, which provides a constant source of life for the branches (15:1–7). If the disciples are to enter into the divine communion of love between the Father and Son, they must obey Jesus and love one another with God's radical, self-giving love (15:8–17). But the Church must also confront "the world," the sum total of all that deliberately rejects God and persecutes Jesus and his disciples (15:18–16:11). Although the Church will be hated and persecuted by the world, Jesus commissions the disciples to go and bear witness to the love of God. To help them in this mission, Jesus promises them the divine help of the Spirit.

The Vine and the Branches (15:1–8)

[1]"I am the true vine, and my Father is the vine grower. [2]He takes away every branch in me that does not bear fruit, and every one that does he prunes so that it bears more fruit. [3]You are already pruned because of the word that I spoke to you. [4]Remain in me, as I remain in you. Just as a branch cannot bear fruit on its own unless it remains on the vine, so neither can you unless you remain in me. [5]I am the vine, you are the branches. Whoever remains in me and I in him will bear much fruit,

because without me you can do nothing. [6]Anyone who does not remain in me will be thrown out like a branch and wither; people will gather them and throw them into a fire and they will be burned. [7]If you remain in me and my words remain in you, ask for whatever you want and it will be done for you. [8]By this is my Father glorified, that you bear much fruit and become my disciples."

OT: Ps 80; Isa 5:1–7

NT: 1 Cor 12:12–28

Catechism: Church as vine, 755; being conformed to Christ, 1694; "Apart from me you can do nothing," 2074; praying in Jesus' name, 2614

Lectionary: Fifth Sunday of Easter (Year B); Common of Saints; Consecration of Virgins and Religious Profession; For the Sick; Sacred Heart; Christian Initiation apart from Easter Vigil; Baptism of Children

15:1–4 With his seventh "I am + predicate" title, **I am the true vine**, Jesus reveals the communion between himself and the disciples to be the inner reality of the Church. The vine is a biblical image for Israel as the people of God: "The vineyard of the LORD of hosts is the house of Israel, / the people of Judah, his cherished plant" (Isa 5:7; see Ps 80:9). As the **true vine**, Jesus is the perfect realization of Israel's vocation to be God's obedient people, for he is completely obedient to the Father's will. The disciple who lives in communion with Jesus is a **branch** united to the **vine** (15:5) and is summoned to practice the same obedience (15:10).

The identification of the **Father** as **the vine grower** likewise recalls Scripture. Both the Psalms and Isaiah depict the Lord as the vine's owner, who plants it and cares for it (Ps 80:9–12; Isa 5:1–7). But when the vine produces the opposite of what the Lord desires and expects—sour grapes instead of edible—he allows his vineyard to be overrun (Isa 5:2–7). The Father wants to cultivate a fruitful vine, which produces love (see 15:16–17). The disciples who do **not bear fruit**, who do not perform works of love, the Father will cut off from the vine. The disciples who do produce works of love, the Father **prunes so that** they can produce even **more fruit**. The verb for "prune" (*kathairō*) also means "cleanse," and the Father has already been at work in Jesus' disciples, purifying them through his **word**, which they have embraced and to which they continually yield (8:31). But for branches to **bear fruit**, they must stay attached to the vine. If the disciples are to produce works of love, they must remain in communion with Jesus: **Remain in me, as I remain in you**.

15:5–6 Jesus clarifies the relationship: **I am the vine, you are the branches**. Like Paul's teaching on the Church as the body of Christ (Rom 12:3–8; 1 Cor 12:12–27), John's teaching on the vine and the branches †signifies that Jesus and his disciples are united to each other in a vital union, the Church. Paul emphasizes the unity of the Church as a body with a diversity of members and roles. John emphasizes the flow of life and power from Jesus, **the vine**, to his disciples, **the branches**. Jesus is the indispensable source of life and empowerment for his disciples, the one upon whom they must constantly and radically depend: **Without me you can do nothing**. The disciples' communion with Christ opens them up to the Father's work of pruning, through which they **will bear much fruit**.[1] However, branches that are cut off from the vine, their life-source, can only **wither**. Disciples who do **not remain in** communion with Jesus are cut off from the source of spiritual life. All that remains for such spiritually dead branches is to be cast **into a fire**.

15:7 The communion between Jesus and his disciples (**If you remain in me and my words remain in you**) enables them to petition the Father with confidence that their request **will be done**. As discussed previously (14:13–14), to pray in communion with the risen Jesus means to be in communion with his total love and obedience to the Father. It is to pray that the Father's will be accomplished in the world and in our lives.[2] Such prayer is anticipated by the people Israel at Mount Sinai, who profess three times, "Everything the Lord has said, we will do" (Exod 19:8; see 24:3, 7). It is the prayer of the Virgin Mary, who completely consents to God's will for her, "May it be done to me according to your word" (Luke 1:38). It is the prayer that Jesus himself offers to the Father in Gethsemane, "Not what I will but what you will" (Mark 14:36), and teaches his disciples to pray, "Your will be done" (Matt 6:10).

15:8 The Father brings people into communion with himself through his Son (6:44), and through this communion he enables them to produce the **fruit** of love (15:2). Through these divinely assisted acts of love, the **disciples** manifest and deepen their communion with Jesus and the Father. The **Father** is **glorified**, revealed, and praised by the lives of Jesus' disciples, who manifest the Father's transforming love at work in them through their relationship with Jesus.

Reflection and Application (15:1–8)

The Father wants us to "bear much fruit" (15:8). He wants us to perform acts of love, whether great or small, in all aspects of our lives, and at all times. The key to this kind of living is remaining on the vine, staying in spiritual communion with Jesus. The image of the vine teaches that Jesus provides his disciples with

1. Catechism 2074.
2. Catechism 2614.

Saint Catherine of Siena on the Vine and the Branches

LIVING TRADITION

Saint Catherine records that in a mystical encounter, God the Father told her:

> I am the gardener, then, who planted the vine of my only-begotten Son in the earth of your humanity so that you, the branches, could be joined to the vine and bear fruit. Therefore, if you do not produce the fruit of good and holy deeds you will be cut off from this vine and you will dry up. For those who are cut off from this vine lose the life of grace and are thrown into the eternal fire. . . . [But if you are attached to the vine] you will produce much fruit, because you will share the vital sap of the vine. And being in the Word, my Son, you will be in me, for I am one with him and he with me. If you are in him you will follow his teaching, and if you follow his teaching you will share in the very being of this Word—that is, you will share in the eternal Godhead made one with humanity, whence you will draw that divine love which inebriates the soul.[a]

a. Catherine of Siena, *The Dialogue*, trans. Suzanne Noffke, OP (New York: Paulist Press, 1980), section 23.

a constant source of life and power to love. We must remain constantly united to Jesus and grow in communion with him through prayer and the sacraments in order to love others as he commands. The more we love and obey Jesus, the more our lives will become conformed to his. We are to become living icons of Jesus such that, when people look at us, they should be able to see God's love shining in the world. Jesus' words are also a warning to Christians not to abandon Jesus and break communion with him. Cut off from their source of spiritual life, such branches will "wither" and die, and end up in "fire" (15:6).

Bearing Fruit through Divine Love (15:9–17)

[9]"As the Father loves me, so I also love you. Remain in my love. [10]If you keep my commandments, you will remain in my love, just as I have kept my Father's commandments and remain in his love.

[11]"I have told you this so that my joy might be in you and your joy might be complete. [12]This is my commandment: love one another as I love you. [13]No one has greater love than this, to lay down one's life for one's friends. [14]You are my friends if you do what I command you. [15]I no longer

call you slaves, because a slave does not know what his master is doing. I have called you friends, because I have told you everything I have heard from my Father. [16]It was not you who chose me, but I who chose you and appointed you to go and bear fruit that will remain, so that whatever you ask the Father in my name he may give you. [17]This I command you: love one another."

OT: Deut 6:4–9; Lev 19:18

NT: Matt 5:43–48; Mark 12:28–34; Phil 2:1–4; 1 John 4:7–12

Catechism: faith, 153–54; charity, 1822–29

Lectionary: Sixth Sunday of Easter (Year B); St. Matthias; Common of Pastors; Common of Saints; Christian Initiation apart from Easter Vigil; Baptism of Children; Holy Orders; Marriage; For Peace and Justice; Consecration of Virgins and Religious Profession; For Election of a Pope or Bishop; For Vocations of Priests and Religious; Sacred Heart

15:9–11 In the Shepherd Discourse, Jesus taught that his relationship with his disciples involved an intimate, mutual knowing, similar to that between the Father and the Son (10:14–15). Here Jesus teaches about the profound love existing among the Father, himself, and his disciples: **As the Father loves me, so I also love you**. From all eternity, the Father infinitely loves the Son (17:23–24, 26), pouring forth all that he is into the Son and teaching him everything (5:20, 26). Jesus loves his disciples with the same infinite, radically self-giving love: "so I also love you." He draws his disciples into this unimaginable communion of love between the Father and Son and invites them to **remain in** this communion of **love**. As the branches are to "remain" on the vine (15:4–5), the disciples are to **remain in** communion with Jesus and the Father's love through loving obedience: **Keep my commandments** (see 14:15, 21, 23). Such trusting, loving obedience preserves and fosters the disciples' communion with Jesus because this is Jesus' own response to the Father as the Son: **Just as I have kept my Father's commandments and remain in his love**. If his disciples love and obey him as he loves and obeys the Father, then they too will share his **joy**, a **complete**, divine joy that comes from knowing the Father and experiencing his love.

15:12–13 The heart of Jesus' moral teaching is one simple **commandment: love one another as I love you** (see 13:34; Matt 5:43–48; Mark 12:28–34). Jesus loves his disciples with the total self-giving love of God himself. This divine love appears most radiantly in the cross, where the Father gives Jesus for the world's salvation (3:16) and Jesus lays down his life in an act of perfect love and obedience to the Father (10:17). For, **No one has greater love than this, to lay down one's life for one's friends.**

Jesus requires that his disciples practice the same kind of radical, self-giving love. God loves first, and the disciples' love for others arises from their encounter

Pope Benedict XVI on God's Love Eliciting Our Love

[God] encounters us ever anew, in the men and women who reflect his presence, in his word, in the sacraments, and especially in the Eucharist. . . . He has loved us first and he continues to do so; we too, then, can respond with love. . . . [Love of others] can only take place on the basis of an intimate encounter with God, an encounter which has become a communion of will, even affecting my feelings. Then I learn to look on this other person not simply with my eyes and my feelings, but from the perspective of Jesus Christ. His friend is my friend. . . . Only if I serve my neighbor can my eyes be opened to what God does for me and how much he loves me.[a]

a. Pope Benedict XVI, *Deus Caritas Est* (God Is Love) 17–18.

with God's love. As 1 John 4:11 nicely summarizes it, "If God so loved us, we also must love one another." The visible †sign of the disciples' love for Jesus, the sign that they are his **friends**, is their obedience to his **command** to love one another.

15:14–15 Jesus elaborates on the love command with a contrast between two kinds of relationships. First, there is the relationship between a **master** and his **slaves**, in which commands are given and obeyed simply on the basis of the master's authority and backed by force. While Jesus is "master and teacher" (13:14), he does not issue the love command in the context of a master-slave relationship but in the context of friendship. **Friends** do good things for each other because of the friendly affection between them. The disciples are to love one another because this is what Jesus, their friend, has done for them and asks of them. The friendship between Jesus and his disciples has arisen because he has given them **everything** that he **heard from** the **Father**, and, implicitly, they have been willing to receive it.

15:16–17 The very fact that the disciples have come to know Jesus is a gift of divine love: **It was not you who chose me, but I who chose you**. Jesus earlier said, "No one can come to me unless the Father who sent me draw him" (6:44). The Father works to bring people to believe in Jesus so that they might receive eternal life through him (6:37–39; 17:6–9). Faith, by which people come to know Jesus, is a free, undeserved gift of divine love, which people must receive and embrace.[3]

The divine choosing of Jesus' disciples brings a commission: **Go and bear fruit that will remain**. The fruit that the Father seeks from the vine's branches

3. Catechism 153–54.

Friendship

BIBLICAL BACKGROUND

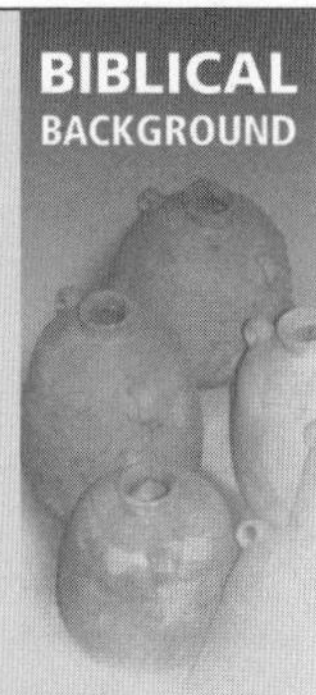

Friendship was a very popular topic among philosophers in Greco-Roman antiquity. The famous Roman orator and statesman Cicero wrote a treatise *On Friendship*, in which he defines friendship as "an accord in all things, human and divine, conjoined with mutual goodwill and affection."[a] Such popular thinking about friendship appears in the New Testament. Paul calls the Philippians to such friendship: Be "of the same mind, with the same love, united in heart, thinking one thing. Do nothing out of selfishness or out of vainglory; rather, humbly regard others as more important than yourselves" (Phil 2:2–3). In both Phil 2 and John 15 there is concern for union and harmony among friends and putting others' good before one's own—and that is love.

a. Cicero, *On Friendship* 6.20, in *On Old Age, On Friendship, On Divination*, trans. W. A. Falconer, LCL 154 (Cambridge, MA: Harvard University Press, 1923), 131.

is that they **love one another**. The disciples' communion with Jesus enables them to produce works of love (15:4–5), and Jesus' friends are those who, like Jesus, obey the Father's will in love (15:7, 14). Accordingly, disciples who pray to **the Father in** Jesus' **name** pray in communion with Jesus in his perfect, loving obedience to the Father's will. They ask the Father to accomplish his plan in the world and their lives and, if they are ready to obey the Father and yield to his will, the Father will **give** them this request.

Reflection and Application (15:9–17)

Jesus' command, "Love one another as I love you" (15:12), is foundational to the entire Christian life (Catechism 1827). It is so simple and yet so difficult. When we look upon the cross in faith, we see the love of God revealed, a love that is totally self-giving for others' good. It is the same love that Jesus tells us we must practice. One reason why it is so difficult to love as Jesus does is that we are sinners, bound up in prideful selfishness. To love as God does, we must be constantly dying to our own sinfulness and selfishness and living for God. And we live for God by obeying the Father's will and loving one another.

We need God's help to love others in this way. To produce the fruits of love, we must remain on the vine and be pruned by the Father. Put differently, if we are to love others as God does, we need to remain and grow in communion with Jesus, through such things as prayer, the sacraments, and works of penance. Through these spiritual practices, we open ourselves to God's action in us whereby we increasingly die to our own sinfulness and become conformed to the Father's will. Thus we will come to joyfully experience the Father' love and be able to love others as he calls us to do.

Confrontation with the World (15:18–16:4a)

[18]"If the world hates you, realize that it hated me first. [19]If you belonged to the world, the world would love its own; but because you do not belong to the world, and I have chosen you out of the world, the world hates you. [20]Remember the word I spoke to you, 'No slave is greater than his master.' If they persecuted me, they will also persecute you. If they kept my word, they will also keep yours. [21]And they will do all these things to you on account of my name, because they do not know the one who sent me. [22]If I had not come and spoken to them, they would have no sin; but as it is they have no excuse for their sin. [23]Whoever hates me also hates my Father. [24]If I had not done works among them that no one else ever did, they would not have sin; but as it is, they have seen and hated both me and my Father. [25]But in order that the word written in their law might be fulfilled, 'They hated me without cause.'

[26]"When the Advocate comes whom I will send you from the Father, the Spirit of truth that proceeds from the Father, he will testify to me. [27]And you also testify, because you have been with me from the beginning.

[16:1]"I have told you this so that you may not fall away. [2]They will expel you from the synagogues; in fact, the hour is coming when everyone who kills you will think he is offering worship to God. [3]They will do this because they have not known either the Father or me. [4a]I have told you this so that when their hour comes you may remember that I told you."

OT: Ps 69

NT: Matt 10:16–25; Mark 13:9–13; Acts 7:54–60

Catechism: the Spirit reveals the Father and the Son, 243–48; effects of Confirmation, 1302–5

Lectionary: Common of Martyrs; Confirmation

15:18 After teaching his disciples that they must love, Jesus tells them that they are going to be hated and persecuted by **the world**.[4] Here "the world" signifies

4. John 15:20–16:4a resembles †Synoptic texts where Jesus teaches his disciples about future persecutions, as in Matt 10:16–25.

human beings and their world as they are in hostile rebellion against God (see sidebar on p. 37). Out of love, the Father sent his Son to save the fallen world (3:16–17), and Jesus will send his disciples to the world as an extension of his own mission (20:21). But the world will treat the disciples in the same way that it treated Jesus: **If the world hates you, realize that it hated me first**.

15:19 The hostile, unbelieving **world hates** the disciples because they **do not belong to the world**; that is, the disciples do not give their allegiance to the world's values and live by its ways. Jesus has **chosen** his disciples **out of the world**, for they have received him and are in relationship with the Father through him. As the Gospel articulates it, one is ultimately on either the world's side or God's side. Friendship with Jesus (15:15) means incurring the world's hatred. Conversely, as James writes, "Whoever wants to be a lover of the world makes himself an enemy of God" (4:4).

15:20–21 After the footwashing, Jesus used this expression, **No slave is greater than his master**, to teach his disciples that they, as his subordinates, must follow his example of humble, self-giving love (13:16; see Matt 10:24–25). He now repeats the phrase to tell them that they must follow him in being **persecuted** and having their **word** rejected, although it will be **kept** by some. The fundamental reason why the world will persecute the disciples is that these disciples are loyal to Jesus. As Jesus says in Matt 10:22, "You will be hated by all because of my name, but whoever endures to the end will be saved." The core of the fallen world is its rejection of God's Word, and since the world has rejected the †incarnate Word, they **do not know the** Father, whom he reveals.

15:22–24 Jesus has **come and spoken** the Father's words (8:38, 40) and has **done works** that are completely unprecedented (his †signs, 9:31–33). Jesus' own person, his words, and his works reveal the Father, and they have provided sufficient opportunity for his contemporaries to receive him in faith (see 10:37–38; 14:11). Yet some of his opponents **have seen** all of this and still knowingly and willfully reject him. Consequently, they have **no excuse for their sin**, sin here meaning "unbelieving rejection of Jesus," and their rejection of him is simultaneously a rejection of the **Father**, "who sent" him (15:21).

15:25 Like Judas's betrayal, the world's rejection of Jesus is foreseen in Scripture (see 12:38–40; 13:18). Jesus quotes Ps 69:5, **They hated me without cause**. The Fourth Gospel interprets the one suffering for the Lord in Ps 69 as a prophetic anticipation of Jesus (see John 2:17; 19:28–30). The description of Scripture as **their law** is strange, since Jesus and his first disciples were all †Jews. This description suggests that John sees the dynamics of the world's spiritual rebellion in the Jewish authorities who have known Jesus, rejected him, and take hostile action against him. The descriptor "their" is not meant to distinguish John's audience from Israel as much as to show the †irony of the situation. By rejecting Jesus, his opponents are unwittingly fulfilling things given in their own Scripture (compare 11:49–52).

15:26–27 But the disciples will not be on their own and helpless in the face of the world's hostility. Once Jesus has entered into the Father's glory, he **will send** the Holy Spirit, **the Advocate**, to his disciples. In this third promise of the Spirit, Jesus says that the Holy Spirit **will testify to me**. The Spirit, who will dwell within the disciples (14:17), will teach them about the risen Jesus and impress his truth upon their hearts, making it come alive in them. The Spirit's internal witness to the powerful reality of the risen Lord will sustain and empower the disciples, who will go to the hostile world and **testify** externally about Jesus (see Acts 5:30–32).[5] As Augustine puts it, the Spirit "will give [testimony], you also will give [testimony]: he in your hearts, you in your voices."[6] Jesus' words echo those in Matt 10:19–20, "When they hand you over, do not worry about . . . what you are to say. . . . For it will not be you who speak but the Spirit of your Father speaking through you." The disciples will be good witnesses because they know what Jesus said and did (they **have been with** him **from the beginning**; see Acts 1:21–22) and, what is more important, **the Spirit of truth** will lead them to understand the mystery of Jesus' life.[7]

16:1–4a Jesus has both prophetically revealed the coming persecutions and promised the Spirit's help so the disciples **may not fall away**, may not abandon their relationship with him on account of persecutions.[8] Similar to some sayings in the †Synoptics, Jesus predicts that his disciples **will** become separated **from the synagogues** (in Matt 10:17; Mark 13:9; Luke 21:12, Jesus predicts various troubles for his disciples in †synagogues).[9] Some will even die as martyrs, killed by those who think such bloodshed is the right thing before **God** (see Acts 7:54–60; Gal 1:13–14). Jesus traces the persecution of his disciples to the spiritual root of the fallen world, which is the rejection of Jesus and **the Father**. And yet, by prophetically revealing these coming persecutions, Jesus shows that, like those of his own passion, they are not beyond God's knowledge or control. Hence, **when** this †**hour comes**, the disciples can **remember that** Jesus prophesied **this** and thus have confidence in his power (13:19; 14:29).

5. Catechism 1303–4.

6. St. Augustine, *Tractates on John* 93.1.

7. Catechism 737.

8. The verb for "fall away" (*skandalizō*) also appears in 6:61, where the NABRE translates it as "shock."

9. See "Historical Context" in the introduction to this volume.

The Filioque

When Roman Catholics profess the creed at Mass, we pray, "I believe in the Holy Spirit, . . . who proceeds from the Father and the Son." The phrase "proceeds from the Father" (John 15:26) appeared in the creed issued by the ecumenical councils of Nicaea (325) and Constantinople (381). Starting in the early Middle Ages, the phrase "and [from] the Son" (Latin *filioque*) was incorporated into Latin versions of the creed in Western Christianity to reinforce the divinity of the Son and the Spirit.[a] Starting in the ninth century, this addition became a major source of controversy between Western and Eastern Christians and contributed to the split between Catholics and Orthodox.[b]

Theologically, the dispute concerns the relations between the persons of the Trinity; specifically, it shows how Catholics and Orthodox articulate the way in which "the Father is the Source of the Trinity."[c] Much progress has been made regarding this topic in ecumenical discussions between Catholics and Orthodox. Indeed, some see it more as a dispute over language and perspective, rather than over doctrinal substance, in which there is basic agreement.[d]

a. So Gilles Emery, OP, *The Trinity: An Introduction to Catholic Doctrine on the Triune God*, trans. Matthew Levering (Washington, DC: Catholic University of America Press, 2011), 140.

b. For an excellent overview, see Brian E. Daley, SJ, "Revisiting the 'Filioque': Roots and Branches of an Old Debate: Part One," *Pro Ecclesia* 10 (2001): 31–62; and "Revisting the 'Filioque': Part Two: Contemporary Catholic Approaches," *Pro Ecclesia* 10 (2001): 195–212. See also Catechism 246–48.

c. Emery, *Trinity*, 149.

d. Ibid., 141–42, 148–49.

Reflection and Application (15:18–16:4a)

The Holy Spirit is essential to the Church's mission in the world. Jesus has chosen his disciples and appointed them to bear the fruit of holiness and love (15:16) and bear witness in the world, which is often hostile to the gospel. The only way we will be able to do this is through the power of the Holy Spirit. To grow in holiness and love, each of us needs to get to know the Holy Spirit more deeply and invite him into our lives. To those who call upon him in faith and confidence, the Spirit gives a personal, experiential knowledge of the risen Jesus, who is Lord of heaven and earth (Matt 28:18): nowadays this is often called "baptism in the Holy Spirit" (see sidebar on p. 48). The Spirit makes the reality and power of the risen Jesus come alive in the hearts of believers. Through his gentle yet powerful activity, the Holy Spirit empowers Christians to live lives of love and holiness and, through their lives, to bear witness in the world to the Father's love revealed in Jesus.

Farewell Discourse III

John 16:4b–33

This last section of the Farewell Discourse centers on two topics. First, Jesus continues to teach about the Holy Spirit, who will reveal the divine mystery of Jesus and his accomplishments to the disciples (16:4b–15). Second, Jesus goes on to speak of a change in affairs that will take place because of the events of his †hour (16:16–33). While the disciples will mourn when Jesus leaves them in death, they will be filled with †eschatological joy when they see him again after his resurrection. Through his death and resurrection, Jesus will put the disciples in a new relationship with the Father, whose love they will come to know in a new, intimate way.

Conviction from the Spirit (16:4b–11)

[4b]"I did not tell you this from the beginning, because I was with you. [5]But now I am going to the one who sent me, and not one of you asks me, 'Where are you going?' [6]But because I told you this, grief has filled your hearts. [7]But I tell you the truth, it is better for you that I go. For if I do not go, the Advocate will not come to you. But if I go, I will send him to you. [8]And when he comes he will convict the world in regard to sin and righteousness and condemnation: [9]sin, because they do not believe in me; [10]righteousness, because I am going to the Father and you will no longer see me; [11]condemnation, because the ruler of this world has been condemned."

OT: Zech 3
NT: 1 Cor 1:18–25; Rev 12:10–12
Catechism: the Spirit brings our sin to light, 388, 1433; Christ's victory over the enemy, 2853
Lectionary: Confirmation

16:4b–6 Having announced the upcoming persecutions of his disciples and having promised them the divine assistance of the Holy Spirit (15:18–16:4a), Jesus reiterates that he will soon be leaving them to go **to the** Father, **who sent** him, by way of his cross and resurrection (13:1, 3; 14:12).[1] The disciples' **hearts** are **filled** with **grief** because Jesus, their beloved teacher and master, will soon be leaving them.

16:7 Jesus now makes an astonishing claim: **It is better for you that I go**. If Jesus does **not go** into the Father's glory by way of his cross and resurrection, the Holy Spirit **will not come** to the disciples, for fallen humanity, enslaved to sin, is not capable of receiving him. **But** once Jesus' humanity has been transformed by the Father's glory, he **will send** the Holy Spirit (Acts 2:33). Having been so glorified, Jesus will no longer be bound by the limits of space and time, and therefore he can be present to the disciples in an infinitely more intimate way through the Spirit than he ever could be before Easter: Jesus will not just be *with* them but will also be *in* them. This is why things will be better for the disciples after Jesus has left them physically.

16:8 Jesus then makes the fourth promise about the Holy Spirit. After the resurrection, when the Spirit comes to dwell in the disciples (14:17), **he will convict the world**. The verb for "convict" implies a trial, a theme that runs throughout the Gospel. It has the sense of bringing bad things to light and showing them to be wrong (see 3:20; Matt 18:15; Eph 5:11).

Jesus has taught that the Spirit's action takes place within the disciples (14:16–17) and is directed to them first (15:26–27). The Spirit will prove to believers that the world, which rejects the Gospel and persecutes them, is wrong **in regard to sin and righteousness and condemnation**. He does this by bringing believers into a personal, experiential contact with the risen Jesus that transforms their lives and makes them utterly convinced of the truth of the Gospel. Through this gentle but powerful consolation, the Spirit gives security and peace to the disciples when they are confronted by the world's rejection and hatred. The Spirit does this work within the disciples so that they can then go into the world and testify with confidence to the love of God in Christ.

16:9 First, the Spirit will prove that the world is wrong about **sin**. The spiritual core of sin is rejecting the divine Word, since **they do not believe in me**.

1. Jesus' remark, **and not one of you asks me, "Where are you going?,"** is often taken as a sign that the Farewell Discourse was composed over time, because Peter has asked Jesus this question in 13:36.

The Spirit reveals to the disciples that the world is wrong to reject God's Word, its only hope of salvation.[2] Put positively, the Spirit reveals to the disciples that by God's gift, they have found the "pearl of great price" (Matt 13:45–46): Jesus gives meaning to the whole of existence and bears them into eternal life.

Second, the Spirit will prove the world wrong about **righteousness**, or justice. When Jesus dies on a cross, to many he will appear as a guilty criminal. As Paul writes, the Christian proclamation that the crucified Jesus is the "the power of God and the wisdom of God" is "a stumbling block to Jews and foolishness to Gentiles" (1 Cor 1:23–24). But Jesus is **going to the Father**. The Spirit will so impress the reality of the glorified Jesus on believers' hearts that they will know that justice and righteousness is on Jesus' side, not the world's, for the Father has vindicated him in raising him from the dead. **16:10**

Third, the Spirit will prove the world wrong about judgment or **condemnation**. Jesus' death on the cross will appear to be his defeat and his enemies' victory. But the opposite is in fact the case: Satan as **the ruler of this world has been condemned**. The Spirit reveals to believers that the blood that Jesus shed on the cross has broken Satan's power and secured his eternal defeat.[3] Thus the angels can sing of the martyrs in Revelation, "They conquered him [Satan] by the blood of the Lamb" (Rev 12:11; see Zech 3). Although the powers of evil abound in the world, Christ has "conquered the world" (16:33). The powers of evil have lost. **16:11**

Reflection and Application (16:4a–11)

Jesus' disciples are messengers of the Father's love to the hostile, unbelieving world. Their mission is going to be a struggle, and it requires the help of the Holy Spirit. They give testimony not only by their words but also by their transformed lives, which display the Father's love available in Jesus. Pope Paul VI speaks to this very point: "For the Church, the first means of evangelization is the witness of an authentically Christian life, given over to God in a communion that nothing should destroy and at the same time given to one's neighbor with limitless zeal. As we said recently to a group of lay people, 'Modern man listens more willingly to witnesses than to teachers, and if he does listen to teachers, it is because they are witnesses.'"[4]

2. Catechism 388, 1433.
3. Catechism 2853.
4. Pope Paul VI, *Evangelii Nuntiandi* (On Evangelization in the Modern World) 41.

The Spirit of the Living God (16:12–15)

[12]"I have much more to tell you, but you cannot bear it now. [13]But when he comes, the Spirit of truth, he will guide you to all truth. He will not speak on his own, but he will speak what he hears, and will declare to you the things that are coming. [14]He will glorify me, because he will take from what is mine and declare it to you. [15]Everything that the Father has is mine; for this reason I told you that he will take from what is mine and declare it to you."

OT: Jer 31:31–34; Ezek 36:24–28
NT: Rom 8:14–17; 1 John 5:6–12
Catechism: Trinity, 221, 687; the Spirit's mission, 258, 729, 737
Lectionary: Trinity Sunday (Year C)

16:12 Jesus makes the fifth promise about the Holy Spirit with the announcement that he has **much more to tell** his disciples. This "much more" concerns his revelation of the Father (8:38, 40), which the disciples are not presently capable of receiving and grasping—**You cannot bear it now**—because they have not yet received the Spirit.

16:13 Jesus develops his teaching that the Spirit will teach and remind the disciples about him (14:26) with the declaration, **When he comes, the Spirit of truth, he will guide you to all truth**. In the Fourth Gospel, the **truth** is Jesus' revelation of the Father and himself as the Son. The Holy Spirit is **the Spirit of Truth** (14:17; 15:26) because he leads the disciples to understand in faith the meaning of Jesus' revelation.[5] As de la Potterie writes, "The task of the Spirit will be to cause the message of Jesus to penetrate into the hearts of the faithful, to give them the understanding of faith."[6] Similarly, 1 John 5:6 says that "the Spirit is the one that testifies," and he testifies to "the one who came through water and blood, Jesus Christ." It is this inner, spiritual awareness of God that Jeremiah and Ezekiel prophesied in connection with the New †Covenant: "I will place my law within them, and write it upon their hearts. . . . Everyone, from least to greatest, shall know me" (Jer 31:33–34); "I will put my spirit within you so that you walk in my statues" (Ezek 36:27).

The Spirit does not work independently of Jesus and the Father.[7] As Jesus does not speak on his own (12:49) but only tells the truth that he heard from

5. Catechism 729, 737.

6. Ignace de la Potterie, SJ, "The Truth in St. John," in *The Interpretation of John*, 2nd ed., ed. and trans. John Ashton (Edinburgh: T&T Clark, 1997), 78; repr. from *Rivista biblica italiana* 11 (1963): 3–24. See also his essay "Anointing of the Christian by Faith," in Ignace de la Potterie, SJ, and Stanislas Lyonnet, SJ, *The Christian Lives by the Spirit*, trans. John Morriss (Staten Island, NY: Alba House, 1971), 79–143; repr. from *Biblica* 40 (1959): 12–69.

7. Catechism 258.

the Father (8:40), so too the Spirit **will not speak on his own, but he will speak what he hears**. He **will** also **declare** to the disciples **the things that are coming**. This includes both the Spirit's charismatic gift of prophecy (1 Cor 12:10) and the disciples' Spirit-given awareness that they already share in ultimate, heavenly realities. The Greek verb translated as "declare" appears in Dan 2:2, 4, 6 †LXX to designate the revelation of †eschatological realities. These eschatological realities, which Jesus has revealed and believers now imperfectly but genuinely possess, the Spirit makes powerfully real in their lives. De la Potterie puts it well: "There are two times of revelation. . . . The first is the time of Christ, who brings revelation objectively and historically, the second is the time of the Spirit, who illuminates the truth of Christ and renders it subjectively present in us."[8]

16:14–15

Jesus then gives the disciples a glimpse of God's inner life. The Spirit will **glorify** Jesus, that is, make Jesus' divine majesty known to believers. The Spirit's work of glorifying Jesus coincides with the Son's glorifying the Father (revealing the Father by doing his saving work; 17:4) and the Father's glorifying the Son (glorifying his humanity in the resurrection and ascension; 17:1, 5).

The relationship of Father and Son is total, self-giving love.[9] All that the Father has, he gives to the Son: **Everything that the Father has is mine.** And all that the Son has, he gives back to the Father, as revealed in his complete gift of his life on the cross. The life of God as an eternal communion of life and love is the heart of Jesus' revelation. And the Spirit makes Jesus' revelation of this infinite exchange of love within God known and powerfully real in the hearts of believers: **He will take from what is mine and declare it to you**. Through the Spirit, we can come to know the Father's love, revealed in Christ, and so cry out, "Abba, Father!" (Rom 8:15; Gal 4:6).

Reflection and Application (16:12–15)

The Church prescribes this reading for Trinity Sunday. The Trinity has *everything* to do with all aspects of Christian life. The Catechism states, "God himself is an eternal exchange of love, Father, Son, and Holy Spirit, and he has destined us to share in that exchange" (221). This sharing is heaven. The Father sent his only Son to suffer, die, and rise, so that humanity could be restored to his friendship and enter into the divine communion. The Spirit has been sent to teach us, strengthen us, and help us replicate in our lives the same pattern of

8. De la Potterie, "Truth in St. John," 78. Catechism 687.

9. Catechism 221. Later Catholic theology will identify the love between the Father and Son as the Spirit himself, as does St. Thomas Aquinas, *Summa theologica* 1, q. 37, a. 1–2.

self-giving love that exists in God. Our task is to yield to the Holy Spirit, who makes the reality of God powerfully alive for us and draws us into communion with him through Jesus. In order to do this, we have to give up our sins and open ourselves up to God. The more attuned we become to the Holy Spirit by renouncing our sins and living a graced life of prayer and the sacraments, the more we will come to know the mystery of love that is the Blessed Trinity.

Sadness Will Give Way to Joy (16:16–24)

[16]"A little while and you will no longer see me, and again a little while later and you will see me." [17]So some of his disciples said to one another, "What does this mean that he is saying to us, 'A little while and you will not see me, and again a little while and you will see me,' and 'Because I am going to the Father'?" [18]So they said, "What is this 'little while' [of which he speaks]? We do not know what he means." [19]Jesus knew that they wanted to ask him, so he said to them "Are you discussing with one another what I said, 'A little while and you will not see me, and again a little while and you will see me'? [20]Amen, amen, I say to you, you will weep and mourn, while the world rejoices; you will grieve, but your grief will become joy. [21]When a woman is in labor, she is in anguish because her hour has arrived; but when she has given birth to a child, she no longer remembers the pain because of her joy that a child has been born into the world. [22]So you also are now in anguish. But I will see you again, and your hearts will rejoice, and no one will take your joy away from you. [23]On that day you will not question me about anything. Amen, amen, I say to you, whatever you ask the Father in my name he will give you. [24]Until now you have not asked anything in my name; ask and you will receive, so that your joy may be complete."

OT: Isa 26:14–19
NT: Mark 13:3–8, 24–27
Catechism: Praying with Jesus in the Spirit, 2611–15

16:16 Jesus shifts to the change in the state of affairs before and after his death and resurrection. He speaks of two different moments when the disciples will not see him and will see him again. The first **little while** refers to the rapidly approaching time of his death, after which the disciples **will no longer see** him. But as he promised (14:19, 28), he will return to his disciples **a little while later** by rising from the dead, and they **will see** him again.

16:17–18 Once again, the disciples do not understand what Jesus is telling them. They question the meaning of his entire **saying** in 16:16, especially the **little while**

Saint Ignatius of Loyola on Dryness in Prayer

The pattern of not seeing and then seeing Jesus can be extended to experiences in the spiritual life and prayer. There are times in the spiritual life when we can be very aware of God's presence and his sweetness (we see Jesus) and times when our prayer is empty and dry (we do not see him). These different states are called "consolation" and "desolation." Saint Ignatius provides helpful teaching about why we sometimes do not see Jesus in prayer:

> There are three principal reasons for our being in desolation: (i) because we are lukewarm, lazy or careless in our commitment to the spiritual life; . . . (ii) to test our quality and to show how far we will go in God's service and praise, even without generous recompense in the form of consolations and overflowing graces; (iii) to give us true information and understanding, so that we may perceive through experience that we cannot ourselves arouse or sustain overflowing devotion, intense love, tears, or any other spiritual consolation, but that everything is a gracious gift from God Our Lord.[a]

a. St. Ignatius of Loyola, "Spiritual Exercises," in *Saint Ignatius of Loyola: Personal Writings*, trans. Joseph A. Munitiz and Philip Endean (New York: Penguin Books, 1996), section 322, p. 350.

and his repeated declaration, **I am going to the Father** (14:12; 16:10). The fact that the disciples **do not know what** Jesus **means** illustrates the state of affairs before Jesus' †hour. Only when the glorified Jesus sends the Spirit of truth to lead them "to all truth" (16:13) will they truly understand and "see" Jesus.

16:19–20 Jesus knows what is going on in his disciples' hearts (see 2:25). They are filled with grief and confusion and **wanted to ask him** about the meaning of his words (16:6). So Jesus explains the contrast between the times before and after his hour with a further contrast between grief and joy. After he dies, his disciples will "no longer see" him (16:16), and they will **weep and mourn** because he is gone. However, **the world**—human beings and their world as they are in rebellion against God—**rejoices** because Jesus is no longer around to expose its ways as sinful. Although the disciples **grieve** now, they will see Jesus again after the resurrection (16:16), and their **grief will become joy** (see 15:11).

16:21–22 To illustrate this transition from pain to joy, Jesus uses the example of **a woman . . . in labor**, a common biblical image for the end of days.[10] Just as a

10. This image often depicts the intense suffering of God's faithful that will immediately precede the arrival of God's end-time salvation (Isa 26:16–17; Mark 13:3–8, 24–27).

woman is **in anguish** as she gives birth, so also are the disciples **now in anguish** because of Jesus' impending death ("anguish" translates the same Greek word that described the disciples' "grief" in 16:6). But once the baby has been born, the mother **no longer remembers the pain** but is filled with **joy**. Similarly, the disciples' grief will pass away, and they **will rejoice** after the resurrection. The risen Jesus **will see** them **again** and fill their hearts with his **joy**. The cause for the mother's joy is her baby's new life; the disciples' joy will stem from their new heavenly life of communion with the Father (15:11).

16:23–24 Jesus' resurrection and exaltation inaugurates a new state of affairs. On **that day**, which includes the whole postresurrection time of the Church, when the disciples see the risen Jesus alive (14:19–20), not only will they be filled with the supernatural joy of the divine communion; they also **will not question** Jesus **about anything**. Throughout the Farewell Discourse, Jesus' disciples have questioned him about his revelation and return to the Father (13:36; 14:5, 8, 22; 16:17–18). But after the resurrection, they will not question him, because they will truly understand him and the meaning of his cross through the action of "the Spirit of truth" (16:13).

Through the Holy Spirit, the risen Jesus will draw his disciples to share in his communion with the Father, and an indication of this new relationship will be their praying to **the Father in** Jesus' **name**. Jesus urges his disciples to pray in this way, and this is the third time he has promised that such prayer will be answered (14:13–14; 15:16). As we have discussed, to pray in Jesus' name is to pray in union with him, who is completely obedient to the Father's will out of love.[11] It is to pray and desire that the Father's will be done (Matt 6:10). If the disciples **ask** the Father to do this, they **will receive** (see Luke 11:9). By being united to Jesus and animated by the Spirit of love and obedience, the disciples will know **joy** that is perfect and **complete**, a joy that comes only from participating in the divine communion.

Things to Come (16:25–33)

[25]"I have told you this in figures of speech. The hour is coming when I will no longer speak to you in figures but I will tell you clearly about the Father. [26]On that day you will ask in my name, and I do not tell you that I will ask the Father for you. [27]For the Father himself loves you, because you have loved me and have come to believe that I came from God. [28]I

11. Catechism 2611, 2614–15.

came from the Father and have come into the world. Now I am leaving the world and going back to the Father." [29]His disciples said, "Now you are talking plainly, and not in any figure of speech. [30]Now we realize that you know everything and that you do not need to have anyone question you. Because of this we believe that you came from God." [31]Jesus answered them, "Do you believe now? [32]Behold, the hour is coming and has arrived when each of you will be scattered to his own home and you will leave me alone. But I am not alone, because the Father is with me. [33]I have told you this so that you might have peace in me. In the world you will have trouble, but take courage, I have conquered the world."

OT: Zech 13:7–9
NT: Rom 8:14–17, 28–30; 1 John 5:1–5
Catechism: fortitude, 1808

16:25 In 16:16–24, Jesus contrasted the times before and after his death and resurrection. To this, he now adds a new contrast between two different modes of revelation. In the state of affairs before his passion, he has spoken **in figures of speech**. Elsewhere in the Gospel this term designates a veiled, figurative language, which Jesus' audience does not readily understand (10:6; 16:29). But after Jesus' resurrection an †**hour is coming when** a new mode of revelation will be established. In the postresurrection state of affairs, Jesus **will** speak **clearly about the Father**. This clear revelatory speech will be the work of the Holy Spirit, who "will speak what he hears" (16:13) and impress the reality of Jesus' revelation onto the disciples' hearts.

16:26 Jesus' resurrection will create a new relationship between his disciples and the Father. **On that** Easter **day**, and throughout the time of the Church, Jesus will draw his disciples into communion with himself through the Holy Spirit dwelling in them, so that they can pray **in** union with Jesus' **name**. In one respect, the risen Jesus exists in heavenly glory, forever fixed in that act of love in which he died, to make perpetual intercession for his own with the Father (Heb 7:25; 1 John 2:1–2). In another respect, the disciples have new access to the Father through their union with the Son. Hence Jesus adds, **I do not tell you that I will ask the Father for you**. Jesus' cross and glorification enables all heavenly gifts to be given to his disciples: the Holy Spirit, his joy, his peace, and the ability to pray in union with his name.

16:27–28 The disciples need to be prepared to receive these heavenly gifts, and the first step is receiving Jesus in faith. Recall that Jesus' entire person and mission are constituted by his relationship with the Father: he **came from the Father**, has **come into the world**, and will now return **to the Father**. Since Jesus reveals the

Father and the disciples have received Jesus in love and faith (you **have loved me and have come to believe that I came from God**), the disciples are being opened up to experience that **the Father himself loves you** (14:21, 23; 17:23). When the disciples are spiritually united to the Son, the Father will look upon them and see in them "the image of his Son" (Rom 8:29). For their part, the disciples, having been filled with the Holy Spirit, will call out to the Father with divine affection, as Jesus does, "Abba, Father!" (Rom 8:15).

16:29–30 But once again, the **disciples** display their pre-Easter lack of understanding. They pick up on Jesus' distinction between **talking plainly** and in a **figure of speech** from 16:25. But they think it has to do with the figurative quality of Jesus' language and not a contrast in modes of revelation before and after the resurrection. The disciples underscore their misunderstanding by making a well-intentioned but misguided profession of faith. They are correct to believe that Jesus **came from God**, but their profession is insufficient because it is based on Jesus' knowledge (**You know everything**) and authority (**You do not need to have anyone question you**).

16:31–32 Jesus exposes the immaturity of the disciples' faith by predicting that **each of** them **will** soon **be scattered to his own home**, literally, "to his own."[12] The disciples will not simply go home, but will be driven back into themselves: their faith in him will fail. Even though the disciples **will leave** him **alone** physically, Jesus is never **alone** spiritually, **because the Father is with** him always. The abiding presence of the Father with the Son is manifested in Jesus' total obedience to the Father's will: "The one who sent me is with me. He has not left me alone, because I always do what is pleasing to him" (8:29).

16:33 Jesus concludes the Farewell Discourse with words of consolation and reassurance. Like his other predictions of future events (13:19; 14:29; 16:1, 4), Jesus has revealed all **this** to his disciples **so that** they **might have peace** and confidence **in** him. The Father has put all things into Jesus' power (13:3), and everything, even the **trouble** that his disciples will encounter in **the world**, is within his sovereign control. Jesus will send them to the hostile, spiritually darkened world so that the light of the Father's love, revealed in him, might radiate out to the world through them (13:35; 17:18, 21, 23). Even though they will experience suffering and persecution, Jesus tells them, **Take courage, I have conquered the world**. Through his death and resurrection, Jesus "takes away the sin of the world" (1:29) and thereby conquers the powers of evil oppressing it. The reality of his victory takes root in believers through faith. Thus 1 John teaches, "The victory that conquers the world is our faith" (5:4). The Holy Spirit makes

12. Compare Mark 14:27, referencing Zech 13:7.

the victory of Christ powerfully alive in believers, so that they know it to be absolutely true. By virtue of this Spirit-animated faith, the disciples should have courage and confidence to meet whatever situations they might encounter in their mission of love to world.[13]

Reflection and Application (16:25–33)

Christians are called to grow continually in faith. Faith involves not only intellectual assent to revealed truths but also the entrusting of one's whole life to the risen Jesus and a constant yielding to the Holy Spirit's action. Here we see that the disciples' faith in Jesus at this time is immature and shaky (16:31–32). Yet their basic welcoming of Jesus has opened them up to the Father's love (16:27). As faith matures, believers become more aware of Jesus' victory over sin and allow the power of his victory to shape their lives (16:33). This is why, John later wrote, "Who [indeed] is the victor over the world but the one who believes that Jesus is the Son of God?" (1 John 5:5).

13. Catechism 1808.

Jesus' Prayer of Communion

John 17:1–26

John 17 is a prayer of Jesus offered to the Father for his disciples. It is sometimes called Jesus' "High-Priestly Prayer" because he appears in the priest's role of intercessor and mediator. The prayer divides into three basic sections: Jesus prays for the mutual glorification of Father and Son to be revealed in him (17:1–8); he prays for his present disciples, especially in their mission to the hostile world (17:9–19); he prays that all his disciples, present and future, will be united with one another and God (17:20–26).

The language of this prayer contains some curious details pertaining to time. On the one hand, the prayer looks forward to the events of Jesus' †hour of glory on the cross (17:5, 11). On the other hand, the prayer sometimes hints that the events of Jesus' hour have already been accomplished and that Jesus is speaking to the Father in heavenly glory (17:4, 22, 24). The fusion of times in this prayer show it to be offered by Jesus in connection with his self-gift to the Father on the cross and continuing forever in his heavenly glory, where he makes constant intercession to the Father on his disciples' behalf (1 John 2:1–2; Heb 7:25). Through this prayer for glory and unity, Jesus provides a glimpse into the communion of Father and Son into which he invites all humanity to enter.

Jesus Prays for the Glorification of Father and Son (17:1–8)

---

[1]When Jesus had said this, he raised his eyes to heaven and said, "Father, the hour has come. Give glory to your son, so that your son may glorify you,

[2]just as you gave him authority over all people, so that he may give eternal life to all you gave him. [3]Now this is eternal life, that they should know you, the only true God, and the one whom you sent, Jesus Christ. [4]I glorified you on earth by accomplishing the work that you gave me to do. [5]Now glorify me, Father, with you, with the glory that I had with you before the world began.

[6]"I revealed your name to those whom you gave me out of the world. They belonged to you, and you gave them to me, and they have kept your word. [7]Now they know that everything you gave me is from you, [8]because the words you gave to me I have given to them, and they accepted them and truly understood that I came from you, and they have believed that you sent me."

OT: Ps 123; Wis 8:13–18
NT: Matt 11:25–27; 1 Cor 13:11–13; 1 John 4:7–12
Catechism: faith, the beginning of eternal life, 163–65; heaven, 1023–28
Lectionary: Seventh Sunday of Easter (Year A)

17:1–2 **Jesus** begins his prayer with a customary Jewish gesture: **He raised his eyes to heaven** (see Ps 123:1; Mark 7:34). By addressing the **Father** directly, Jesus offers us a glimpse of the intimacy between them (see John 11:41–42). The Gospel has been building toward Jesus' **hour**, when he will be glorified in his cross and resurrection (12:23) and "pass from this world to the Father" (13:1). Now that **the** †hour **has come**, Jesus asks the Father to **give glory to your son, so that your son may glorify you** (see 13:31–32). As previously discussed (see sidebar on p. 39), "the glory of the Lord" is the sensible, radiant manifestation of God's awesome presence. Jesus' prayer for mutual glorification is a request for the divine majesty—the eternal exchange of life and love within God—to be revealed in his hour. The cross reveals the love of the Father, who gives his all, his Son, for the world's salvation (3:16–17), and the love of the Son, who gives his all, his life, in a perfect act of love and obedience to the Father (14:31). The Father will then confirm Jesus' identity as the Son by transforming his humanity in divine glory through the resurrection (12:16; 20:28) and sending the Holy Spirit to dwell in his disciples. In this way, Jesus' hour reveals the very life of God, his glory, which is radical, self-giving love (1 John 4:9–11).

17:2 The Father has already given Jesus **authority over all people** (3:35; 5:27; 13:3). And now Jesus asks the Father to glorify him **so that** when he has been crucified, resurrected, and exalted to glory, he **may give eternal life to** the disciples whom the Father **gave him**. The whole life of the †incarnate Word has been directed to this goal: to redeem and draw all humanity to share in God's eternal life. Once Jesus' flesh has been given on the cross and then resurrected to glory, it becomes the source of eternal life for all (see 6:54).

17:3 Jesus specifies in what **eternal life** consists: to **know** the Father, **the only true God, and the one whom** he **sent, Jesus Christ.**[1] Only the Son "has seen" and knows the Father (1:18; 6:46); after becoming incarnate, he reveals the Father to human beings (1:18; 14:7, 9). As Jesus says elsewhere, "No one knows the Son except the Father, and no one knows the Father except the Son and anyone to whom the Son wishes to reveal him" (Matt 11:27; see Luke 10:22). While the Holy Spirit is not explicitly mentioned here, his presence is implied. Only through the Holy Spirit do the disciples come to know the truth about Jesus (14:26; 16:13–15), and by knowing him, to know the Father (14:7). The book of Wisdom declares, "Immortality lies in kinship with [divine] Wisdom" (8:17); similarly, it is in relationship with the Son that human beings come to know the Father—in the present time by faith and in eternity by knowledge.[2] As St. Paul writes, "At present we see indistinctly, as in a mirror, but then face to face. At present I know partially; then I shall know fully" (1 Cor 13:12). Eternal life is the "communion of life and love with the Trinity" (Catechism 1024): knowing the Father, through the Son, and in the Holy Spirit.[3]

17:4–5 Jesus **glorified** the Father **on earth by** revealing the divine majesty and **accomplishing** his **work**. Jesus' whole life has centered on doing the Father's will: "My food is to do the will of the one who sent me and to finish his work" (4:34; see 6:38). Throughout his ministry, Jesus has been revealing the divine glory by doing the Father's works (5:36; 9:3; 11:4), and he will do so in an unparalleled way on the cross. About to enter his †hour, Jesus prays that the **Father** will **glorify** him with the divine **glory** that he, as the eternal Son, **had with** the Father **before the world began**. He asks the Father to transform his humanity with the divine glory through the events of his hour and so reveal the deity of the incarnate Son.

17:6–7 Jesus continues his prayer by recounting his revelatory work. As the incarnate Son, Jesus **revealed** the Father's **name**, meaning his reality, to the disciples through his own person and his accomplishment of the Father's work. The disciples are the Father's gift to the Son: **They belonged to you, and you gave them to me** (see 6:37, 39). Jesus said, "No one can come to me unless the Father who sent me draw him" (6:44). His disciples have been "taught by God" (6:45) and have come to Jesus by consenting to the Father's work in them (6:29). They **have kept** the Father's **word** by receiving Jesus and his revelation in faith, for Jesus is the Father's Word (1:1), and his spoken words are those of the Father (12:49; 14:24). Through their faith in Jesus, the disciples **know that everything** about

1. The third-person reference to "Jesus Christ" suggests that John, under the Spirit's guidance, has made explicit the theological substance of Jesus' teaching by so articulating these words.

2. Catechism 163.

3. Catechism 1023, 1028.

Saint Thomas Aquinas on Faith as the Beginning of Eternal Life

Thomas Aquinas teaches that heavenly life consists in the "beatific vision": the direct, experiential knowledge of God through which he perfects human beings and fulfills all their desires.[a] While we cannot have such direct knowledge of God in this life, faith provides us with an indirect, imperfect knowledge of heavenly realities. In other words, the things we now believe in faith are the same things we will experience directly in heaven. In this respect, Thomas Aquinas can define faith as the beginnings of heavenly life on earth:

> Therefore [Heb 11:1] says, [Faith is] "the substance of things to be hoped for." [And I Cor 13:12:] "We see now through a glass in a dark manner; but then face to face"; as if to say: Then we shall be blessed when we see face to face that which we now see in a mirror and in a dark manner.
>
> Hence, in these words the order of the act of faith to its end is shown, since faith is ordered to the thing hoped for [i.e., heavenly knowledge of God].[b]

a. St. Thomas Aquinas, *Summa theologica* 1–2, q. 3, a. 8.

b. St. Thomas Aquinas, *Commentary on the Epistle to the Hebrews*, trans. Chrysostom Baer, OPraem (South Bend, IN: St. Augustine's Press, 2006), 11.1, section 557.

him—his words, deeds, and his very self—is **from** the Father. To believe in Jesus is to receive him, his revelation, as being uniquely from the Father (1:18; 6:46).

17:8 Now Jesus explains how the disciples know that everything about him is from the Father. First, he has faithfully spoken the Father's **words** as he was sent to do, and the disciples have **accepted** Jesus' revelatory words, taking them in and believing them to be from the Father.[4] Having so internalized Jesus' words, they have **truly understood that** he **came from** the Father. Jesus has planted a knowledge of the Father in their hearts, and by letting his revelation take root and grow through the Spirit's action in them, the disciples come to a living, experiential knowledge of the truth of Jesus' words: "Everything you gave me is from you" (17:7).

Reflection and Application (17:1–8)

Jesus opens a window onto his relationship with the Father, and we see that it is marked by complete selflessness. The Father glorifies the Son, and the Son

4. The verb for "accept" or "receive" (*lambanō*) is often a synonym for "believing" in John (see 1:12; 3:11–12, 32–33; 12:48).

glorifies the Father. The Father gives his all in the Son, and in turn the Son gives his all back to the Father. It is in this total giving of self that we can perceive something of the reality of "God is love" (1 John 4:8). By revealing this exchange to be the very life of God, Jesus simultaneously calls his disciples to practice this kind of love. God's life is to become our life, which means that our lives must become characterized by love. As 1 John 4:16 states, "God is love, and whoever remains in love remains in God and God in him."

Jesus Prays for His Disciples in Their Mission to the World (17:9–19)

[9]"I pray for them. I do not pray for the world but for the ones you have given me, because they are yours, [10]and everything of mine is yours and everything of yours is mine, and I have been glorified in them. [11]And now I will no longer be in the world, but they are in the world, while I am coming to you. Holy Father, keep them in your name that you have given me, so that they may be one just as we are. [12]When I was with them I protected them in your name that you gave me, and I guarded them, and none of them was lost except the son of destruction, in order that the scripture might be fulfilled. [13]But now I am coming to you. I speak this in the world so that they may share my joy completely. [14]I gave them your word, and the world hated them, because they do not belong to the world any more than I belong to the world. [15]I do not ask that you take them out of the world but that you keep them from the evil one. [16]They do not belong to the world any more than I belong to the world. [17]Consecrate them in the truth. Your word is truth. [18]As you sent me into the world, so I sent them into the world. [19]And I consecrate myself for them, so that they also may be consecrated in truth."

OT: Exod 29:1–9; Dan 7:7–8, 23–27; 11:36–37
NT: Eph 4:1–5; 2 Thess 2:3–12; Heb 9:11–14; 1 John 5:18–20
Catechism: Church's unity, 813–22; sanctifying grace, 1996–99
Lectionary: Seventh Sunday of Easter (Years A and B)

17:9–10 Jesus now prays for his present disciples, whom he will send to the hostile, unbelieving world (17:18). In the first section of the prayer, Jesus has revealed the mutual, selfless sharing between Father and Son. Now he places the disciples within this communion through the language of mutual belonging. The disciples "belonged" to the Father (17:6), and since the Father gives **everything** to the Son, they also belong to Jesus. He also includes his disciples in the exchange of glory that he spoke of in 17:1–5 by saying, **I have been glorified in them**. As Jesus reveals the Father's glory by accomplishing his saving work, so the disciples similarly reveal the divine majesty of the glorified Jesus: "By this is my Father glorified, that you bear much fruit and become my disciples" (15:8).

Jesus prays for his disciples, adding the qualifier, **I do not pray for the world**. Recall that John often uses "the world" to mean human beings and their world insofar as it is fallen, in rebellion against God, and under the power of sin (see sidebar on p. 37). Jesus does not pray for "the world" insofar as it is "the world," as it rejects the Father and the Son. Jesus is going to send his disciples to the hostile, unbelieving world as an extension of his own mission (17:18; 20:21). Through their visible unity, faithfulness, and love, they bear witness to the reality of the Father's love in Jesus, so that the world may come to believe and be redeemed (17:21, 23). Creation ceases to be "the world" as it receives Jesus and enters into redemption. C. K. Barrett puts it well: "To pray for the [world] would be almost an absurdity, since the only hope for the world is precisely that it should cease to be the [world]."[5]

17:11–12 Although Jesus **will no longer be in the world**, his disciples will still be **in the world**, and they are going to face its hatred in the form of persecutions, hostility, and temptation (15:18–21). While the world *hates* the disciples because of their relationship to Jesus (15:19, 21; 17:14), the Father *loves* them for the same reason (14:21, 23; 16:27). Since the disciples will experience the world's attacks, Jesus asks the **Father** to continue protecting them (**Keep them in your name**), as Jesus himself did while physically present among them (**I protected them in your name**). The divine protection of the disciples recalls Jesus' words about his sheep: "No one can take them out of my hand, . . . and no one can take them out of the Father's hand" (10:28–29). Protected by Jesus, none of his disciples **was lost except** for Judas, **the son of destruction**. Judas's defection was not due to any failure of Jesus' part but so **that** God's plan, given in **scripture, might be fulfilled** (see 13:18).

God's protection of the disciples preserves them in communion: **so that they may be one just as we are**. This is the first of four passages in John 17 in which Jesus prays for the unity of his disciples (also 17:21, 22, 23). Two things come to light in this petition. First, the basis for the unity among the disciples is the unity between the Father and the Son.[6] As Ephesians states, "One body and one Spirit, as you were also called to the one hope of your call; one Lord, one faith,

5. C. K. Barrett, *The Gospel according to St. John*, 2nd ed. (Philadelphia: Westminster, 1978), 506; a point affirmed by Raymond E. Brown, SS, *The Gospel according to John*, AB 29A (New York: Doubleday, 1970), 2:764.

6. Catechism 813.

The Son of Destruction and Antichrist

BIBLICAL BACKGROUND

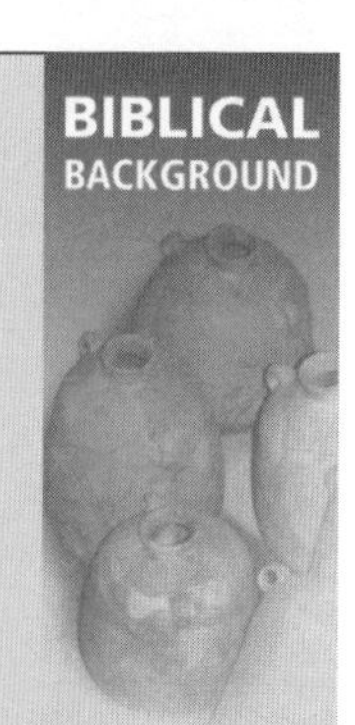

The title "son of destruction" and its connection to the fulfillment of Scripture recall several biblical texts that speak of an †eschatological enemy or enemies who lead a final persecution of God's people in the end time (e.g., Dan 7:7–8, 23–27; 11:36–37; 2 Thess 2:3–12; Rev 19:19–21). This eschatological opposition sometimes appears as a political oppressor who makes himself out to be divine (Rev 13:1–10), or as a false prophet who leads people away from God by false teaching (13:11–18). In some cases, the roles are combined into a single figure (2 Thess 2:3–12). Paul uses the same title "son of destruction" in 2 Thess 2:3 (NABRE: "the one doomed to perdition") to designate the end-time adversary of Christ, more commonly known as antichrist, whose deception is "a pseudo-messianism by which man glorifies himself in place of God and of his †Messiah come in the flesh (cf. 2 Thess 2:4–12; 1 Thess 5:2–3; 2 John 7; 1 John 2:18, 22)" (Catechism 675). The Fourth Gospel teaches that these eschatological realities are already present during the ministry of Jesus. The reality of antichrist is thus present in Judas, who turns away from Jesus and leads the opposition against him under the devil's influence (see John 13:27; 18:1–9; 1 John 4:2–3).

one baptism; one God and Father of all" (4:4–6). The Father and Son are one in sharing the same divine life (John 5:26), marked by intimate, personal knowledge (10:14–15) and self-giving love (15:9). The disciples are introduced into the divine communion by their faith in Jesus' revelation of the Father's "name" (17:6) and grow in it through love. As we shall see, their invisible communion with God becomes visible in their earthly community of faith and love, the Church (see 17:21, 23). Second, the placement of this unity petition after the mention of the disciples' being in the world (17:11) suggests that the world's attacks are going to threaten the disciples' unity. It seems that the purpose of the world's attacks is to get the disciples to break their communion with Jesus and to affiliate with the world and its ways, in rebellion, sin, and hatred (3:19–21; 7:7). To the extent that the world's ways exercise influence over Jesus' disciples in the form of divisions and discord, sin and scandal, the Church's unity is weakened, and the power of its witness to the world about the Father's love in Jesus is compromised.

17:13 By participating in the divine communion, the disciples come to **share** Jesus' **joy**. This joy is a fruit of his communion with the Father, to whom he now goes. Once Jesus has been resurrected and exalted to heavenly glory, he will incorporate his disciples into his communion with the Father, and they too

Pope St. John Paul II on Christian Unity

The words "that they may be one" in John 17:11 provide the title for Pope St. John Paul II's encyclical on ecumenism, *Ut Unum Sint*, in which he states:

> The unity of divided humanity is the will of God. For this reason he sent his Son, so that by dying and rising for us he might bestow on us the Spirit of love. On the eve of his sacrifice on the Cross, Jesus himself prayed to the Father for his disciples and for all those who believe in him, that they *might be one*, a living communion. This is the basis not only of the duty, but also of the responsibility before God and his plan, which falls to those who through Baptism become members of the Body of Christ, a Body in which the fullness of reconciliation and communion must be present.[a]

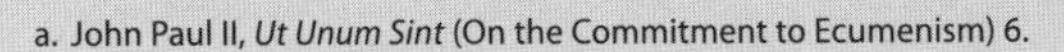

a. John Paul II, *Ut Unum Sint* (On the Commitment to Ecumenism) 6.

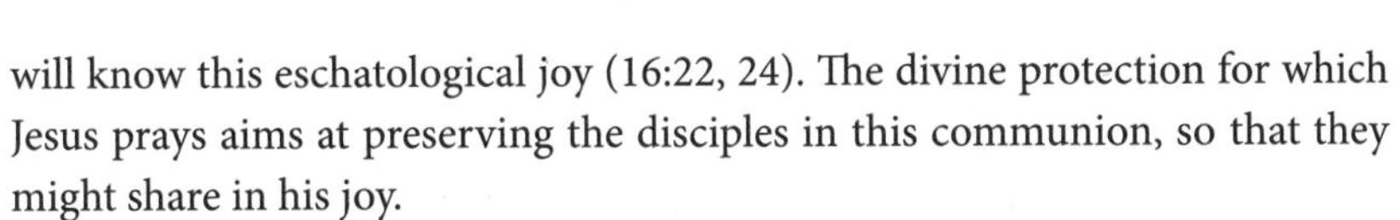

will know this eschatological joy (16:22, 24). The divine protection for which Jesus prays aims at preserving the disciples in this communion, so that they might share in his joy.

17:14–16 Since the disciples receive the Father's **word** through Jesus, the Word, they receive his gift of participating in his communion with the Father. They therefore, like Jesus, **do not belong to the world**. Consequently, **the world hated them** as it hated Jesus (15:18).[7] But the disciples cannot escape from the world (see 1 Cor 5:9–11), and Jesus does not ask the Father to **take them out of the world**. Instead, they must go to the world and testify to the Father's love in Christ (17:18; 20:21)!

"In the world," Jesus said, "you will have trouble" (16:33). The "ruler of the world" (14:30) is the devil. He has been the primary enemy of Jesus in the Gospel, and he will also be the primary enemy of his disciples in their mission to the world, despite the fact that Jesus' exaltation secures his defeat (12:31). Accordingly, Jesus repeats his prayer for the divine protection of his disciples, **Keep them from the evil one**, a phrase similar to the final petition of the Our Father: "deliver us from the evil one" (Matt 6:13). This divine protection comes to the disciples through the indwelling Holy Spirit (1 John 4:4) and the related gift of participation in the divine communion as God's children in Christ (known in Catholic doctrine as sanctifying grace). As 1 John 5:18 says, "The one begotten by God he protects, and the evil one cannot touch him."

7. Use of "hated" in the past tense is a case where the prayer points to a time after Jesus' glorification. See the introduction to this chapter.

Saint Thérèse of Lisieux on the Spiritual Power and Protection of Sanctifying Grace

Sanctifying grace is the human being's "*participation in the life of God*" (Catechism 1997). It is received in baptism, cleanses the soul of sin, and continues to work in the baptized to make each believer holy and pleasing in God's eyes (Catechism 1996–99). Sanctifying grace is lost when a person knowingly, willingly, and deliberately commits mortal sin (Catechism 1861), but it can be restored through the sacrament of reconciliation (Catechism 1446). In her autobiography, St. Thérèse of Lisieux recounts a dream in her childhood from which she learned the protective power of sanctifying grace:

> I dreamed one night I went to take a walk all alone in the garden. . . . [While I was walking], there was a barrel . . . and on this barrel two *frightful little devils*. . . . All of the sudden they cast fiery glances at me and at the same moment appeared to be more frightened than I was, for they jumped from the barrel and went to hide in the laundry that was just opposite. Seeing they weren't so brave, I wanted to know what they were going to do, and I went up to the window. The poor little devils were there, running on the tables, not knowing what to do to hide from my gaze. . . . This dream, I suppose, has nothing extraordinary about it, and still I believe God permitted me to remember it in order to prove to me that a soul in the state of grace has nothing to fear from demons who are cowards, capable of fleeing before the gaze of a little child![a]

a. St. Thérèse of Lisieux, *Story of a Soul: The Autobiography of Thérèse of Lisieux*, 3rd ed., trans. John Clarke, OCD (Washington, DC: ICS Publications, 1996), 28.

17:17–18 Jesus asks the Father to **consecrate** his disciples. The language of consecration is characteristic of liturgy and priesthood. Things that are consecrated, or made holy, are set apart from the ordinary and dedicated for the special service of the Lord (e.g., priests, Exod 29:1; sacred vessels and furnishings, Exod 30:26–30; sacrifices, Lev 6:18–23). Jesus previously associated consecration and mission by referring to himself as "the one whom the Father has consecrated and sent into the world" (10:36). Just as the Father consecrated Jesus and **sent** him **into the world**, so too must the disciples be consecrated when Jesus sends **them into the world**. Jesus specifically prays that the disciples be consecrated **in the truth**, meaning in Jesus himself, who is both the Father's **word** and **truth**. He prays that the disciples be enveloped in the Father's love, which makes them holy and empowers them for their mission to the world.

Ignace de la Potterie sums these points up well: "This sanctification that Jesus asks of the Father is nothing other than their going deeper into the truth, in the revelation of the Father's name; it is, then, a deepening on the part of believers in their life of sonship because of their union with Christ. . . . It is in the Christ-Truth, in Jesus who makes himself known as the Son of God, that the Father's name is revealed to them. And it is also in him, Jesus, that the possibility of living fully as children of God is opened up to them."[8]

17:19 But for the disciples to be **consecrated in truth**, Jesus must first go to the cross and complete his mission from the Father. This is the significance of his remark, **I consecrate myself for them**. The preposition "for" (Greek *hyper*) recalls the good shepherd who lays down his life "for" (*hyper*) the sheep (10:11) and Jesus' words, "The bread that I will give is my flesh for [*hyper*] the life of the world" (6:51). Jesus consecrates himself by offering his own life as a sacrifice of love to the Father on the cross. Since Jesus is the one offering the sacrifice, he also serves as the priest. As Hebrews states, Jesus, the high priest of the New †Covenant, offered "his own blood, thus obtaining eternal redemption. . . . The blood of Christ, who through the eternal spirit offered himself unblemished to God, cleanse[s] our consciences from dead works to worship the living God" (9:12, 14). This sacrifice of Jesus, the gift of his flesh (6:51), is sacramentally present in the Eucharist. Jesus identifies his flesh, given on the cross, as "bread" (6:51) and commands his disciples to eat "this bread" (6:58), which is "the flesh of the †Son of Man" (6:53). The disciples' participation in the divine communion, made possible by Jesus' self-sacrifice on the cross and deepened by the Eucharist, sustains them in their mission.

Reflection and Application (17:9–19)

Jesus teaches that unity is essential to the life of his disciples because it is the visible manifestation of their invisible sharing in the divine communion. Along with love and obedience, Jesus names the unity of disciples as strengthening their witness to the world. While all Christians are united by virtue of a common baptism, various events in Christian history have led to real divisions among Christians. The "promotion of the restoration of unity among all Christians" is known as ecumenism, and many Catholic, Protestant, and Orthodox Christians have committed their lives to this important task.[9] Whether among ordinary

8. Ignace de la Potterie, *La Vérité dans Saint Jean* (1977; repr., Rome: Editrice Pontificio Istituto Biblico, 1999), 2:782–73, our translation.

9. Catechism Glossary, "Ecumenism." The Second Vatican Council (*Lumen Gentium* 15) teaches, "The Church recognizes that in many ways she is linked to those who, being baptized, are honored with the name of Christian, though they do not profess the faith in its entirety or do not preserve unity of communion with the successor of Peter."

believers or official panels of experts, ecumenical work involves collaboration and honest dialogue, so Christians can understand one another and clarify topics of agreement and disagreement.[10] Jesus' prayer in John 17 teaches that Christian unity is fundamentally a gift from God. Ecumenical work, therefore, needs to be deeply informed by a spirit of repentance, humility, love, and prayer, because these dispose us to God's action. The reunion of Christians will be a work of the Holy Spirit, and the work of ecumenism will truly flourish through the holiness and love of its participants.

Jesus Prays for the Unity of His Church (17:20–26)

[20]"I pray not only for them, but also for those who will believe in me through their word, [21]so that they may all be one, as you, Father, are in me and I in you, that they also may be in us, that the world may believe that you sent me. [22]And I have given them the glory you gave me, so that they may be one, as we are one, [23]I in them and you in me, that they may be brought to perfection as one, that the world may know that you sent me, and that you loved them even as you loved me. [24]Father, they are your gift to me. I wish that where I am they also may be with me, that they may see my glory that you gave me, because you loved me before the foundation of the world. [25]Righteous Father, the world also does not know you, but I know you, and they know that you sent me. [26]I made known to them your name and I will make it known, that the love with which you loved me may be in them and I in them."

OT: Ezek 36:24–28
NT: Matt 28:16–20; 1 John 3:1–3
Catechism: communion of saints, 946–59; heaven, 1026–29
Lectionary: Seventh Sunday of Easter (Year C)

17:20–21 The participation in the divine communion that Jesus offers is not limited only to that first group of disciples but also extends to include all future disciples in later generations. The description of future disciples as **those who will believe in me through their word** implies that the disciples' mission to the world has as its goal bringing people to know Jesus and the Father (see Matt 28:19). Jesus has given the Father's Word, which is identical to his very self, to the disciples (John 17:14), and this same Word, which remains in the disciples (8:31; 15:7), continues to sound out in the world and encounter people through their witness.

10. Catechism 821.

Saint Cyril of Alexandria on the Disciples' Union of Love as an Icon of God

Christ wishes the disciples to be kept in a state of unity by maintaining a like-mindedness and an identity of will, being mingled together as it were in soul and spirit and in the law of peace and love for one another. He wishes them to be bound together tightly with an unbreakable bond of love, that they may advance to such a degree of unity that their freely chosen association might even become an image of the natural unity that is conceived to exist between the Father and the Son.[a]

a. Cyril of Alexandria, *Commentary on John* 11.9, in ACCS 4b:245.

Jesus' prayer that his disciples, both present and future, **may all be one** implies that the communion in which his disciples all participate transcends time and place.[11] This is the case because it is the communion of the Father and the Son (**as you, Father, are in me and I in you**) and his disciples share in it (**that they also may be in us**). The disciples' invisible participation in the divine communion is manifested visibly in the bonds of faith and love existing in their historical community, the Church. When the Church is strongly and vibrantly united in faith and love, it becomes a †sign and testimony of the unity between Father and Son. The Church's unity is a prophetic witness to the unbelieving **world**, inviting them to **believe** in the truth revealed by Christ.

17:22

Through his revelation and incorporation of his disciples into the divine communion, the exchange of glory between the Father and Son, Jesus has **given** his disciples **the glory** that he himself received from the Father (see 17:1, 4–5). In this way, he provides the basis for the oneness of his disciples: **so that they may be one, as we are one**. As Raymond Brown writes, "The oneness of the believers flows from [Jesus'] giving to the believers the glory that the Father has given him, and so unity comes down from the Father and the Son to the believers."[12]

17:23

These relations of mutual indwelling between Jesus and his disciples (**I in them**; see 6:56; 14:20) and between the Father and Jesus (**and you in me**; see 10:38; 14:10) are the communion in which the disciples are **brought to perfection**. Humanity's participation in the divine communion is the goal of the Father's saving plan, indeed, the goal of the whole of human history: Jesus

11. This is a basis for what is known in Catholic doctrine as "the communion of saints" (Catechism 946–59). Since all believers participate in the one life of the risen Jesus, they are all united together across time and into eternity.

12. Brown, *John*, 2:776.

"takes away the sin of the world" (1:29) and brings human beings to share his own eternal communion with the Father as God's "children" (1:12).[13] The communion of Father and Son is an eternal exchange of life and love, and the disciples' participation in this communion becomes manifest through their love: "No one has ever seen God. Yet, if we love one another, God remains in us, and his love is brought to perfection in us" (1 John 4:12). The visible unity and love of the disciples is testimony to **the world** of their being **loved** and transformed by the Father, through Jesus, whom he **loved** and **sent** for the world's salvation (3:16–17).

17:24 The longing of Jesus' heart is for his disciples to **be with** him forever in the Father's house (14:2). In this heavenly destination, they will **see** the eternal **glory** of the Son, given him by the Father **before the foundation of the world**, in his own glorified humanity. The disciples' participation in the divine communion begins now through faith and baptism and will culminate in this heavenly "beatific vision" (Catechism 1028). As 1 John 3:2 states, "Beloved, we are God's children now; what we shall be has not yet been revealed. We do know that when it is revealed we shall be like him, for we shall see him as he is."

17:25–26 Only the eternal Son, who became †incarnate in Jesus, knows the **Father** and reveals him (1:18; 6:46). While **the world does not know** the **Father** because it rejects the Son, the disciples **know that** the Father **sent** Jesus because they have received his revelation in faith. During his earthly ministry, Jesus **made known** the Father's **name** to them, and **will** continue to **make it known** through the indwelling Holy Spirit (see 16:13). Through the Holy Spirit, **the** divine **love with which** the Father has **loved** the Son from all eternity becomes a living reality **in** Jesus' disciples. As they come to know the Father, whom Jesus has revealed, more deeply through the Holy Spirit, the disciples' love and participation in the divine communion will increase, until at last they reach the goal of remaining forever in the Father's house (14:2–3).

13. Catechism 221.

The Hour Begins

John 18:1–27

From the beginning of the Gospel, Jesus' earthly life has been moving toward his †hour: the divinely appointed time when he will preeminently reveal the Father's love and accomplish his work of salvation. Now it has arrived. John's passion narrative, while in many ways similar to the †Synoptic accounts, has several distinct theological emphases. First, the *kingship* of Jesus is prominent in John. Jesus is the sovereign Lord, who is in complete control over the events of his passion. Since Jesus possesses divine power (10:30), the events of his passion happen because he allows them to happen. Second, the emphasis on Jesus' kingly sovereignty and power underscores the *freedom* with which he goes to the cross. As Jesus earlier said, "No one takes [my life] from me, but I lay it down on my own. I have power to lay it down, and power to take it up again" (10:18). By freely going to the cross, Jesus offers his life as a perfect gift of love, given to the Father for the world's salvation. Third, by freely laying down his life in obedience to the Father, Jesus reveals *the infinite depths of the Father's love and mercy toward sinners*. Perceiving the revelation of divine love in Jesus' cross requires faith, and John invites us to view the passion with the eyes of faith through his use of †irony: "On the spiritual level the situation is exactly the opposite of what it is on the natural level."[1] On the surface Jesus' death on the cross seems to be defeat and humiliation, but in fact it is God's victory and triumph. Through the cross, God takes on and overcomes sin and death with his infinitely greater merciful love.

1. Ignace de la Potterie, SJ, *The Hour of Jesus: The Passion and Resurrection of Jesus according to John*, trans. Dom G. Murray, OSB (Staten Island, NY: Alba House, 1989), xiii.

Jesus Goes to His Arrest (18:1–14)

[1]When he had said this, Jesus went out with his disciples across the Kidron valley to where there was a garden, into which he and his disciples entered. [2]Judas his betrayer also knew the place, because Jesus had often met there with his disciples. [3]So Judas got a band of soldiers and guards from the chief priests and the Pharisees and went there with lanterns, torches, and weapons. [4]Jesus, knowing everything that was going to happen to him, went out and said to them, "Whom are you looking for?" [5]They answered him, "Jesus the Nazorean." He said to them, "I AM." Judas his betrayer was also with them. [6]When he said to them, "I AM," they turned away and fell to the ground. [7]So he again asked them, "Whom are you looking for?" They said, "Jesus the Nazorean." [8]Jesus answered, "I told you that I AM. So if you are looking for me, let these men go." [9]This was to fulfill what he had said, "I have not lost any of those you gave me." [10]Then Simon Peter, who had a sword, drew it, struck the high priest's slave, and cut off his right ear. The slave's name was Malchus. [11]Jesus said to Peter, "Put your sword into its scabbard. Shall I not drink the cup that the Father gave me?"

[12]So the band of soldiers, the tribune, and the Jewish guards seized Jesus, bound him, [13]and brought him to Annas first. He was the father-in-law of Caiaphas, who was high priest that year. [14]It was Caiaphas who had counseled the Jews that it was better that one man should die rather than the people.

OT: Gen 2:4–3:24; Pss 16; 75

NT: Mark 14:32–52

Catechism: all sinners are authors of Christ's passion, 598; Christ's life is an offering to the Father, 607; Jesus embraces the Father's redeeming love, 609; Gethsemane, 612

Lectionary: Good Friday

18:1 After praying for all his disciples, **Jesus went out with his disciples across the Kidron valley**. The Kidron is a riverbed located outside Jerusalem on the eastern side. Farther to the east, on the far side of the Kidron, is the Mount of Olives. The †Synoptics all mention Jesus as going there after the Last Supper (Matt 26:30; Mark 14:26; Luke 22:39). Only John refers to Jesus' destination as **a garden**. The larger †canonical context invites a connection with the garden of Eden. In that garden, the serpent enticed Adam and Eve to sin against God (Gen 3:1–6).[2] As a result, humanity came under God's condemnation (John

2. Cyril of Alexandria, *Commentary on John* 11.12.

Fig. 11. The Kidron Valley and the Mount of Olives

3:36) and became enslaved to the power of sin (8:34). Now, in this garden, Jesus obediently embraces his Father's will for the world's salvation.

18:2–3

To emphasize Judas's treachery, John mentions the familiarity that **Judas his betrayer** has with **the place**. This garden is a favorite place where **Jesus** frequently **met . . . with his disciples** (see Luke 21:37; 22:39). Judas betrays Jesus in this same place, even though it is associated with their friendship and relationship as master and disciple. When we last saw Judas, "Satan entered him" (13:27), and he went out into the "night" (13:30), the spiritual darkness. Now Judas reappears, leading the arrest party, which for John symbolizes the whole of sinful humanity. In the arrest party, there are both †Jews (**guards from the chief priests and the †Pharisees**) and Gentiles (**a band of** Roman **soldiers**).[3] We also see the betrayal of Jesus by his own disciples: Judas leads the arrest party, and in the next scene, Peter denies Jesus three times. All sinners are implicated in and responsible for Jesus' death.[4]

Only John mentions that the arrest party carries **lanterns** and **torches**. Since Jesus is arrested at night, there is deeper symbolism. The †hour of Jesus' passion is the great showdown, where God confronts and conquers Satan, "the ruler

3. Jews ("children of Israel") and Gentiles ("the nations") are the two basic categories in biblical anthropology.

4. Catechism 598.

of this world," and the power of sin and evil (12:31; see Col 1:13). At the Last Supper, Jesus said that "the ruler of the world," the devil, "is coming" (14:30). Now the devil arrives in the person of Judas, leading the symbolic totality of sinful humanity against the divine Word through whom the world was made (1:3, 10). Since the arrest party does not follow "the light of the world" (8:12; 9:5), they walk in spiritual darkness and must carry other sources of light—lanterns and torches.

18:4 Since "the Father had put everything into his power" (13:3), Jesus has complete control over the events of his passion; the other individuals mentioned in the Gospel have power over Jesus only because he gives it to them (19:11).

Jesus displays his kingly sovereignty by confronting those who have come to arrest him. The arrest party does not storm into the garden and seize him by surprise. Rather, **Jesus** knew **everything that was going to happen to him**, and he **went out** to confront them! Jesus' question, **Whom are you looking for?**, recalls his initial words to the first disciples (1:38) as well as previous efforts of opponents looking for Jesus to kill him (5:18; 7:1, 11; 8:37, 40).

18:5–6 The arrest party seeks **Jesus the Nazorean**, and Jesus identifies himself with the divine name: **I AM** (see sidebar on p. 89). Jesus' self-identification as "I AM" appears three times in the arrest account (18:5–6, 8) to reaffirm Jesus' identity as the Lord. The response of **Judas** and the arrest party to Jesus' declaration is the typical response to a †theophany: **they turned away and fell to the ground**. By pronouncing his divine name, Jesus displays his divine identity and sovereignty, before which his opponents are utterly powerless.[5] Thus the psalmist prays, "The voice of the LORD is power" (29:4). Similarly, St. Paul writes, "At the name of Jesus / every knee should bend, / of those in heaven and on earth and under the earth" (Phil 2:10; see Isa 45:22–24).

18:7–9 With his opponents at his feet, Jesus **again asked, "Whom are you looking for?"** After they reply, **Jesus the Nazorean**, Jesus once more identifies himself as **I AM**. Then, in another display of divine sovereignty, Jesus gives orders to the arrest party: **If you are looking for me, let these men go**. John does not report the disciples as abandoning Jesus in fear and panic, as Matthew and Mark do (see Matt 26:56; Mark 14:50–52). Instead, John emphasizes that the disciples avoid capture because Jesus has so decreed it. The disciples' release **was to fulfill** Jesus' own prayer in 17:12: **I have not lost any of those you gave me**. Jesus' order protects his disciples. Unlike the hired man who runs away, the good shepherd confronts the danger and protects his sheep (10:11–13).

5. Raymond E. Brown, SS, *The Death of the Messiah: From Gethsemane to the Grave*, ABRL (New York: Doubleday, 1994), 1:261.

18:10–11 **Simon Peter** takes forceful action to prevent Jesus' arrest by cutting off the **ear** of **the high priest's slave**. But Jesus orders Peter to sheathe his sword and not hinder his arrest. The explanation for this lies in the rhetorical question: **Shall I not drink the cup that the Father gave me?** The "cup" is a biblical image for what God has decreed for the life of an individual or group. The psalmist prays, "Lord, my allotted portion and my cup, / you have made my destiny secure" (16:5). In many cases, God fills the cup with his wrath, the punishment that sinners incur (Ps 75:9; Isa 51:17; Rev 14:9–10). Jesus' words about the cup recall Synoptic accounts of his prayer in Gethsemane: "Father, if you are willing, take this cup away from me" (Luke 22:42).[6] In John, "the cup" is akin to Jesus' "hour." It is that which the Father has willed for him, and which Jesus himself wills, to accomplish the work of salvation: to lay down his life and take it up again (10:17–18). Jesus freely lays down his life in obedience to the Father—he willingly drinks the cup—and no one, not even Peter, will hinder him from making the perfect gift of his life on the cross.

18:12–14 With his kingly sovereignty established, Jesus allows himself to be arrested. Both the Roman **soldiers** under the command of **the tribune**, a Roman military officer, **and the Jewish guards seized Jesus** and **bound him**. The arrest party **brought him to Annas first** (an incident not reported in the Synoptics). Annas, a former high priest, was a major figure in first-century Jewish leadership in Jerusalem (Luke 3:2; Acts 4:6). Not only was he **the father-in-law of Caiaphas**, the current **high priest**, but several of his other sons served as high priest in later years.

Unlike the Synoptics, John does not include a lengthy description of Jesus' legal proceedings before the Jewish authorities after his arrest (see Mark 14:53–65). John placed the authorities' decision to seek Jesus' execution after the raising of Lazarus in order to show the connection between Jesus' death and his power to give life (11:45–53). John simply reminds us of these earlier deliberations: **It was Caiaphas who had counseled the Jews that it was better that one man should die rather than the people.**

Reflection and Application (18:1–14)

A gift must be freely given. Earlier in the Gospel, Jesus has declared that he is going to lay down his life as a gift: "No one takes [my life] from me, but I lay it down on my own" (10:18). The emphasis here on Jesus' sovereignty testifies to the perfect freedom with which he relinquishes his life. In other words,

6. The Johannine equivalent appears in 12:27.

Jesus completely and willingly chose to die on the cross for the world's salvation (Catechism 609). The Blessed Trinity could have chosen to redeem the world in other ways, but God chose to do so through the cross of Jesus. For in the cross, we see the radical, self-giving nature of divine love and the extent to which God goes to prove his love for us. As St. Paul writes in Rom 5:8, "God proves his love for us in that while we were still sinners Christ died for us." That is why during the Easter Vigil liturgy, the prayer of Easter Proclamation, the Exsultet, speaks of the sin of Adam as "O happy fault that earned so great, so glorious a Redeemer!"[7] We are invited to remember that God freely chose the humiliation and agony of the cross to demonstrate how great is his love for us, a love that embraces the worst parts of human existence and goes to the absolute end for us (13:1).

Jesus before Annas and Peter's Denials (18:15–27)

[15]Simon Peter and another disciple followed Jesus. Now the other disciple was known to the high priest, and he entered the courtyard of the high priest with Jesus. [16]But Peter stood at the gate outside. So the other disciple, the acquaintance of the high priest, went out and spoke to the gatekeeper and brought Peter in. [17]Then the maid who was the gatekeeper said to Peter, "You are not one of this man's disciples, are you?" He said, "I am not." [18]Now the slaves and the guards were standing around a charcoal fire that they had made, because it was cold, and were warming themselves. Peter was also standing there keeping warm.

[19]The high priest questioned Jesus about his disciples and about his doctrine. [20]Jesus answered him, "I have spoken publicly to the world. I have always taught in a synagogue or in the temple area where all the Jews gather, and in secret I have said nothing. [21]Why ask me? Ask those who heard me what I said to them. They know what I said." [22]When he had said this, one of the temple guards standing there struck Jesus and said, "Is this the way you answer the high priest?" [23]Jesus answered him, "If I have spoken wrongly, testify to the wrong; but if I have spoken rightly, why do you strike me?" [24]Then Annas sent him bound to Caiaphas the high priest.

[25]Now Simon Peter was standing there keeping warm. And they said to him, "You are not one of his disciples, are you?" He denied it and said, "I am not." [26]One of the slaves of the high priest, a relative of the one whose ear Peter had cut off, said, "Didn't I see you in the garden with him?" [27]Again Peter denied it. And immediately the cock crowed.

7. *The Roman Missal* (London: Catholic Truth Society, 2010), 389.

NT: Mark 14:53–65

Catechism: God comes to meet man, 50; God has said everything in his Word, 65; sin's damage and definition, 1811; sin exposed 1851

Lectionary: Good Friday

18:15–18

John has arranged 18:15–27 in a †concentric literary structure, in which Peter's denials (18:15–18 and 25–27) frame the central scene of Jesus' appearance before Annas (18:19–24). This literary structure highlights the scene with Jesus and invites us to see it in light of the surrounding scenes with Peter.

With Jesus having been taken to the former high priest, **Simon Peter and another disciple followed**. This **other disciple** is probably the Beloved Disciple, because he is often coupled with Peter and left unnamed. The Beloved Disciple **was known to the high priest**, which suggests his priestly or aristocratic connections. These gave him access to **the courtyard of the high priest**, while **Peter stood at the gate outside**. The disciple then **spoke to the gatekeeper** and obtained access for **Peter**.

After **Peter** entered, **the gatekeeper** asked him, **You are not one of this man's disciples, are you?** At the Last Supper, Peter, full of naive self-confidence, insisted that he would be willing to die for Jesus. But Jesus revealed Peter's frailty, predicting that he would deny him three times (13:37–38).[8] Answering the gatekeeper, Peter denies his relationship with Jesus for the first time: **I am not**.

Also in the courtyard are a group of **slaves and guards**, including some of those who made up the party that arrested Jesus (18:3). Since the night **was cold**, they **were standing around a charcoal fire**. So **Peter** joined them to keep **warm**. Somewhat like Judas, who brought the arrest party and betrayed Jesus, Peter finds himself among Jesus' opponents in this cold, dark night.

18:19–24

The focus shifts from outside, where Peter is denying Jesus, to inside the house of Annas, the former **high priest**. John does not directly mention any questions from Annas but relates that they concerned Jesus' **disciples** and **doctrine**. By relating Annas's questioning in an indirect summary, John makes Jesus' direct speech the focus of the scene.

As to his teaching, **Jesus** declares its public and universal character: **I have spoken publicly to the world**, and **In secret I have said nothing**. As the †incarnate Word, Jesus says and does all that the Father has given him. His revelation is not a secret meant for only a select few but is openly directed to all people and in all places.[9] The public character of his revelation is supported by

8. See Raymond E. Brown, SS, *The Gospel according to John*, AB 29A (New York: Doubleday, 1970), 2:616.

9. Catechism 50, 65.

the public settings for his teaching: either **in a †synagogue** (6:22–59) **or in the temple area** (5:14–47; 7–8; 10:22–39).

As to his disciples, Jesus turns the tables by questioning and telling Annas: **Why ask me? Ask those who heard me what I said to them. They know what I said.** †Ironically, at the moment when Jesus is saying this, Peter, who has heard Jesus speak and knows what he said, is denying him in the courtyard.

In response to Jesus' boldness, **one of the temple guards . . . struck Jesus** and asked, **Is this the way you answer the high priest?** The guard regards Jesus' words as insubordinate and disrespectful, for Annas, being the former high priest, was a man of great social standing. At a deeper level, as de la Potterie has argued, the guard can be taken as a "representative of all those who have rejected the revealing word of Jesus to the world."[10] Jesus has just referred to his public revelation to the whole world, and some in the world, typified by the guard, reject him.

Jesus challenges the guard to produce evidence that would prove him to be in the wrong: **If I have spoken wrongly, testify to the wrong**. Since Jesus speaks only "the truth . . . from God" (8:40), the guard implicitly cannot do so. Hence Jesus asks, **But if I have spoken rightly, why do you strike me?** Jesus reveals the Father's truth to the world, he speaks rightly, and the guard's blow symbolizes the rejection of his revelation.

The scene ends with **Annas** sending Jesus **to Caiaphas the high priest**, but we hear nothing more of the proceedings before Caiaphas (as given in the †Synoptics, e.g., Mark 14:53–65).

18:25–27 The narrative shifts back to **Peter** outside, in the courtyard, where he is again questioned about his relationship with Jesus, this time by the slaves and guards. Is Peter a disciple of Jesus? Once more, Peter **denied it**. The situation becomes even more difficult for Peter because among the **slaves** is **a relative of the one whose ear Peter had cut off**. John was deliberate about specifically naming Peter as the one who cut off the ear of a slave named Malchus (18:10). Now Peter is confronted by an eyewitness, with personal ties to the man whom he wounded, who claims to have seen Peter **in the garden** with Jesus. Faced with this pressure, **Peter denied** Jesus for a third time. Then, as Jesus predicted (13:38), **the cock crowed**.

Reflection and Application (18:15–27)

John 18 gives us a sad account of Peter's denial of Jesus. Since we have all been unfaithful to Jesus, we should see some reflection of ourselves in Peter

10. De la Potterie, *Hour*, 51.

(Catechism 1851). Peter wanted to follow Jesus as a disciple (6:68), learned from him, ate at the Last Supper with him, and insisted that he would follow Jesus even to death (13:37). Yet despite his best efforts and intentions, Peter fails miserably when forced to choose in a difficult situation. Since the number three often symbolizes completeness, Peter completely disavows Jesus. Whenever we sin, we act just like Peter: we deny Jesus by our sinful thoughts, words, and deeds.

The example of Peter can be a healthy warning for us not to underestimate our own weaknesses and the lingering effects of original sin. Warming himself by the fire with the guards who arrested Jesus, Peter has put himself in a difficult situation. Some of these guards, who are Jesus' opponents, pressure Peter over his relationship with Jesus. We must be careful not to put ourselves into situations where we will be pressured to sin and deny our relationship with Jesus.

The older form of the Roman Holy Week Liturgy subtly presented Judas and Peter as two traitors and then leads us to recognize ourselves as traitors with a choice: repent like Peter or give up like Judas and despair of mercy. As we shall see with Peter, God's mercy is infinitely greater than the worst of our sins. God is always ready to forgive those who return to him (see reflection on John 21:15–19).

The Trial before Pilate

John 18:28–19:16a

John's account of Jesus' trial before Pilate is longer and more complex than its †Synoptic counterparts. The trial is divided into seven scenes, arranged in a †concentric literary structure.[1] The scenes labeled A and A_1, B and B_1, C and C_1 parallel each other. The literary structure marks the only unparalleled scene, the proclamation of Jesus' kingship (D), as the focal point of the trial:

A Pilate talks to the Jewish authorities outside (18:28–32)
  B Pilate talks to Jesus inside (18:33–38a)
    C Pilate talks to the Jewish authorities outside (18:38b–40)
      D Jesus hailed as King (19:1–3)
    C_1 Pilate, Jesus, and the Jewish authorities outside (19:4–8)
  B_1 Pilate talks to Jesus inside (19:9–12)
A_1 Pilate, Jesus, and the Jewish authorities outside (19:13–16a)

Several important features in John's trial narrative should be noted. First, the account is filled with †irony: while one thing seems to be the case, the reality is different, often quite the opposite. For instance, the Roman soldiers put a crown of thorns on Jesus as though he is king. But while they intend it as mockery, their proclamation of Jesus as king is actually true. Second, this narrative, like the story of the man born blind in John 9, illustrates John's theological understanding of judgment. Jesus comes into the world, and his presence

1. Following Ignace de la Potterie, SJ, *The Hour of Jesus: The Passion and Resurrection of Jesus according to John*, trans. Dom G. Murray, OSB (Staten Island, NY: Alba House, 1989), 58–61.

requires a response from people (3:19–21). Judgment is determined by each one's response to him. Since Jesus offers the gift of eternal life, the acceptance of him leads to the reception of eternal life. However, since rejecting Jesus means rejection of his gift of eternal life, the negative response leaves a person under condemnation and the power of sin. Third, John combines irony and judgment in his complex portrayal of Pilate. John's portrayal of Pilate shows him to be both arrogant and cowardly. Pilate blusters about his power and acts condescendingly toward his Jewish subjects. Yet he waffles and tries to escape making a decision about Jesus, a decision that he cannot avoid no matter how much he tries. Pilate's indecisiveness is dramatized by his trips back and forth between the Jewish authorities outside the praetorium and Jesus inside. While Pilate is in the position of authority to judge Jesus, ironically, it is Pilate, not Jesus, who is really on trial.

Scene 1 [Outside]: What Charge Do You Bring? (18:28–32)

[28]Then they brought Jesus from Caiaphas to the praetorium. It was morning. And they themselves did not enter the praetorium, in order not to be defiled so that they could eat the Passover. [29]So Pilate came out to them and said, "What charge do you bring [against] this man?" [30]They answered and said to him, "If he were not a criminal, we would not have handed him over to you." [31]At this, Pilate said to them, "Take him yourselves, and judge him according to your law." The Jews answered him, "We do not have the right to execute anyone," [32]in order that the word of Jesus might be fulfilled that he said indicating the kind of death he would die.

NT: Luke 23:1–5

Catechism: divisions among the Jewish authorities concerning Jesus, 596; responsibility and Jesus' death, 597–600

Lectionary: Good Friday

18:28 John does not report anything about Jesus' appearance before Caiaphas. Instead, he focuses the whole of Jesus' trial on this sequence with Pilate. The proceedings begin when some Jewish authorities bring **Jesus from Caiaphas to the praetorium**. The praetorium (derived from the Latin *praetor*, meaning "commander" or "general") was the Jerusalem headquarters of the Roman prefect, or governor, who normally resided at Caesarea Maritima, on the Mediterranean Sea. The praetorium was most likely a palace along the western wall of

The Church's Condemnation of Anti-Semitism

The Second Vatican Council teaches:

> True, the Jewish authorities and those who followed their lead pressed for the death of Christ; still, what happened in His passion cannot be charged against all the †Jews, without distinction, then alive, nor against the Jews of today. Although the Church is the new people of God, the Jews should not be presented as rejected or accursed by God, as if this followed from the Holy Scriptures. All should see to it, then, that in catechetical work or in the preaching of the word of God they do not teach anything that does not conform to the truth of the Gospel and the spirit of Christ. Furthermore, in her rejection of every persecution against any man, the Church, mindful of the patrimony she shares with the Jews and moved not by political reasons but by the Gospel's spiritual love, decries hatred, persecutions, displays of anti-Semitism, directed against Jews at any time and by anyone.[a]

The Catechism (598) similarly makes clear that all sinners are responsible for Jesus' death: "The Church has never forgotten that 'sinners were the authors and ministers of all the sufferings that the divine Redeemer endured' (*Roman Catechism* 1.5.11; cf. Heb 12:3). Taking into account the fact that our sins affect Christ himself (cf. Matt 25:45; Acts 9:4–5), the Church does not hesitate to impute to Christians the gravest responsibility for the torments inflicted upon Jesus, a responsibility with which they have all too often burdened the Jews alone."

a. Second Vatican Council, *Nostra Aetate* (Declaration on the Relation of the Church to Non-Christian Religions) 4. See also Catechism 595–96.

Jerusalem, built by Herod the Great.[2] The Jewish authorities **did not enter the praetorium** so as not to be rendered ritually impure through contact with a Gentile and thus unable to **eat the Passover**.[3] Throughout the trial, the Jewish

2. See Urban C. von Wahlde, "Archaeology and John's Gospel," in *Jesus and Archaeology*, ed. James H. Charlesworth (Grand Rapids: Eerdmans, 2006), 572–73; Raymond E. Brown, SS, *The Death of the Messiah: From Gethsemane to the Grave*, ABRL (New York: Doubleday, 1994), 1:705–10.

3. See E. P. Sanders, *Judaism: Practice and Belief, 63 BCE–66 CE* (Philadelphia: Trinity Press International, 1992), 73–75. A complication arises here for understanding the chronology of the last events of Jesus' mortal life. John and the †Synoptics agree that Jesus died on a Friday afternoon, the "day of preparation" for Passover, which started that same Friday night along with the sabbath (Mark 15:42; John 19:31). John 18:28 suggests that the Passover meal was to be eaten on Friday night; the Synoptics suggest that the Last Supper, eaten on Thursday night, was the Passover meal (Mark 14:12). Most likely, the agreement between John and the Synoptics that Jesus died on Friday is historically accurate, and the Last Supper, celebrated on Thursday evening, was not the regular Passover seder that all Jews ate but Jesus' own Passover meal, celebrated a day earlier. See Brown, *Death of the Messiah*, 2:1350–78; John P. Meier, *A Marginal Jew*, ABRL (New York: Doubleday; New Haven: Yale University, 1991), 1:386–402.

Pontius Pilate

BIBLICAL BACKGROUND

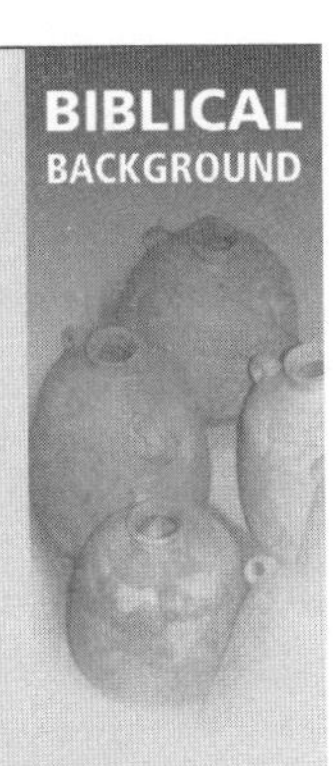

In AD 6, the Roman emperor Caesar Augustus placed Samaria and Judea under the direct rule of a Roman governor called a prefect. From 26–36, the Roman prefect was Pontius Pilate. Outside of the New Testament, we learn of several events in Pilate's career from the first-century Jewish writers Josephus and Philo of Alexandria.[a] For instance, Pilate ordered a public display in Jerusalem of Roman standards bearing the image of the Roman emperor, which triggered Jewish protest because such images violated the commandments (Exod 20:4). A Jewish delegation appealed to Pilate in Caesarea to remove the images, and after five days of appeal, he threatened to have them killed if they did not quit. But the Jewish delegation passively resisted and showed their willingness to die for their religious traditions. Upon seeing their display, Pilate himself backed down and had the standards removed. Pilate's career as prefect ended in AD 36 when he was deposed by his superior, the legate of Syria, after he violently suppressed an assembly of Samaritans with †messianic intentions. In many ways, John's portrayal of Pilate coheres with the portrait given in these other sources. Pilate asserts his Roman power and acts condescendingly toward his Jewish subjects, and he has no qualms about using violent force. But he also can be pressured into some courses of action, especially when his political and social standing is vulnerable.[b]

a. Josephus, *Jewish Antiquities* 18.3.1–3; 18.4.1–2; and *Jewish War* 2.9.2–4; Philo, *On the Embassy to Gaius* 299–305.

b. Philo, *On the Embassy to Gaius* 303–5.

authorities remain fixed both in their location outside the praetorium and in their rejection of Jesus.

The seemingly insignificant detail, **It was morning**, has both literal and spiritual implications. Literally, Jesus was brought to Pilate in the early morning hours. Spiritually, the light of the morning sun points to the brilliance of God's glory and love to be revealed this day in Jesus' cross. Through the cross, the light of the world will conquer the "night" (13:30) of spiritual darkness.

18:29–32

Pilate, the Roman prefect, comes **out** and asks **what charge** they **bring** against Jesus. In this Gospel, the Jewish authorities do not make a specific accusation (compare Luke 23:2), but they indirectly declare their own verdict that Jesus is **a criminal**. Without any charges, **Pilate** concludes that this matter is not his problem. The language of **yourselves** and **your law** suggests that Pilate sees this as an intra-Jewish dispute and that he seeks to remain uninvolved.

The Jewish authorities then hint that this case calls for the death penalty: **We do not have the right to execute anyone**. In Roman provincial rule, only the Roman prefect had the power over life and death, the power to administer capital punishment. Since the Jewish authorities cannot execute anyone, Jesus' death, which they seek, would have to come about by order of the Roman prefect. Jesus has declared three times that he would be "lifted up" (3:14; 8:28; 12:32) on a cross. The shifting of the executing decision to the Roman prefect was so **that the word of Jesus might be fulfilled** about **the kind of death he would die**. As a matter of prophetic fulfillment, Jesus' death on a Roman cross comes about as part of God's plan for the world's salvation.[4]

Reflection and Application (18:28–32)

In the creed we profess that Jesus suffered and was crucified "under Pontius Pilate." Pilate is the only human being specifically mentioned in the creed aside from Jesus and Mary. The creed includes this historical reference to Pilate to teach that Christianity deals with real, historical events. Put negatively, Christianity is not a collection of ahistorical myths, metaphors for our experiences, or generic philosophical truths to guide our thinking and living. Rather, Christians believe that God truly acts in a milieu of real people, in the course of real events—in creation, in the people Israel, in Christ, and in the Church—to bring about the salvation of the world. Since God became flesh in a historically particular human being, Jesus of Nazareth, it is through that same particular human being, crucified and resurrected to glory, that we are able to enter into the communion of eternal life with the Triune God.

Scene 2 [Inside]: Jesus' Kingship and Kingdom (18:33–38a)

[33]So Pilate went back into the praetorium and summoned Jesus and said to him, "Are you the King of the Jews?" [34]Jesus answered, "Do you say this on your own or have others told you about me?" [35]Pilate answered, "I am not a Jew, am I? Your own nation and the chief priests handed you over to me. What have you done?" [36]Jesus answered, "My kingdom does not belong to this world. If my kingdom did belong to this world, my attendants [would] be fighting to keep me from being handed over to the Jews. But as it is, my kingdom is not here." [37]So Pilate said to him, "Then

4. Catechism 600.

you are a king?" Jesus answered, "You say I am a king. For this I was born and for this I came into the world, to testify to the truth. Everyone who belongs to the truth listens to my voice." [38]Pilate said to him, "What is truth?"

OT: Isa 11:1–9; Dan 7:13–14

NT: Acts 17:1–9; 1 Cor 15:20–28; Rev 1:5–8

Catechism: the kingdom of God, 541–42, 2816–21; the Church instituted by Christ, 763

Lectionary: Good Friday; Solemnity of Christ the King (Year B)

18:33

Pilate went inside **the praetorium and summoned Jesus.** As in the †Synoptics, he first asks Jesus, **Are you the King of the Jews?** In John's passion narrative, "king" is the central title for Jesus. Previously, Jesus has been hailed as "king" by various Jewish persons (1:49; 6:15; 12:13) who saw him as the promised †messiah, the one whom God would raise up to overthrow the Gentile overlords and rule over a restored monarchy in Israel (see Isa 11:1–9; *Psalms of Solomon* 17:21–25). Jesus, however, has used other biblical images to present the true nature of his messianic kingship (John 12:12–15; see Zech 9:9–10). A Roman authority like Pilate would principally be concerned with the political aspect of Jewish messianism. For the Romans, the emperor held supreme power. Anyone claiming on his own to be king would be a rival to the emperor and thus an affront or threat to Roman imperial rule (see Acts 17:7).

18:34–35

Jesus' counterquestion implicitly raises the issue of what sort of king Pilate might have in mind. **Pilate** then distances himself from his Jewish subjects: **I am not a Jew, am I? Your own nation and the chief priests handed you over to me.** Since no charges were specified, Pilate asks Jesus **what** he has **done** that led the Jerusalem authorities to call for his death.

18:36

Pilate thinks of kingship in terms of earthly political realities. Jesus responds to Pilate's question with a three-part answer about his kingdom in which he reveals the true nature of his kingdom and invites Pilate to think about him in terms appropriate to his heavenly origin.

Jesus first declares, **My kingdom does not belong to this world**. The only other mention of "kingdom" in John is 3:3, 5. There Jesus taught that seeing and entering God's kingdom requires a new, spiritual life from heaven, which is received through a new birth of water and Spirit, through baptism. This new heavenly life is a share in the divine communion by becoming the Father's "children" through his Son Jesus (1:12; 12:36). The "kingdom" is fundamentally this communion between human beings and God. Since Jesus is in eternal communion with the Father as his Son and has become a human being, the reality of the kingdom is embodied in Jesus himself.[5]

When Jesus says, **My kingdom does not belong to this world**, he speaks of his kingdom's nature in terms of its origins. The Greek phrase translated in the NABRE as "belong to this world" literally means "from this world" (NRSV). Elsewhere Jesus declares that he does "not belong to this world" (8:23) and his disciples "do not belong to the world" (15:19; 17:14–16). This is because Jesus has his origin with the Father as the Son, and the disciples receive a new spiritual life from God as his children through Jesus. The **kingdom**, the communion of human beings with the Father through Jesus, comes about by God's initiative and action. Thus the kingdom originates from God, not the world.

Jesus' statement, **my kingdom is not here**, reiterates this point. The Greek adverb translated as "here" suggests a point of departure or origin, "from here" (see 2:16; 7:3; 14:31).[6] Jesus is not saying that his kingdom is absent from the world or has no bearing on worldly realities. Rather, John's Gospel teaches that heavenly realities, such as communion with God, are genuinely enjoyed by believers, who live presently in the world. The present, albeit imperfect, possession of these heavenly realities will lead into the complete possession of these same realities for all eternity on the last day (John 5:24, 28–29; 6:39–40; 11:25; see 1 Cor 15:20–28). The kingdom, which is present in Jesus and shared genuinely but imperfectly by the community of his disciples, can thus be *in* the world but not *of* the world (John 17:14–18).

Jesus illustrates with a contrasting example: **If my kingdom did belong to this world, my attendants [would] be fighting to keep me from being handed over to the †Jews** (compare Matt 26:53). But Jesus' kingdom does not act in this way, because his kingdom is God's work.[7] Recall that Peter fought violently to prevent Jesus' arrest, but Jesus stopped him so that he could freely do the Father's will in obedience and love (18:10–11). This is the manner in which his kingdom operates. Jesus thus shows that his kingdom is "of God" and not "of the world."

18:37 **Pilate** does not understand Jesus because he thinks about his kingdom in earthly terms, not heavenly terms. After hearing Jesus mention "kingdom," Pilate takes Jesus to be affirming political kingship: **Then you are a king?** Jesus responds by defining the nature of his kingship. As St. Augustine observes, with the response, **You say I am a king**, Jesus "neither denies himself [to be] a king

5. Catechism 541–42, 763, 2816.

6. This aspect of the adverb *enteuthen* is captured in the RSV ("from the world") and NRSV ("from here").

7. So St. Thomas Aquinas, *Commentary on John* 18.6, sections 2353–54.

Saint Augustine on God's Kingdom Being "in the World" but Not "of the World"

LIVING TRADITION

What is his kingdom except those believing in him, to whom he says, "You are not of the world, as I also am not of the world" [see John 15:19; 17:16]? He wanted them, though, to be in the world, and for this reason he said to the Father concerning them, "I pray not that you should take them out of the world, but that you should keep them from evil" [John 17:15]. Consequently, here too he does not say, "My kingdom is not" *in* this world, but "is not *of* this world." . . . For his kingdom *is here* right up to the end of the world, having cockles intermixed in it right up to the harvest; for the harvest is the end of the world when the harvesters, that is, the angels, will come and gather out of his kingdom all scandals [Matt 13:38–41]—and this certainly would not happen if his kingdom were not here. But nevertheless it *is not from here*, because it resides in the world as an exiled foreigner; for indeed he says to his kingdom, "You are not of the world, but I have chosen you out of the world" [John 15:19].[a]

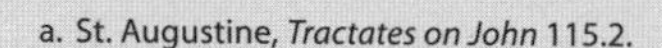

a. St. Augustine, *Tractates on John* 115.2.

(for he is a king whose kingdom is not of this world) nor does he say that he is such a king whose kingdom is thought to be of this world."[8]

Jesus explains his kingship in terms of his heavenly identity and mission as the †incarnate Word: he **came into the world, to testify to the truth**. Jesus' kingship consists in his being the obedient Son, who reveals the Father and accomplishes his saving work. He does both in a supreme way by giving his life in love on the cross, for there he reveals that "God is love" (1 John 4:8–10). On the cross, Jesus is "the faithful witness [Greek *martys*, martyr], . . . who loves us and has freed us from our sins by his blood, who has made us into a kingdom" (Rev 1:5–6).

The Father draws people to believe in Jesus (6:29, 37–38, 44) and forms believers into the community of the Church: **Everyone who belongs to the truth listens to my voice**. To "belong to the truth" implies that one does not "belong to this world" (18:36). Jesus speaks "the truth . . . from God" (8:40), and those who receive and yield to his revelation become children of the Father and so enter the communion of the kingdom: "Whoever belongs to God hears the words of God" (8:47). Consequently, the members of Jesus' kingdom must listen to his voice, as sheep listen to the shepherd (10:4), and live as Jesus did: faithfully witnessing to the truth and obeying the Father's will, activities both driven by love.

8. St. Augustine, *Tractates on John* 115.3.

18:38a Pilate concludes that Jesus is not a threat to Roman imperial rule. He cynically asks, **What is truth?** Of what consequence is this talk about truth when compared with the brute force of Roman imperial power? But Pilate's question is deeply †ironic. While Pilate may scoff, Jesus, who stands before him at that very moment, is himself "the truth" (14:6). The truth is quite literally staring Pilate in the face and speaking to him, and yet Pilate does not see or hear that truth. He refuses to recognize Jesus' heavenly origin; he does not receive Jesus' testimony.

Reflection and Application (18:33–38a)

The Church proclaims this Gospel passage in the liturgy of Christ the King, the last Sunday in Ordinary Time (see also the Reflection on 19:8–12). As the incarnate Son of God, who rose from the dead and sits at the Father's right hand, Jesus has "all power in heaven and on earth" (Matt 28:18). As the victorious †Son of Man, "His dominion is an everlasting dominion / that shall not pass away" (Dan 7:14).

Jesus exercises his kingly power by bearing witness to the truth in love. He does so by giving his life on the cross, and through the kingly power of truth and love in his cross, he has "conquered the world" (John 16:33). Jesus incorporates his disciples into his victory over the world and its wicked ways, and he continues to exercise his kingly rule in the world through his members. Christ's kingship is manifested in Christians, who live as he did: they bear faithful witness to the truth with great love. The only way that we can bear faithful, loving witness in the world is through his power working in us, and his power comes to us through our communion with him. If we allow God to impress his truth and love on our hearts through practices of holy living, prayer, and the sacraments, he will transform our lives so that we can be instruments of Christ the King in the world. As we do so the Spirit will prove the world wrong (see 16:8), and the victory of God's kingdom over the world's injustice, aggression, and thirst for dominating power will become manifest.

Scene 3 [Outside]: Barabbas or Jesus? (18:38b–40)

[38b]When he had said this, he again went out to the Jews and said to them, "I find no guilt in him. [39]But you have a custom that I release one prisoner to you at Passover. Do you want me to release to you the King of the

Jews?" [40]They cried out again, "Not this one but Barabbas!" Now Barabbas was a revolutionary.

NT: Mark 15:6–15; Luke 23:1–5
Lectionary: Good Friday

18:38b–39 Pilate now goes **out** and declares for the first time: **I find no guilt in him** (see Luke 23:4). He cites **a custom**, unattested outside the New Testament, of letting **one prisoner** go **at Passover** (see Mark 15:6–7).[9] Perhaps resenting the demands of the Jewish authorities, Pilate condescendingly mocks them by asking if he should free **the King of the Jews**, a title he knows they reject.

18:40 The Jewish authorities, however, call for **a revolutionary** named **Barabbas**. Barabbas appears as the exact opposite of Jesus. The Greek term for "revolutionary" (*lēstēs*) is the same term for the "robber," the rival of the good shepherd (10:1). Moreover, in Aramaic, the name "Barabbas" means "son of the father," another point of contrast with Jesus, the Son of God the Father. Jesus' kingship consists in revealing the truth and loving obedience to the Father. But Barabbas is a criminal, who uses violence to achieve his goals—the way of the world. Pilate has determined that Jesus is not a threat and would like to release him. But now he is confronted with the request to release Barabbas, who is unquestionably a threat. Thus Pilate's first attempt to release Jesus fails, and the Jewish authorities begin to pressure him. He must choose between Jesus, whom he has found innocent, and Barabbas, whom he knows is guilty. In making this decision about Jesus, Pilate will implicitly make his decision as to whether he will receive the truth that Jesus reveals.

Scene 4: The King Is Crowned (19:1–3)

[1]Then Pilate took Jesus and had him scourged. [2]And the soldiers wove a crown out of thorns and placed it on his head, and clothed him in a purple cloak, [3]and they came to him and said, "Hail, King of the Jews!" And they struck him repeatedly.

OT: Deut 25:1–3; Isa 50:4–11; 52:13–53:12
NT: Matt 27:27–31
Lectionary: Good Friday

9. Some have pointed to *Mishnah Pesahim* 8:6, with its instruction to have a Passover lamb slaughtered "for one whom they have promised to bring out of prison," as an oblique reference to a custom of Passover amnesty. See Raymond E. Brown, SS, *The Gospel according to John*, AB 29A (New York: Doubleday, 1970), 2:854–55.

19:1 In Matthew and Mark, Jesus' scourging follows Pilate's verdict and immediately precedes the crucifixion—in usual Roman practice (Matt 27:28–31; Mark 15:15–20). John places it here, before Jesus' condemnation, so as to make it the centerpiece of the trial narrative, because here Jesus is crowned and hailed as the king.

Pilate tries another strategy to release Jesus. He first orders him to be **scourged**. Whipping or scourging was a punishment for crimes among both Jews (e.g., Deut 25:1–3; 2 Cor 11:24) and Romans (Acts 22:24–25). The scourging of Jesus recalls the Servant of the Lord in Isaiah: "He was pierced for our sins, / crushed for our iniquity. / . . . / By his wounds we were healed" (Isa 53:5). Since it could take a long time for a person to die by crucifixion, sometimes several days, the fact that Jesus died within a few hours of being crucified suggests that his scourging was particularly severe.

19:2–3 The Roman **soldiers** ridicule and humiliate Jesus. All of the mockery concerns the title "king." They put **a crown of thorns** on **his head** and dress **him in a purple cloak**—purple was the color of royalty since genuine purple dye was very expensive. They also mock him with the greeting, **Hail, King of the Jews!**, a form of address resembling that given to the Roman emperor, "Hail, Caesar!"

The Romans **struck him repeatedly**, as the Jewish guard in Annas's house "struck" Jesus (18:22). In both cases, †Jews or Gentiles strike Jesus soon after he speaks about his revelatory teaching (18:20–21, 37), thus indicating their rejection of it.[10] Just as both Jews and Gentiles, representing the world, were led by Judas to arrest Jesus (18:3), so now we see both Jews and Gentiles rejecting Jesus' revelation. These events also recall what was prophesied about the Servant of the Lord in Isaiah: "I have given my back to scourges and my cheeks to blows" (Isa 50:6 †LXX).[11]

The mockery of Jesus as the king is very †ironic. The Romans' mockery of Jesus is in fact true. Jesus is the king, and he is hailed as such by worldly powers! This scene highlights the irony in Jesus' passion. Although his suffering and death appear to be his defeat, they are actually his royal victory over the sinful world.

Scene 5 [Outside]: Pilate Presents the King (19:4–7)

[4]Once more Pilate went out and said to them, "Look, I am bringing him out to you, so that you may know that I find no guilt in him." [5]So Jesus

10. De la Potterie, *Hour*, 51–52.

11. Our translation of the LXX. The Greek word behind "blows" is *rhapisma*, the same word translated as "strike" in John 18:22; 19:3.

came out, wearing the crown of thorns and the purple cloak. And he said to them, "Behold, the man!" [6]When the chief priests and the guards saw him they cried out, "Crucify him, crucify him!" Pilate said to them, "Take him yourselves and crucify him. I find no guilt in him." [7]The Jews answered, "We have a law, and according to that law he ought to die, because he made himself the Son of God."

OT: Lev 24:10–16; 1 Kings 1:38–40
NT: Luke 23:6–16
Catechism: divisions among the Jewish authorities, 595–96; responsibility for Jesus' death, 597–98
Lectionary: Good Friday

19:4–5 As in 18:38–40, **Pilate** again tries to release Jesus. Having concluded that Jesus is not a threat to Rome (**I find no guilt in him**), Pilate now presents the beaten and bloodied Jesus, **wearing** the mocking royal apparel, to the Jewish authorities, thereby to persuade them that Jesus is not to be taken seriously: **Behold, the man!** To paraphrase Pilate's sentiment: "How can such a pathetic man be taken seriously as a king? I certainly don't take him seriously. Why should you?" But Pilate's actions are ironic. By bringing Jesus out in royal dress, Pilate presents Jesus to the public as the king. This scene recalls the first public appearance of newly crowned kings, who were publicly presented to their subjects for royal acclamation (e.g., 1 Kings 1:38–40; 2 Kings 11:12).[12]

19:6 But instead of hailing Jesus as king, **the chief priests and the guards** shout, **Crucify him, crucify him!** The situation now becomes more difficult for Pilate. Earlier the Jewish authorities hinted at the death penalty (18:31) and refused Pilate's offer to release Jesus (18:39–40). Now they explicitly call on him to execute Jesus. The opposition to Jesus is not budging and will not bargain with Pilate.

After affirming Jesus' innocence for a third time, Pilate throws the burden of decision making back to the Jewish authorities: **Take him yourselves and crucify him. I find no guilt in him**. Pilate could be toying with the Jewish authorities here: he openly disagrees with them and asks them to do something that they want to do but cannot. Yet beneath his Roman bravado, Pilate is struggling. In his desperation to avoid making a decision of lasting consequence about Jesus, he suggests a course of action that even he knows is impossible (18:31). But, as John has demonstrated throughout the Gospel, everyone must either receive or reject the divine Word; it is impossible not to respond to him.

19:7 The Jewish authorities voice their reason for taking action against Jesus: **We have a law, and according to that law he ought to die, because he made**

12. Brown, *John*, 2:889–90.

himself the Son of God. The language "made himself the Son of God" recalls other instances in the Gospel where Jesus' opponents have sought his death because he was "making himself equal to God" (5:18; 8:53, 58–59). To his opponents, Jesus is only a man, one who claims divine identity and prerogatives (10:33). These claims are tantamount to blasphemy and, according to Lev 24:16, blasphemy warrants the death penalty.

Scene 6 [Inside]: "No Power over Me" (19:8–12)

[8]Now when Pilate heard this statement, he became even more afraid, [9]and went back into the praetorium and said to Jesus, "Where are you from?" Jesus did not answer him. [10]So Pilate said to him, "Do you not speak to me? Do you not know that I have power to release you and I have power to crucify you?" [11]Jesus answered [him], "You would have no power over me if it had not been given you from above. For this reason the one who handed me over to you has the greater sin." [12]Consequently, Pilate tried to release him; but the Jews cried out, "If you release him, you are not a Friend of Caesar. Everyone who makes himself a king opposes Caesar."

OT: Isa 52:13–53:12

NT: Acts 14:8–18

Catechism: authority, 1897–1904; the natural law, 1954–60; duties of civil authorities, 2235–37; the political community and the Church, 2244–46

Lectionary: Good Friday

19:8 Pilate has not considered Jesus to be a serious threat thus far. But when he hears talk about Jesus being "Son of God" (19:7), he **became even more afraid**. A Roman pagan like Pilate could hear this and think that Jesus might be a demigod like Hercules or Perseus. A similar situation appears in Acts 14, when the people of Lystra, after seeing Paul heal a paralyzed man, hail him as "Hermes" and Barnabas as "Zeus" and declare, "The gods have come down to us in human form" (Acts 14:11–12).

19:9 Pilate takes **Jesus** back inside **the praetorium** and asks, **Where are you from?** Pilate's question recalls the recurring theme of Jesus' identity in terms of his origins (see John 7–9). But the question simultaneously reveals Pilate's own unbelief and misunderstanding. If Pilate had accepted Jesus' invitation to think in heavenly terms, he would know that Jesus' origin is with the Father. Similarly, if Pilate had received Jesus' word as "the truth," (18:37), he would not have to ask "What is truth?" (18:38). Since Jesus already told Pilate that he "came into the world, to testify to the truth" (18:37), and since Pilate chose not to receive that truth, **Jesus did not answer him** here (see Mark 15:5). Jesus' silence recalls the Servant of the Lord in Isa 53:7: "Like a lamb led to slaughter / . . . / he did not open his mouth."

19:10 **Pilate** becomes angry that Jesus does not answer him, a man who wields the power of the Roman Empire. So he tries to intimidate Jesus by asserting his **power** over Jesus' life and death. †Ironically, Pilate's blustering underscores his responsibility. Only Pilate has the power to execute Jesus, and he must make a decision about him.

19:11 But **Jesus** is not the least bit intimidated by Pilate. Jesus reveals the truth about the power dynamics in this trial: **You would have no power over me if it had not been given you from above**. Since Jesus possesses divine authority, he is in complete, sovereign control of his passion (10:17–18; 13:3). Pilate claims to exercise supreme power over life and death, but Jesus unmasks Pilate's power as limited and delegated. Only Jesus has the supreme power of God, and Pilate has power over Jesus only because the Father has permitted it.

For this reason, Jesus says, **the one who handed me over to you has the greater sin**. Whereas Pilate will condemn Jesus out of fear and self-interest, Judas and the authorities, who delivered Jesus to Pilate, have known Jesus, his teaching and his works, and still have willfully rejected him (15:24–25).

19:12 After **Pilate tried to release him** a third time, the voice of the Jewish authorities sounds out: **If you release him, you are not a Friend of Caesar. Everyone who makes himself a king opposes Caesar**. The matter now becomes personal for Pilate, because the Jewish authorities subtly threaten his own political and social standing. The title "Friend of Caesar" was an honorific designation given to persons enjoying the special favor of the Roman emperor.[13] If Pilate frees Jesus the "king," he knowingly releases a claimant to kingship in opposition to Roman sovereignty. Pilate could lose own his power and social status if it is reported that he failed to enforce Roman supremacy. But if Pilate executes Jesus, he will preserve his own power at the expense of killing the innocent.

Reflection and Application (19:8–12)

The Christian profession "Jesus Christ is Lord" implies that no earthly reality, political body, or head of state is almighty.[14] Since human beings are naturally social and thus form communities, human communities require structures

13. See BDAG 395–96; Epictetus, *Discourses* 3.4.2; 4.1.8; 4.1.45–48.

14. Similarly N. T. Wright, *The Resurrection of the Son of God* (Minneapolis: Augsburg Fortress, 2003), 568.

Pope St. John Paul II on Truth, Goodness, and Political Life

Jesus tells Pilate that his worldly power as a Roman prefect is not absolute but is subject to a higher authority. In his encyclical *Centesimus Annus*, Pope John Paul II similarly warns about political and social structures that do not recognize their own subordination to the transcendent standards of truth and goodness, which are knowable by human reason (see Catechism 1902, 1954–56, 1960):

> Totalitarianism arises out of a denial of truth in the objective sense. If there is no transcendent truth, in obedience to which man achieves his full identity, then there is no sure principle for guaranteeing just relations between people. . . . The culture and praxis of totalitarianism also involve a rejection of the Church. The State or the party which claims to be able to lead history towards perfect goodness, and which sets itself above all values, cannot tolerate the affirmation of an *objective criterion of good and evil* beyond the will of those in power, since such a criterion . . . could be used to judge their actions. This explains why totalitarianism attempts to destroy the Church, or at least to reduce her to submission.
>
> Nowadays there is a tendency to claim that agnosticism and skeptical relativism are the philosophy and the basic attitude that correspond to democratic forms of political life. Those who are convinced that they know the truth and firmly adhere to it are considered unreliable from a democratic point of view, since they do not accept that truth is determined by the majority, or that it is subject to variation according to different political trends. Yet if there is no ultimate truth to guide and direct political activity, then ideas and convictions can easily be manipulated for reasons of power. As history demonstrates, a democracy without values easily turns into open or thinly disguised totalitarianism.[a]

a. John Paul II, *Centesimus Annus* (On the Hundredth Anniversary of *Rerum Novarum* [On Capital and Labor]) 44–46. What he described as the potential of democratic societies to degenerate into a kind of totalitarianism when objective truth and goodness are disregarded, Pope Benedict XVI has called the "dictatorship of relativism." See Pope Benedict XVI, *The Light of the World: The Pope, the Church, and the Signs of the Times*, trans. Michael J. Miller and Adrian J. Walker (San Francisco: Ignatius Press, 2010), 50–59.

of governance, which can rightfully exercise power in the world (Catechism 1879, 1897–98). But human political communities are subject to transcendent standards of truth and goodness, which are knowable by human reason and provide the basis for public reasoning about just laws, practices, and policies (Catechism 1898–99, 2235). These same naturally knowable truths are brought to light more clearly by divine revelation; and the Church, as the custodian of revelation, often speaks prophetically about political and social matters that impact the good of human beings and society (Catechism 2245–46).

The Church celebrates the supreme lordship of Jesus Christ over all creation on the Feast of Christ the King. Pope Pius XI instituted this feast in 1925, after World War I and the rise of atheistic communism in Russia showed the human degradation facilitated by the disregard for God, objective truth, and love in public life.[15] As Pope St. John Paul II observed nearly eighty years later, the history of the twentieth century showed that human beings "attempted to build the city of man without reference to [God]. It ended by actually building that city *against* man! Christians know that it is not possible to reject or ignore God without *demeaning man*."[16] The Feast of Christ the King aims to reorient our hearts to the absolute sovereignty of Jesus Christ so that truth and goodness may reign in the world and provide the foundation for a just society and lasting peace.

Scene 7 [Outside]: The Verdict (19:13–16a)

[13]When Pilate heard these words he brought Jesus out and seated him on the judge's bench in the place called Stone Pavement, in Hebrew, Gabbatha. [14]It was preparation day for Passover, and it was about noon. And he said to the Jews, "Behold, your king!" [15]They cried out, "Take him away, take him away! Crucify him!" Pilate said to them, "Shall I crucify your king?" The chief priests answered, "We have no king but Caesar." [16a]Then he handed him over to them to be crucified.

OT: Exod 12:1–20; Isa 43:1–8; Jer 23:7–8

NT: Mark 15:6–15; Luke 23:18–25

Catechism: divisions among the Jewish authorities concerning Jesus, 595–96; Christ's death is the unique and definitive sacrifice, 613–14

Lectionary: Good Friday

19:13 Running out of options and with his own power in jeopardy, **Pilate** again **brought Jesus out**. This is the climax of the trial narrative, and it showcases John's theology of judgment, which centers on people's reception or rejection of the divine Word. Jesus is presented before "the world," and the response of "the world" becomes the basis of its own judgment.

15. Pope Pius XI, *Quas Primas* (On the Feast of Christ the King) 24.

16. Pope John Paul II, "Evening Vigil with Young People: Address by the Holy Father John Paul II," on the seventeenth World Youth Day, Toronto, July 27, 2002.

In an †ironic detail, Pilate **seated** Jesus **on the judge's bench**, a public location where judicial decisions were rendered (see Acts 18:12–17). While Jesus is on trial in one sense, the opposite is really the case. As in John 9, the other participants, not Jesus, are actually being judged in this trial; the verdict is based on their responses to Jesus.[17]

19:14a These events took place **about noon** on Friday, the **preparation day for Passover** (Passover would begin at sundown on that Friday). This is the very day and time when the priests in the temple would begin sacrificing the lambs for Passover (see Exod 12:6). At the beginning of the Gospel, the Baptist announced that God's promised act of salvation, the new exodus (1:23; Isa 40:1–3; 43:1–3, 16; Jer 23:7–8), was about to happen, and he testified that Jesus is "the Lamb of God, who takes away the sin of the world" (1:29). Now, Jesus, the Passover lamb of the new exodus, approaches his death.[18] He is "like a lamb led to slaughter" (Isa 53:7), at the very moment when the Passover lambs are being sacrificed in the temple.

19:14b–15 With his weaknesses exposed (19:11–12), Pilate puts on a strong face by again ridiculing his Jewish subjects. With Jesus in public view, Pilate proclaims, **Behold, your king!** Once again, the Jewish authorities respond with hostile rejection: **Take him away, take him away! Crucify him!** (see Luke 23:21).

After Pilate asks, **Shall I crucify your king?** (see Mark 15:12), the **chief priests** respond, **We have no king but Caesar**. In 11:45–53, we saw that the relationship between the Jewish authorities in Jerusalem and the Romans was a factor in their decision to seek Jesus' death. Members of the †Sanhedrin feared that a †messianic movement would form around Jesus, leading to a violent Roman suppression and the destruction of the temple. Now, at the conclusion of the trial narrative, the Jewish authorities reject the divine, messianic kingship of Jesus to curry favor with the Romans by aligning themselves with the Roman emperor as king.

19:16a Caught between accepting or rejecting Jesus, Pilate ultimately rejects him and gives him **over to them to be crucified**. While the Jewish authorities reject Jesus for theological and political reasons, Pilate rejects him out of fear and self-interest. Pilate fears that he will lose his power, and this self-interest leads him do something that he knows is wrong: crucify an innocent man. For all of his arrogant blustering, Pilate is a coward.

17. The Greek verb for "seated" (*ekathisen*) can also be translated "he sat down," suggesting that Pilate, not Jesus, sat on the judge's bench. The NIV, RSV, and NRSV prefer the latter translation, and the NJB has the former translation. For discussion of both possibilities, see Brown, *John*, 2:880–81; Ignace de la Potterie, SJ, "Jesus King and Judge according to John 19:13," *Scripture* 13 (1961): 97–111.

18. Catechism 613.

No Greater Love

John 19:16b–42

The mystery of the cross stands at the heart of Christian faith. The Fourth Gospel uses many scriptural references to reveal its spiritual depths: the cross is the royal victory and enthronement of Jesus, the promised †messiah-king (19:19); Jesus is the new Passover lamb, sacrificed in the new exodus (1:29; 19:36); like the bronze serpent, the crucified Jesus is a source of merciful healing for sinners who look on him in faith (3:14–15); Jesus embodies the suffering of those spoken of in the Psalms (John 19:24) and of the Servant of the Lord in Isaiah; Jesus is the new dwelling of God among humanity, the new temple, from whose opened side flow the life-giving waters of mercy and spiritual life (19:34, 37).

At the center of all of this, John invites us to look upon the crucified Jesus and see the revelation that "God is love" (1 John 4:8–10). The cross reveals that God holds nothing back in order to bring about the salvation of sinners, whom he loves to infinite depths. The Father gives his Son, and the Son, out of love and obedience, willingly lays down his life so that sinners "might have life and have it more abundantly" (10:10). By making a perfect gift of his life on the cross, Jesus reveals the infinite depths of God's self-giving love for us. Through the cross, Jesus reveals the meaning of his own words: "No one has greater love than this, to lay down one's life for one's friends" (15:13).

The Crucifixion (19:16b–22)

[16b]So they took Jesus, [17]and carrying the cross himself he went out to what is called the Place of the Skull, in Hebrew, Golgotha. [18]There they crucified

him, and with him two others, one on either side, with Jesus in the middle. [19]Pilate also had an inscription written and put on the cross. It read, "Jesus the Nazorean, the King of the Jews." [20]Now many of the Jews read this inscription, because the place where Jesus was crucified was near the city; and it was written in Hebrew, Latin, and Greek. [21]So the chief priests of the Jews said to Pilate, "Do not write 'The King of the Jews,' but that he said, 'I am the King of the Jews.'" [22]Pilate answered, "What I have written, I have written."

OT: Lev 24:10–23
NT: Matt 25:31–33; Mark 15:21–27
Catechism: Jesus' kingship, 440
Lectionary: Good Friday

19:16b–17 The †Synoptics report that Simon of Cyrene helped Jesus carry his cross (Mark 15:21). In John, Jesus carries **the cross** by **himself**, perhaps to emphasize that his passion is a completely free act, a perfect gift of himself, and no one interferes. Jesus **went out** of Jerusalem, for the Romans conducted crucifixions in very public places, such as along roadsides, and according to the †Torah, executions were to take place outside the city (see Lev 24:14, 23). The location of Jesus' crucifixion, **the Place of the Skull** or **Golgotha**, had long served as a rock quarry, and perhaps it received its nickname as "Skull Place" from the terrain, along with its being a place of execution.[1] Today the Church of the Holy Sepulchre stands over this location.

19:18 As in the Synoptics, the Roman soldiers **crucified** Jesus with **two others**, and John specifies that he was **in the middle**. For John, the crucifixion is Jesus' royal enthronement. The king occupies the central position, with attendants at his sides (Matt 25:31–33; Rev 4:1–6). †Ironically, while the cross appears to be defeat for Jesus, the vision of faith recognizes the cross as his kingly victory over the "sin of the world" (1:29).[2]

19:19–20 John sees the universal proclamation of Jesus' kingship in the action of **Pilate**, who ordered **an inscription written and put on the cross**. This was the *titulus*, a placard that specified the crime for which the condemned was being executed. All four Gospels link Jesus' execution by Rome to the claim of his kingship: **Jesus the Nazorean, the King of the Jews** (see Matt 27:37; Mark 15:26; Luke 23:38).

1. Golgotha reflects the Aramaic *gulgulta'*, which means "skull." For background, see Urban C. von Wahlde, "Archaeology and John's Gospel," in *Jesus and Archaeology*, ed. James H. Charlesworth (Grand Rapids: Eerdmans, 2006), 576–80.

2. Catechism 440.

Fig. 12. Cast of the remains of a crucified man's foot

John emphasizes the public character of Pilate's proclamation: **Many of the Jews read** it because Jesus' cross was **near the city** and the inscription **was written in Hebrew, Latin, and Greek**, the languages of Jews and Gentiles, representing all people.[3] While Pilate writes the inscription in condemnation of Jesus, he ironically proclaims Jesus' kingship to the whole world.

19:20–22

The **chief priests** protest because they do not want people to be misled by the claim of kingship on the inscription (7:12, 47). They want **Pilate** to change the wording to **He said, "I am the King of the Jews"** in order to reflect their judgment that Jesus was "making himself" God and king (5:18; 19:7). The authorities' protest shows their ongoing opposition to Jesus, even while he hangs on the cross. After previously bowing to their pressure, Pilate reasserts his authority by refusing their request: **What I have written, I have written**. Pilate forces his subjects to live with his proclamation, precisely what the Jewish authorities had disavowed in the trial (19:15).

Jesus' Garments (19:23–24)

[23]When the soldiers had crucified Jesus, they took his clothes and divided them into four shares, a share for each soldier. They also took his tunic, but the tunic was seamless, woven in one piece from the top down. [24]So they said to one another, "Let's not tear it, but cast lots for it to see whose it will be," in order that the passage of scripture might be fulfilled [that says]:

> **"They divided my garments among them,**
> **and for my vesture they cast lots."**

This is what the soldiers did.

OT: Ps 22
NT: Matt 25:31–46; Mark 15:22–34
Catechism: Christ and the poor, 544, 786; love for the poor, 2443–49
Lectionary: Good Friday

3. The letters "INRI," often appearing on crucifixes, abbreviate Pilate's inscription, written in Latin from the Vulgate: *Iesus Nazarenus, Rex Iudaeorum* (Jesus the Nazorean, the King of the Jews).

Crucifixion

BIBLICAL BACKGROUND

The famous Roman orator and statesman Cicero referred to crucifixion as "that most cruel and disgusting penalty."[a] Crucifixion was a brutally sadistic form of execution practiced by the Romans, among others, in antiquity. It was reserved for noncitizens and slaves who were guilty of capital crimes against Roman rule.

Crucifixion was the complete degradation of a human being. The condemned was first flogged and tortured, and then he would carry the crossbeam out to a public location. He would be stripped and affixed alive to an already-standing post with ropes and nails. Since no major organs were damaged, crucifixion could bring a slow, extremely painful death, often taking several days. The first-century Roman philosopher Seneca wrote the following about the awful death by crucifixion:

> Can anyone be found who would prefer wasting away in pain, dying limb by limb, or letting out his life drop by drop, rather than expiring once for all? Can any man be found willing to be fastened to the accursed tree, long sickly, already deformed, swelling with ugly tumours on chest and shoulders, and draw the breath of life amid long-drawn-out agony?[b]

An important dimension to crucifixion was its public character. The Romans crucified criminals in public places to heap shame upon them and send a message to deter others from challenging their power. Ancient writers also speak of the Romans crucifying both Jews and Christians as a form of public entertainment.[c] Crucifixion was an extremely violent, public expression of the power of Roman rule.[d]

a. Cicero, *Against Verres* 2.5.165, in *The Verrine Orations I*, trans. L. H. G. Greenwood, LCL 221 (Cambridge, MA: Harvard University Press, 1928), 651.
b. Seneca, *Epistle* 101, in *Epistles 93–124*, trans. Richard M. Gummere, LCL 77 (Cambridge, MA: Harvard University Press, 1925), 167.
c. Josephus, *Jewish War* 5.11.449–51; Philo, *Against Flaccus* 72.84–85; Tacitus, *Annals* 15.44.
d. This sidebar is indebted to Gerald G. O'Collins, "Crucifixion," *ABD* 1:1207–10.

19:23 Four Roman **soldiers** start to divide Jesus' garments among themselves. There are two kinds of garments and two kinds of actions taken by the Romans. First, there are Jesus' **clothes**, which the soldiers **divided into four shares**. Second, there is his **tunic**, a long undershirt, which **was seamless** and **one piece**.

19:24 Since tearing the one-piece tunic would ruin it, the soldiers **cast lots for it**. John sees the division of Jesus' clothes and the casting of lots for his tunic foreshadowed in Ps 22:17: **They divided my garments among them, / and for my vesture they cast lots**. Psalm 22 figures prominently in the Gospel accounts of Jesus' crucifixion (Mark 15:24, 29, 34). While the †Synoptics' references to

Ps 22 underscore Jesus' suffering, John emphasizes the soldiers' actions as the fulfillment of God's plan in **scripture**. Jesus' life has unfolded in accordance with the divine plan, and even now, as he hangs dying and seemingly powerless on the cross, the Scriptures continue to bear witness to him (5:39).

Some Church Fathers saw in Jesus' untorn tunic a symbol of the Church's unity.[4] John uses the Greek terms for tear (verb, *schizō*; noun, *schisma*) to designate the divisions among the crowds and authorities over Jesus (7:43; 9:16; 10:19). However, Jesus calls his disciples to be one in him and so share in his relationship with the Father (10:16; 17:11, 21–23). Since unity marks Jesus' disciples, they, unlike the other groups in the Gospel, are not to be divided or torn (21:11). If John subtly invites us to see in Jesus' intact tunic a symbol for the disciples' unity, the symbolism sets up the next scene, which focuses more directly on the Church.[5]

Reflection and Application (19:23–24)

Even though John places less attention on Jesus' suffering than Matthew and Mark do, we should not overlook the brutal reality of this scene. As mentioned in the sidebar (p. 318), crucifixion was the sadistic degradation of a human being. Jesus has been stripped and nailed to a cross to die. Now his executioners take from him what little he had left: his clothes.

The crucifixion shows that Jesus has chosen to identify himself with the poor and those who are victimized by evil. As the Catechism states, "Jesus shares the life of the poor, from the cradle to the cross; he experiences hunger, thirst, and privation (cf. Matt 21:18; Mark 2:23–26; John 4:6–7; 19:28; Luke 9:58)" (544). Christ himself is present among the poor and needy, and therefore, love and practical care for them are not an optional or tangential part of Christian life. As suggested in Matt 25:31–40, "It is by what they have done for the poor that Jesus Christ will recognize his chosen ones" (Catechism 2443).

The Family of God (19:25–27)

[25]Standing by the cross of Jesus were his mother and his mother's sister, Mary the wife of Clopas, and Mary of Magdala. [26]When Jesus saw his mother and the disciple there whom he loved, he said to his mother,

4. Cyprian, *Unity of the Church* 7; John Chrysostom, *Homilies on John* 85.2; Augustine, *Sermon* 218.9.

5. So Ignace de la Potterie, SJ, *The Hour of Jesus: The Passion and Resurrection of Jesus according to John*, trans. Dom G. Murray, OSB (Staten Island, NY: Alba House, 1989), 103–4.

"Woman, behold, your son." [27]**Then he said to the disciple, "Behold, your mother." And from that hour the disciple took her into his home.**

OT: Isa 60:1–4; 66:7–13

NT: Luke 2:34–35; Rom 8:14–17; 1 John 3:1–3; Rev 12

Catechism: Mary ever virgin, 501; the Church, body of Christ, 787–96; Mary united with her Son, 964; Mary's prayer, 2618

Lectionary: Good Friday; Our Lady of Sorrows; Common of the Blessed Virgin

19:25 As in the †Synoptics, a group of Jesus' women disciples, including **Mary of Magdala**, witness his crucifixion (Mark 15:40). Only John mentions the **mother** of Jesus at the cross. Whereas the Synoptics report the women as watching only at a distance (Matt 27:55), John mentions them as **standing by the cross**. Jesus spoke of his death as having a gathering and unifying effect: "When I am lifted up from the earth, I will draw everyone to myself" (12:32; see 11:51–52). This assembly of disciples at the foot of the cross displays Jesus' disciples as beginning to gather into one around him.

19:26–27 Like the wedding at Cana, the account of Jesus' mother and the Beloved Disciple at the foot of the cross narrates an event that reveals a spiritual mystery. In a basic sense, Jesus entrusts his mother to the care of the Beloved Disciple in an act of love for her.[6] In antiquity, women without a male protector, especially those of lower classes, had little or no social standing and few societal protections. They depended on a male, usually a husband or son, for survival.[7] When Jesus dies, Mary will be left without a husband or son to care for her, and so Jesus gives her into the Beloved Disciple's care for her own survival. But this act has dimensions deeper than Jesus' practical care for his mother.

In John, Mary appears only here and at the wedding at Cana (2:1–12), and in both cases, Jesus addresses her as **Woman** (2:4). As mentioned previously, the title "the mother of Jesus" allows Mary to serve a larger, symbolic role in the Gospel narrative than if she had simply been named. At Cana, she appeared as the model of the Church, the singular embodiment of the faithful people of God. At the cross, she appears as the mother of the Church. In this scene, John subtly draws on the biblical imagery of both "Mother Zion" (Isa 60:1–4; 66:7–9) and Eve, to whom the titles "woman" and "mother" are given (Gen 2:23; 3:20).[8]

6. So Augustine, *Tractates on John* 119.2; Cyril of Alexandria, *Commentary on John* 12. See Ignace de la Potterie, SJ, *Mary in the Mystery of the Covenant*, trans. Bertrand Buby, SM (Staten Island, NY: Alba House, 1992), 211–13.

7. Hence widows were considered among the most vulnerable in society (Isa 1:17; James 1:27).

8. The interpretation of Mary as a new Eve appears in many of the Church Fathers, although largely in connection with her obedience at the Annunciation. See Justin Martyr, *Dialogue with Trypho* 100; Irenaeus, *Against the Heresies* 3.22.4; Tertullian, *On the Flesh of Christ* 17; Augustine, *On Holy Virginity* 6; and *On Christian Struggle* 24.

Jesus' words from the cross are framed in the same "see and say" revelatory pattern, which appeared in John 1: one person "sees" another and "says" or declares that person's role in God's plan.[9] Here, Jesus sees and speaks to his **mother** and the Beloved **disciple**. Through this formula, Jesus articulates the spiritual relationships that constitute the Church as the disciples' communion with God and one another through Jesus. Jesus first says to his mother, **Behold, your son**. Who is the "son" to whom Jesus refers? In one sense, "son" refers properly to Jesus himself, for as her biological son he is addressing Mary. But the context also suggests that "son" applies to the Beloved Disciple because of what Jesus says to him: **Behold, your mother**. By naming his own mother as the mother of the Beloved Disciple, Jesus reveals a spiritual relationship between himself and the Beloved Disciple: both of them are Mary's sons.[10]

We have seen that John often uses family language to articulate the communion with the Father that Jesus makes possible. As the "only Son" (1:18), Jesus brings his disciples to share in his own eternal relationship with the Father, to share in his Sonship, making them God's children (1:12; see Rom 8:14–15; 1 John 3:1).[11] In these words from the cross, Jesus reveals the spiritual relationship among himself, his mother, and the Beloved Disciple in the Church as the family of God. If the Beloved Disciple shares spiritually in Jesus' own life as the Son, then, by implication, he also has Mary for his spiritual mother. The mother of Jesus becomes a new Eve, the spiritual mother of Jesus' disciples, those who share in his life. The first Eve became "the mother of all the living" (Gen 3:20), and the second Eve becomes the mother of all believers, those being re-created by the Holy Spirit of the new creation (see 7:37–39).[12] Similarly, Rev 12:17 refers to Christians as the "offspring" of the woman clothed with the sun, the mother of the †Messiah.

The disciples' communion with God also affects their relationship with one another. The evangelist concludes, **From that hour the disciple took her into his home**. This also has a deeper spiritual meaning than the disciple simply taking Mary into his care. The verb **took** is translated elsewhere in the Gospel as "receive," often to express the receiving of heavenly realities.[13] The Beloved Disciple receives the mother of Jesus **into his home** as his own. This action †signifies that the spiritual reality of the Church, the relationship of communion

9. See the comments on 1:29.

10. So too Origen, *Commentary on John* 1.6.

11. Catechism 501, 787, 790.

12. Catechism 2618.

13. So de la Potterie, *Hour*, 117–20; see John 1:11–12; 3:27, 32–33; 5:43; 13:20; 20:22.

with the Father through the Son, has been received by the disciple and has transformed his own relationships.

Reflection and Application (19:25–27)

One of the most difficult experiences in human life is to witness the suffering of a loved one. While we might not be afflicted in the exact same way, we nevertheless share the suffering of our loved ones in a very real way. Since we love, we suffer with those who suffer.

The Church prescribes this reading for the Feast of Our Lady of Sorrows, a feast that speaks to this experience. At Jesus' presentation in the temple, Simeon prophesied to Mary, "You yourself a sword will pierce, . . . that the thoughts of many hearts may be revealed" (Luke 2:35). The sword of sorrow pierces Mary's heart as she stands at the foot of the cross and watches her only Son die. She is powerless to change anything, and all she can do is simply be present to her Son. As we share the suffering of our loved ones, so too does Mary share in the suffering of her dying Son.[14] When we find ourselves sharing our loved ones' pain, we can turn to the intercession of Mary, Our Lady of Sorrows, who has been in the same place we are. We are encouraged to ask Our Lady of Sorrows to intercede for us in such times, so that through her prayers and maternal tenderness, we might find help and consolation.

Loving to the End (19:28–30)

[28]After this, aware that everything was now finished, in order that the scripture might be fulfilled, Jesus said, "I thirst." [29]There was a vessel filled with common wine. So they put a sponge soaked in wine on a sprig of hyssop and put it up to his mouth. [30]When Jesus had taken the wine, he said, "It is finished." And bowing his head, he handed over the spirit.

OT: Exod 12:21–23; Ps 69
NT: Matt 27:45–56
Catechism: Christ offers his life to the Father, 606–7, 2605
Lectionary: Good Friday; Triumph of the Holy Cross

19:28 When Jesus went to meet those who came to arrest him, he knew "everything that was going to happen to him" (18:4). After revealing the spiritual

14. Catechism 964.

relationships that constitute the Church (19:25–27), Jesus was **aware that everything was now finished**. The "everything" is the Father's work of salvation. There is wordplay here in Greek. The Greek verb for **finished** (*teleō*) is related to the verb for **fulfilled** (*teleioō*). John often uses the verb *teleioō* to talk about Jesus' "accomplishing" the Father's work (4:34; 5:36; 17:4). These verbs are related to the noun *telos*, which means "end" or "goal." By laying down his life, Jesus loves his disciples to the "end" (*telos*) (13:1), thus accomplishing the Father's work of salvation. In this way, Jesus reveals the utmost depths of God's love for the world (3:16).

Fig. 13. Hyssop

John then connects Jesus' **thirst** with the fulfillment of **scripture**. The topic of thirst appeared in Jesus' dialogue with the Samaritan woman (4:7–42). He first asked the woman for water to drink, but as the dialogue unfolded, he revealed that she was the one thirsting for the "living water," the Holy Spirit, which only Jesus can give (4:10, 13–14). Jesus' thirst is not ultimately for physical water for himself. Rather, he thirsts to finish the Father's will, to drink his "cup" (18:11), and pour out the living water, the Holy Spirit, in fulfillment of God's promises in Scripture (see sidebar on p. 47).

19:29 The Roman soldiers, who do not grasp the spiritual meaning of Jesus' words, found **a vessel filled with common wine**. The word for **common wine** (*oxos*) recalls Ps 69:22 †LXX, "For my thirst they gave me vinegar [*oxos*]." Having already quoted Ps 69 in relation to Jesus' passion (2:17; 15:25), John invites us to see Jesus' suffering anticipated in the psalmist's suffering. As in Luke 23:36, the Romans apparently give Jesus the sour, vinegary wine to mock him. They offer the dying Jesus something undrinkable to drink when he cries out in thirst.

John's statement that the Romans lifted up a "sponge soaked in wine on a sprig of hyssop" has a spiritual meaning. Hyssop is a small, branchy plant, which could not bear the weight of a soaked sponge. But hyssop plays an important role in Israelite liturgical rites in Scripture. During the exodus, the Israelites were instructed to use hyssop to smear the blood of the Passover lamb on their door frames to save them from the death of the firstborn (Exod 12:22). Hyssop also features in the priestly rites to purge people and their homes from the impurity of leprosy (Lev 14:4–7, 49–53) and contact with corpses (Num 19:6, 9, 11–12, 18–20) so that they could draw near God's presence in the tabernacle or temple. Hyssop dovetails with John's presentation of Jesus, "the Lamb of God, who takes away the sin of the world" (1:29), whose blood saves us from spiritual death and purifies us to dwell in the "Father's house" (14:2).

19:30 Of the four Gospels, only John states that **Jesus** drank **the wine** offered him on the cross. Jesus told Peter that he (Jesus) must "drink the cup that the Father gave" him (18:11), he must fulfill the Father's will. In the last act of his mortal life, Jesus drinks and declares, **It is finished**. Jesus offers his life in a perfect act of love and obedience to the Father and so accomplishes the work of salvation. Jesus has loved "to the end" of his life and to the utmost (13:1).[15]

The phrase **handed over the spirit** has a double meaning. For one, it means that Jesus died. But the phrase also reminds us of the connection between the †hour of Jesus and the coming of the Holy Spirit (16:7), which the risen Jesus will send to his disciples (20:22).

Reflection and Application (19:28–30)

The Gospel and Letters of John teach that Jesus' death reveals that "God is love" (1 John 4:8), showing us how unimaginably great is God's love for us. At the Last Supper, Jesus taught that true, godly love is self-sacrifice for others' good (15:12–13), and he enacts this love by dying on the cross. The cross of Jesus reveals God's love because it shows how far God goes for our salvation. God gives absolutely everything; he holds nothing back for the good of his beloved, the salvation of the human race. The Father "so loved the world that he gave his only Son" for the world's salvation (3:16). The Son became †incarnate in Jesus, and out of love and obedience, he lays down his life on the cross (10:17–18). The Father gives his all, his beloved Son; by freely giving his all on the cross, Jesus, the incarnate Son of God, reveals that "God is love" (1 John 4:8).

15. Catechism 607.

Jesus calls us to put into practice the same kind of self-sacrificial love. As 1 John 4:11 states, "Beloved, if God so loved us, we also must love one another." Being Jesus' disciples means practicing the same kind of radical, self-giving love in our families, communities, and in all our relationships. As Jesus said, "This is how all will know that you are my disciples, if you have love for one another" (13:35).

Blood and Water (19:31–37)

[31]Now since it was preparation day, in order that the bodies might not remain on the cross on the sabbath, for the sabbath day of that week was a solemn one, the Jews asked Pilate that their legs be broken and they be taken down. [32]So the soldiers came and broke the legs of the first and then of the other one who was crucified with Jesus. [33]But when they came to Jesus and saw that he was already dead, they did not break his legs, [34]but one soldier thrust his lance into his side, and immediately blood and water flowed out. [35]An eyewitness has testified, and his testimony is true; he knows that he is speaking the truth, so that you also may [come to] believe. [36]For this happened so that the scripture passage might be fulfilled:

> **"Not a bone of it will be broken."**

[37]And again another passage says:

> **"They will look upon him whom they have pierced."**

OT: Exod 12:43; Deut 21:22–23; Ps 34:12–23; Ezek 47; Zech 12:10–13:6

NT: 1 John 5:6–12

Catechism: the heart of Jesus, 478; water as symbol of the Holy Spirit, 694; blood and water as signs of baptism and the Eucharist, 1225

Lectionary: Good Friday; Sacred Heart (Year B); Baptism of Children; Triumph of the Holy Cross; Precious Blood

19:31–32 Jesus died on Friday afternoon, the **preparation day** for Passover, which started (along with **the sabbath**) at sundown. The Jewish authorities do not want the bodies of the crucified men left on the cross overnight because of Deut 21:22–23, which requires that they be buried before sundown. They **asked Pilate** to have the legs of the crucified men broken. This would hasten their deaths by making it impossible for them to support their body weight in order to breathe. Pilate obliges, and the Romans **broke the legs of** the two men **crucified with Jesus.**

19:33–34, 36–37 Since Jesus **was already dead,** the Romans **did not break his legs** but stabbed **his side** with a spear. John discerns profound mysteries in these two events, each of which fulfills **scripture**. First, John sees a relationship between the Romans'

not breaking the **dead** Jesus' **legs** and the regulations regarding the Passover lamb: **Not a bone of it will be broken**. This citation closely resembles the †LXX text of Exod 12:10, 46 and Num 9:12, prescribing that none of the Passover lamb's bones should be broken. This is a further indication that Jesus is the Passover lamb of the new exodus, whose blood saves us from the spiritual slavery of sin and death. John also affirms that although Jesus died by capital punishment, he was in fact righteous. He does this by alluding to Ps 34:21, which says of the just man, God "watches over all his bones; / not one of them shall be broken."

Even more significant is the **blood and water** that **flowed out** from Jesus' pierced **side**. This flow of blood and water shows that Jesus was truly dead.[16] The salvation of the world has been worked out in the death of a real human being. As 1 John 5:6 teaches, "This is the one who came through water and blood, Jesus Christ, not by water alone, but by water and blood"; here water alludes to baptism, and blood indicates his death. Jesus really did lay down his life out of love and obedience to the Father, and he gave us a concrete, genuine proof that "God is love" (1 John 4:8).[17]

John connects the piercing of Jesus' side with Zech 12:10: **They will look upon him whom they have pierced**. This verse appears within a set of oracles concerning God's action to purify and save his people on the Day of the Lord (12:1–13:6).[18] John cites the second part of the verse, but we need to consider the first part as well: "I will pour out on the house of David and on the inhabitants of Jerusalem a spirit of mercy and supplication" (12:10). There is a connection between the death and mourning over the pierced one and the outpouring of God's Spirit of mercy on his people. This passage from Zechariah dovetails with other biblical texts in which God promises to pour out his Spirit in the last days (see sidebar on p. 47).

Shortly after the oracle in Zech 12:10 is the declaration: "On that day a fountain will be opened for the house of David and the inhabitants of Jerusalem, to purify from sin and uncleanness" (13:1). The prophet speaks of God opening up a fountain, probably within the temple, and water flowing from it to bring purification and forgiveness of sins.[19] This text recalls other scriptural passages that speak of the waters of salvation flowing out of God's dwelling in the end times. For instance, the prophet Joel announces that on the day of salvation, "a

16. Gail R. O'Day, "The Gospel of John," in *The New Interpreter's Bible*, vol. 9 (Nashville: Abingdon, 1995), 834.

17. The insistence on the reality of Jesus' death is important because the genuineness of Jesus' humanity and thus the reality of his death became a point of controversy in the early Church, as evidenced in the Johannine Epistles (1 John 4:2–3) and in various forms of gnosticism.

18. David L. Petersen, *Zechariah 9–14 and Malachi* (Louisville: Westminster John Knox, 1995), 109–10, 120–21.

19. Ibid., 123–24.

spring will rise from the house of the LORD" (4:18). Ezekiel receives an elaborate vision of God's †eschatological temple, out of which flows a paradisal stream of life-giving waters of the new creation (Ezek 47). John's quotation of Zech 12 thus evokes a tapestry of biblical texts in which God promises to pour out his Spirit and the waters of forgiveness and regeneration on the day of salvation.

In John's Gospel, the other references to blood and water allude to the sacraments of baptism and the Eucharist. Aside from 1:13, the only other place in the Gospel where blood is mentioned is the Bread of Life Discourse (6:51–58), in which Jesus commands his followers to eat and drink his eucharistic flesh and blood. Those who eat and drink receive communion with Jesus (6:56), eternal life (6:54), and a share in the end-time resurrection (6:54). John uses water as a symbol for the disciples' new spiritual life from heaven, received through the new birth of water and the Holy Spirit, that is, baptism (3:5; 4:10–14; 7:38). Blood and water have sacramental dimensions in John's Gospel, for through them Jesus gives the gift of eternal life.

When the biblical context is brought to bear on the flow of blood and water, a profound spiritual reality comes to light. The blood and water †signify that Jesus' death is the source of spiritual life for all who are "in darkness" (8:12) and dead in sin (8:24). Just as Zech 12:10 spoke of God pouring out his Spirit in connection with the death of the pierced one, so Jesus, whose body was pierced with a lance, "handed over the spirit" (19:30; see 20:22). Just as Ezekiel, Joel, and Zechariah prophesied the life-giving waters of mercy and regeneration flowing from God's temple on the day of salvation, water flows out from Jesus' side, from "the temple of his body" on the cross (2:21). These waters of mercy, regeneration, and new life in the Spirit—these waters flow in the sacrament of baptism, through which people are "born of water and Spirit" (3:5) and receive a new, spiritual life from heaven. The blood of Jesus, shed on the cross and resurrected to glory, is offered sacramentally to believers in the Eucharist. By drinking his blood, believers grow in communion with Jesus and share in his eternal, resurrected life (6:54). These gifts of mercy, re-creation, and eternal life in the Spirit have been made available to us through the sacraments and through Jesus' death on the cross.[20]

19:35 The reality of these events and the spiritual understanding of the mystery within them are based on the **testimony** of an **eyewitness**. Testimony and bearing witness are important theological themes in the Gospel. Jesus himself bears witness "to the truth" (18:37), and many others in the Gospel bear witness to Jesus: the Baptist, Jesus' works, the Scriptures, and the Father himself (5:32–39). Now a new witness is introduced, and his testimony is the basis for the Gospel

20. Catechism 1225.

Saint John Chrysostom on the Blood and Water

Regarding the blood and water that flowed from Jesus' side on the cross:

> It was not accidentally or by chance that these streams came forth, but because the Church has been established from both of these. Her members know this, since they have come to birth by water and are nourished by Flesh and Blood. The Mysteries [the sacraments] have their source from there, so that when you approach the awesome chalice you may come as if you were about to drink from His very side.[a]

a. St. John Chrysostom, *Homilies on John* 85.3, in *Commentary on Saint John the Apostle and Evangelist: Homilies 48–88*, trans. Sister Thomas Aquinas Goggin, SCH, FC 41 (New York: Fathers of the Church, 1959), 435.

account. The purpose of his testimony to **the truth** is clear: **so that you also may [come to] believe.**[21] Like the other witnesses in the Gospel, this eyewitness of the crucifixion gives testimony for the avowed purpose of fostering faith in Jesus. While only a hint here, the context suggests that the Beloved Disciple is this eyewitness (19:26–27), and as we shall later see, the Gospel's author (21:24).

The King's Burial (19:38–42)

[38]After this, Joseph of Arimathea, secretly a disciple of Jesus for fear of the Jews, asked Pilate if he could remove the body of Jesus. And Pilate permitted it. So he came and took his body. [39]Nicodemus, the one who had first come to him at night, also came bringing a mixture of myrrh and aloes weighing about one hundred pounds. [40]They took the body of Jesus and bound it with burial cloths along with the spices, according to the Jewish burial custom. [41]Now in the place where he had been crucified there was a garden, and in the garden a new tomb, in which no one had yet been buried. [42]So they laid Jesus there because of the Jewish preparation day; for the tomb was close by.

OT: Tob 1:3, 16–20; Ps 45; Ezek 36:33–36
NT: Luke 23:50–56
Catechism: Jesus' burial, 624–27
Lectionary: Good Friday

21. See the comments on 20:31 for discussion of the bracketed text.

Saint Faustina Kowalska and the Divine Mercy

In April 2000, Pope St. John Paul II established the second Sunday of Easter as "Divine Mercy Sunday."[a] This feast celebrates the infinite mercy of God given to us through the death of Jesus, which brings about the forgiveness of sins and makes possible reconciliation with God and among people. Devotion to the Divine Mercy is informed by the private revelations and mysticism of the twentieth-century Polish nun St. Faustina Kowalska (1905–38).[b] Images of the Divine Mercy feature red and white rays emanating from Jesus' heart, and these are associated with the blood and water flowing from his pierced side. The rays are interpreted in St. Faustina's *Diary*: "During prayer I heard these words within me: The two rays denote Blood and Water. The pale ray stands for the Water which makes souls righteous. The red ray stands for the Blood which is the life of souls."[c]

Saint Faustina offered herself to Jesus so that sinners, especially those who think that their sins are too great or too many to be forgiven, would return to God with trust in his mercy, which is infinitely greater than the worst of all our sins:

> I want to make amends to You for the souls that do not trust in Your goodness. I hope against all hope in the ocean of Your mercy. My Lord and my God, my portion—my portion forever, I do not base this act of oblation on my own strength, but on the strength that flows from the merits of Jesus Christ. I will daily repeat this act of self-oblation by pronouncing the following prayer which You Yourself have taught me, Jesus:
>
> "O Blood and Water which gushed forth from the Heart of Jesus as a Fount of mercy for us, I trust in You!"[d]

a. Pope John Paul II, "Homily of the Holy Father: Mass in St. Peter's Square for the Canonization of Sr. Mary Faustina Kowalska," April 30, 2000.
b. On private revelations, see Catechism 67.
c. Sister M. Faustina Kowalska, *Divine Mercy in My Soul: The Diary of the Servant of God Sister M. Faustina Kowalska* (Stockbridge, MA: Marian Press, 1987), section 299.
d. Ibid., section 309.

19:38–39 Jesus' burial is coordinated by two Jewish religious authorities, who were seemingly secret disciples: **Joseph of Arimathea** and **Nicodemus**. Up till now, they had not made their discipleship public because they were afraid of the other religious authorities who strongly opposed Jesus (see 12:43–44).

Being an authority in Jerusalem, Joseph has access to **Pilate** and obtains custody of Jesus' corpse (see Luke 23:50–53). Nicodemus, a member of the †Sanhedrin (7:50–51) **who had** previously **come to** Jesus **at night** (3:1–2), now brings **a mixture of myrrh and aloes** to his burial. The theme of Jesus' kingship, so prominent in John's passion narrative, subtly appears in the details of his burial. The myrrh and aloes evoke the description of the Davidic king's robes as scented with "myrrh [and] aloes" in Ps 45:9. Moreover, reminiscent of Mary of Bethany (12:1–8), Nicodemus brings a huge amount of ointment, befitting a royal burial.

19:40 By burying his **body**, Joseph and Nicodemus perform a culturally significant act of respect and faithfulness to **Jesus**. Burying the dead was an important service of love in Jewish piety (Tob 1:16–20; 4:3–4); conversely, lying unburied was a great source of shame for the deceased (Tob 6:15).[22] Through this public act of piety, Joseph and Nicodemus make known their relationship with Jesus.

John's description of **the Jewish burial custom** reminds us of the raising of Lazarus. Just as Lazarus was "tied hand and foot with burial bands" (11:44), Jesus' corpse was **bound . . . with burial cloths**. The mention of **the spices** reminds us of Martha's worry about the "stench" of the dead body (11:39). These connections indicate that like Lazarus, Jesus was truly dead.[23]

19:41–42 As the passion narrative started in "a garden" (18:1), so also does it end in **a garden**, where there was a **tomb**. Archaeological excavations suggest that at the time of Jesus' death, the area near Golgotha contained significant vegetation and tombs "hewn out of the rock" (see Mark 15:46).[24] Since **the tomb was close by** and daytime was running out on the **preparation day**, Joseph and Nicodemus put the body of **Jesus there**.

John's description of Jesus' tomb points us to a new beginning. The tomb was **new**, unoccupied, and **in which no one had yet been buried** (see Luke 23:53). The location of this tomb in a garden (Greek *kēpos*) is significant. Many biblical prophets spoke of the future age of salvation as a new creation, which they described in the language and imagery of Eden. Ezekiel articulates the voice of the redeemed after God's act of salvation: "This once-desolate land has become like the garden [†LXX *kēpos*] of Eden" (Ezek 36:35; see Isa 58:11). As the passion narrative concludes, Jesus is buried near the place where he died. The new tomb in the garden points us forward to the dawning of the new creation: the resurrection of Jesus.

22. See Craig S. Keener, *The Gospel of John: A Commentary* (Peabody, MA: Hendrickson, 2003), 2:1158–59.

23. Catechism 624, 627.

24. Von Wahlde, "Archaeology and John's Gospel," 578–82.

Encountering the Risen Lord

John 20:1–31

The resurrection of Jesus is the foundation of Christian faith. John 20 depicts the movement of different individuals toward faith in the reality of Jesus' resurrection in four carefully constructed scenes. John uses different verbs of seeing to describe peoples' movement to faith in the risen Jesus.[1] Various individuals may see the empty tomb, the graveclothes, and even the angels in the tomb, and yet not fully believe in his resurrection. Only a personal encounter with the risen Jesus can bring about Easter faith. When people arrive at this belief, they declare, "I have seen the Lord" (see 20:18, 25, 29), and this statement, understood most of the time as an experience born of faith, is still the foundation of Christian witness. The personal encounter with the risen Lord that leads to faith can come through a resurrection appearance (as it did for Mary Magdalene and the first disciples) or through the testimony of those disciples, handed on in the Gospel and through the Church (20:29–31). John 20 also depicts the risen and glorified Jesus sending the Holy Spirit upon his disciples to empower them for their mission to the world.

The Empty Tomb (20:1–10)

[1]On the first day of the week, Mary of Magdala came to the tomb early in the morning, while it was still dark, and saw the stone removed from the tomb.

1. Following Ignace de la Potterie, SJ, *The Hour of Jesus: The Passion and Resurrection of Jesus according to John*, trans. Dom G. Murray, OSB (Staten Island, NY: Alba House, 1989), 166–69.

[2]So she ran and went to Simon Peter and to the other disciple whom Jesus loved, and told them, "They have taken the Lord from the tomb, and we don't know where they put him." [3]So Peter and the other disciple went out and came to the tomb. [4]They both ran, but the other disciple ran faster than Peter and arrived at the tomb first; [5]he bent down and saw the burial cloths there, but did not go in. [6]When Simon Peter arrived after him, he went into the tomb and saw the burial cloths there, [7]and the cloth that had covered his head, not with the burial cloths but rolled up in a separate place. [8]Then the other disciple also went in, the one who had arrived at the tomb first, and he saw and believed. [9]For they did not yet understand the scripture that he had to rise from the dead. [10]Then the disciples returned home.

OT: Jon 2:3–10
NT: Matt 28:11–15; Luke 24:1–12; Rom 6:3–11; 1 Cor 15:1–11
Catechism: the empty tomb, 640; Jesus' resurrection as a transcendent event, 647
Lectionary: Easter Sunday; Mary Magdalene; John, Apostle and Evangelist

20:1–2 **Early** on Sunday **morning, Mary of Magdala**, whom we first met at the crucifixion (19:25) and whom the †Synoptics count among Jesus' women disciples from Galilee (Luke 8:1–3), **came to** Jesus' **tomb**. The notice **while it was still dark** gives insight into her spiritual disposition after Jesus' death. Mary saw Jesus die on the cross, and the predawn darkness symbolizes her own sadness and loss of hope: Jesus, the light of the world, has died.

Mary finds something completely unexpected: **the tomb** is open because **the stone** has been **removed from** it. Caught off guard by the opened tomb, Mary **ran** back **to Simon Peter** and the Beloved **disciple** and reported, **They have taken the Lord from the tomb, and we don't know where they put him**. Mary thinks that someone broke into Jesus' tomb and stole his corpse. The Gospel of Matthew reports that a rumor of grave robbery circulated in antiquity to explain why Jesus' tomb was empty (see Matt 28:11–15).

20:3–6 Informed by Mary Magdalene, **Peter** and the Beloved **disciple** run to the tomb to investigate (see Luke 24:9–12). The Beloved Disciple **ran faster than Peter and arrived at the tomb first**. When Peter last appeared, he denied his relationship with Jesus, and the Beloved Disciple's last appearance was at the foot of the cross, receiving the mother of Jesus as his own spiritual mother. The Beloved Disciple is the first to arrive at the empty tomb: love speeds him on his way to Jesus, and he arrives even before Peter, the "rock" and chief of the Twelve (1:42).[2]

2. So too Raymond E. Brown, SS, *The Gospel according to John*, AB 29A (New York: Doubleday, 1970), 2:1004–7.

Fig. 14. Rock tomb with a rolling stone

Having arrived first, the Beloved Disciple looked into the tomb **and saw the burial cloths**. He does not enter, but instead he waits for **Peter** to arrive. Even though his love may be more intense, the Beloved Disciple waits for Peter to enter **the tomb** first, perhaps because of Peter's status among the disciples.

20:7 John's description of the graveclothes suggests several important things about what happened to Jesus.[3] The first, the presence of **the burial cloths** in the tomb refutes the speculation that Jesus' body had been stolen, because grave robbers would not have unwrapped the corpse before stealing it. Second, the graveclothes point toward something unprecedented happening to Jesus through a contrast with the raising of Lazarus. When Jesus called Lazarus out of the tomb, Lazarus "came out, tied hand and foot with burial bands, and his face was wrapped in a cloth" (11:44), and Jesus then gave the order to unwrap him. But Jesus, who is not in the tomb, is not bound by the graveclothes or face **cloth** nor in need of anyone to untie him. Something radically different has happened to Jesus. Whereas Lazarus was resuscitated to mortal life and would die again, Jesus' resurrection is not resuscitation but God's raising and transforming him to an immortal, glorified mode of existence. As St. Paul writes, "Christ, raised

3. Gail R. O'Day, "The Gospel of John," in *The New Interpreter's Bible*, vol. 9 (Nashville: Abingdon, 1995), 841.

from the dead, dies no more; death no longer has power over him" (Rom 6:9). Third, the fact that the head covering was **rolled up in a separate place** suggests conscious, deliberate action. As Moloney points out, many verbs pertaining to what happened in the tomb, such as the stone being "removed" (20:1) and the face cloth being "rolled up" (20:7), are in the passive voice, which points to God as the agent.[4] Jesus' tomb is empty because God has directly acted here.

20:8 Having first seen the graveclothes from the tomb's entrance, the Beloved Disciple **went** in after Peter, and he **saw and believed.** The nature of the Beloved Disciple's faith is open to different interpretations. Some scholars think that his is a full-fledged faith in the resurrection, which he arrives at without seeing the risen Jesus. However, there are good reasons to think that the Beloved Disciple has only an initial faith at this point, perhaps simply believing that God has in some way acted here.[5] The form of the Greek verb "believed"[6] can mean "began to believe."[7] Moreover, as we shall see, John seems to articulate the disciples' full Easter faith with verbs in the perfect tense (20:18, 25, 29). Finally, John follows up this description of the Beloved Disciple's faith with a statement about the disciples' ignorance regarding the resurrection (20:9).

20:9–10 The New Testament speaks of Jesus' resurrection, like his death, as part of God's plan (Mark 8:31; Luke 24:26), foretold in the Scriptures (Luke 24:27; Acts 17:2–3; 1 Cor 15:4). But how or where precisely this is foretold is not obvious. While scriptural texts speak of the resurrection of the righteous,[8] of God delivering his faithful ones from death,[9] and of the vindication of the Suffering Servant,[10] none offer straightforward, literal predictions of the resurrection of a crucified †messiah. Accordingly, these disciples **did not yet understand the scripture that he had to rise from the dead**. Similarly, when Mary Magdalene came to the open tomb "in the dark," her first thought was grave robbery, not resurrection. Only when the Holy Spirit comes and leads them to a deeper, "spiritual understanding" of the Scriptures will the disciples be able to understand how Jesus' death and resurrection has been part of God's plan from the beginning. But as they were in a state of ignorance and unenlightened by the Spirit, **the disciples returned home**.

4. Francis J. Moloney, SDB, *The Gospel of John* (Collegeville, MN: Liturgical Press, 1998), 518–20, referring to Donatien Mollat, "La découverte du tombeau vide," in *Études johanniques* (Paris: Éditions du Seuil, 1979), 137–38.

5. Catechism 640.

6. John 20:8, Greek *episteusen*.

7. As also in John 2:11, 22; 4:41; 7:31; 8:30.

8. Dan 12:2–3; 2 Macc 7.

9. Compare John 2:3–10 and Matt 12:40; Ps 16:7–11 and Acts 2:22–28.

10. Isa 52:13; 53:10–12.

Reflection and Application (20:1–10)

The Beloved Disciple arrives first at Jesus' tomb and also at some degree of faith in the resurrection, due to his love for Jesus. The Disciple's love for Jesus results from Jesus' love for him. God's love awakens and enflames disciples' love, which leads them into a greater knowledge of Jesus. Theologian Hans Urs von Balthasar wrote the following about how God's love can bring us to know him:

> After a mother has smiled at her child for many days and weeks, she finally receives her child's smile in response. She has awakened love in the heart of her child, and as the child awakens to love, it also awakens to knowledge. . . . God interprets himself to man as love in the same way: he radiates love, which kindles the light of love in the heart of man, and it is precisely this light that allows man to perceive this, the absolute Love.[11]

Mary Magdalene's Movement to Easter Faith (20:11–18)

[11]But Mary stayed outside the tomb weeping. And as she wept, she bent over into the tomb [12]and saw two angels in white sitting there, one at the head and one at the feet where the body of Jesus had been. [13]And they said to her, "Woman, why are you weeping?" She said to them, "They have taken my Lord, and I don't know where they laid him." [14]When she had said this, she turned around and saw Jesus there, but did not know it was Jesus. [15]Jesus said to her, "Woman, why are you weeping? Whom are you looking for?" She thought it was the gardener and said to him, "Sir, if you carried him away, tell me where you laid him, and I will take him." [16]Jesus said to her, "Mary!" She turned and said to him in Hebrew, "Rabbouni," which means Teacher. [17]Jesus said to her, "Stop holding on to me, for I have not yet ascended to the Father. But go to my brothers and tell them, 'I am going to my Father and your Father, to my God and your God.'" [18]Mary of Magdala went and announced to the disciples, "I have seen the Lord," and what he told her.

OT: Song 3:1–5; 5:6–8
NT: Matt 28:1–10; Luke 24:13–35; Rom 8:14–17
Catechism: Jesus' resurrection appearances, 641–44; Jesus' ascension, 659–64
Lectionary: Mary Magdalene

11. Hans Urs von Balthasar, *Love Alone Is Credible*, trans. D. C. Schindler (San Francisco: Ignatius Press, 2004), 76.

20:11 After Peter and the Beloved Disciple returned home, **Mary stayed outside the tomb weeping**. She grieves deeply over one whom she greatly loved and whose body is missing. The repeated mention of Mary's weeping recalls Jesus' words about his †hour: "You will weep and mourn, while the world rejoices; you will grieve, but your grief will become joy" (16:20). Now she grieves, but John's audience knows that her weeping will soon become joy.

20:12–13 While Peter and the Beloved Disciple saw only graveclothes in the tomb, when Mary looked in, she **saw two angels in white sitting there, one at the head and one at the feet where the body of Jesus had been**. The †Synoptics all mention angels at the empty tomb, who announce Jesus' resurrection to the women (Matt 28:2–7; Mark 16:5–7; Luke 24:4–7). In John, they ask, **Woman, why are you weeping?** When people in Scripture see angels, they are often overcome by fear at their glorious appearance (Dan 10:4–9; Matt 28:2–4) and sometimes attempt to worship them (Rev 19:9–10). Astonishingly, Mary shows no fear at the angelic appearance, but restates her claim about the disappearance of Jesus' corpse (see 20:2). As de la Potterie points out, while Mary had said "*the* Lord" and "*we* don't know" in 20:2, she now says ***my* Lord** and ***I* don't know where they laid him**.[12] The shift to the singular pronouns indicates that Mary now speaks of her own relationship with Jesus and what these events mean to her personally. Like the beloved in the Song of Songs, who searches for her love, she asks the angelic watchmen, "Him whom my soul loves—have you seen him?" (Song 3:3).

20:14 The distraught Mary then **turned around and saw Jesus there, but did not know it was Jesus**. As on the road to Emmaus, the risen Jesus can withhold recognition of his identity; he reveals himself to those whom he chooses and when he chooses (Luke 24:15–16, 30–32). John's language recalls the relationship between perception and faith that we saw in 20:2–10. Just as Peter saw the empty tomb and the graveclothes but did not arrive at faith in the resurrection, so too here Mary *sees* but does not *know*. She does not yet have the gift of faith in the risen Jesus.

Like the angels, the risen **Jesus** first asks, **Woman, why are you weeping?** Then he adds, **Whom are you looking for?** Two aspects of these questions require attention. First, Jesus has used the address "Woman" on several occasions in the Gospel, and in each case, Jesus was redefining relationships with those addressed (see 2:4; 4:21; 19:26). Jesus' second question recalls the initial words he spoke to his first disciples, "What are you looking for?" (1:38). These hints suggest that a new beginning is taking place. The risen

12. De la Potterie, *Hour*, 171–72, emphasis added.

Jesus is redefining his relationship with his disciples in the time after the resurrection.

20:15 Mary mistook Jesus for **the gardener** (Jesus' tomb was located in a garden; 19:41), and her question expresses her ongoing belief that Jesus' corpse has been stolen: **Sir, if you carried him away, tell me where you laid him, and I will take him**. Having come to the tomb "in the dark," Mary remains fixated on a past reality. She is convinced that Jesus remains dead because she has not wavered in her belief that his corpse has been stolen—even when she saw angels in the empty tomb!

20:16 The risen **Jesus** opens her eyes to the reality of his resurrection when he speaks her name, **Mary!** Jesus pronounces Mary's name just as the good shepherd "calls his own sheep by name and leads them out" (10:3). As the sheep respond to the shepherd, Mary, a faithful disciple, recognizes his voice (see 10:4), and addresses **him** as **Rabbouni**, "my **Teacher** and master." Mary now believes that Jesus is no longer dead but truly alive. Her sadness has become joy (16:20). However, Mary thinks her relationship with Jesus is the just same as it was before he died, for she addresses him with the title "Rabbi" or "Teacher" (1:38, 49; 3:2).

20:17a But the resurrection of Jesus has changed absolutely everything, including the relationship between him and his followers. The disciples, such as Mary, can relate to him no longer as an earthly teacher but as the risen Lord. Jesus' order, **Stop holding on to me**, is meant in a figurative sense: Mary can no longer hold on to her past notions of discipleship.

His explanation, **for I have not yet ascended to the Father**, speaks of this new state of affairs. The exaltation of the risen Jesus at the Father's right hand, and the sending of the Holy Spirit, completes the Father's saving work. It marks the entrance of Jesus' glorified humanity into God's own life and thus gives humanity access to communion with the Father, the purpose for which Jesus came.[13] Jesus precedes his disciples to glorified life with the Father, opens the way to the Father, and enables them to follow (13:36).

20:17b The risen Jesus now gives Mary a mission, and his instructions have great theological depth: **Go to my brothers and tell them, "I am going to my Father and your Father, to my God and your God."** Jesus' death and resurrection has radically changed the relationship between human beings and God. By completing the Father's saving work, Jesus gives his disciples a share in his own relationship with the Father—his sonship—by making them God's children (1:12–13). For the first time, Jesus speaks of the disciples as "brothers" because,

13. Catechism 661, 663

Saint John Chrysostom on Jesus' Words to Mary Magdalene

LIVING TRADITION

It seems to me that she wished to enjoy His presence still, in the same way as before, and because of her joy at seeing Him, had no realization of His greatness, even though He had become much more excellent in bodily appearance. Thus, to lead her to abandon this notion and to refrain from addressing Him too familiarly, . . . He elevated her thoughts so that she would treat Him with a more reverential attitude.

Accordingly, if He had said: "Do not touch me as you did before, because things are not the same now, and I will not associate with you in [the] future in the same way as before," it would seem somewhat harsh and boastful. But when he said: "I have not yet ascended to my Father," even though the words were without offense, they meant the same thing.[a]

a. St. John Chrysostom, *Homilies on John* 86.2, in *Commentary on Saint John the Apostle and Evangelist: Homilies 48–88*, trans. Sister Thomas Aquinas Goggin, SCH, FC 41 (New York: Fathers of the Church, 1959), 449–50.

on account of Jesus' saving act of love, they now share the same Father (see Rom 8:14–17). The risen Jesus has opened the way to eternal communion with God.

20:18 Mary fulfills her role as "apostle to the apostles" by declaring, **"I have seen the Lord," and what he told her**. John expresses Mary's proclamation of faith in the perfect tense to indicate her complete transformation to mature faith in the risen Jesus. Mary has progressed from being "in the dark," fixated on the reality of Jesus' death, to belief that Jesus has been raised. And the risen Jesus has brought her to a higher level of relationship, for his disciples can relate to him no longer only as teacher but also as **the Lord** himself, who is simultaneously their "brother."

Reflection and Application (20:11–18)

Mary Magdalene gives a saintly example of the intense love that must animate every disciple's search for the Lord. She seeks Jesus with the intensity of the beloved in the Song of Songs: "I sought him / whom my heart loves— / I sought him but I did not find him" (3:1). When the risen Jesus reveals himself to Mary, she "held him and would not let him go" (Song 3:4). But Mary had to let go of the past and allow the risen Jesus to transform her life. Having encountered the risen Lord, she was given a mission to bear witness to the reality of his resurrection: "I have seen the Lord."

Saint Bede on the Gift of Divine Sonship

Every Church of Christ . . . as well as any holy soul, is a sister of the Lord and Savior, not only on account of the assumption of the very same nature by which he himself became a human being, but also on account of the free gift of grace by which he gave those who believe in him the power to become children of God, so that he who was the only Son of God by nature might become "the firstborn among many brothers and sisters" (Rom 8:29) by grace. Hence the sweetness of that word of his spoken to Mary: "Go to my brethren and say to them, I am ascending to my Father and your Father, to my God and your God" (John 20:17).[a]

a. Bede the Venerable, *Expositio in Cantica Canticorum*, in *The Song of Songs: Interpreted by Early Christian and Medieval Commentators*, trans. and ed. Richard A. Norris Jr. (Grand Rapids: Eerdmans, 2003), 289.

Mary's transformation and mission is the same for every follower of Christ. We are called to seek Jesus intensely and with great love, allowing him to possess our hearts and change our lives. Like Mary, Jesus' other disciples are also given a mission. Mary's mission is the mission of the Church and all Christians in the world: to bear witness to the reality of the risen Jesus and the transforming power of his love available to all who seek it. The only way in which Christians can carry out this mission is if our lives are first grounded in a personal encounter with the risen Lord and with the grace of his Holy Spirit. A thriving relationship of faith, hope, and love in the living and ever-present Lord is the house built on rock (Matt 7:24), which enables us to say with Mary, "I have seen the Lord."

The Disciples' Movement to Easter Faith (20:19–25)

[19]On the evening of that first day of the week, when the doors were locked, where the disciples were, for fear of the Jews, Jesus came and stood in their midst and said to them, "Peace be with you." [20]When he had said this, he showed them his hands and his side. The disciples rejoiced when they saw the Lord. [21][Jesus] said to them again, "Peace be with you. As the Father has sent me, so I send you." [22]And when he had said this, he breathed on them and said to them, "Receive the holy Spirit. [23]Whose sins you forgive are forgiven them, and whose sins you retain are retained."

[24]Thomas, called Didymus, one of the Twelve, was not with them when Jesus came. [25]So the other disciples said to him, "We have seen the Lord." But he said to them, "Unless I see the mark of the nails in his hands and put my finger into the nailmarks and put my hand into his side, I will not believe."

OT: Gen 2:7–8; Ezek 36:24–28; 37:1–14

NT: Luke 24:36–49; Acts 2:1–4, 29–36; Gal 5:22–23; Rev 5:6–10

Catechism: the risen Jesus, 641–46; the Holy Spirit and the Church, 737–41; the sacrament of Reconciliation, 1461–67

Lectionary: Second Sunday of Easter; Pentecost Sunday; Holy Orders; For Peace and Justice; St. Thomas the Apostle

20:19a As he did in regard to Mary Magdalene, John provides insight into the spiritual disposition of Jesus' **disciples** as they are gathered in Jerusalem. Mary came to Jesus' tomb "while it was still dark" (20:1). The disciples are similarly gathered in the **evening** darkness, †signifying the absence of Christ the light and their own hopelessness. Moreover, the disciples are filled with **fear** of the Jewish authorities who pushed for Jesus' execution, and thus **the doors were locked.**

20:19b During the Farewell Discourse, Jesus told his disciples that they would "weep and mourn" (16:20) and be "in anguish" (16:22) when he left them. He also reassured them, "I will come back to you" (14:28) and "you will see me" (16:16). Now **Jesus** fulfills this promise: he **came and stood in their midst**. And he speaks the words of *shalom*, the †eschatological reconciliation between God and his people: **Peace be with you** (see Isa 52:7; 57:19). Before he departed, Jesus told his disciples, "Peace I leave with you; my peace I give to you. . . . Do not let your hearts be troubled or afraid" (14:27). The risen Jesus now gives the disciples the gift of his peace, which drives away their fear, for he incorporates them into communion with the Father. Through his cross and resurrection, Christ has "conquered the world" (16:33) and its ruler (12:31), and he has made his disciples "children of God" (1:12). There is, then, no reason for his disciples to fear.

20:20 The presence of the wounds of crucifixion on the risen Jesus' body is significant. They indicate that the body resurrected to glory is the same one that died on the cross (see Luke 24:39).[14] Resurrection is not the return of a human being to ordinary mortal life but total transformation into a glorified mode of existence. As St. Paul wrote, the natural body is transfigured by the Holy Spirit into a glorified, "spiritual body" (1 Cor 15:44). The wounds on Jesus' resurrected body reveal that he is forever fixed in the act of love in which he died. The love

14. Catechism 645.

and sacrifice that he offered on the cross are forever present before the Father as "expiation for our sins, and . . . for those of the whole world" (1 John 2:2). Jesus' wounds also signify that the victory of the resurrection comes only through the cross. Similarly, the Lamb in the book of Revelation bears the wound of his slaughter by which he accomplished the work of redemption (Rev 5:6, 9). In this way, St. Thomas Aquinas, drawing on the Venerable Bede, can speak of the wounds on Jesus' resurrected body as "trophies" of his victory.[15]

Donatien Mollat found significance in John's use of the verb "showed."[16] After the temple incident (2:14–17), the †Jews asked Jesus to "show" them a sign to legitimate his words and deeds (2:18). Jesus responded with a statement about raising up the temple of his body (2:19). Now, when Jesus shows the disciples his risen body with its wounds, he provides the †sign that legitimates his words and deeds: his resurrection.[17]

The **disciples** were in a state of grief, hopelessness, and fear, but they now **rejoiced when they saw the Lord**. We again recall Jesus' words during the Farewell Discourse: "I will see you again, and your hearts will rejoice, and no one will take your joy away from you" (16:22). The risen Jesus fills his disciples with the eschatological gifts of peace and joy, which proceed from sharing in the divine communion. These same gifts Paul counts among the fruits of the Spirit (Gal 5:22–23), and in this scene, Jesus pours out the Holy Spirit upon his disciples.

20:21–22 After repeating his words of **Peace**, Jesus draws the disciples into his own mission: **As the Father has sent me, so I send you**. The Gospel has frequently spoken of Jesus as the envoy of the Father, sent to reveal him and accomplish his saving work (e.g., 12:44–50). Now the risen Jesus commissions the disciples as his envoys and sends them into the world (see 17:18). The fellowship of Jesus' disciples, the Church, is an extension of the work of the Father and the Son in the world.

In order to be an extension of Jesus' work, the disciples need to be united to him, as branches to the vine (15:4–5), and receive his divine assistance and power (see Luke 24:49). Accordingly, Jesus **breathed on them and said, "Receive the holy Spirit."** This scene is John's presentation of the reality of Pentecost: the risen Jesus sending the Holy Spirit upon his disciples (see Acts 2:1–4, 33).

As Raymond Brown observes, the Holy Spirit "consecrates" the disciples for their mission, as Jesus himself was "consecrated and sent into the world"

15. St. Thomas Aquinas, *Summa theologica* 3, q. 54, a. 4.
16. Donatien Mollat, "L'Apparition du Ressuscité et le Don de L'Esprit," in *Études johanniques*, 152–53.
17. Catechism 651.

by the Father (10:36).[18] Through the Spirit, the disciples are united to the risen Jesus and receive a share in his own life, and thus in the divine communion. The indwelling Holy Spirit is a sign of their having a share in God's eschatological salvation, for the Spirit makes the disciples a "new creation" (see sidebar on p. 47). The Greek verb for "breathed" recalls Gen 2:7 and Ezek 37:9, which speak of God breathing life into his creatures at the first creation and in the eschatological new creation.

20:23 The risen Jesus connects the Holy Spirit with Church's power to forgive sins: **Whose sins you forgive are forgiven them, and whose sins you retain are retained**. Jesus was first hailed in the Gospel as "the Lamb of God, who takes away the sin of the world" (1:29). He declared that his saving work liberates humanity from slavery to the power of sin (8:34–36). By incorporating the disciples into his own mission, Jesus also gives them the authority to take away people's sins, that is, to administer God's mercy, through the power of the Holy Spirit. As discussed previously (at 20:7), the passive voice ("forgiven," "retained") suggests that here God is acting through his Church. Thus the forgiveness administered by the Church on earth stands in heaven (see Matt 18:18).

20:24–25 **Thomas**, however, **was not with them when Jesus came**. Like Mary Magdalene, the disciples have encountered the risen Jesus, have been brought to the fullness of Easter faith, and now announce to Thomas, **We have seen the Lord** (compare v. 18). But Thomas is unwilling to **believe** their testimony. If he is to believe, he requires tangible proof, **the mark of the nails in his hands** and the wound in **his side**, which he can physically sense (**see** and touch with his **finger** and **hand**).

The Movement to Easter Faith of Thomas and Future Believers (20:26–31)

[26]Now a week later his disciples were again inside and Thomas was with them. Jesus came, although the doors were locked, and stood in their midst and said, "Peace be with you." [27]Then he said to Thomas, "Put your finger here and see my hands, and bring your hand and put it into my side, and do not be unbelieving, but believe." [28]Thomas answered and said to him, "My Lord and my God!" [29]Jesus said to him, "Have you come to believe because you have seen me? Blessed are those who have not seen and have believed."

18. Brown, *John*, 2:1036–37.

The Council of Trent on the Sacrament of Penance

LIVING TRADITION

The Church's Magisterium has rarely made official pronouncements about the meaning of specific biblical texts. One of those few pronouncements, however, concerns Jesus' words in John 20:23, which the Council of Trent (the council of the Catholic Counter-Reformation, 1545–63) defined as the institution of the sacrament of penance:

> The Lord . . . instituted the sacrament of penance, principally when after his resurrection he breathed upon his disciples, and said: "Receive the Holy Spirit. If you forgive the sins of any, they are forgiven; if you retain the sins of any, they are retained."
>
> The universal consensus of the Fathers has always acknowledged that by so sublime an action and such clear words the power of forgiving and retaining sins was given to the Apostles and their lawful successors for reconciling the faithful who have fallen after baptism.[a]

a. Denzinger 1670.

[30]Now Jesus did many other signs in the presence of [his] disciples that are not written in this book. [31]But these are written that you may [come to] believe that Jesus is the Messiah, the Son of God, and that through this belief you may have life in his name.

OT: Ps 35:22–28

NT: Luke 24:36–43

Catechism: faith, 153–62; Christ's risen humanity, 645–46; saving significance of the resurrection, 651–55

Lectionary: Second Sunday of Easter; St. Thomas the Apostle

20:26 On the Sunday after Easter, Jesus' **disciples were again inside**, now with **Thomas**. As in 20:19, **the doors were locked**, but John makes no mention of the disciples' fear. The presence of the Holy Spirit, given by the risen Jesus, has driven their fear away. As before, **Jesus came** and **stood in their midst**, and he repeated his gift of **Peace**.

20:27 Jesus addresses **Thomas** directly. He knows what is in Thomas's heart, and his words to Thomas closely resemble Thomas's own request for tangible proof in 20:25: **Put your finger here and see my hands, and bring your hand and put it into my side**. Thomas demanded proof in order to believe, and Jesus shows his wounds in order to bring Thomas to faith: **Do not be unbelieving, but believe**.

20:28 Upon seeing the wounds of the risen Jesus, **Thomas** responds with the most robust profession of faith in the Gospel: **My Lord and my God!** The pairing of the titles **Lord** (*kyrios*) and **God** (*theos*) recall the naming of God as "the LORD God" or "the LORD, your God" and the address "O Lord GOD." This pairing is found throughout the Old Testament, as in the psalmist's prayers to "my God and my Lord" (Ps 35:23). Through this title, Thomas identifies the risen Jesus with the Lord God, †YHWH himself.

The risen Jesus has completed the work of his †hour and has returned to the Father in glory.[19] Thomas's profession recalls the Gospel's opening verse, which declares "the Word was God" (1:1). Before he came to his hour, Jesus prayed, "Glorify me, Father, with you, with the glory that I had with you before the world began" (17:5). However, it is crucial to recognize that Jesus' glorification in his hour is not a straightforward return to his preexistent glory as the Word, because "the Word became flesh" (1:14). The glorification of Jesus in his hour is the glorification of his *humanity*. The glorified humanity of Jesus provides the way for his disciples, who will come to share in his resurrection, to enter the "Father's house" (14:2). Thomas makes this profession of faith because he recognizes the wounds on the glorified body of Jesus as a †sign, a disclosure of his divinity through his glorified humanity.

20:29 Since ancient Greek manuscripts do not use punctuation marks, it is not clear whether Jesus' words to Thomas in 20:29a are a question or a statement. The NABRE translates it as a question, **Have you come to believe because you have seen me?**, which hints at disapproval that Thomas needed tangible proof to believe. However, it is also possible to translate it as a statement, "You have believed because you have seen me," in which case Jesus does not disapprove of Thomas's faith but simply declares that Thomas has arrived at full Easter faith because of the tangible proof that has been given him.[20]

The beatitude, **Blessed are those who have not seen and have believed**, moves the attention to later generations of disciples, including the Gospel's readers, who have not encountered the risen Jesus in the same way as those first disciples did on Easter. But the fact that later generations of disciples did not see the Lord firsthand does not make their faith in the risen Jesus any less genuine. The Gospel stresses the importance of the apostolic witness to Jesus (19:35; 21:24) by the disciples who received tangible proof of Jesus' resurrection. Jesus prayed for later generations of believers "who will believe in me through their

19. So Rudolf Bultmann, *The Gospel of John: A Commentary*, ed. R. W. N. Hoare and J. K. Riches, trans. G. R. Beasley-Murray (Philadelphia: Westminster, 1971), 695; Brown, *John*, 2:1046; O'Day, "Gospel of John," 850.

20. Catechism 156.

word" (17:20), and as we shall see in John 21, the testimony of those disciples is given to later generations in the words of this Gospel we are now reading.

20:30 Most scholars think that 20:30–31 was the original ending to the Gospel and that chapter 21 was later added as an epilogue. However, while these verses bring the Gospel as a whole to a close, we should not overlook their close connection with the preceding scenes. Indeed, we can read them as a conclusion to the resurrection appearances in John 20, and read John 21 as the conclusion to the Gospel proper.[21]

Jesus' resurrection appearances to the disciples and to Thomas both feature him showing the wounds on his glorified body, which leads the disciples to faith in him. In this respect, the wounds on his glorified body act as signs: they reveal that he has overcome death and that his claims to be divine are true. John's declaration that **Jesus did many other signs in the presence of [his] disciples that are not written in this book** can be taken in reference to other disclosures that the risen Jesus made to those disciples.

20:31 The appearance to Thomas concluded by turning the focus to later generations of disciples, and John continues this shift by directly addressing the Gospel's audience: **But these are written that you may [come to] believe that Jesus is the Messiah, the Son of God.**[22] The Gospel explicitly serves the purpose of nurturing faith in Jesus in the Gospel's readership. While later generations do not encounter the risen Jesus in the same way as those first disciples, they do come to believe through their testimony, which has been recorded in the Fourth Gospel. The Gospel itself is John's testimony to the reality and power of the risen Jesus, and by reading it, later generations of readers can believe in Jesus as the Son of God.

Taken as a conclusion to the resurrection narrative in John 20, this statement reveals a powerful dimension of how the Fourth Gospel understands itself. The preceding episodes with Mary Magdalene, the disciples, and Thomas have all shown that only a personal encounter with the risen Jesus causes faith in him

21. See Edwyn Clement Hoskyns, *The Fourth Gospel*, ed. Francis Noel Davey (London: Faber & Faber, 1947), 549–50; Paul S. Minear, "The Original Functions of John 21," *Journal of Biblical Literature* (1983): 85–98; O'Day, "Gospel of John," 850–52.

22. The bracketed phrase "come to" reflects a famous problem in the manuscript tradition of John. Some ancient witnesses read "you may believe," and other ancient witnesses read "you may come to believe." The implication of the first reading is that the Gospel is written for believers to bolster their faith; the second reading suggests that the Gospel is fundamentally written as an evangelization tool for nonbelievers. The problem cannot be resolved on the basis of the manuscript evidence alone, and so the Gospel's content must be a factor. In this respect, Raymond Brown's observation is fitting: "John's primary purpose of deepening the faith of believers has a secondary goal of thereby bringing others to make an act of faith" (*An Introduction to the Gospel of John*, ed. Francis J. Moloney, ABRL [New York: Doubleday, 2003], 183).

as the risen Lord. In 20:30–31, the Evangelist claims that the Gospel has been written so that its readers may come to believe in Jesus. The implication is that the Fourth Gospel understands itself as mediating an encounter with the risen Jesus that is as genuine as the encounters of those who saw him. The readers of the Fourth Gospel can encounter the risen Jesus by reading its contents in faith.

Faith in Jesus as **the †Messiah, the Son of God**, made possible in part by the Gospel itself, leads to the reception of **life in his name**. Throughout the Gospel, we have seen the importance of receiving or accepting the divine Word (1:11–12). To those who receive him, the divine Word gives "power to become children of God" (1:12). By receiving the †incarnate Word in faith, Jesus' disciples receive the gift of eternal life that he offers: participation in the divine communion. The Gospel is an invitation to heavenly life, to communion with God. The evangelist encourages us to accept this invitation by believing in the risen Jesus, to whom he bears witness in his Gospel.

The Church's Witness to the Risen Lord

John 21:1–25

Chapter 21 expresses the mission of the Church and the relationship of disciples with the risen Jesus. The chapter opens with a richly symbolic story to present the Church's mission to bring people to Christ, who feeds them with his eucharistic food. The second part of the chapter shifts to Peter and the Beloved Disciple, who will bear witness to the risen Lord in the life of the Church in different ways. Most scholars regard John 21 as an epilogue to the Gospel, appended later, after the conclusion in 20:30–31. Yet this chapter plays an integral role in the overarching plan of the Gospel, bringing to a conclusion important themes such as testimony and the pairing of Peter and the Beloved Disciple, as well as the Gospel narrative itself.

The Risen Lord and the Church's Mission (21:1–14)

---

[1]After this, Jesus revealed himself again to his disciples at the Sea of Tiberias. He revealed himself in this way. [2]Together were Simon Peter, Thomas called Didymus, Nathanael from Cana in Galilee, Zebedee's sons, and two others of his disciples. [3]Simon Peter said to them, "I am going fishing." They said to him, "We also will come with you." So they went out and got into the boat, but that night they caught nothing. [4]When it was already dawn, Jesus was standing on the shore; but the disciples did not realize that it was Jesus. [5]Jesus said to them, "Children, have you caught anything to eat?" They answered him, "No." [6]So he said to them, "Cast the net over the right side of the boat and you will find something." So they cast it, and

were not able to pull it in because of the number of fish. [7]So the disciple whom Jesus loved said to Peter, "It is the Lord." When Simon Peter heard that it was the Lord, he tucked in his garment, for he was lightly clad, and jumped into the sea. [8]The other disciples came in the boat, for they were not far from shore, only about a hundred yards, dragging the net with the fish. [9]When they climbed out on shore, they saw a charcoal fire with fish on it and bread. [10]Jesus said to them, "Bring some of the fish you just caught." [11]So Simon Peter went over and dragged the net ashore full of one hundred fifty-three large fish. Even though there were so many, the net was not torn. [12]Jesus said to them, "Come, have breakfast." And none of the disciples dared to ask him, "Who are you?" because they realized it was the Lord. [13]Jesus came over and took the bread and gave it to them, and in like manner the fish. [14]This was now the third time Jesus was revealed to his disciples after being raised from the dead.

NT: Mark 1:16–20; Luke 5:1–11; 24:13–35

Catechism: the Church's apostolate, 863–65; pope and bishops, 880–87, 895; Christ's presence in the Eucharist, 1373–81

Lectionary: the Holy Eucharist

21:1 John 21:1–14 centers on the self-revelation of the risen **Jesus** to the **disciples.**[1] John communicates this point by framing the account with two mentions of the verb **revealed,** in verses 1 and 14. Two narrative threads serve the theme of revelation: the miraculous catch of fish and the meal that Jesus provides. Both are †signs leading to the recognition that the risen Jesus is "the Lord" (21:7, 12).

This resurrection appearance occurs at **the Sea of Tiberias** in Galilee (see also Matt 28:16; Mark 16:7). The site recalls the multiplication of loaves and fish, which took place alongside the same lake (6:1–15). Both accounts present Jesus as providing food to those in need.

21:2–3 Assembled in Galilee is a group of seven disciples: **Simon Peter, Thomas, Nathanael, Zebedee's sons** (whom we know from the †Synoptics as James and John), **and two others.** The Synoptics attest to several of Jesus' apostles being Galilean fishermen (Mark 1:16–20), but in John it is mentioned only here. This scene resembles the miraculous catch of fish in Luke 5:1–11. Both episodes are concerned with the apostles' mission to make disciples, to be "fishers of men" (Mark 1:17). The risen Jesus has commissioned the disciples as his envoys, sending them to the world (John 17:18; 20:21). In this fishing episode, John reveals some spiritual dimensions of the disciples' mission to the world.

1. So Gail R. O'Day, "The Gospel of John," in *The New Interpreter's Bible*, vol. 9 (Nashville: Abingdon, 1995), 856–59.

The opening description emphasizes the disciples' failure and need. They follow **Simon Peter** out **into the boat** to go **fishing**, and they fish throughout the **night**, a customary time for fishing on the Sea of Galilee. But as we have seen, darkness often symbolizes separation from Jesus as well. Jesus had previously said, "Without me you can do nothing" (15:5), and not surprisingly, the disciples **caught nothing**. The implication is that they can fulfill their mission only if the risen Jesus is with them.

21:4–5

After the disciples have fished in the dark, the risen **Jesus** appears **on the shore** in the bright light of **dawn**. As with Mary Magdalene (20:14) and the disciples on the road to Emmaus (Luke 24:16), the risen **Jesus** prevents the disciples from recognizing him, but they are close enough to shore to hear him ask, **Children, have you caught anything to eat?** The Greek phrasing of this question expects **no** for an answer and thus means, "Children, you haven't caught anything to eat, have you?" As with the multiplication of the loaves, a miracle is introduced with emphasis on the disciples' present lack (6:5–9), for which Jesus will provide a superabundance.

21:6

After the disciples answer in the negative, Jesus gives them a command: **Cast the net over the right side of the boat and you will find something**. At Cana, the mother of Jesus instructed the attendants who had no wine, "Do whatever he tells you" (2:5), and when they did what Jesus said, he provided a superabundance of wine for the wedding.[2] Now the disciples, who have nothing to eat, follow Jesus' instructions and make a catch so great that they **were not able to pull it in the boat.** In both cases, Jesus provides abundantly for those who follow his directions.

21:7

Like Jesus' other miracles in John, the miraculous catch of fish is a sign that reveals something about Jesus and his mission. The Beloved Disciple, whose love accelerates the process of his gaining spiritual insight, recognizes it as a sign and realizes that **the Lord** is speaking to them from the shore. He tells **Peter**, and Peter's subsequent actions are almost comical. Wanting to be presentable before Jesus, he **tucked in his garment, for he was lightly clad**. But then he **jumped into the sea**, even though he was dressed. He is so eager to see Jesus that he swims to shore and does not wait for the others.

21:8–9

The other disciples tow the catch from **the boat**, and once ashore, they see Jesus has been preparing food for them: **a charcoal fire with fish on it and bread**. The breakfast recalls the miracle in which Jesus multiplied a little bread and fish to feed a great crowd (6:5–13). Similarly here, the disciples did not catch

2. Ibid., 856.

any food while they were fishing at night (21:5). After providing a miraculous catch, the risen Jesus feeds his disciples.

21:10–11 **Jesus** instructs his disciples to **bring** the catch to him. **Peter** obeys Jesus' command and performs an extraordinary action: single-handedly, he **dragged the net ashore**, which the disciples previously could not even pull into their boat (21:6). The meaning of the **one hundred fifty-three large fish** is unclear, but it is generally regarded as a sign of the universality of the disciples' mission.[3] More important is the detail that Peter's **net was not torn** despite the huge number of fish.[4] Various groups have been torn or divided over Jesus (7:43; 9:16; 10:19). Jesus' disciples, however, are to be "one flock" (10:16) and "brought to perfection as one" (17:23). The untorn net, like Jesus' untorn tunic (19:23–24), symbolizes the unity of his disciples.

Here the Church's mission comes to light. The disciples, whom the risen Jesus has sent into the world, are to go and bear witness to him, much as they go out fishing. Without Jesus' assistance, they will fail in their mission. But if they are obedient to him and cooperate with the Spirit working in them, they will bring others to faith in Jesus: "those who," as Jesus prays, "will believe in me through their word" (17:20), "those who have not seen and have believed" (20:29). The disciples are to bring all people to Christ, just as they bring the catch to him. Illumined by the Church's tradition, the scene of Peter hauling the untorn net ashore can be seen as indicating the special role of Peter's ministry in the apostolic mission of bringing disciples to Christ and preserving their unity.[5]

21:12–14 With the catch on the shore, the risen **Jesus** invites his disciples to eat. During the Farewell Discourse, when he told them that they would see him again, after the resurrection, he announced, "On that day you will not question me about anything" (16:23). Accordingly, **none of the disciples dared to ask him, "Who are you?"** Just as they did with the miraculous catch (21:6–7), the disciples now recognize that the one who feeds them is the risen **Lord.**

The meal that Jesus provides for his disciples has eucharistic overtones. John's description of Jesus' actions—coming over he **took the bread and gave it to them, and in the like manner the fish**—recalls both the multiplication of loaves and fish (6:11) and other New Testament texts concerning the Eucharist (Mark 14:22–23). New Testament writings also speak of the Eucharist as a privileged setting in which the risen Jesus is present: for example, the risen Lord revealed himself to the two disciples on the road to Emmaus "in the breaking of the

3. For the major theories, see Raymond E. Brown, SS, *The Gospel according to John*, AB 29A (New York: Doubleday, 1970), 2:1074–75.

4. The Greek verb for "torn" is *schizō*; the related noun is *schisma*.

5. Catechism 882.

Adoro Te Devote: St. Thomas Aquinas's Hymn to the Eucharist

The disciples' faith enables them to recognize the risen Jesus in the meal that he provides them. Similarly, the eyes of faith allow us to see the risen Jesus present in the holy Eucharist under the appearances of bread and wine (Catechism 1373–81). In his hymn to the Eucharist, *Adoro Te Devote* ("I devoutly adore You"), St. Thomas Aquinas speaks of how faith enables us to move beyond our sense perceptions to the presence of Jesus in the Eucharist:

> Devoutly I adore You, hidden Deity,
> Under these appearances concealed.
> To You my heart surrenders self
> For, seeing You, all else must yield.
> Sight and touch and taste here fail;
> Hearing only can be believed.
> I trust what God's own Son has said.
> Truth from truth is best received.[a]

a. St. Thomas Aquinas, "Devoutly I Adore You, Hidden Deity," in *The Aquinas Prayer Book: The Prayers and Hymns of St. Thomas Aquinas*, ed. and trans. Robert Anderson and Johann Moser (Manchester, NH: Sophia Institute Press, 2000), 69.

bread" (Luke 24:35). The food that the risen Jesus provides for his disciples and to which they are to draw all believers is the Eucharist, the sacrament of his real presence, for "whoever eats this bread will live forever" (6:58).

John's identification of this appearance as **the third time Jesus was revealed to his disciples** presumes that the first two appearances are to the disciples without Thomas (20:19) and with Thomas present (20:26). The appearance to Mary Magdalene is not counted, either because John is thinking of appearances to the disciples as a group rather than to individuals or because a woman's testimony did not have legal standing in Judaism at that time (compare 1 Cor 15:3–8).

Peter's Witness to the Risen Lord (21:15–19)

[15]When they had finished breakfast, Jesus said to Simon Peter, "Simon, son of John, do you love me more than these?" He said to him, "Yes, Lord, you know that I love you." He said to him, "Feed my lambs." [16]He then said to him a second time, "Simon, son of John, do you love me?" He said

to him, "Yes, Lord, you know that I love you." He said to him, "Tend my sheep." [17]He said to him the third time, "Simon, son of John, do you love me?" Peter was distressed that he had said to him a third time, "Do you love me?" and he said to him, "Lord, you know everything; you know that I love you." [Jesus] said to him, "Feed my sheep. [18]Amen, amen, I say to you, when you were younger, you used to dress yourself and go where you wanted; but when you grow old, you will stretch out your hands, and someone else will dress you and lead you where you do not want to go." [19]He said this signifying by what kind of death he would glorify God. And when he had said this, he said to him, "Follow me."

OT: 2 Sam 5:1–5; Ezek 34:11–16

NT: Matt 16:13–20; 1 Peter 5:1–4

Catechism: the papacy, 881, 890–92; Jesus is model for clergy, 896, 1551; continual conversion, 1427–29; martyrdom, 2473–74

Lectionary: third Sunday of Easter (Year C); Solemnity of Peter and Paul; Common of Pastors [for a pope]; Holy Orders

21:15–17 **Jesus** initiates a very personal dialogue with **Simon Peter**, which focuses on the way Peter will bear witness to the risen Lord. It takes place after the **breakfast**, which was prepared on "a charcoal fire" (21:9)—a detail that recalls Peter's threefold denial of Jesus in Annas's courtyard, where he stood warming himself by "a charcoal fire" (18:18). Peter denied Jesus three times, thereby rejecting Jesus and his own status as a disciple. Thus Jesus does not address him as "Peter" but as **Simon, son of John**, his name before becoming Jesus' disciple and the "rock." Moreover, when Jesus asks Peter if he loves him **more than these**, he reminds Peter about his solitary boast to be willing to lay down his life for Jesus and Jesus' prophecy of Peter's threefold denial (13:37–38).[6] Jesus now invites Peter to repent and profess his love for him three times and, in doing so, to restore their relationship.[7]

Jesus asks Simon three times, **Do you love me**, and three times he answers, **You know that I love you.**[8] After each profession of love from Peter, Jesus assigns him a responsibility as the shepherd of his sheep: **Feed my lambs. . . . Tend**

6. O'Day, "Gospel of John," 860–61.

7. Catechism 1428–29.

8. There is a subtle variation in the Greek verbs for "love." Jesus' first and second questions use the Greek verb *agapaō*, the verbal form of *agapē*, which in the New Testament usually refers to God's love. All three responses from Peter and Jesus' third question use the Greek verb *phileō*, the verbal form of *philia*, which designates the love between friends. While some have tried to distinguish between different forms of love in the questions and answers, we do not think that there is a difference, for John uses both verbs interchangeably and as synonyms throughout the Gospel; thus *agapaō* and *phileō* are applied to Jesus' love for Lazarus (11:3, 5), *phileō* is applied to the Father's love for the Son (5:20), and both verbs are applied to the Father's love for Jesus' disciples (16:27; 17:23).

my sheep. . . . Feed my sheep. Throughout the Bible, those people appointed by God to lead and govern his people are often spoken of as shepherds (e.g., 2 Sam 5:2; Ezek 34:2; 1 Pet 5:2), and in the Fourth Gospel, this scene recalls the Good Shepherd Discourse (10:1–18). Jesus is the good shepherd, and he gives Peter a unique share in his work of shepherding. As shepherd of Christ's sheep, Peter has a special role as leader and custodian of Jesus' disciples (see Matt 16:17–19; Luke 22:32). Modeled on the good shepherd, Peter's office as shepherd is one of self-sacrificial service and care for the sheep (10:11–15). It is built upon Peter's own discipleship and personal love for Jesus, for in 21:19, Jesus gives Peter the command that applies to all disciples: "Follow me." At the heart of both discipleship and leadership in the Church is a personal love for Jesus.

21:18–19 The good shepherd "will lay down [his] life for the sheep" (10:15). Like Jesus, Peter's role as the shepherd of Jesus' sheep extends to the laying down of his own life, culminating in his martyrdom. Peter previously professed his willingness to lay down his life for Jesus (13:37), and Jesus said that Peter "will follow later" (13:36). Now Jesus tells Peter, **When you were younger, you used to dress yourself and go where you wanted.** But as the shepherd, Peter will have to lay down both his will and his life for Christ: **But when you grow old, you will stretch out your hands, and someone else will dress you and lead you where you do not want to go.** The phrase "**stretch out your hands**" refers to crucifixion, and Peter was martyred by crucifixion during the persecution of Christians in Rome around AD 65.[9] The Evangelist clarifies that Jesus has been talking about Peter's **death** by which **he would glorify God**. Peter, therefore, will bear witness to the Lord by serving as the leader of Christ's disciples and by laying down his life as a martyr—recall that the term "martyr" is from the Greek word for "witness."

With the command **Follow me**, Jesus emphasizes that Peter's own relationship with him as a disciple lies at the heart of his role as shepherd. When speaking about his own death, Jesus said, "Whoever serves me must follow me, and where I am, there also will my servant be" (12:26). For Peter to serve as the shepherd of Jesus' sheep, he must follow Jesus completely, even to the point of laying down his life (13:37). He must carry out his role as shepherd by imitating Christ the good shepherd, who lays down his life for the sheep (10:15) and thus performs the greatest act of love (15:13).

9. See *1 Clement* 5.2–4; Eusebius, *Ecclesiastical History* 2.25. Early Christian tradition holds that St. Peter was martyred during the reign of Emperor Nero in the Circus of Nero, which was located in an area called Vaticanus. Today, Vatican City stands on the place where Nero's Circus stood. The site has been venerated from Christian antiquity, since Peter's burial place lies underneath St. Peter's Basilica.

Reflection and Application (21:15–19)

This exchange between Jesus and Peter provides much food for thought about the ministry of the pope and basic aspects of the Christian life, such as sin, repentance, and discipleship. When Peter denied Jesus three times, he rejected his relationship with Jesus. In this scene, which recalls Peter's denials, we see the tremendous love and mercy of Jesus for Peter. Jesus makes the first move and initiates the conversation with Peter. He invites Peter to repent and return to him by professing his love. With Peter's threefold profession of love, his threefold denial is undone, and Jesus restores the relationship between them. Jesus' mercy is so complete that he does not hold Peter's past sins against him. Instead, Jesus gives Peter the honor and responsibility of serving as the delegated shepherd of his sheep.

The same dynamics of repentance and forgiveness apply to all disciples, for Peter is still a sheep in relation to Jesus. No matter how serious or how many the sins we have committed (Peter's were very serious), the love and mercy of Jesus is infinitely greater. He seeks us out and invites us to return to him. This scene should give us confidence that when we seek reconciliation with Jesus, he forgives us completely and forever. As Pope Francis has beautifully taught, God "does not tire of forgiving us if we are able to return to him with a contrite heart."[10]

The Beloved Disciple's Witness to the Risen Lord (21:20–25)

[20]Peter turned and saw the disciple following whom Jesus loved, the one who had also reclined upon his chest during the supper and had said, "Master, who is the one who will betray you?" [21]When Peter saw him, he said to Jesus, "Lord, what about him?" [22]Jesus said to him, "What if I want him to remain until I come? What concern is it of yours? You follow me." [23]So the word spread among the brothers that that disciple would not die. But Jesus had not told him that he would not die, just "What if I want him to remain until I come? [What concern is it of yours?]"

[24]It is this disciple who testifies to these things and has written them, and we know that his testimony is true. [25]There are also many other things that Jesus did, but if these were to be described individually, I do not think the whole world would contain the books that would be written.

NT: 1 John 1:1–4; 2 John; 3 John
Catechism: Scripture, 101–4

10. Pope Francis, "Angelus," March 17, 2013.

21:20 The focus shifts from **Peter** to the Beloved **Disciple**. Every time that Peter and the Beloved Disciple have appeared together in the Gospel thus far, the Beloved Disciple has had a special privilege or insight that Peter did not have at first. But now the Beloved Disciple is **following** Peter the shepherd, who is himself following Jesus (21:19).

21:21–22 Peter asks Jesus about the Beloved Disciple, and Jesus replies with a cryptic saying: **What if I want him to remain until I come?** Instead of worrying about the Beloved Disciple, Peter should keep his attention focused on Jesus; hence Jesus repeats the instruction, **You follow me**.

21:23 Jesus' saying about the Beloved Disciple was interpreted in different ways. One interpretation **among the brothers**—likely the Christians affiliated with the Beloved Disciple (1 John 3:13; 3 John 3)—was **that** this **disciple would not die**. They interpreted Jesus to mean that the Beloved Disciple would live to see the †Parousia, the glorious manifestation of the Lord Jesus on the last day (5:28–29; 6:39–40, 54). To clear up this misunderstanding, the author clarifies that Jesus never said anything about the Beloved Disciple not dying, only about his remaining. The need to clear this up may have been prompted by the Beloved Disciple's death.

21:24–25 The Beloved Disciple remains not by living forever but through the abiding presence of his testimony for subsequent generations. The Beloved Disciple **testifies to these things**, and **his testimony is true**. This statement recalls 19:35, which spoke of the Beloved Disciple's reliable testimony (see 3 John 12). Now we learn that this same disciple, who witnessed the crucifixion, **has written** his testimony in the Gospel, which we have been reading!

Since the **many other things that Jesus did** are so profound, **the whole world would** not **contain the books that would be written** about them. Whereas Peter bears witness to the risen Lord by his office of shepherd and martyr, the Beloved Disciple bears witness through the testimony of his Gospel. The Beloved Disciple will remain until the Parousia through his Gospel, the written record of his testimony: his "fruit that will remain" (15:16).

Reflection and Application (21:20–25)

The Fourth Gospel preserves the testimony of the Beloved Disciple, which brings about an encounter with the divine Word to all who read it in faith, from the time of its author until today. As the Catechism (104) states, quoting the Second Vatican Council, "In the sacred books, the Father who is in heaven comes lovingly to meet his children, and talks with them (*Dei Verbum* 21)." By reading in faith the pages of Sacred Scripture, including this Gospel, we truly encounter the Word of God, who makes himself present to us. And we, like the people in the Gospel narrative, must respond to him. It is the hope of the Evangelist and his purpose in writing that we might receive the divine Word in faith and remain in his love. For only by doing so do we "become children of God" (1:12) and "have life in his name" (20:31).

Suggested Resources

Catholic authors are designated with an asterisk (*).

From the Christian Tradition

*Aquinas, Thomas. *Commentary on the Gospel of John*. Translated by Fabian Larcher, OP, and James Weisheipl, OP. 3 vols. Washington, DC: Catholic University of America Press, 2010. The complete text of Aquinas's university lectures on the Fourth Gospel, which integrate the commentary of his predecessors, especially Origen, John Chrysostom, and Augustine.

*Augustine. *Tractates on the Gospel according to John*. 5 vols. Translated by John W. Rettig. Fathers of the Church 78, 79, 88, 90, 92. Washington, DC: Catholic University of America Press, 1988–95. Augustine's highly influential 124 sermons on John. Theologically and rhetorically brilliant.

Elowsky, Joel C., ed. *John*. Ancient Christian Commentary on Scripture: New Testament 4a–b. Downers Grove, IL: InterVarsity, 2006–7. Excerpts of interpretations from many early Christian readers.

Scholarly Commentaries

*Brown, Raymond E., SS. *The Gospel according to John*. 2 vols. Anchor Bible 29–29A. New York: Doubleday, 1966–70. The landmark commentary by a major American Catholic scholar.

Keener, Craig S. *The Gospel of John: A Commentary*. 2 vols. Peabody, MA: Hendrickson, 2003. A major scholarly treatment, featuring a staggering wealth of learning about the ancient world.

O'Day, Gail R. "The Gospel of John." In *The New Interpreter's Bible*, vol. 9, 491–865. Nashville: Abingdon, 1995. Insightful literary and theological analysis with helpful reflections for preaching.

Theology of the Gospel of John

*De la Potterie, Ignace, SJ. *The Hour of Jesus: The Passion and Resurrection of Jesus according to John*. Translated by Dom G. Murray, OSB. Staten Island, NY: Alba House, 1989. An exemplary study of John 18–20, which integrates historical, literary, and theological analysis in concert with the Church's tradition.

Smith, D. Moody. *The Theology of the Gospel of John*. New York: Cambridge University Press, 1995. A succinct presentation of mainline scholarship on John's theology.

Popular and Pastoral Commentaries

*Raymond E. Brown. *The Gospel and Epistles of John: A Concise Commentary*. Collegeville, MN: Liturgical Press, 1988. A shorter, more accessible presentation of Brown's study of John.

———. *A Retreat with John the Evangelist: That You May Have Life*. Cincinnati: St. Anthony Messenger Press, 1998. A lighter, spiritual reflection on the Gospel, based on Brown's scholarly work.

Glossary

apocalyptic (from Greek *apocalyptō*, "to unveil or reveal"): a distinct theological and literary genre especially popular in the centuries immediately before and after Jesus' life. Apocalyptic centers on the revealing of heavenly mysteries about the ultimate meaning of the cosmos or history, and these revelations are expressed literarily in bizarre symbolism. Apocalyptic literature often spoke to God's faithful, who are suffering unjustly, to reassure them that God is sovereign and that his justice will prevail in the end.

canon: the official list of divinely inspired books that make up the Bible.

concentric literary structure: a way of structuring narrative material such that the focal element appears at the center, like a bull's-eye, and the elements that lead up to and away from the center parallel or mirror each other. John has composed the trial of Jesus before Pilate in an elaborate concentric structure (see the diagram in the opening discussion of John 18:28–19:16a).

covenant: a solemn promise that creates a kinship bond between those who enter into it. In a covenant relationship, one or both parties swear promises to the other, to which are attached blessings and penalties for keeping or breaking the covenant promises.

Dead Sea Scrolls: a library of ancient religious writings, collected by a Jewish sect who lived on the shores of the Dead Sea from the mid-second century BC until AD 70. These texts, discovered in 1947, contribute to a fuller picture of Jewish life and belief before and during Jesus' day (ca. 4 BC–AD 30).

eschatology: a branch of theology that deals with the last or ultimate things. In Scripture studies, it often refers to the definitive action of God at the end time, in which he will save his people, punish the wicked, renew creation, and fully establish his kingly rule in the world.

hour: a technical expression in John for the divinely appointed time of Jesus' cross and resurrection, through which he will preeminently reveal the Father's love and accomplish his saving work.

incarnation: the Second Person of God metaphysically uniting himself to a human nature in Jesus of Nazareth, yet without ceasing to be God.

irony: a literary device in which one thing seems to be the case to a speaker or actor, but another thing, often its exact opposite, is actually the case. For instance, Roman soldiers crown Jesus with thorns to mock him as king, but ironically what they express as mockery is in fact true: Jesus is the king.

Jews: a term that John sometimes uses in reference to those Jewish religious authorities in Jerusalem who aggressively opposed Jesus and sought his death. See sidebar, "John and the Jews," on p. 101.

LXX: the Roman numeral for seventy, used as the abbreviation for the Septuagint based on the legend that it was produced by seventy scholars.

Messiah (from Hebrew *mashiakh*, "anointed one"; Greek translation is *Christos*): narrowly, a new Davidic king, whom God promised to raise up to deliver his people from their enemies and rule over a restored Israelite monarchy in righteousness and peace. Broadly, it can refer to any number of end-time saviors whom Jews expected God to send.

Mishnah: a collection of Jewish law, compiled around AD 200, which preserves the traditions and teachings of many great rabbis. Some of its contents, if used critically, can illumine Jewish life and belief before the Roman destruction of the temple in AD 70.

Parousia: the public manifestation of the Lord Jesus in glory at the end of days, when he will raise and judge the dead and fully establish the kingdom of God in power on the earth; the second coming of Christ.

Pharisees: a movement within Judaism emerging in the mid-second century BC, made up of laity and generally lower-ranking priests with characteristic beliefs (e.g., an authoritative oral law along with the written Scripture) and practices (e.g., wide-ranging extension of purity laws). While some Pharisees had political power in Jesus' day, the group as a whole did not. Their spiritual descendants, the rabbis, emerged as authoritative teachers following the destruction of the temple in AD 70.

Prophet-like-Moses: a prophet foretold in Deut 18:15–19 whom God promises to raise up to speak his word to Israel. This text helped to generate the expectation of a messianic figure who would be a great prophet and teacher at the end of days. Evidence for this messianic expectation is found in the Dead Sea Scrolls.

Sanhedrin: a council of high-ranking priests, theologians, and aristocrats that had religious and political authority in Jerusalem and was subject to the Roman prefect in Jesus' day.

Septuagint: a Greek translation of the Old Testament produced in about 200 BC; the version of the Bible most often quoted in the New Testament (see **LXX**).

sign: the technical term for Jesus' miracles in John's Gospel. As signs, Jesus' miracles are sensible revelations of spiritual truths about himself and his saving work. They are a means by which people are brought to faith in Jesus, but only if they are appropriately viewed as revelatory signs that say something about Jesus, and not simply as mighty deeds.

Son of Man: the apocalyptic figure who appears "with the clouds of heaven" and receives God's kingship in Dan 7:13–14. In John, Jesus uses this title to present himself as the one who comes down from heaven to reveal the Father and accomplish his saving work by being lifted up on the cross (see sidebar on p. 52).

synagogue (from Greek "come together"): originally, a Jewish institution for prayer and community life in the Holy Land and in Jewish communities throughout the Greco-Roman world.

Synoptic (from Greek "see together"): a descriptive term applied to the Gospels of Matthew, Mark, and Luke, inasmuch as these Gospels can be lined up in parallel columns and seen together because of their similarities in content, sequence, and wording.

theophany: an appearance of God in some sensible medium, often provoking fear and awe in those who receive it.

Torah: the Hebrew word meaning "instruction" or "law." The term is applied to God's instructions given to Israel through Moses at Mount Sinai for how Israel is to live as a holy, righteous people in covenant relationship with him. The term, synonymous with "the law of Moses," is applied particularly to the first five books of the Bible, and sometimes to the whole Old Testament in general.

YHWH: the transliteration of the four Hebrew consonants of the sacred, personal name of God revealed to Moses at Mount Sinai (Exod 3). Its likely pronunciation is "Yahweh." Out of respect, in Jewish tradition this name is never spoken. Instead, the Hebrew word meaning "the Lord" (*'adonai*) is substituted. Similarly, the Septuagint renders this sacred name as Greek *kyrios*, meaning "Lord." See sidebar on p. 89.

Index of Pastoral Topics

This index indicates where the Gospel of John provides material related to topics that may be useful for evangelization, catechesis, apologetics, or other forms of pastoral ministry.

Index of Sidebars

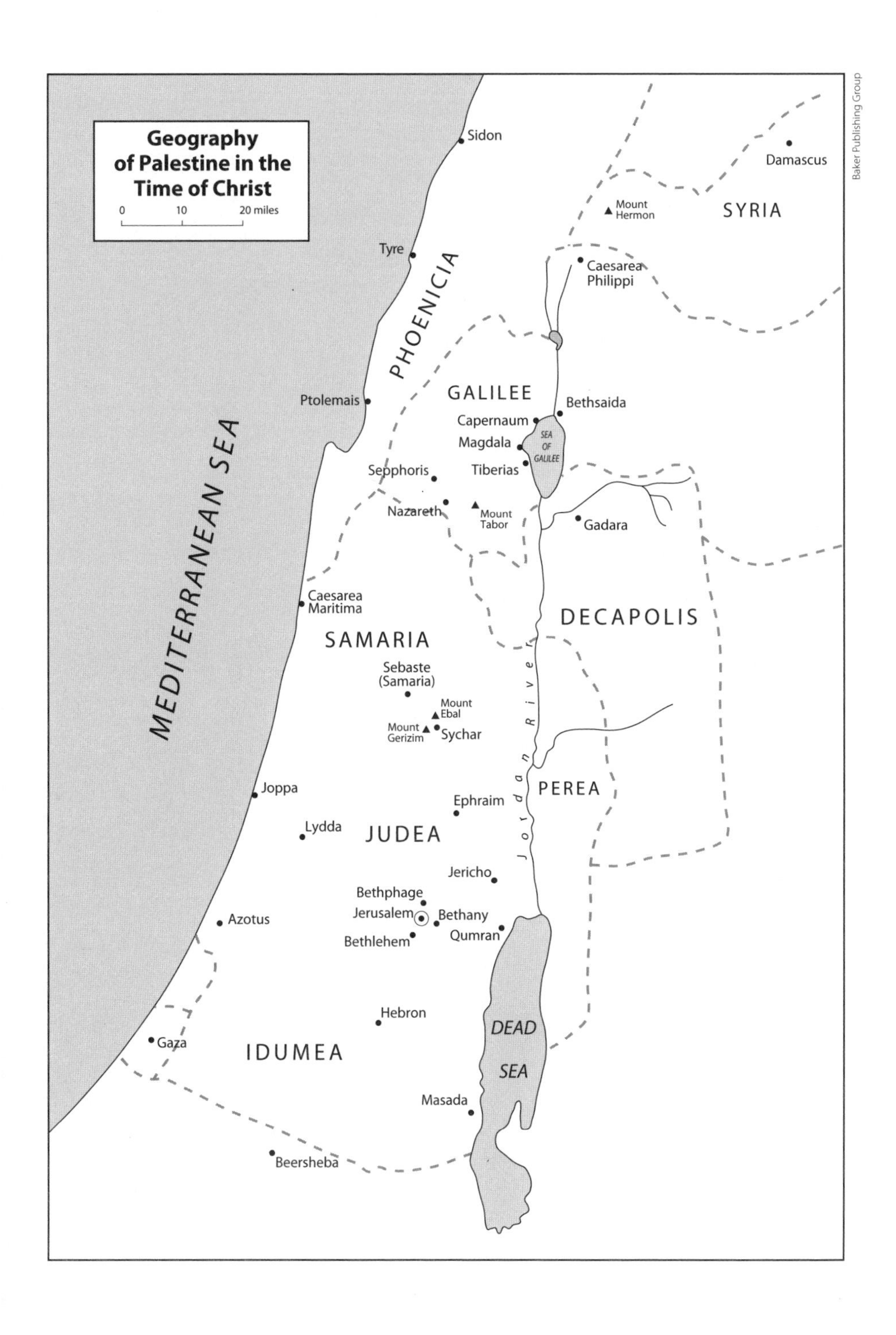

Geography of Palestine in the Time of Christ
0
10
20 miles
MEDITERRANEAN SEA
Sidon
Damascus
Mount Hermon
SYRIA
Tyre
PHOENICIA
Caesarea Philippi
GALILEE
Ptolemais
Bethsaida
Capernaum
Magdala
SEA OF GALILEE
Sepphoris
Tiberias
Nazareth
Mount Tabor
Gadara
Caesarea Maritima
DECAPOLIS
SAMARIA
Sebaste (Samaria)
Mount Ebal
Mount Gerizim
Sychar
Jordan River
Joppa
PEREA
Ephraim
Lydda
JUDEA
Jericho
Bethphage
Jerusalem
Bethany
Azotus
Qumran
Bethlehem
Hebron
DEAD SEA
Gaza
IDUMEA
Masada
Beersheba